Introducing Globalization

To our children, Rachael and Charlie, who will grow up in a globalized world.

Introducing Globalization: Analysis and Readings

Editors:
Richard W. Mansbach
Iowa State University

Edward Rhodes
George Mason University

Los Angeles | London | New Delhi
Singapore | Washington DC

Los Angeles | London | New Delhi
Singapore | Washington DC

FOR INFORMATION:

CQ Press

An Imprint of SAGE Publications, Inc.

2455 Teller Road

Thousand Oaks, California 91320

E-mail: order@sagepub.com

SAGE Publications Ltd.

1 Oliver's Yard

55 City Road

London, EC1Y 1SP

United Kingdom

SAGE Publications India Pvt. Ltd.

B 1/I 1 Mohan Cooperative Industrial Area

Mathura Road, New Delhi 110 044

India

SAGE Publications Asia-Pacific Pte. Ltd.

3 Church Street

#10–04 Samsung Hub

Singapore 049483

Printed in the United States of America

Library of Congress Cataloging-in-Publication Data

Introducing globalization : analysis and readings / editors, Richard W. Mansbach, Edward Rhodes.

p. cm.

ISBN 978-1-60871-742-2 (pbk.)
1. Globalization—Textbooks. I. Mansbach, Richard W., 1943–II. Rhodes, Edward, 1959–

JZ1318.I586 2013
303.48'2—dc23   2012008919

This book is printed on acid-free paper.

Certified Chain of Custody
Promoting Sustainable Forestry
www.sfiprogram.org
SFI-01268

SFI label applies to text stock

Acquisitions Editor: Elise Frasier
Editorial Assistant: Nancy Loh
Production Editor: Astrid Virding
Copy Editor: QuADS Prepress (P) Ltd.
Typesetter: C&M Digitals (P) Ltd.
Proofreader: Ellen Brink
Cover Designer: Myself Included Design
Marketing Manager: Jonathan Mason
Permissions Editor: Adele Hutchinson

12 13 14 15 16 10 9 8 7 6 5 4 3 2 1

CONTENTS

PREFACE

Globalization has become a buzzword for a world in which new technologies have enabled the unprecedented movement of persons, things, and ideas; people have become ever more interdependent; territory and geography have begun to lose their traditional significance; and boundaries have become more and more porous. The traditional focus on the interstate system has necessarily broadened to include transnational advocacy groups, intergovernmental networks, immense globe-girdling corporations, highly mobile groups of terrorists and criminals, and new and more specialized international institutions involved in all the realms of human activity. Simultaneously, power and authority have grown more diffuse, involving international, transnational, regional, and subnational authorities; religions and religious groups have once again become important factors in global affairs; and markets have become regional and even global in scope. As a result, courses in international relations, foreign affairs, and global politics necessarily include materials on globalization, and courses specializing in globalization have proliferated. Nevertheless, as will become apparent, virtually every aspect of globalization is vigorously contested, including its definition and historical origins.

We have assembled this reader to give students a sense of and a "feel" for the impact of globalization in a variety of contexts at the level of those most affected by it. Materials have been selected in an effort to represent the ways in which globalization is altering the lives of people in diverse settings—Europe, North America, Africa, Asia, the Middle East, and so forth. Our selections also involved an effort to paint globalization's impact on a highly diverse cast of individual actors with different identities—prosperous and poor, men and women, highly and less well educated, and so forth—in order to show how perceptions of the phenomenon vary depending on one's perspective. Finally, the readings seek to show how globalization is altering our lives in almost all respects—political, economic, cultural, normative, and institutional.

Organization of the Reader

The reader is organized into 14 chapters. The first involves the different ways in which globalization has been defined and the different "schools" of globalization theorists. As we shall see, such differences also extend to tracing the history of globalization and its origins. Chapter 2 focuses on the technological foundations of contemporary globalization, especially the Internet and social networks, and the dangers as well as virtues of such technologies. Chapter 3 examines what many believe is the core of globalization, that is, its economic dimension and the institutions and neoliberal ideology that are its pillars. Chapter 4 turns to globalization's political dimension, examining in particular the ideas and institutions of global civil society and global governance in a world increasingly beyond the control of any single nation-state or group of states. Chapter 5 examines the consequences of globalization for international security and the traditional international relation concepts of distribution of power and sources of violence. Chapter 6 turns to the impact of globalization on culture. Is an homogenized globalized culture emerging that is erasing cultural differences, or can local cultures survive the spread of globalized tastes? One way in which national culture is altered is by migration, the topic to which we turn in Chapter 7. What are the sources of migration, what is the impact of migrants on local mores, and how are indigenous populations reacting to the influx of "aliens" in their midst?

Chapter 8 turns to a very different aspect of globalization, its environmental dimension. The chapter examines the proliferation of "extreme natural hazards," for example, global warming and deforestation, which threaten the well-being and perhaps even the survival of vast numbers of the world's population. No single country can cope with such hazards, and indeed, globalization enthusiasts often applaud what they believe to be the erosion of the territorial nation-state as the world is globalized. Chapter 9 confronts the question of the future of the nation-state in a globalizing world. Nationalism, the topic of Chapter 10, is frequently the reaction of those who fear the erosion of state authority or its culture. However, while nationalism is a key form of "localism" in reaction to globalization, the process also involves the spread of new norms and ideas. Such ideas may weaken state sovereignty, as is the case with human rights, the topic of Chapter 11.

Chapter 12 involves a shift from the empirical aspects of globalization to its normative implications. Put simply, is globalization, overall, a "good" or a "bad" phenomenon? As with other aspects of the subject, this question elicits little agreement. Not surprisingly, those who benefit from globalization applaud its virtues, while those left behind emphasize its vices. Critics of globalization have become especially vociferous since the global economic and financial crises that began in the United States in 2007–2008 spread rapidly and were thus globalized. For this reason, alternative visions of globalization, the topic of Chapter 13, have become more attractive to many people. Among the most important of these are a vision that seems more just and equitable in its impact and an Islamic perspective that advocates emphasizing the *umma*, or global community of Muslims. In light of the role of globalization in creating and then spreading the economic "contagion," the topic of our final chapter—the future of globalization—is more pressing than at any time in recent decades. Will the globalized world, which Thomas Friedman famously described as "flat," once again become "round" as sovereign states reassert their authority, borders are thickened, and interdependence is diluted, or will the processes of globalization once again intensify?

Acknowledgments

Our thanks go to those at CQ Press who have been generous with their time and effort, including Elise Frasier, who got this project off the ground; Nancy Loh, for her valuable assistance; Astrid Virding, who oversaw the book's production; Lauren Johnson, who spent vast amounts of time tracking down permissions around the world; and Shamila Swamy, who did a careful and splendid job of copyediting. We also wish to thank those who reviewed the original proposal and whose suggestions were invariably helpful, including Jeanie Bukowski, Bradley University; Peter Dombrowski, Naval War College; Yosef Lapid, New Mexico State University; James A. Mitchell, California State University, Northridge; Frances Pilch, U.S. Air Force Academy; and Franke Wilmer, Montana State University.

Chapter 1

WHAT IS GLOBALIZATION AND WHAT ARE ITS ORIGINS?

Every aspect of globalization invites controversy, including its definition. This chapter seeks to make you think about the competing notions and definitions of globalization and helps you explore the relationship between these various conceptions of "globalization" and alternative theoretical perspectives on the phenomenon. If globalization, for instance, implies the declining importance of geographical distance and of (physical, political, social, and cultural) boundaries, this suggests a range of processes by which change occurs to human identity, human institutions, and human "interests."

1.1

THE MANY MEANINGS OF GLOBALIZATION

Richard W. Mansbach[1]

We recognize that the world is in flux but are uncertain about how and why it is changing, how extensive the changes are, and where the world is headed. We describe the present era as that of "globalization," yet we argue about what that means. The journalist Thomas Friedman, a globalization enthusiast, recalls how on a visit to India Nandan Nilekani, CEO of Infosys, had said to him, "Tom, the playing field is being leveled," because knowledge was available to all countries. "What Nandan is saying, I thought to myself, is that the playing field is being flattened. . . . Flattened? I rolled that word around in my head for a while and then, in the chemical way that these things happen, it just popped out: My God, he's telling me the world is flat!"[2] Friedman sees globalization as a novel phenomenon, but whether we perceive it to be so depends largely on one's historical perspective.

Introduction

Globalization is a very big idea. We are all affected by it, yet its meaning and consequences remain subjects of heated debate. As it is a complex idea, defining it is challenging. Understanding its impact is made more difficult owing to the growing velocity with which ever more things, people, and ideas move around the world. Are globalizing trends intensifying or attenuating? Can they be reversed, or will human interdependence continue to thicken? Does globalization merely connect sovereign states and/or individuals in novel ways, or does it transcend them? Does it render obsolete the traditional distinctions in international relations between "domestic" and "foreign" and "public" and "private"? These are just a few of the myriad crucial questions one must deal with when confronting globalization.

Inasmuch as there is no consensus as to what globalization is, it is hardly surprising that there is no agreement as to what is causing it or what its consequences are. Globalization is said to be driven by forces as diverse as technology, market capitalism, democracy, corporate growth, transnational linkages, economic interdependence, Western culture, and modernity itself. The consequences attributed to it are equally diverse. Does globalization augur an end to territoriality and the demise of territorial states and the state system and, therefore, the discipline of "international relations" as it has been studied for several centuries? Will globalization bring an end to cultural diversity around the world? Or does it mark the triumph of liberal democracy and neoliberal economics? Divergent answers to such question reveal the competing theoretical, empirical, and normative positions of observers of world affairs.

Some observers believe that globalization applies only to the economic aspects of global life, whereas others perceive its impact in all spheres of human affairs—political, cultural, military, criminal, and even spiritual. Some see globalization in the spread of English, designer jeans, and hamburgers. Others see it in the growing trade and economic interdependence among societies and the global spread of financial markets and production networks (and, as a result, the rapid spread of financial and economic crises). Still others conceive of globalization as the spread of common ideas and the end of a world divided by ideologies like communism. Some equate globalization with "Americanization," while others insist that it is "modernization." What virtually everyone concedes is that globalization involves proliferating connections among societies and peoples, growing porosity of national frontiers, proliferation of transnational processes, and the growing importance of authoritative actors other than national governments, such as transnational corporations, social networks, and international organizations.

What follows briefly describes several competing definitions of globalization that we have found helpful based on a typology developed by the British political theorist David Held and his colleagues, who distinguish among three perspectives that they label "skeptical," "hyperglobalist," and "transformationalist."[3] Each perspective makes different assumptions and draws different inferences about the phenomenon. Thereafter, we will contrast globalization with the forces of "localization," with which globalization competes.

Skeptics

Skeptics believe that contemporary globalization is neither unprecedented nor revolutionary, and they claim it is reversible (and has in the past been reversed). Globalization, in their view, remains limited to *economic interdependence*, that is, a condition in which the economic destinies of key actors are linked. In an economically interdependent interstate world, the prosperity of every society depends on what other societies do. Thus, when China refuses to devalue its currency, it keeps the cost of its exports low and sells more overseas, while limiting its purchases of foreign goods. The outcome is one in which the United States is less able to export its products to China, while China finds it easier to export its goods to the United States. Skeptics focus especially on levels of interstate trade and whether trade is increasing or decreasing, and they contend that, notwithstanding the expansion of global trade after World War II, trade levels were actually higher in the late 19th century, when Great Britain ruled the waves. Thus, the effects of contemporary globalization are exaggerated.

Their historical analysis leads skeptics to conclude that globalization is reversible. After all, the open economic system of the 19th century based on free trade thrived until the onset of World War I in 1914. A decade later, the Great Depression began, and international trade collapsed under the weight of unilateral tariff increases and currency depreciations—"beggar-thy-neighbor" policies—as countries sought to restore prosperity at the expense of one another. Then came a second world war.

World trade and interstate economic interdependence were not restored until after World War II and the establishment under American leadership of the International Monetary Fund, the World Bank, and the General Agreement on Tariffs and Trade at the 1944 Bretton Woods Conference. If the United States were to turn its back on free trade, according to skeptics, global economic interdependence would erode, much as it did earlier when Britain was no longer able to provide global leadership. Skeptics believe that globalization would not survive if today's major powers became disillusioned with globalization's consequences, as they did earlier in the 20th century, and that this would bring about the collapse of key public and private institutions that sustain it.

In other words, globalization is hardly an inexorable, irreversible process. Instead, its future depends on, among other things, great-power rivalry, whether major countries are satisfied with the status quo, whether people remain satisfied with the rewards of capitalism, and whether the global economic system experiences severe economic crises or the trauma of a major war. These are all factors that preoccupy traditional theorists and practitioners of international relations, and there is nothing especially novel about contemporary globalization. Governments retain economic authority, and North America, Europe, and Japan remain economically preeminent, much as they were in earlier eras. Of course, this last assertion seems increasingly obsolete in light of the dramatic economic rise of countries such as Brazil, India, and China.

Although skeptics recognize the expansion of global markets in recent decades, they insist that those markets are still controlled by major states. They believe that regional trade groups like the European Union (EU), rather than enhancing global trade, are acting as impediments to a genuinely globalized economic system because they raise tariffs on goods imported from outside their boundaries. Indeed, they emphasize that most trade is still regional in scope.

As the above suggests, skeptics also retain the belief that sovereign states rather than other actors remain dominant and are capable of managing and even reversing globalization. States may reassert their authority and disrupt global interdependence, even though it may be costly to do so, and powerful countries remain responsible for the existence and survival of international economic institutions like the World Trade Organization and World Bank (International Bank for Reconstruction and Development). Thus, in the view of skeptics, the interstate system that emerged after the Thirty Years' War (1618–1648) and the Peace of Westphalia remains intact; and transnational corporations and international organizations, though important, remain subject to the authority of governments. Those who believe that state sovereignty has diminished do not realize that sovereignty always was less complete than observers claimed it to be.[4] Moreover, even global corporations, according to skeptics, remain essentially national in attitude.

Hyperglobalizers

Those termed hyperglobalizers also perceive globalization as an essentially economic phenomenon. Where they differ from the skeptics is their conviction that contemporary economic links are historically unprecedented, that they involve new actors—state and nonstate—and that Westphalian states no longer control their economic fates. While economic interdependence in the past consisted largely of interstate trade and foreign investment consisted mainly of the purchase of foreign securities, contemporary trade is largely among and within transnational corporations and their subsidiaries, and much of it consists of services; and foreign investment is largely "direct," that is, involving the acquisition or construction of production facilities.

Hyperglobalizers regard the end of the Cold War and the collapse of the Soviet bloc, or "Second World," as having given birth to a truly global capitalist economic system. Indeed, with Russia's entry into the World Trade Organization in 2011, all major states are integrated into the global trading system. Moreover, there is now a single, integrated and internationalized global market in which ideas and capital move effortlessly and instantaneously across vast distances, and giant transnational corporations have global production, sales, and distribution networks. Capital is mobile, investment moves with unprecedented speed and freedom, and manufacturing and finance are no longer national. Unlike earlier firms, these corporations have global sales, customers, and production facilities, and they trade in the currencies of the countries in which they are sited and design integrated global sales and production strategies. Although transnational corporations still earn much of their profits from their "home region," they also invest anywhere where profits and market share can be maximized.

What hyperglobalizers *do* consider to be novel is the rapidity with which ever more goods, capital, people, and ideas move around the globe. This mobility contrasts vividly with the world before globalization, in which states controlled their borders and media and could limit the movement of people, money, and even ideas. Currency could be exchanged only with difficulty in most countries, and investment had to meet political as well as economic criteria. Today, in contrast, producers, investors, and consumers think, advertise, purchase, and sell globally in markets that transcend porous state boundaries. This view of globalization suggests that contemporary globalization augurs a new stage of human history in which nation-states are no longer the only or even the most important entities in the global economy. Economically, at least, hyperglobalizers view states as obsolete. Giant transnational corporations have become the principal economic actors, and they, like capital markets, have no national home.

There are, in fact, two versions of hyperglobalism. The first describes the position of economic neoliberals, who view capitalism, the free market, deregulation, and private enterprise as virtues and see the dominance of states by markets as the source of global prosperity. The unrestricted movement of capital, trade, and ideas, in their view, will make the global economic system more efficient than ever before and enrich everyone. Neoliberal enthusiasts point to the dramatic rise in international trade and daily foreign exchange turnover in recent decades. Global interest rates and macroeconomic policies, they point out, are converging, reflecting the deepening interdependence of major economies. Global trade continued to rise until the global recession, as did flows of direct foreign investment. However, these advocates of globalization ignore that while a "borderless" world may increase global wealth, it may also spread economic distress, as it did after America's subprime mortgage crisis in late 2007 rapidly circumnavigated the globe.

A second group of hyperglobalizers dislike globalization, perceiving it as an imperial project supported by Western capitalists. They argue that economic globalization promotes greater inequality within and between countries, whereby wealth is concentrated in the hands of a few and unregulated competition among states reduces the living standards of citizens. Some of those who hold this view are influenced by Marxism and recall how globalization was a principal cause for the ultimate collapse of the Soviet bloc, which could not function effectively in an economic environment of complex capitalist networks and integrated production and marketing. Unrestrained competition, they argue, forces states to reduce the costs of their exports in order to undersell their rivals for fear of losing jobs and industries that will relocate where costs are lower. Hence, states are forced to reduce government services, lower taxes, eviscerate safety and environmental rules that raise costs, and reverse welfare policies in a "race to the bottom."

Transformationalists

A third perspective, that of transformationalists, reflects a belief that globalization is unprecedented and multidimensional and that it is producing profound changes in politics and economics that, in turn, are remaking the essential nature of global life. As a process, globalization according to transformationalists also has technological, cultural, security, migration, human rights, and environmental dimensions.

Among the changes it is bringing are a decline in the significance of territory and the disappearance of the distinction between "foreign" and "domestic" as a result of the porosity of states' boundaries, which once impeded the movement of persons, things, and ideas. Transformationalists also perceive a growing privatization of all aspects of life, from welfare to warfare. In a word, transformationalists equate globalization with modernity, a consequence of revolutionary new technologies. Epitomizing the transformational perspective, James Rosenau argues that "a process of 'deterritorialization'" is under way.

> With satellite dishes allowing pictures to ignore airspaces easily, with the Internet enabling messages to bypass borders readily, with computer linkups facilitating the swift, unhindered transfer of money around the world, with jet aircraft making it possible for people to move speedily across boundaries, the concept of territory as a bounded land mass is undergoing diminution and revision as new spatial entities—such as offshore banks, global factories, ethnic diaspora, and transnational organizations—evolve that cannot be linked to a singular geographic locale and that enable people to overcome the obstacles to movement.[5]

As a result of new information and communication technologies, transformationalists conclude that national borders are becoming irrelevant and that governments must share political authority with a host of overlapping and layered polities, such as religious and ethnic groups. If territory is less relevant, then territorial states also become less important. As the role of citizenship diminishes, multiple identities become significant, much as they had been before the emergence of the modern nation-state. Where citizens' loyalties and identities in recent centuries focused principally on territorial nation-states, they now increasingly encompass religion, gender, ethnicity, tribe, and even profession.

Transformationalists envision new forms of multilayered "global governance" by a wide variety of polities—governmental and nongovernmental; public and private; and national, subnational, international, and even supranational—often with overlapping memberships. At the heart of such governance, they applaud the formation of webs of nongovernmental organizations—including humanitarian groups like Doctors Without Borders, human rights organizations like Amnesty International, and environmental groups like Greenpeace—that provide expert information to publics and governments and advocate policies to cope with global problems before which individual states seem helpless.

In a word, the essential nature of social and political space, once contained within well-defined territorial units, is undergoing rapid change, and this requires that we "remap" global politics. Globalization, transformationalists point out, enables people to interact with one another regardless of where they reside, and this means that global interconnectedness is among *people* rather than among *states*. This interconnectedness extends political and social relations beyond states' boundaries. As a result, events that occur in one place may have ripple effects on people and places remote from where they took place. Thus, new technologies including the Internet, mobile phones, and satellite dishes enable domestic unrest in one country like Tunisia or Egypt to spread like wildfire across much of North Africa, the Middle East, and beyond.

The authors of this book accept the transformationalist perspective. The several dimensions of globalization that are described in later chapters are linked. Thus, as the economy becomes more globalized, it may produce inequalities in the developing world that, on the whole, erode human rights. Violence, poverty, increasing population density, or environmental disasters in poor countries may produce massive migrations to rich countries in Europe and North America, where populations are rapidly aging. Such migrations may in turn produce a mixing of cultures or trigger violent nationalism aimed at the newcomers, who are ethnically and religiously different from indigenous citizens. For their part, migrants may remit earnings to their homelands in a process that can provide an enormous economic infusion for countries like El Salvador, Mexico, or the Philippines.

On the other hand, the export of globalizing ideas associated with neoliberal capitalism from the West to traditional societies profoundly affects local cultures. And the spread of norms such as individualism, consumerism, entrepreneurship, and secularism to traditional societies may produce a backlash by elites seeking to defend their positions and privileges and reinforce local cultural and religious mores. Indeed, this is one explanation for the upsurge of militant Islam in countries like Pakistan.

The most important linkage may be that between economic and political factors. Thus, it is widely believed among liberals that economic globalization enlarges the size of the global middle class by increasing global wealth. A wealthy middle class, in turn, is seen as preferring democratic to authoritarian institutions and procedures, the rule of law to arbitrary power, and individual freedom to collectivism. Finally, democratic societies are believed to favor peace more than do authoritarian societies. In this way, globalization is seen to be associated with the emergence of a "democratic peace" in world affairs.

Localization

Global politics features localizing as well as globalizing dynamics. Globalization enthusiasts perceive the forces of localization as conflictive and insular, whereas critics of globalization point out the diversity that is preserved by localization. Globalization erodes and transcends borders and boundaries, whereas localization reinforces boundaries and impedes the movement of persons, things, and ideas. Globalization involves rendering the political frontiers and sovereign barriers of states less relevant as they are transcended by economic, political, and social forces and as numerous groups—transnational, international, regional, national, and local—become enmeshed in governance. In short, globalization entails overcoming impediments to the movement of persons, things, and ideas, whereas localization involves processes and institutions that are rooted in territory and that impede such movement.

Localization may take the form of economic protectionism, anti-immigration policies, national sentiments, ethnic secessionism, and religious communalism. Balance of power, alliances, power politics, a cyber attack, arms racing, export substitution, economic protectionism, and great-power unilateralism all reinforce localization. Events like Russia's war with Georgia in 2008 and the resulting independence of South Ossetia and Abkhazia from Georgia are localizing because they result in reinforcing the role of territory and erecting new boundaries. In contrast, economic integration, free trade, and granting international institutions additional authority are globalizing in their impact.

Both globalization and localization are, therefore, features of contemporary global life, and interaction between them produces contradictions. The two occur simultaneously, they are linked, and it is frequently difficult to see which is dominant or sometimes even to tell them apart. Indeed, the term *glocalization* was coined to refer to the simultaneous presence of globalizing and localizing dynamics where precise boundaries between the two do not exist and where neither dominates the other. Successful transnational corporations reflect the virtues of glocalization when they "think globally, act locally." Thus, firms like McDonald's take advantage of the global convergence of tastes by developing products that can be sold worldwide. Nevertheless, many tastes remain localized, placing limits on homogenization and forcing firms to tailor products to local tastes. Thus, McDonald's serves "Chicken Maharaja Mac" and the vegetarian "McAloo Tikki" (potato burger) in India because Hindus do not eat beef. In Japan, the firm caters to local tastes by serving "Ebi Filet-O" (shrimp burgers), "Koroke Burger" (a sandwich consisting of mashed potato, cabbage, and katsu sauce), and "Ebi-Chiki" (shrimp nuggets), and in Hong Kong, "rice burgers" are popular.[6]

Nongovernmental organizations frequently operate in a "glocalized" fashion. Environmental groups, for instance, combine the global and the local by focusing activities on local events of importance to local residents, like the building of a dam or the burning of waste in incinerators. Such events, however, are microcosms of global issues, and organizations have the capacity to publicize these actions to publics around the world. The welding of local and global perspectives is frequently visible in antiglobalization demonstrations that mix opponents of local policies with those opposed to international policies. Transnational media like CNN and Al Jazeera, using satellite links, play a key role in linking the "global" and the "local." "Local" events like a popular uprising in Cairo or an Asian tsunami acquire global interest owing to technologies that enable empathy and virtual travel on the part of observers.

Global cities are "glocalized" worlds. Key corporate functions, including financial, legal, managerial, and planning tasks required for global management—skills needed by the global economy—are concentrated in "world cities" like New York, London, Frankfurt, Tokyo, and Shanghai. These are *globalized* cities that are located *within* the sovereign boundaries of nation-states, especially wealthy developed states. Such cities are sites for private governance functions performed by transnational corporations and homes for state-of-the art infrastructure and technology. They are also places where cultures mingle and where transnational identities come alive in neighborhoods and migrant communities.

The relationship between the local and the global, then, is complex. In some contexts, they clash, and in others, they reinforce each other. As Thomas Friedman declares, "The challenge in this era of globalization—for countries and individuals— is to find a healthy balance between preserving a sense of identity, home and community and doing what it takes to survive within the globalization system," so that society can prosper in the globalized world. "But no one," he continues,

> should have any illusions that merely participating in this global economy will make a society healthy. If that participation comes at the price of a country's identity, if individuals feel their olive tree crushed, or washed out, by this global system, those olive tree roots will rebel. They will rise up and strangle the process.[7]

The Origins of Globalization

There are various views regarding the origins of globalization, and to some extent, these views reflect the definition and perspective of observers. As we have seen, those described earlier as "skeptics" do not think that contemporary globalization is novel. Although they differ about its precise origins, most agree that it arose in the late 18th or early 19th centuries, reflecting the effects of the Industrial Revolution, the growth in free trade and foreign investment, the growth of European overseas empires, and the impact of British hegemony in global economic affairs.

Industrialization, according to one team of observers, involved "a marked break with the past, when trade's weight in the world economy scaled new heights and prices converged dramatically, with the process reaching its first crescendo around 1913,"[8] and "the really big leap to more globally integrated commodity and factor markets took place in the second half of the [19th] century." In consequence, by the outbreak of World War I,

> there was hardly a village or town anywhere on the globe whose prices were not influenced by distant foreign markets, whose infrastructure was not financed by foreign capital, whose engineering, manufacturing, and even business skills were not

imported from abroad, or whose labor markets were not influenced by the absence of those who had emigrated or those who had immigrated.[9]

In contrast, hyperglobalizers, who believe that contemporary economic interdependence is unprecedented, date the origins of globalization from the 20th century. Some contend that it emerged from the catastrophes of the Great Depression and World War II, viewing the Bretton Woods Conference and the onset of American economic hegemony as key moments in the process. Globalization in their view reflects the desire of American leaders to encourage and sustain an open trading system and global economic growth and to promote the spread of values such as individualism, democracy, and free enterprise. As noted earlier, Bretton Woods, which reflected American policy preferences, witnessed the establishment of the international economic institutions that would become the pillars of economic globalization, and the end of the Cold War produced a truly global economic system by ending the economic isolation of Russia, its successor states, and the former satellite states of Eastern Europe.

Like hyperglobalizers, transformationalists see globalization as being of relatively recent origin, dating from the emergence of new information and communication technologies, although "it certainly is plausible," declares the political scientist Jack Donnelly, "to suggest that, whatever the historical parallels or antecedents, at least the pace of change is accelerating, with important qualitative differences." As such, globalization is "a characteristic of the decades on either side of the year 2000."[10] Since transformationalists emphasize the impact of new technologies, they believe that globalization dates back to the invention of the Internet in the 1960s or the more recent proliferation of mobile phones, small computers, and space satellites and the spread in recent decades of online social networks such as Bebo, Douban, Facebook, Habbo, Linkedin, Myspace, Qzone, and Twitter, which overcome physical geography and allow virtually instantaneous communication. These technologies that link previously disparate communities increase the velocity with which people, things, and ideas move and cross boundaries, and thereby also produce new vulnerabilities to global changes.

Others see the roots of globalization as historically much older and agree with Peter Heintz that, at most, the past three centuries "have been an apprenticeship for living in one world."[11] Barry Gills and William Thompson write of "globalizations," arguing that globalization processes "have long pedigrees" and "are anything but novel."[12] The reason that we think of globalization as novel "has to do with the way we tell stories about the past" that focus on "relatively local and largely disconnected events."[13] "History," they conclude, "is a matter of perspective. Local perspective yield local histories. Global perspective yield global perspectives."[14] Globalization, then, "is not only a phenomenon of the modern age," and understanding the phenomenon "requires placing it in the context of world historical development."[15]

Jan Nederveen Pieterse, thus, views globalization as a "deep historical process." "Taking a long view," the characteristics of globalization include ancient population movements across and between continents, long-distance trade, the spread of major religions like Christianity and Islam, the spread of knowledge and technology ranging from Arabic numerals to war chariots, and the meeting and mixing of different cultures.[16] Like Nederveen Pieterse, Nayan Chanda also sees globalization as beginning in the distant past, with the emigration of our original ancestors from Africa, traders seeking commercial opportunities, the proselytizers of the world's religions, adventurers and explorers, soldiers and conquerors, slaves, tourists, and migrants in search of a better life. "In the *longue durée* historical perspective," writes Chanda, "globalization has been growing ever since homo sapiens settled into sedentary cultures in river valleys. Connections that began as short forays for trading, exploration, evangelism, and imperial expansion have accelerated over the millennia."[17] Thus, "if one looked under the hood of our daily existence, one could see a multitude of threads that connect us to faraway places from an ancient time."[18]

Among the historical processes that produced globalization, observers see wars as particularly important. As Anthony McGrew writes,

> From the Chinese armadas of the thirteenth century through the medieval Crusades, to the New Imperialism of the late nineteenth century, military conquest and force have been vital instruments in drawing the world's distant regions and discrete civilizations into tightening webs of recursive interaction.[19]

The three global wars of the 20th century—World Wars I and II and the Cold War—globalized security issues and spread modern technologies.

Like war, exploration and colonialization were also key processes in facilitating globalization through expanding trade, globalizing capitalism, exporting political institutions, and spreading dominant cultures. "From the late fifteenth century," writes one observer, "the European powers embarked on a project of exporting their own cultural practices and exploiting the resources of people across the world. Colonization laid the routes for globalization."[20] Another declares that "historians have noted the importance of the first circumnavigation of the Earth in 1519–1521."[21]

Perhaps the most reasonable approach to the origins of globalization is that, while contemporary globalization is unprecedented, its roots lie in ancient history and its evolution has been discontinuous. This is Alison Jagger's position:

> Globalization in the broadest sense is nothing new. Intercontinental travel and trade, and the mixing of cultures and populations are as old as humankind; after all, the foremothers and forefathers of every one of us walked originally out of Africa.[22]

However, the neoliberal capitalism that dominates contemporary globalization entails "a retreat from the liberal social democracy of the years following World War II back toward the non-redistributive laissez-faire liberalism of the seventeenth and eighteenth centuries."[23]

Conclusion

Globalization and localization processes wax and wane. Earlier epochs have witnessed a retreat from or movement toward highly globalized worlds. Some periods feature the integration of independent polities into empires characterized by economies of scale, cultural homogenization, and centralized governance, followed by their breakup into small polities with localized political and economic systems. In its day, Rome ruled much of the Western world until it crumbled in the face of repeated assaults from without. It was succeeded in medieval Europe by a system of overlapping polities, with the Frankish

Holy Roman Empire and the Church of Rome at the acme of a feudal pyramid atop a diverse array of regional and local political entities. In the Far East, a great empire emerged from China's warring states era in the 3rd century BCE, and in the Near East an Islamic empire expanded with unprecedented speed after the 7th century CE.

We live in a world of shifting boundaries, proliferating actors, and evolving authority. The role of territory is declining, and the mobility of things, persons, and ideas is accelerating. The spatial issue is made more complex because global institutions, practices, and processes are located within territorial states, even as their impact overwhelms the boundaries of those states. Such institutions, practices, and processes inhabit sovereign states but are at the same time transnational and "denationalized." Thus, we must reconceptualize "international relations" as "global relations" and move away from organizing our analyses solely around territorial states and toward contemplating a world in which political space is based on the distribution of identities and affiliations.

As we shall see in a later chapter, whether globalization or localization is inherently preferable or normatively superior is a question for which there are no easy answers. Judgments like these depend on personal values and interests, and it is possible to marshal persuasive arguments in favor of both. Both processes benefit some people and harm others; both produce "winners" and "losers."

Notes

1   For a lengthy and in-depth analysis of some of the issues dealt with in this brief essay, see Yale H. Ferguson and Richard W. Mansbach, *Globalization: The Return of Borders to a Borderless World?* (Abingdon, UK: Routledge, 2012), chapter 1.

2   Thomas Friedman, *The World Is Flat* (New York: Farr, Straus & Giroux, 2005), 7.

3   David Held, Anthony McGrew, David Glodblatt and Jonathan Perraton, *Global Transformations: Politics, Economics, and Culture* (Stanford, CA: Stanford University Press, 1999), 2–10.

4   See Stephen D. Krasner, *Sovereignty: Organized Hypocrisy* (Princeton, NJ: Princeton University Press, 1999).

5   James N. Rosenau, *Distant Proximities* (Princeton, NJ: Princeton University Press, 2003), 176.

6   See Beatrice Adams, "McDonald's Strange Menu Around the World," *Trifter*, July 19, 2007, http://trifter.com/practical-travel/budget-travel/mcdonald%E2%80%99s-strange-menu-around-the-world/.

7   Thomas L. Friedman, *The Lexus and the Olive Tree,* rev. ed. (New York: Farrar, Straus and Giroux, 2000), 41.

8   Michael D. Bordo, Alan M. Taylor, and Jeffrey G. Williamson, "Introduction," in Michael D. Bordo, Alan M. Taylor, and Jeffrey G. Williamson, eds., *Globalization in Historical Perspective* (Chicago: University of Chicago Press, 2003), 4.

9   Kevin H. O'Rourke and Jeffrey G. Williamson, *Globalization and History* (Cambridge, MA: MIT Press, 1999), 2.

10 Jack Donnelly, "Human Rights, Globalizing Flows, and State Power," in Alison Brysk, ed., *Globalization and Human Rights* (Berkeley, CA: University of California Press, 2002), 226.

11 Peter Heintz, "Introduction: A Sociological Code for the Description of World Society and Its Change," *International Social Science Journal* 34:1 (1982), 7. As cited in Barrie Axford, *The Global System: Economics, Politics, and Culture* (New York: St. Martin's Press, 1995), 33.

12 Barry K. Gills and William R. Thompson, "Globalizations, Global Histories and Historical Globalities," in Gills and Thompson, eds., *Globalization and Global History* (Oxford, UK: Routledge, 2006), 1.

13 Ibid.

14 Ibid, 2.

15 David Held and Anthony McGrew, "The Great Globalization Debate: An Introduction," in Held and McGrew, eds., *The Global Transformations Reader: An Introduction to the Globalization Debate,* 2nd ed. (Cambridge, UK: Polity Press, 2003), 7.

16 Jan Neederveen Pieterse, *Globalization and Culture: Global Mélange* (Lanham, MD: Rowan & Littlefield, 2004), 24–25.

17 Nayan Chanda, "Runaway Globalization Without Governance," *Global Governance* 14 (2008), 119.

18 Nayan Chanda, *Bound Together: How Traders, Preachers, Adventurers, and Warriors Shaped Globalization* (New Haven, CT: Yale University Press, 2007), x.

19 Anthony McGrew, "Organized Violence in the Making (and Remaking) of Globalization," in Held and McGrew, eds., *Globalization Theory: Approaches and Controversies* (Cambridge, UK: Polity Press, 2007), 15.

20 Nikos Papastergiadis, *The Turbulence of Migration: Globalization, Deterritorialization and Hybridity* (Cambridge, UK: Polity Press, 2000), 76.

21 Mauro F. Guillén, "Is Globalization Civilizing, Destructive or Feeble? A Critique of Five Key Debates in Social Science Literature," *Annual Review of Sociology* 27 (2001), 237.

22 Alison M. Jaggar, "Is Globalization Good for Women?" *Comparative Literature* 53:4 (Autumn 2001), 298.

23 Ibid, 299.

1.2

GLOBALIZATION PREDATES WAL-MART BY THOUSANDS OF YEARS

Peter Hadekel

> In the following selection, the author describes a recent book that argues that economic globalization has a very long history. It suggests that early civilizations featured highly successful economic systems, some with similarities to contemporary economic practices and others that seem unique to their time and place. The lesson to be drawn from this is that there is no single approach to achieving global economic prosperity.

Many of us tend to assume that globalization of the economy is a recent trend.

But thousands of years before Wal-Mart figured out how to source products in China, savvy traders were trading successfully with other parts of the world.

Source: Peter Hadekel, "Globalization Predates Wal-Mart by Thousands of Years; 'We Have a Lot to Learn From Business History of Ancient World,'" *Montreal Gazette,* May 27, 2009.

McGill University management professor Karl Moore has spent much of his academic life studying business history, looking for patterns and clues that might apply to modern-day globalization.

His latest book, co-written with historian David Lewis, is *The Origins of Globalization*—a look back at the business history of the ancient world.

Perhaps surprisingly, Moore has found that we have a lot to learn from Mesopotamia, Egypt, ancient Greece, Rome and the Chinese dynasties.

One of the most valuable lessons is that "there's more than one way to have a successful economy," Moore said in an interview. And that's a useful reminder to those who preach that the "Anglo-American" business model is the only way to go.

"We looked at 3,000 years of business history and we saw quite different approaches.

"When we looked at Assyria and Phoenicia, the temple was the central institution. They were kind of the investment bankers of the day, so that if you wanted to get some investment funding, you would go to visit your priest."

Ancient Egypt was very much an example of state socialism—a command-and-control economy run with some success by the pharaohs.

"When we move on to Greece, it was much more entrepreneurial. That was partly because of the geography—city states like Athens and Sparta were fighting."

Those military prerogatives led to a more entrepreneurial society.

Greece was really the first example of a free market, the authors note. Rome, by contrast, was where family capitalism first began—more about who you knew than anything else.

"It was really following the military as they expanded.

"So what we saw is a number of different models of economies that were successful.

"Of course, the issue is: what's a successful economy? Is it about the distribution of wealth, the lack of poverty? We can debate what is success. But we've seen long-lasting economies."

What's the relevance of all this today? A dose of humility, Moore says. History clearly shows that there have been many different ways to create prosperity, and there's no overarching ideology to economic development.

"There was a time in the late '80s, early '90s, when there was a kind of sense of American triumphalism," Moore said. "The Anglo-American system had triumphed, communism was discredited with the fall of the Berlin Wall, Europe was in low growth, Japan was in a recession, China and India were really not on the radar.

"It seemed that the Anglo-American system was alone in the world." And its proponents weren't shy about saying that "the rest of the world should be like us."

Fast-forward to today and the U.S. looks hobbled by problems of its own making, while large parts of the emerging world are growing at much faster rates.

History gives us a good perspective on what kinds of economies work, he says.

"There are three things you have to look at: culture, history and social institutions. Not one size fits all.

"The American system is great for America, most of the time, but it doesn't mean that's the form the Swedes or the Japanese should adopt."

The global economy needs to make room for diversity, he adds.

The book makes plenty of interesting connections: economic activity in ancient Assyria and Babylon was the precursor for multinational enterprise, dominated by successful trading houses. Roman commercial organizations were the first de facto corporations. Chinese culture and history bequeathed a system allowing its modern-day economy to flourish while central power and control remains.

The book's conclusion is simple enough. There is more than one path to success, and we can all learn from the good and bad decisions of the past.

1.3

GENGHIS KHAN STARTED GLOBALIZATION

from *Chinadaily.com.cn*

> The next selection reflects a Chinese approach to the origins of globalization. It argues that the seeds of globalization were planted eight centuries ago when the conqueror, Genghis Khan, was expanding the Mongol empire into Asia and Europe. This empire, according to a Chinese scholar, promoted economic and cultural expansion and exchange and overwhelmed the political boundaries that it confronted.

We think of globalization as selling Coca-Cola in Calcutta or Starbucks in Shanghai. But researchers claim the process dates back 800 years, to the time when Genghis Khan was building his empire.

It was under Genghis Khan's empire that the Eurasian landmass began to demonstrate the characteristics of global exchanges, according to Hao Shiyuan, a researcher at the Chinese Academy of Social Sciences (CASS).

Thanks to the expansion of the empire, "economic and cultural exchanges became possible to the maximum extent and previously isolated civilizations became linked," said Hao, director of the academy's Institute of Ethnology and Anthropology, at an international symposium on the founding of the Mongol Empire held by the CASS in Beijing yesterday.

"This is what globalization features: shrinking space, shrinking time, and disappearing borders," said Hao. Globalization is leading to the integration of the world's markets, culture, technology, and governance, in a similar way to the spread of communications, trade, transport and technology in Genghis Khan's era, said Hao.

Establishing the Mongol Empire, the largest contiguous land empire in history, covering modern Mongolia, China, Korea, Russia, Iran, Iraq, Afghanistan, and Syria in the

Source: "Genghis Khan Started Globalization," *Chinadaily.com.cn,* June 5, 2006.

13th century, Genghis Khan has been described as 'World Conqueror,' 'Emperor of All Men' and 'Scourge of God.' But whatever title he is given, nothing can eliminate his contribution to the integration of ethnicities, nationalities and civilizations in ancient times.

An in-depth understanding of the historical context and social system of the time is needed to evaluate Genghis Khan and his contribution to history, said B. Enkhtuvshin, vice-president of the Mongolian Academy of Sciences, at the symposium.

"Genghis Khan promoted globalization as has no ruler before him," said the Mongolian academician, who is also director of the International Institute for the Study of Nomadic Civilizations.

More than 50 experts and researchers from China, Mongolia, Russia, Japan and the United States attended the symposium, commemorating the 800th anniversary of the founding of the Mongol Empire.

1.4

GLOBALIZATION NOT MADE IN THE WEST

Robbie Robertson

> Are the origins of globalization exclusively Western? The following selection published in a Korean newspaper denies this Eurocentric claim, suggesting that a long historical view reveals that it has an Asian heritage. The expansion of Chinese civilization and trade bore considerable similarities to contemporary globalization trends that linked previously isolated societies. Disease disrupted this early globalization, while creating the opportunity for European–Chinese contacts, which in turn led to the discovery of America. European colonialism and imperialism then ensued, and with them features of 18th- and 19th-century globalization dynamics.

SUVA, Fiji - The question, what is the most serious threat to our contemporary wellbeing, might evoke the answer: "Globalization." Globalization, many of us believe, is a powerful juggernaut of transnational forces intent on devouring the world for profit, and destroying local cultures and environments in the process. However, from the perspective of history, things look different.

Source: Robbie Robertson, "Globalization Not Made in the West," *The Korea Herald,* April 18, 2005. Originally published in *YaleGlobal Online,* April 13, 2005.

The Non-Western Roots of Globalization

First, although globalization is often viewed as the consequence of new technologies and changing political priorities after the Cold War, it is in fact a much older force for change.

A historical view of globalization, stressing the common heritage of humanity, enables us to contextualize changes such as industrialization without assigning superiority to the West. The result is a much more inclusive interpretation of globalization.

Second, a historical interpretation enables us to treat globalization as a process facilitating the most radical transformation of societies that humans have ever experienced: a transformation called democratization.

Globalization, then, is not about rampant capitalism, technology or homogenization. It is about the changed environments people create and manipulate as their societies globally interconnect, environments that have become increasingly commercialized, urbanized, and democratized.

Humans first experienced this transformative effect 1000 years ago, when the most advanced society of the time fueled continental interconnectedness. China's trade surpluses fed a network of regional linkages that stretched across the world's most populous continent.

But the momentum did not last. China succumbed to Mongolian warlords and much of Afro-Eurasia fell victim to the plague they carried across the continent. Like HIV/AIDS and SARS today, the plague was an early indicator that interconnectedness possesses real dangers. In the 14th century, China lost one-quarter of its population and Europe, one-third. The resulting disruption encouraged European states to connect directly with China. In the process, they discovered the Americas, using its wealth to buy their way into the intra-Asian trade and establish a new Atlantic economy. Thus, human interconnectedness became globalized, and a whole new environment for human activities emerged.

Today, the history of this early transformation is usually read in terms of civilizations and economic activity: Because Europeans initiated global networks, many observers stress European exceptionalism as its cause; because of the tremendous growth in commercial activities, many also give centrality to capitalism.

But the transformation was much more extensive and destabilizing than these interpretations suggest. It accelerated the global distribution of plants and animals, transformed human diets, spawned rapid population growth, and stressed environments as land-use patterns changed and urbanization increased.

Authorities everywhere struggled to accommodate these unprecedented changes. Spain's rulers tried to convert their newfound wealth into the basis for hegemony within Europe, but in the end, power flowed to societies that gave space to wealth-generating merchants. This democratizing consequence of globalization challenged the interests of elites. They sought stability through exclusions of religion and race, as well as imperial and commercial monopolies. Frequently, they turned to war and conquest—outcomes that reduced global interconnectivity. Most elites little understood the transformations they confronted.

Industrialization is a case in point, normally portrayed as an example of British exceptionalism, or of Europe's "enlightenment." Rarely is it presented as an outcome of global production and trade in cotton and the expanding consumer markets globalization occasioned. Many analysts give centrality to technology in stimulating change. Yet human interconnectedness alone enabled industrialization to resonate so rapidly and globally.

However, there can be no doubting the impact of what became a second wave of globalization. Industrialization enabled environments to carry larger populations, which in turn generated new social and political dynamics. More than ever before, technology generated huge profits, which made it desirable as an economic activity. Certainly the military power it generated attracted the attention of states.

Yet most leaders still failed to grasp that security and well-being came from social empowerment, not conquest. They feared democratization and tried to reduce its impact. They sought colonial successes as alternatives. With competition increasingly drawn in Darwinian terms, they were prepared to go to war in order to retain hegemonic status at home and abroad. They failed, and World War I cost their nations tremendously—and not only in lives: It cost them the confidence that once energized the second wave of globalization.

Economic collapse quickly generated a brutal depression. The resulting inward-looking economic policies simply reinforced the drive to empire and conquest that had already exacted a high price. During the 1930s and 1940s, they provoked a second round of bloodletting.

From World War II, a very different third wave of globalization emerged. The demise of many former ruling classes created the democratic space for political stability in industrialized nations and for international cooperation.

It also enabled the dissolution of empires. Thus decolonization, too, was a product of globalization. But decolonization could not guarantee meaningful participation in the new global environment for the emergent Third World. Colonialism left its peoples poorly equipped, and development strategies gave little weight to the democratic imperative. Consequently, a democratic global divide emerged that still holds the potential to destabilize human interconnectedness.

In addition, the third wave began with a new global ideological division, an unprecedented arms race, and a destructive Soviet-American rivalry. It was not an auspicious start. However, as the Cold War ended, corporate transnationalism assumed center stage.

When postwar prosperity faltered in the 1970s, corporations exploited fears of recession to deregulate domestic economies and transform global regulatory systems to their advantage. As capital became more transnational, it harnessed a new generation of technological change to fashion global production networks. But it was not the only global force to survive the Cold War.

Postwar democratization had sent shockwaves of empowerment through industrialized societies. They reached deep into societies to transform working and domestic lives, family and social relationships, gender and race relations. They created wealthier, more educated, and longer-living populations able to connect with industry in new and innovative ways. Civil societies represented the symbiosis between economic growth and democratization. They stressed the role of human agency in development and generated alternative global goals.

Such transformations demonstrate the dynamic character of the third wave of globalization. Human interconnectivity has always expanded the environments in which humans operate. But, as we have seen, it also generates challenges.

Three challenges stand out: first, the challenge of extending and deepening democratization globally. Increases in inequalities, exacerbated by war and debt, have lost the third wave of globalization much of its legitimacy. However, like the empires of old, the industrialized world cannot survive as a world unto itself. Human interconnectivity makes that impossible.

Second, there exists the environmental challenge of addressing issues of sustainability globally. Just as democracy cannot survive in a sea of poverty, so it cannot survive in an environmentally damaged and disease-ridden world.

The third challenge is multicultural. We need to adjust to the diversity that globalization presents. With human migration greater and more rapid than at any time in the past, all forms of exclusivity risk instability. They deny common citizenship and collective responsibility as tools for sustainability in increasingly multicultural societies.

All three challenges represent divides that could cripple globalization and its human dynamic. Only democratization broadens the scope for wealth generation and capacity-building, and creates the skills needed to manage increasingly complex societies.

1.5

ASIA SHOULD CHANGE ITS WEST-CENTRIC LOOKING GLASS

from *Chinadaily.com.cn*

> The next selection emphasizes that globalization did not have exclusively European roots. It argues that much of Asia was globalized before the 20th century but that this has been largely ignored, even by Asians themselves. Contemporary views of globalization, according to the article, have a pro-Western bias, a bias apparent in debates about issues such as the deterioration of the global environment. Instead, the article suggests, Asians need to look more closely at their own history and reduce what is termed the "Dubai syndrome," that is, a dependence on Western practices and institutions.

For a continent that is the cradle of civilization, it is sad that only meanings invented elsewhere get affixed to words. An example is "globalization," which is seen as a

Source: "Asia Should Change Its West-Centric Looking Glass," *Chinadaily.com.cn,* December 3, 2009.

phenomenon of recent origin. The fact is that many parts of Asia were globalized long before the second half of the 20th century. The Mesopotamians, Chinese, Indians and Persians were trading even before the Roman Empire was built.

So why is it that we continue to see "globalization" as something new, something introduced to Asia by "outsiders"? Why is Asia still suffering from a "colonial" hangover—of judging everything from outsiders' perspective? This attitude is deep-rooted not only in commerce, but also education. Take the field of international relations for example. Every country has its own approach to geopolitics and needs to view facts from its own perspective. Yet for decades the three biggest powers in Asia—China, India and Japan—have been sending hundreds of students to the US or European countries to study international relations. Many of those who return from abroad with multiple degrees subconsciously imbibe the biases and deficiencies of the US-European viewpoint on Asia, and thus get disconnected from their own countries' realities. And quite a few of them become important policymakers in their home countries. The true meaning of "globalization" is to make the home country the hub and let its "spokes" radiate across the globe. But, for much of the Asian policymaking community, the hub is either the US or the European Union (EU), or both.

We need to ensure that future international relations students are anchored to the needs of their own societies. Of course, those who choose to stay back in the US and or a European country are free to see matters from the West's perspective.

India, where at least 310 million people are close to starvation levels, spends tens of millions of dollars every year on endowments and scholarships to send students to the US and the EU. Recently, a large group of young Indian parliamentarians were sent to the US to study international relations at the expense of taxpayers. These future leaders were drilled in curricula that understandably place the interests of the US at the core. The money would have been worth being spent if the government of India had given it to its universities to set up international relations departments. Although the US and EU make no pretence that their policies are geared exclusively toward furthering their own interests, many of their counterparts in Asia appear reluctant to adopt such robustness in defending the interests of their own peoples.

The debate on climate change is an example of how much the entire world has been influenced by "globalization," defined as a West-centric viewpoint. Any individual moving away from such a territory-specific calculus is seen as "anti-globalization," while people in Asia who support US and EU policies are called "good global citizens." Watching some of the more prominent international TV channels one would get the feeling that the horrors of climate change have been caused by the economic growth of China and India, when the truth is that 87 percent of the damage is the direct consequence of human activity in the US, the EU and other developed countries.

What developing countries like China, India, Brazil and South Africa need to do is to publish a joint white paper, detailing the origin of environmental degradation over the past couple of centuries and giving the per capita greenhouse gas emission of every country in the developed world.

Although the "globalizers" talk of "one Europe," they refuse to acknowledge the existence of "one Asia." Instead, they have broken Asia into different segments, and treat each as separate from the rest, when in fact the continent forms a single geopolitical mass. For example, there is "East Asia," "Southeast Asia," "South Asia," "Central Asia" and the "Middle East". And since President Dimitry Medvedev considers Russia to be "100 per cent European" three-fourths of the largest country gets excluded from Asia. Asians should be aware of international relations theories that divide Asia into separate parts and hence prevent a pan-Asian view from evolving.

This propensity to view all matters from the lens of the self-appointed "globalizers" can be termed the "Dubai syndrome". Those who have visited the UAE city must have seen how comprehensive the influence of Western "experts" on its decision-making process is. To a lesser degree, such outsourcing of brainpower is characteristic of several of Dubai's neighbors.

Other countries too have suffered for outsourcing their decisions. From 1955 to 1995, South American countries provide several examples of collapsed economies for adhering to the so-called "Friedmanite" economics, which in effect made monopolitics out of foreign companies and denied incentives to domestic enterprises.

Dubai is the most recent example. But outsourcing of "mind space" to the "globalizers" has for long been an unfortunate feature of Asia. And since the problems in Dubai have been caused by decisions taken on the advice of external banking institutions, shouldn't they bear the cost of such errors? Indeed, the Gulf Cooperation Council has already suffered—a loss of more than $1.3 trillion because of the greed of the "globalized" financial fraternity.

Dubai is a warning to Asia. The continent needs to look at itself from its own perspective, the way the developed world has been doing. Once the UAE city emerges from the mess created because of its blind faith in Western advisers, whose only intention was to make quick profits, hopefully its leadership will follow policies that are helpful to its people. Asia must avoid a repeat of the "Dubai syndrome," by looking at the world through a lens that has the continent at the core.

Chapter 2

TECHNOLOGY AND GLOBALIZATION

Technology is often portrayed as shrinking today's world and erasing its political borders. Chapter 2 looks at the impact of technological change in shaping the pace and character of "globalization," both historically and in recent decades. In a historical context, it leads us to consider the effects of technology, ranging from the stirrup and the sailing vessel to the printing press and the telegraph, on the scale and permeability of political, economic, social, and cultural institutions and identities. For reasons of space, however, we will focus on more recent technologies. The chapter also investigates the "stickiness" of the changes facilitated or caused by technological development. Finally, the chapter asks us to explore how contemporary technologies, such as jet aircraft, satellite communication, and the Internet, are driving developments in globalization.

No one can say with certainty whether technological innovations will ultimately be beneficial. Consider the Human Genome Project and the science of genetic engineering. On the one hand, genetic engineering promises greater crop yields and new treatments for ancient diseases. On the other, genetically modified plants or fish may eliminate native species and reduce the gene pool and biodiversity. Although technology does *not* necessitate globalization, it enables and drives it. Technology, however, is not necessarily benevolent. For instance, as we will see in Chapter 5, the same technologies that have contributed to globalization also have raised the specter of war in cyberspace.

2.1

THE TECHNOLOGICAL FOUNDATIONS OF GLOBALIZATION[1]

Richard W. Mansbach

The process of contemporary globalization, like globalization in the past, is inextricably linked to the development of modern information and communication technologies (ICTs). These technologies have been characterized by dramatic innovation, including the introduction of the Internet in 1995, which cost less than the telephone and increased the volume of communication that could be sent. A key step took place in 1997, when the world's major states, representing much of world economic production, signed the Information and Technology Agreement, which committed them to eliminate tariffs on major technology products by the year 2000. ICTs have significant political consequences because they facilitate mobilization and coordination in cyberspace by dissidents, criminals, insurgents, terrorists, corporate managers, and others.

Technological change has always been a key factor in global politics, shaping everything from the ways in which people organize for political ends to the ways they trade with or kill one another. From the humble stirrup, the Byzantine incendiary "Greek fire," and gunpowder to the printing press, the mechanical clock, the steam engine, the airplane, radio and television, and nuclear fission, dramatic changes in global politics have been linked to technological innovation. The stirrup, probably invented in China in the 4th century CE and spread westward across the Asian steppes by tribal horsemen, revolutionized warfare by providing a stable platform for archers. The mariner's astrolabe, in wide use by the late 15th century, which made it possible to determine a ship's latitude by celestial measurement, and the accurate mechanical clock introduced in the 18th century, which allowed the measurement of longitude, fostered the age of European exploration and colonialism. The printing press, invented in the 15th century, permitted the unprecedented spread of ideas that fostered the Renaissance and the Protestant Reformation. The invention of canning in 1809 by the French brewer Nicholas Appert revolutionized warfare, allowing armies to fight all the year round and making it possible to feed vast numbers of soldiers, who no longer had to forage for themselves. The steamship and medicines like quinine made it possible for Europeans to penetrate previously inaccessible regions, and modern firearms enabled them to conquer much of the world.

The military historian Martin Van Creveld points out that technology, "which between 1500 and 1945, was such a great help in constructing the state, has turned around and is often causing states to lose power in favor of various kinds of organizations which are either not territorially based, or lacking in sovereignty, or both."[2] Centuries earlier, when gunpowder and cannon smashed stone fortresses and brought down knights in armor, military security depended on the size of a polity's territory. Technology largely fostered state power as long as its products—for example, plows, cannon, and muskets—could be used independently. This changed with the spread of technologies that functioned as *networked systems*—railways, telegraphs, and telephones—which national boundaries impeded.

Recent decades have witnessed a dramatic acceleration in technological innovation. Contemporary technologies are altering the meaning of time and space, and the changes are reducing the central role formerly played by territory with regard to the world economy, warfare, political mobilization, and identity formation. These innovations underpin much of what is novel about contemporary globalization. Technology is overcoming sovereign boundaries and is arguably making the world "flat," as Thomas Friedman famously described it.

The impact of new technologies has, however, been uneven. Their greatest impact has been in North America, Western Europe, and Japan, although this impact is rapidly increasing in the developing economic powers of China, India, and the countries of

Southeast Asia. Their impact is least evident in poor regions like Africa. By 2010, there were almost 2 billion Internet users. Asia hosts over 828,000,000 users, including 384 million in China alone. In contrast, Africa and the Middle East host relatively few users, some 67 and 57 million, respectively.[3] What is sometimes called the "digital divide" is also apparent in Internet penetration, which ranges from a high of more than 70% in North America to a low of less than 11% in Africa. Worldwide, ICTs are concentrated among employees of corporations, government bureaucracies, and universities, and those who can afford to purchase home computers and the services of Internet providers. However, technology affects those at the bottom as well, as when the media make the poor painfully aware of their relative deprivation or when mobile phones allow the rural poor to save money or learn the prices they will receive for their products.

Some observers believe that ICTs and more education are increasing human skills in ways that allow them to become politically active in unprecedented ways. Advances such as the Internet afford people the information needed to discover whether their interests are being served by their governments, in much the same way as did the printing press, telephone, radio, and television in earlier eras. As citizens' skills increase, their sense of empowerment grows, along with their willingness to act outside traditional avenues of political discourse. Mass media like CNN and Al Jazeera give them the facts they need to discern whether their interests are being sacrificed to those of leaders who are authoritarian, incompetent, and/or corrupt.

Satellite television exposes viewers to a variety of new opinions and information, and the Internet is becoming crucial for exchanging views, disseminating information, creating virtual communities, and mobilizing citizens' political activities. Internet bloggers influence and inform people around the world by transmitting information and opinion. As a result, the desire of citizens to control their destinies is likely to intensify, thereby undermining rule from the top. In sum, political participation is growing and manifesting itself in unconventional ways, ranging from street demonstrations and formation of new political parties to political agitation and terrorism. The unconventional political activities promoted by ICTs are nowhere more evident than in the Occupy movement, which began in September 2011 in Zuccotti Park, located in New York City's Wall Street financial district, in protest against economic inequality and injustice and then spread like wildfire nationally and internationally. Today, the mobilization of whole populations against foreign occupation (Iraq and Afghanistan) or authoritarian rule (Tunisia, Egypt, Bahrain, and Libya) makes the costs of such practices prohibitively high.

Those who seek to reform globalization have also extensively used new digital media, which they see as creating nonhierarchical, horizontal networks among individuals. The Internet, cell phones, and other digital technologies help antiglobalization activists coordinate activities and provide new ways of globalizing local events and publicizing such events. Activists communicate, provide one another with information and training, and mobilize in cyberspace.

Although we understand some of the changes in global life wrought by new technologies like ICTs, predicting their precise impact is probably impossible. Will genetic engineering of plants and animals be used to produce "genetic power," perhaps to sterilize an enemy's biosystem, or will it be used to create "food independence" for those who suffer from malnutrition? Will the cell phone prove more valuable to terrorists moving from place to place to escape detection or to agricultural workers in the developing world seeking an optimal price for their produce?

Technology and the Global Economy

Brain power and knowledge have become critical economic resources, increasingly replacing muscle power as sources of wealth. This insight led Richard Rosecrance to conceptualize what he called the "virtual state" built on information processing and services. He described a new global division of labor "between 'head' countries, which design products, and 'body' nations, which manufacture them."[4] "Head" countries, like Israel and Singapore, are "info-tigers" that specialize in innovative research and services like marketing, transport, and insurance, while "body" countries, like China and Vietnam, depend on manufacturing. The two types of countries rely on each other to create an integrated global market based on transnational production and instantaneous communication among corporate subsidiaries.

The revolutions in transportation, information, and communication are integrating the global economy; reducing costs; and enabling the creation of networked-based productivity. These increase interdependence and enable corporations and their markets to transcend territorial boundaries. Such markets are made possible by the instantaneous transmission of vast amounts of funds and information from anywhere to everywhere, enabling corporations and banks to use integrated global production and marketing strategies that take advantage of global capital markets and investment. The Internet extends the reach of the capital, bond, and trading markets and ensures the rapid reaction of markets to events.

Not only do technologies like the Internet complicate states' efforts to manage private investment and currency flows and interest rates, they undermine the capacity of states to protect citizens' intellectual property. Everything from books and articles to works of art are accessible in "virtual" form, both legally and illegally, on the Internet. Moreover, if investors lose confidence in national currencies or the capacity of states to pay their debts, the new technologies foster rapid and destructive capital flight and currency speculation that magnify existing economic problems and spread them around the world in a matter of seconds. Banks and even states, electronically connected by the global financial market, may find themselves suddenly on the verge of economic collapse. Hedge funds, derivatives, securitization, and other exotic financial instruments can bring national economies to the brink of disaster by the rapid movement of funds from one country to another. In these and other ways, new technologies undermine the economic authority and autonomy of sovereign states, including major actors like the United States, Britain, and Germany.

Technology and Political Stability

The capacity to control and filter political information and communication has historically been a key factor of state power, and government control of the media helped ensure unity and stability at home. As long as TV, radio, and the press were the only sources of news, it was relatively simple for authoritarian governments to manage the dissemination of information. Satellite transmissions complicated matters, and China restricted satellite-delivered TV service to hotels and residential complexes for foreigners. New ICTs further eroded state control. The overthrow of Iran's Shah in 1979 was partly the result of distributing tapes with speeches by Ayatollah Ruhollah Khomeini. Chinese democracy protesters used fax machines to spread the news about the 1989 massacre in Tiananmen Square. The Internet further decentralized information production and dramatically empowered protest groups and NGOs, which could, regardless of geographic location, express political and ideological views and mobilize and coordinate antigovernment or antiglobalization demonstrations in cyberspace.

The new technologies appear especially dangerous to authoritarian regimes. The stability of such societies is threatened by private weblogs that can transmit information and opinion that such regimes do not wish to be aired. Online blogs are also sites for mobilizing undesirable public protests. Thus, in Russia, Alexei Navalny, a 35-year-old, Yale-educated blogger, has become the focus for large-scale protests against irregularities in the country's disputed parliamentary elections and against the corrupt authoritarianism of Vladimir Putin and his political allies. "He has no political party but Navalny has become possibly Russia's most popular political blogger by using his computer keyboard to illustrate the absurdities of a corrupt bureaucracy."[5]

The Internet, especially chat rooms, poses unprecedented problems for state control of information. Authoritarian governments, like those in China and Iran, try to censor the Internet, with variable success. In 2009, Iranians protesting the country's rigged presidential elections made use of social sites including Twitter, Facebook, and YouTube to keep the world informed of events there. "Yes, this revolution is being tweeted, blogged and Facebooked."[6] The same cyber community played a key role in fostering antiregime sentiment in Tunisia and forcing President Zine al-Abidine Ben Ali to flee in early 2011 and then in spreading unrest throughout the Middle East and North Africa, which brought down President Hosni Mubarak's government in Egypt, produced civil war in Libya that led to the overthrow of Muammar Qaddafi, and caused mass demonstrations and violence elsewhere, including Syria, Yemen, and Bahrain.

China's government, like Iran's, is alarmed by the threat to internal security that the Internet, Twitter, and other online communities seem to pose, and Beijing has sought to limit access to these media. China's *People's Daily* has an Internet division that deletes criticisms of the Communist Party. Beginning in 1998, China's government introduced a system to block Internet content, called the Golden Shield or Great Firewall of China. "In China," writes correspondent James Fallows, "the Internet came with choke points built in."

Even now, virtually all Internet contact between China and the rest of the world is routed through a very small number of fiber-optic cables that enter the country at one of three points. Thus, Chinese authorities can easily do something that would be harder in most developed countries: physically monitor all traffic into or out of the country by installing at each of these few "international gateways" a device called a "tapper" or "network sniffer," which can mirror every packet of data going in or out.[7]

China's government also issued Computer Information Systems Internet Secrecy Administrative Regulations to limit the release of information on the Internet, including a prohibition against disseminating so-called state secrets. The regulations censor chat rooms, electronic mail, and Internet sites. Whoever puts an item on the Internet, whether the original source or not, is held legally responsible for it. China's democracy movement and the Falun Gong movement have used e-mail to mobilize activities.

Globalization of Hate

The Internet spreads hate as well as increasing understanding, and extremists use it to spread their views and recruit like-minded individuals. Racist groups, child pornographers, and others whose views are offensive also use the technology to attract a following. In the United States, some Internet bloggers disseminate anti-Semitic, homophobic, and racist views.

Latin American guerrilla movements use the Internet to communicate directly with supporters, publicize their views and actions, and promote their agendas. Al Qaeda's leaders repeatedly use the Internet to air their views, and militant jihadist sites on the web encourage Muslims to engage in violence. Video terrorism has been practiced by radical Muslim groups broadcasting the beheading of hostages. Among the examples of video beheadings are those of American hostages Nick Berg in 2004 and Kenneth Bigley in 2008 by the al-Zarqawi terrorist organization in Iraq and of six Russian soldiers in Dagestan by Chechen rebels in 2008. Jihadist sites also broadcast the "martyrdom" speeches of suicide bombers. "At its best," writes Thomas Friedman, "the Internet can educate more people faster than any media tool we've ever had. At its worst, it can make people dumber faster than any media tool we've ever had. The lie that four thousand Jews were warned not to go into the World Trade Center on September 11 was spread entirely over the Internet and is now thoroughly believed in the Muslim world. . . . Worse, just when you might have thought you were all alone with your extreme views, the Internet puts you together with a community of people from around the world who hate all the things and people you do."[8]

Technology, Drugs, and Bugs

The Internet can also assist transnational criminals. Along with mobile phones, it provides drug smugglers with an inexpensive means of communication and can facilitate illicit laundering of funds. Criminals use disposable cell phones and instant messaging to arrange trafficking and sales. And identity theft has become a major headache, with millions of victims in recent years.

The United States has tried to cope with criminal secrecy by persuading its allies to allow computer eavesdropping by law enforcement agencies. One idea is to restrict private use of advanced data-scrambling technology that protects e-mail privacy. The proposal would create a system in which law enforcement officials could obtain the mathematical keys to computer-security codes held in escrow by agents without a court-ordered wire-tapping warrant.

Modern transportation also facilitates the spread of disease. The spread of infectious diseases like SARS and the swine and avian influenza pandemics, as well as the increase in the incidence of HIV/AIDS, highlights how rapidly new diseases spread in a globalized world and the difficulty of coping with them. The Atlanta-based Centers for Disease Control and Prevention have initiated the Border Infectious Disease Surveillance program, which is a system for responding to infectious diseases prevalent along the American–Mexican border, including hepatitis, measles, rubella, dengue, and typhus.[9]

In a globalized world, "bioinvasion," involving the movement of a species from its indigenous location into new regions via ships or planes, is a major problem. In 1999, a West Nile–like virus arrived in New York, possibly carried there on a jet or an exotic bird or illegal organ transplants smuggled into the United States. A bioinvasion unbalances the existing ecosystem, producing economic harm (e.g., the destruction of fisheries) or threatening human health (e.g., the spread of paralytic shellfish poisoning). An example of a destructive marine invasion was the *Mnemiopsis leidyi*, a jellyfish that travelled in ballast water on a ship from the United States to the Black Sea, where it devastated the local fishing industry. Another is *Mytilopsis*, the black-striped mussel, which spread from South America to Australia, India, Fiji, Singapore, Taiwan, Japan, and elsewhere in Southeast Asia.

The Technological Bases of Cultural Influence

The Internet and online communities spread values such as consumerism, individualism, and secularism, which subvert the legitimacy of traditional elites, religion, and culture. Local elites frequently regard the spread of such ideas and the fashions and tastes that accompany them as cultural imperialism, a manifestation of "Westernization" or "Americanization." Others regard the spread of such values as legitimate "soft power." "The one country," declare Joseph Nye and William Owens, "that can best lead the information revolution" is the United States because of its dominance of "important communications and information processing technologies." This edge, they believe, is "a force multiplier of American diplomacy, including 'soft power'—the attraction of American democracy and free markets."[10]

David Rothkopf regards America's role as "the world's only information superpower" as an enormous advantage:

> Setting technological standards, defining software standards, producing the most popular information products, and leading in the related development of the global trade in services are as essential to the well-being of any would-be leader as once were the resources needed to support empire or industry.[11]

While some countries fear such influence, others like China are beginning to challenge American dominance in cultural "soft power."

Notwithstanding states' efforts to manage the Internet and other media, these technologies have made it difficult for states to maintain a homogeneous culture and identity. They also complicate the assimilation of minorities and migrants, which states regard as important in maintaining national identity, because they enable migrants to remain in contact with their homelands. Although globalization in general fosters knowledge of

English, the language of global technology and commerce, migrant groups find it easier than in the past to maintain their own cultural traditions and language. And as the new technologies overwhelm traditional structures, they also erode national identities and infuse societies with alternative identities based on gender, profession, race, ethnicity, or religion. With the proliferation of multiple identities, people acquire new definitions of who they are. Therefore, countries around the world have employed a variety of strategies to adopt, yet limit the impact of, globalized values, seeking to minimize the political and social turmoil that such values threaten to create.

ICT innovations are also playing a major role in creating new globalized elites consisting of businessmen, knowledge workers, academics, aid workers, employees of international organizations, government officials, and other professionals whose activities are transnational and who are enmeshed in the global economy and are involved in global governance. The members of such elites are "denationalized," remain in contact however remote geographically they are from one another, and communicate and coordinate activities by phone, e-mail, and teleconferencing. They tend, too, to share tastes and norms in dealing with issues like human rights, democracy, and neoliberal capitalism. Many are what Robert Reich calls "symbolic analysts" who "may be connected to larger organizations, including worldwide webs," and "sit before computer terminals—examining words and numbers, moving them, altering them trying out new words and numbers, formulating and testing hypotheses, designing or strategizing," and spending "long hours in meetings or on the telephone, and even longer hours in jet planes and hotels—advising, making presentations, giving briefings, doing deals."[12]

The Emergence of Global Public Opinion

Global media using ICTs, along with the proliferation of nongovernmental and international organizations, have produced at long last *genuine* global public opinion. This development is reflected in several ways. News of humanitarian disasters—like the deadly 2004 Asian tsunami, the catastrophic 2010 Haiti earthquake, and the devastating 2011 giant tsunami and the resulting nuclear crisis in Japan—quickly spread around the world, attracting large amounts of humanitarian assistance. NGOs like Amnesty International and Human Rights Watch publicize human rights abuses, and "name and shame" may lead to global condemnation and international sanctions. Aggression, for example, Iraq's invasion of Kuwait in 1990, is quickly publicized and opinion mobilized against it.

Publicity of the sort described above is a resource of the weak when confronting the strong. We live in a "CNN age," in which protests, demonstrations, and other manifestations of disaffection become widely known in minutes if the media are present.

Technology and Deterritorialization

Overall, contemporary information and transportation technologies overcome geography and physical distance in politics, economics, and war and render geography ever less an impediment to the movement of persons, things, and ideas. The Internet is especially critical in overcoming geography. It has done this by enabling global marketing, electronic commerce, the rapid movement of financial assets, the global spread of ideas and opinions, the coordination of economic strategy by corporations, and the global diffusion of news and information. Distance is no longer a major obstacle to global activities ranging from economic transactions and mobilization of political activity to projecting military force and exchanging information by e-mail and mobile telephone.

Our conception of political space as consisting of exclusive territorial states demarcated by sovereign boundaries is giving way to a conception of a pluralist world of numerous political entities that overlap and are heterogeneous. At the same time that state authority is declining and state boundaries are becoming more porous, transnational processes, sustained by instantaneous communication and rapid transportation, are proliferating. Transnational corporations, terrorist networks, economic markets, and ethnic groups have their own versions of "territory," the boundaries of which coincide less and less with those of states. Moreover, some "virtual" polities exist only in cyberspace. Overlapping identities and groups have altered the essential character of political space and boundaries.

In sum, there has been a proliferation of crisscrossing subnational, transnational, international, and supranational actors in global politics, alongside and sharing adherents with territorial states. This trend has moved the globalizing world away from the neat territorial boxes characteristic of the political maps of recent centuries and has given rise to new forms of political activity that are neither domestic nor interstate but are "intermestic." Indeed, the overlap and layering of local, regional, national, and transnational authorities are analogous to conditions in medieval Europe.

Conclusions

Most observers agree that, for better or worse, the Internet, cell phones, space satellites, and other contemporary information and transportation technologies are altering the way we produce, sell, consume, learn, wage war, socialize, and mobilize activities. There are, of course, others who believe that these technologies are, in the main, only benefiting the rich countries and that they will actually widen the gap between rich and poor. Whoever is correct, it is certain that the new technologies have opened up new possibilities, even probabilities, but do not determine the manner in which these are exploited or whether in the long run they will prove beneficial or harmful. If history is any guide, the answer is probably that they will have both effects.

Notes

1   Elements of the arguments in this essay appear in Yale H. Ferguson and Richard W. Mansbach, *Remapping Global Politics: History's Revenge and Future Shock* (Cambridge, UK: Cambridge University Press, 2004), especially chapter 3.

2   Martin Van Creveld, *The Rise and Decline of the State* (Cambridge, UK: Cambridge University Press, 1999), 337.

3   "Internet Stats Today," *Internet World Stats News,* January 2010, http://internetstatstoday.com/?p=1295.

4   Richard N. Rosecrance, *The Rise of the Virtual State: Wealth and Power in the Coming Century* (New York: Basic Books, 1999), xi.

5   Guy Falconbridge, "Protests Pitch Russian Blogger Against Putin," *Reuters*, December 11, 2011, http://www.reuters.com/article/2011/12/11/us-russia-navalny-idUSTRE7BA0FX20111211.

6   John Palfrey, Bruce Etling, and Robert Faris, "Reading Twitter in Tehran?" *Washington Post National Weekly Edition*, June 29–July 12, 2009, 26–27, and "Twitter 1, CNN 0," *The Economist*, June 20, 2009, 26.

7   James Fallows, "The Connection Has Been Reset," *Atlantic Magazine*, March 2008, http://www.theatlantic.com/magazine/archive/2008/03/-ldquo-the-connection-has-been-reset-rdquo/6650/.

8   Thomas L. Friedman, *Longitudes and Attitudes: Exploring the World After September 11* (New York: Farrar, Straus & Giroux, 2002), 169.

9   Centers for Disease Control and Prevention, "Border Infectious Disease Surveillance," http://www.cdc.gov/omhd/Populations/HL/HHP/Border.htm.

10 Joseph S. Nye Jr. and William A. Owens, "America's Information Edge," *Foreign Affairs* 75:2 (March/April 1996), 20.

11 David Rothkopf, "In Praise of Cultural Imperialism?" *Foreign Policy* 107 (Summer 1997), 46–47.

12 Robert Reich, *The Work of Nations* (New York: Alfred A. Knopf, 1991), 179.

2.2

FROM THE STREETS TO THE INTERNET: THE CYBER-DIFFUSION OF CONTENTION

Jeffrey M. Ayres

> The second selection, by the political scientist Jeffrey Ayres, describes the impact of the Internet on political protest. Using the case of the Multilateral Agreement on Investment to illustrate his argument, Ayres contends that the Internet encourages the global mobilization of online opinion and protest. Ayres cautions, however, that the Internet can also spread misinformation and thereby create confusion that could trigger a global "electronic riot."

From May 1995 to April 1998, trade ministers from the world's leading industrialized countries met to hammer out a new global agreement on rules for foreign investment. Without much fanfare, these negotiators from the 29-member Organization for Economic Cooperation and Development (OECD) quietly moved toward completion of the Multilateral Agreement on Investment (MAI) at the OECD's headquarters in

Source: Excerpted from Jeffrey M. Ayres, "From the Streets to the Internet: The Cyber-Diffusion of Contention," *Annals of the American Academy of Political and Social Science* 566 (November 1999), 132–43.

Paris. There were some stumbling blocks: countries piled on sought-after exemptions to protect certain industries, and the developing countries outside the OECD complained about being squeezed out of the secret negotiations. Nonetheless, all expectations were that a new investment treaty would be completed and signed by the end of 1998.

Suddenly, however, overwhelmed by a tsunami of protest from around the world, negotiators suspended talks and left the proposed MAI in limbo. Why this sudden and dramatic reversal of fate for an agreement three years in the works, and one backed by the richest and most powerful countries in the world? Was it a retreat in the face of tens of thousands of protesters taking to the streets of the OECD capitals to protest the deal's perceived threat to national sovereignty, environmental protections, and social benefits? Was it a withdrawal in reaction to populist mobilizations that shut down public transport, bringing cities to a standstill? On the contrary, the rather remarkable collapse of the MAI illustrated the changed dynamics of contention in the global age. The failure to ratify the MAI was in response to a successful Internet campaign by nongovernmental organizations. This campaign against the MAI signaled a shift in the politics of protest: welcome to contentious politics Internet-style, where the rules have changed and the ideas and tactics of protest diffuse quickly to the far ends of the globe.

The Internet, which includes Web sites, listservs, and e-mail, is promoting a revolution in both the means of communication and the dynamics of popular contention. Perhaps nowhere is globalization's impact being more visibly and dramatically felt than in this revolution of communications technology. This cyber-diffusion—the rapid, computer-generated dissemination of information around the world, without concern for geographic location—has not only changed the nature and process of contention but has encouraged a significant rethinking of those concepts available for understanding this contention. From the rainforests of the Mexican state of Chiapas, to the streets of small-town U.S.A., to the capitals of Europe, the Internet is one of the hottest tools in the burgeoning arsenal of protest. Yet the tale of Internet-inspired diffusion is a cautionary one, without a predictable end. . . .

Typically, movements and their participants are outsiders, lacking in adequate formal representation and remaining outside established political institutions. Movements also tend to rely frequently, but not exclusively, on noninstitutional tactics, creating disruption to promote social and political change. . . .

Popular contention thus covers a broad spectrum of protest activity, from a possible continuum of movements, coalitions, networks, pro-tests, petitions, and declarations. . . .

Research on the diffusion of contention . . . has stressed the importance of intervening sociocultural conditions for the spread of collective protest through a population. . . .

So-called cultural linkages rooted in strong interpersonal networks are deemed essential to both the diffusion of protest between ideologically similar movements within a single country . . . and the cross-national diffusion of movement strategy and ideas. . . .

At first glance, the Internet-inspired diffusion of contention might fall neatly into the category of impersonal channels. Yet the Internet challenges the dynamics of diffusion in ways beyond those encouraged by the so-called CNN effect of television. First, the diffusion of ideas and tactics occurs between individuals and groups much more quickly, potentially reducing the relevance of cultural connections or interpersonal networks for the spread of contention. Second, the process of Internet-carried contention may be less contained or constrained by activist-led movements but, rather, unleashed into a type of global electronic riot. . . .

Regardless of the form that this contention may be taking, Internet-inspired protest seems likely to be influenced by domestic and international political conditions. . . .

. . . That contentious collective action has become transnational is evident by the diffusion of tactics and strategies across borders, the sharing of targets, and the coordination of activities between movements. . . .

. . . To be sure, international movements are nothing new; such movements arose a century ago against slavery and for the promotion of worker's rights, while the antinuclear, antiapartheid, and human rights movements of the past couple of decades exemplify more recent transnational political behavior. . . . What has changed in the diffusion of contentious collective action is the globalization of the world economy.

Globalization

Global economic processes, from the internationalization of trade and finance to the rise and spread of regional economic integration projects, have shaped new opportunities for both domestic and transnational contentious action. The rise of global and regional trade pacts combined with the interdependence of communications technology has encouraged a transnationalization of a variety of social forces, from multinational corporations to antinuclear activists. In particular, international processes have encouraged a shift in the mobilization strategies and resulting forms of collective action. Transnational collective actors have sprouted up in recent years in conjunction with a variety of international arrangements, from human rights and environmental regimes to neo-liberal trading arrangements. Many of these transnational collective actors cross national borders and work on international issues, mimicking the same mobilization strategies successfully adopted at the national level. In particular, such transnational collective action can be conceived under the contentious politics framework, as it exhibits a variety of forms of noninstitutionalied behavior, waxing and waning in response to the highs and lows of specific international issues and struggles.

The Internet contributes to this internationalization of contentious activity. It is an efficient and accessible way for individuals and groups to target new and emerging international structures, such as the World Trade Organization and the European Union. In effect, the Internet has become an international opportunity in its own right, as it provides disparate groups around the world with a means for collectively contesting new and emerging global arrangements. . . .

. . . For states constrained by new regulations inherent in regional economic trade pacts, the international environment is playing an ever more critical role in structuring the potential for cross-border collective action.

Contemporary globalization has thus had critical outcomes for the changing dynamics of contentious activity: it has weakened the mobilization potential of states and has created new opportunities for transnational mobilization and the diffusion of protest.

International processes have straitjacketed the state's ability to perform many of the interventionist functions of the past. Global and regional trade pacts, investment firms, and multinational corporations are having important structural effects on a state's national political opportunity structure. At the same time, international processes have created new targets, new international allies, new issues, and new and common strategic repertoires around which nonstate actors are rallying. This is where the Internet and its plethora of resources come into play in the cyber-diffusion of protest.

Wired Activism

Within this global context, the Internet adds a whole new element to the "routine mix of strategies and tactics" described as "strategic repertoires" available to those engaged in contention. . . . In fact, the Internet is far from routine in its impact on contentious strategies, as it offers a diverse menu of options to those seeking new channels for protest. Organizational Web sites present a variety of options, including posting messages on a discussion board, joining a listserv to receive up-to-date information on a campaign or new event through an e-mail account, sending e-mail to politicians, government agencies, or other activists, and searching on related links for additional information related to various campaigns. This last option is an important facet of a Web site, as such sites serve as information clearinghouses for vast amounts of material relevant to protest.

With this collection of resources, the Internet removes barriers to the rapid diffusion of protest ideas, tactics, and strategies. First, the speed by which information can be disseminated affects the global diffusion of protest dramatically. When a message is posted on a Web site, it is immediately accessible, crossing time and geographic boundaries without a concern for time zones, media coverage, or customs barriers. As Maude Barlow, an activist involved in the campaign against the MAI, noted in 1998, "If a negotiator says something to someone over a glass of wine, we'll have it on the Internet within an hour, all over the world." This comment by the head of the 100,000-person-strong Council of Canadians (COC), a public interest group that mobilized via the Internet against the MAI, suggests how strategic a tool the Internet has become for actors engaged in contention. The Globalization and MAI Information Web site, managed by volunteers in Vancouver, British Columbia, for example, has compiled an international smorgasbord of hyperlinks to individual campaigns around the world, immediately accessible to groups and individuals to peruse at the click of a computer keyboard.

Similarly, the Internet has significantly reduced those barriers of place that certainly slowed if not hindered the spread of information. Through the process of cyber-diffusion, groups as remote as Zapatista rebels in the Mexican state of Chiapas can attract a global audience to their cause, encouraging supportive protest in New York City without ever leaving the rainforest. . . . [A] committed, Internet-connected activist can attend to the "virtual barricades" from a bedside table on a small island in the South Pacific. . . . Internet-inspired protest simply diffuses much more quickly and efficiently across geographic boundaries, and, at a minimum, it complements street protest.

The ability of the Internet to quickly and effectively disseminate information across borders also bolsters its potential as a medium for empowerment. . . . The MAI campaign especially highlighted the Internet's potential for enhancing efficacy across borders; those Canadians who logged onto the MAI-Not Web site received encouragement from New Zealand activists via daily e-mail in support of the MAI campaign. "New Zealanders are talking about the tremendous fight Canadians are putting up against the MAI every day . . . each day I switch on my email and there you are, carrying on the flag of freedom and democracy, and we're encouraged all over again to keep going. Here's smiling at you Canada."

Surfing MAI

The recent global protests against the MAI provide an intriguing example of the Internet's power to diffuse contentious political behavior. This global campaign, culminating in the April 1998 decision by OECD ministers to halt negotiations, capitalized on the Internet's speed, disregard for geographic boundaries, efficacious potential, and ease of public accessibility. . . .

The Internet provided an ideal forum for the rapid diffusion of opposition to the MAI. The Washington, D.C.-based group Public Citizen, for example, placed an early rough draft of the treaty on its Web site (www. citizen.org) in February 1997. From that time until the April 1998 breakup of the MAI talks, word of the previously secretly negotiated deal spread like wildfire.

Criticisms of the treaty emerged on hundreds of Web sites, discussion boards, and list serves, where daily traffic in MAI e-mail discussions became common-place. . . .

The Globalization and the MAI Information Centre, a Web site (www.islandnet.com/-ncfs/maisite) hosted by the National Centre for Sustainability, of Victoria, British Columbia, provides a glimpse of the Internet's central role as anti-MAI information disseminator. An active site for unfolding news on the MAI negotiations and international campaigns in protest, this site welcomes individuals surfing the Internet with an attractively designed interface that is easy to understand and use. Is a person seeking the names and addresses of elected representatives and media contacts across the United States and Canada? Does he or she want information on how to create an "MAI-free zone" in a local community? Is he or she interested in participating in international discussion and feed-back regarding the development of a "Citizen's MAI," an interactive process facilitated by the Internet? All these and many more activities are accessible, and a mere click of the computer keyboard away, for a budding activist seeking to participate in the myriad of transnational protests against the MAI.

The anti-MAI activities of the COC provided a case study of how the Internet has changed the strategies of advocacy groups. The COC, already a 10-year veteran of large-scale campaigns against the U.S.- Canada Free Trade Agreement (FTA) and the North American Free Trade Agreement (NAFTA), became a major global clearinghouse for anti-MAI information. Its Web site (www.Canadians.org) contained up-to-date material on the MAI, including discussion papers, press releases, and links to dozens of Web campaigns against the MAI in locations such as the United States, the United Kingdom, and Australia. The COC also provided names and contact information for dozens of Canadian organizations opposed to the MAI, including group e-mail addresses and related Web sites. . . .

[D]uring the MAI campaign, information critical of the MAI was immediately disseminated across Canada via the Internet as soon as it was received by the COC. "If we know of something that is sensitive to one government, we get it to our ally in that country instantly," boasted the head of the COC.

Ultimately, the COC was only one of hundreds of organizations across the developed and developing world that fed a steady stream of anti-MAI information onto the Internet for global public consumption. It lifted the curtain of secrecy that had for years shrouded the OECD MAI talks, and it forced negotiators to begin to openly address concerns that had been dramatically amplified on the Internet. The Internet's global reach, its speed, its immediacy, and its public accessibility proved to be deciding factors in pooling the concerns of disparate people from far ends of the earth. . . .

Conclusion

There is wide agreement that the Internet is dramatically changing the dynamics of political participation. There are now many more opportunities for citizens to communicate with representatives at various levels and to gain access to political information more quickly and efficiently. The question that continues to be debated for some time, however, is whether this change has generally positive or negative consequences. Some weave a tale of the Internet's efficacious potential as it heralds the dawn of a third epoch of democracy. Others spin a decidedly cautionary scenario of the Internet's potential for innovative demagoguery.

Some words of caution are, in fact, in order, particularly with regard to the role that the Internet is undeniably playing in the rapid diffusion of contentious politics. It is certainly not clear, first of all, that the Internet can or will replace the importance of cultural and interpersonal linkages for the sustained diffusion of protest across geographic boundaries. It helps that English is the predominant language used on the Internet—another facet of globalization that may undercut the importance of cultural linkages through the impact of the Internet's potential as a force for cultural homogenization. Yet it is clearly too early to assume that those cultural affinities that have traditionally sped the diffusion of information and protest are now irrelevant.

Moreover, while there is little question of the Internet's ability to quickly disseminate information, there is a great deal of uncertainty about the value of this information. That is, much of the material available on the Internet is often unreliable and clearly unverifiable. . . .

Impressions, fears, opinions, and conclusions are all traded equally on the Web. On the Internet, the information critical of the MAI was immediate and potentially threatening to millions of people around the world, and the Internet was a route that diffused this information within hours. This fact was not lost on the OECD ministers, who clearly lost the MAI public relations battle as the waves of unsettling and frequently unverifiable information on the MAI circled the globe. . . .

This leads to an interesting question: has the Internet, as an important medium for the diffusion of protest, ushered in the dawn of a new form of organized, popular protest, or has it introduced a pattern of repeated global electronic riots? Are we going to witness a revenge of the mob, with electronic panics replacing coordinated protests by social movements? One is certainly freed from such traditional constraints as leaders, organizational membership, geographic place, and time. Yet whether or not the Internet has opened the door to misinformed reactions and uncoordinated chaotic behavior remains to be seen.

Perhaps the Internet does indeed herald a return to old-fashioned collective behavior—the riots, panics and sporadic protests of old . . . only this time on a global scale. What the Internet does not herald is the birth of a global civil society, nor has it ushered in an era of sustained transnational diffusion of social movements. The Internet certainly encourages a rethinking of what is meant by contentious political behavior at the dawn of the twenty-first century, as its role in diffusing protest is unmistakable. Where that will lead the public in the new century is open to debate.

2.3

TRAINING FOR HACKERS STIRS WORRY ABOUT ILLEGAL ACTION

Cui Jia

> Information and communication technologies can have both beneficial and harmful effects. Computer hacking is among the most harmful of these. The following selection describes the widespread training of computer hackers in China and how they use that training to carry out illegal activities including the theft of personal information.

First the bad news: Hackers last year caused an estimated economic loss of 7.6 billion yuan ($1 billion) in China. Using a brutal one-two punch, hackers have stolen people's bank account numbers and passwords and damaged the Internet users' computers and servers in the process. That's according to the National Computer Network Emergency Response Technique Team/Coordination of China. And then there is worse news: Hacker training, like in some other countries, has almost become an industry in China; last year it generated an estimated income of 238 million yuan. Large numbers of hacker schools have been set up—mostly online—around China. (The exact number remains unknown.) "Our school simply helps ordinary citizens learn about self-defense in cyberspace, although it's called 'Hacker Base'," said a customer service employee with Beijing-based hackerbase.com, which provides Internet-security training courses. But, the employee

Source: Cui Jia, "Training for Hackers Stirs Worry About Illegal Action," *Chinadaily.com.cn,* August 4, 2009.

said, it is very easy for their students to hack into other computers after learning the security weaknesses of the Internet. Students, though, are told not to use their skills for illegal purposes, she said.

The employee added, however, that it is not the responsibility of the school if students use their information to do something illegal.

"Lots of hacker schools only teach students how to hack into unprotected computers and steal personal information," said Wang Xianbing, a security consultant for hackerbase.com. "They then make a profit by selling users' information." For investing hundreds of yuan in hacker school, students could obtain the skills to make a fortune, Wang said.

"Hacker school is a bit like driving school—they teach you how to drive but it's up to you if you are going to drive safely or kill someone," said Wang. A 25-year-old hacker school student from Shanghai surnamed Wang, said most of his "classmates" simply enroll in hacker school for personal reasons, such as spying on relatives, showing off their computer-savvy skills or taking revenge on a rival's websites, rather than making money.

"Instructing people on how to hack into other people's computers to make profit is clearly a crime," said Li Xuxi, a lawyer from Beijing Zi Guang law firm. Such hacker schools should be closed and those responsible be punished, said Li. As the number of China's hacking incidents increases, more hackers are being caught and some are receiving sentences. In the latest case, a computer hacker in Hubei province was sentenced this year to one and half years in prison for replacing the picture of an official on a government website with a girl in a bikini.

2.4

BREAKING UP DARK CLOUDS IN CYBERSPACE

Ronal Deibert and Rafal Rohozinski

> Hackers break into sensitive computer sites not only to steal information from individuals but to access secrets that can undermine national security. In a word, hacking frequently involves espionage.

Crime and espionage form a dark underworld of cyberspace. Whereas crime is usually the first to seek out new opportunities and methods, espionage usually follows in its

---

Source: Ronal Deibert and Rafal Rohozinski, "Breaking Up Dark Clouds in Cyberspace; The Need for Security Must Be Balanced With the Equally Important Need for an Open, Accessible Internet," *The Globe and Mail,* April 6, 2010.

wake, borrowing techniques and tradecraft. The Shadows in the Cloud report, released today, illustrates the increasingly dangerous ecosystem of crime and espionage and its embeddedness in the fabric of global cyberspace.

As our everyday lives move online, criminals and spies have migrated to this domain. They leverage complex, adaptive attack techniques to take advantage of the fissures that have emerged in an era where "e" is everything. Every new software, social networking site, cloud-computing system, or web-hosting service represents opportunities for the predatory criminal ecosystem to subvert, adapt, and exploit.

This situation has also emerged because of poor security practices among individuals, businesses and governments. The age of mass Internet access is less than 20 years old. Public institutions—particularly those in developing countries—have embraced these new technologies faster than procedures have been created to deal with the vulnerabilities they introduce. Today, data is transferred from laptops to USB sticks, over wireless networks at cafe hot spots, and stored across cloud-computing systems whose servers are located in far-off jurisdictions. The sheer complexity makes thinking about security in cyberspace mind-bogglingly difficult. Paradoxically, documents and personal information are probably safer in a file cabinet, under the bureaucrat's careful watch, than they are on today's networked PC.

The ecosystem of crime and espionage is also emerging because of strategic calculus. Cyberspace is the great equalizer. Countries no longer need to spend billions of dollars to build globe-spanning satellites to pursue high-level intelligence gathering, when they can do so by harvesting information from government computers connected to the Internet.

Governments are engaged in a rapid race to militarize cyberspace, to develop tools and methods to fight and win wars in this domain. This arms race creates an opportunity structure ripe for crime and espionage to flourish. In the absence of norms, principles and rules of mutual restraint, opportunists, criminals, spies and others rush to fill the vacuum.

Against this context, the absence of Canadian policy for cyberspace is notable. For years, Canadian telcos have acted as the frontline against a surging tide of criminal botnets, MALware, and other MALicious online behavior—largely in the absence of government policy. At least one Canadian institution was ensnared in the Shadow network we uncovered, but no doubt others have been that escaped our gaze.

Canada's cybersecurity strategy has been long promised, but a domestic cybersecurity plan is only a partial solution. In a networked world, you are only as secure as the weakest link—and that link can be anyone, including your allies and partners. Notably, our investigation discovered that Canadian visa applications submitted to Indian consulates in Afghanistan were stolen along with those of 12 other nationalities.

Fixing cybersecurity requires a global effort, and one in which Canada's security and foreign policy must be attuned and synchronized to the unique needs of cyberspace. We should take the lead in pushing for a global convention that builds robust mechanisms of information sharing across borders and institutions, defines appropriate rules of the road for engagement in the cyberdomain, puts the onus on states to not tolerate or encourage MALicious networks whose activities operate from within their jurisdictions.

At the same time, Canada should work to defend the openness of the global Internet commons—to ensure that policies and practices appropriate to security in the information age do not restrict, constrain, or threaten to roll back the gains in development, human rights and democracy—values we as Canadians embrace—and which cyberspace has helped propel globally over the past 20 years.

Today, no country is secure in the global sea of information. Preserving cyberspace requires a strategy to address the dark side of the Internet. This requires urgent international co-operation, level-headed judgment and a commitment to preserve our values of freedom of speech and access to information, so as to ensure that in our quest for online security we do not secure ourselves into a new dark age.

2.5

ARAB WORLD SHAKEN BY POWER OF TWITTER AND FACEBOOK

John Timpane

Cyber-Resistance

> The social networking websites Twitter and Facebook have become two of the most popular sites on the Internet. Their potential political impact became clear, however, in the role they played in bringing about the overthrow of Tunisia's dictator. Thereafter, they helped coordinate and spread resistance against dictators throughout the Middle East between 2010 and 2012. Authoritarians who once controlled their countries' mass media from the center found that these social media were in the hands of others who made use of them to spread "subversive" ideas and encourage activities that brought an end to political inertia in the region and precipitated revolutionary change in the political life of the region.

When dictator Zine el-Abidine Ben Ali fled Tunisia on Jan. 14, it was the first time in history that Twitter, Facebook, and other social media had helped bring down a government.

With Egypt now in its third day of Facebook-organized political flash mobs, it may not be the last.

Recent uprisings midwifed by Twitter, Facebook, YouTube, and the cable news network Al-Jazeera might not be a "Twitter revolution." But the Middle East has been shaken, and social media have done some of the shaking.

"In the Arab world, this has never happened before," says John Entelis, director of Middle Eastern studies at Fordham University. "A dictator has been deposed by the

Source: John Timpane, "Arab World Shaken by Power of Twitter and Facebook," *Philadelphia Inquirer,* January 27, 2011.

people. That is an extraordinary first step, even if nothing else comes of it. And believe me, the whole Arab world is watching."

Mustapha Tlili, director of New York University's Center for Dialogues and himself Tunisian, says: "For the first time, we became a world moral community, thanks to Twitter."

Tlili says dictators in the region's other countries can block social media, but not forever, "so they must deal with the way social media make it easy to flout authority, organize opposition, and appeal to the moral conscience of the world."

In Tunisia, nothing happened overnight. Demonstrations had been widespread since December on issues including unemployment, economic conditions, and official corruption.

On Dec. 17, in Sidi Bouzid, deep in the interior, Mohamed Bouazizi set himself aflame in front of a government building, in protest after police confiscated his produce stand.

Horrible images of his act circulated lightning-fast on the Internet. Protests followed. The world witnessed what Neil Postman wrote in his prescient 1985 book, *Amusing Ourselves to Death*: "Introduce speed-of-light transmission of images and you make a cultural revolution."

"Thanks to Twitter, YouTube, and Facebook, images of those first protests went around the world instantly, and everyone knew about it," says Tlili. "Even 20 years ago, you could have had those uprisings in the interior and few would have known."

Bouazizi's image went out in thousands of tweets, e-mails, and Facebook posts. He became an image of resistance. About a dozen copycat self-immolations occurred in neighboring countries. A purported last note to his mother appeared on a Facebook page in Bouazizi's name: "I will be traveling my mom, forgive me, Reproach is not helpful, I am lost in my way it is not in my hand, for give me if disobeyed words of my mom, blame our times and do not blame me, i am going and not coming back . . ."

Al-Jazeera—drawing indignant criticism from the regime—covered the growing protests. "Al-Jazeera has been very in-your-face covering the uprisings," Entelis says.

David Nassar, chief executive officer of Hotspot Digital and a Middle East expert, says, "Here as elsewhere, cable news has been a breath of fresh air, a powerful unifying force in the Arab world."

One thing about information: Once it's out, you can't put it back. As Richard Goedkoop, associate professor of communication at La Salle University, puts it, "The sheer multiplicity of venues and sources makes it impossible for would-be dictators to get the genie back in the bottle. And once info is out at all, it's easily, infinitely copiable."

Protests punctuated Bouazizi's two weeks in the hospital. He died Jan. 5, and the cycle repeated: Protesters texted and tweeted info and images, organized flash-demonstrations, and warned of police activity. Al-Jazeera kept the camera steady, covering Bouazizi's death and funeral, the unrest that followed, and the often violent government response. More repression, more protest, more tweets, more coverage. Within nine days, Ben Ali was gone.

This tech-powered uprising marks a generation gap, in Tunisia and elsewhere in the Arab world.

"This is being driven by youth, and their familiarity with technology is helping them," Nassar says. "There is a divide between them and the older men who hold power."

He says several Arab countries—"Tunisia, Egypt, Morocco, Lebanon, Algeria, even, increasingly, Syria"—have created an educated middle class that is largely unemployed, leading to social tension.

"You hear them called the 'lost generation,'" Nassar says.

For Tunisia's young technocrats, says Tlili, "social media are second nature, in a country with a tradition of science and scholarship going back to the 16th century, when Spanish Muslims emigrated to Tunisia, bringing with them culture and sophistication."

That sophistication shows in the way protesters use mobile media.

"At one point, young people had transported a man to hospital, and doctors were rushing to save his life," says Tlili. "But people were there with their iPhones and were shouting, 'Wait! We want to share the picture before you clean him up!'"

Response from neighboring dictators was unhappy, to say the least. Protests arose in Jordan, Yemen, and Algeria, where Facebook again played a role. Government responded brutally, and Algerian President Abdelaziz Bouteflika complained about Wikipedia and Facebook. Libya's Moammar Gadhafi appeared in a video—widely seen on Al-Jazeera and YouTube—in which he called the Internet "a great vacuum" that "sucks everything." In Egypt, protests were carefully planned via Facebook, and 30-year ruler Hosni Mubarak finds himself under siege.

Behind the scenes rages a struggle for media control. Government blocks or muddles Twitter and cell-phone use; tech-savvy protesters find workarounds that get out the message. Facebook pages, Twitter tweets, and YouTube posts appear and are taken down. (Twitter confirmed it had been blocked in Egypt. Facebook spokesman Andrew Noyes told CNET on Wednesday that Egypt had not blocked Facebook.)

It would be misleading to overstress the impact of media. Mona el-Ghobashy, assistant professor of political science at Barnard College, says: "The prospects for Tunisia-style reform in Egypt are dim. The Egyptian government is well-versed in managing and containing even large-scale protests, and has been doing so for decades."

On the other hand, says Entelis, "no one saw this coming in Tunisia, either. The main thing is, the unthinkable first step has happened."

2.6

TWITTER TOPPLES TUNISIA?

Kathryn Blaze Carlson

The social networking website Twitter has become one of the most popular sites on the Internet. Its potential political impact became clear, however, in the role it played in bringing about the overthrow of Tunisia's dictator. Thereafter, it helped spread resistance against dictators throughout the Middle East. The next selection, from a Canadian newspaper, describes the role it played in events in Tunisia.

Source: Kathryn Blaze Carlson, "Twitter Topples Tunisia?" *National Post,* January 22, 2011.

When President Zine El Abidine Ben Ali fled Tunisia on Jan. 14, Tunisians declared victory and social-networking site Twitter went berserk with traffic. Soon after, Tunisia—where Internet penetration is roughly 35%, and where cellphone use is reportedly upward of 95%—joined Iran and Moldova on the list of countries that have undergone a "Twitter Revolution." But some say Tunisia's Twitter Revolution was different in one very important way: activists used Twitter to help protesters navigate the on-the-ground tumult, warning of sniper locations, for example. One man even tweeted that Twitter saved his life. Then Friday, Ali Larayedh, leader of Tunisia's once-outlawed opposition Islamist party, told the *New York Times,* "None of us expected the Ben Ali government to go down as fast as [a text] message." To understand the unique role of Twitter and other social networks in the Tunisian revolt, the National Post's Kathryn Blaze Carlson spoke separately with Zeynep Tufekci, assistant professor of sociology at the University of Maryland in Baltimore County, Nasser Weddady, a Mauritania-born expert in Internet activism and a director at the American Islamic Congress in Boston, and Ethan Zuckerman and Jillian York, both of Harvard University's Berkman Center for Internet and Society.

Q:	Why are people calling the revolt in Tunisia a Twitter Revolution?
Jillian York:	It's pretty easy for people to ascribe the term Twitter Revolution to what's going in Tunisia, especially because it's sort of the third time that it's happened. Twitter though, as well as Facebook and blogs, were used in a really unique way this time around.
Nasser Weddady:	You might never have heard about [the revolt in Tunisia] if it wasn't for the folks on Twitter, who were basically engaging in massive information warfare. At the time when the Tunisian dictator fled, there were six tweets on Tunisia every second.
Ethan Zuckerman:	I think Twitter is where North Americans finally woke up to the news that something was going on in Tunisia. But this was far from being a revolution "organized" by Twitter.
Q:	How was the use of Twitter in this revolt different than in, say, the 2009 Iran protests?
JY:	[In Tunisia], there was already a very strong online anti-censorship movement prior to this happening. You already had an Internet elite who were connected to one another, and they were able to leverage those ties to get information out. You had people who were genuinely linking up with each other through social networks to figure out what's going on.
NW:	In Iran, the information was coming out as a jumble. When the Tunisian situation broke out, people like myself were ready and better knew how to get the message out.

Zeynep Tufekci:	The Iranian uprising was not successful; the Tunisian one was. This shows that social media is not a magical tool that guarantees that a popular uprising will succeed. It is just one variable among many that determine the outcome of social protests.
Q:	Tunisians were using Twitter for logistics, from warning of sniper locations to calling for blood donation at hospitals to organizing protests. Does this mark a new era in Twitter use, where people use it to navigate danger and save lives under tumultuous circumstances?
ZT:	Twitter is a very good tool for using in emergencies thanks to its short message format, multi-platform access and the ability to use cell-phones. This was also shown during the Haitian earthquake, Tucson shootings, etc. So, yes, social media in general, and Twitter in particular, are now woven into the fabric of our responses to tumultuous circumstances.
NW:	There was a report on a French TV station called TF1, where a Tunisian man said, "Twitter a sauve ma vie," which means, "Twitter saved my life." What happened was that at one point the presidential guard went on a rampage. The man said he was about to leave his house, but he saw masked, armed gunmen. He went online and tweeted, and asked for help. People saw this in Tunisia and started calling the army's emergency lines, reporting his exact location. The army showed up immediately and arrested these people. This is the power of social media.
JY:	It does seem like a new thing; it's not something that I had seen before. But I saw more [logistical information] being shared on Facebook, behind closed doors using private messaging. I had one friend who sent a message to a group of people to stay away from a specific neighbourhood in Tunis because of snipers. Another person sent out a message saying, "I'm going to be [at a particular place] this afternoon, and I should be back online by 10:30 p.m." That way, if that person is not back online by 10:30 p.m., somebody is going to be concerned. I saw a lot of that happening.
Q:	In your opinion, how much did social networking factor into President Ben Ali's decision to flee?
ZT:	It's possible that social-media tools puncture the bubble dictators create around themselves, where a lot of yes-men and -women tell them their captive population surely loves them. Witness [Libyan leader Muammar Gaddafi's] reaction, blaming the Internet for undermining the values of his people and causing them to not appreciate his [and Ben Ali's] dictatorship. He knows where one threat to his regime is.

EZ: I think [the question] is totally absurd. Ben Ali looked out a window and saw the streets filled with demonstrators—a dictator's worst nightmare—and saw that it was time to leave. People who frame questions like this are willfully deceiving themselves about the importance of social-media technology.

Q: How did social networking affect Al-Jazeera's coverage, which was broadcast into Tunisia via satellite and which offered an alternative to the censored, state-run media?

JY: One thing that I think is really fascinating, and different from the case in Iran, is that the information that was being put on Twitter and Facebook was often used by Al-Jazeera in their reporting.

ZT: Thousands of "citizen-journalists" uploaded photos, videos, texts, appeals and more to social-media sites, which were then rebroadcast by Al-Jazeera. Social media enabled the citizens of Tunisia to bypass censored state media and talk to each other.

2.7

TERROR'S WEB WORLD

from *The Globe and Mail*

Among the most harmful of the Internet's consequences has been its use to recruit potential terrorists and make available information of value to them regarding tactics and weapons. This is the focus of our next selection.

CSIS estimates there are 4,500 terrorist-affiliated websites with such information as how-to guides for running training camps and pointers on where to plant a bomb. "These websites are the new [Osama] bin Laden," said Chris Hamilton, senior fellow at the Washington Institute for Near East Policy. "It's hard for bin Laden to communicate with his followers because he is in hiding, so these websites allow terror organizations to run without too much leadership."

* * *

Source: "Terror's Web World," *The Globe and Mail,* June 6, 2006.

Cyber-Terrorism

THE PORTAL
GETTING IN
Terrorist-affiliated websites are surprisingly easy to find. Starting from the Yahoo search engine, users can type in Irhab, the Arabic word for terrorism. Arabic conversations flash up on the message boards, some laying out how to join the insurgency in Iraq, others providing tips on guerrilla warfare, firing missiles and using poisons.

* * *

THE JIHADI SITES
FIND INSTRUCTIONS
From Yahoo, links can be followed to jihadist websites. Some, such as this one, give detailed instructions on making bombs from simple ingredients, including ammonium nitrate. Instructions are in both English and Arabic.

* * *

THE U.S. SITE
BUILD A SUICIDE BELT
This image is taken from a how-to video on constructing a suicide belt. The video describes what materials to use, how best to hide the belt, where to stand to cause the most destruction and how to use shrapnel to maximize the number of casualties. Sometimes these instructions are overlaid with pieces of Western classical music.

* * *

HOW-TO-VIDEOS
MAKE MISSILES
"Terrorist organizations don't hide their websites. Some even have English translations, although the most inflammatory rhetoric is rarely translated," said Jonathan Halevi, director of the Orient Research Group and a retired counterterrorism expert with the Israeli army. This image shows how to construct a homemade missile with simple and easy-to-acquire ingredients.

* * *

INFLAMMATORY VIDEOS
WATCH KILLINGS
Sometimes the most inflammatory videos are placed on U.S. and Canadian servers to hide them from authorities, Mr. Halevi said. The jihadist websites provide the URL links to these servers, where in just a few seconds, users can upload videos of beheadings, Westerners being shot and the top 10 assassinations of Americans. This image is taken from an al-Qaeda magazine and details how to handle a gun, abduct someone and keep fit by weightlifting.

2.8

CHAMPIONS OF DEMOCRACY, OR PEOPLE WITH BLOODIED HANDS?

Simon Mann, Julia May, and David Wroe

> WikiLeaks, a small nonprofit group dedicated to publishing classified information from around the world, was established in December 2006 by an Australian, Julian Assange. In April 2010, WikiLeaks released a video online that showed a U.S. helicopter in Baghdad killing a dozen Iraqis, including two journalists. Later that year, the WikiLeaks website released logs of events in the Iraqi and Afghan wars and thereafter began to publish 250,000 classified U.S. diplomatic cables that had been passed on to it by an American soldier. There ensued a global uproar as disturbing confidential information about the confidential views of American diplomats became publicized globally. Our next two selections—one published in an Australian newspaper and the other from a Canadian newspaper—contain opposing views on the morality of what WikiLeaks had done.

Someone said you cannot stop an idea whose time has come. It is time for WikiLeaks, whether the US likes it or not. The damage has been done.

WikiLeaks has not done the unimaginable, because this is not the first time that US "secrets" have been leaked. It is more about the manner in which the "leaks" occurred.

There is clearly an insider (in the US system), the conduit (WikiLeaks/Julian Assange) and collaborators (the media).

And, in all fairness, Assange is a visionary of sorts. He did not set up WikiLeaks with the intention to "steal" classified or secret information. He merely set up a platform for the thousands of whistleblowers out there. Assange is a service provider.

That there is someone inside the US system who is disgruntled enough to give out sensitive information should be US's biggest concern. The US should be for the "enemy" within.

The chorus of voices suggesting charges of espionage, treason and terrorism against Assange, and lately death threats, are being directed at the wrong person.

Or is Washington ready to take Sara Palin's and other ultra-nationalists suggestions and "pluck Assange from the streets," rendition him to the US and "neutralize" him?

Has technology changed the world the way we know it? Yes. The US is a creator, seller and an advocate of the same technology used against it. It should simply up its game, since Assange is not a lone player.

Source: Simon Mann, Julia May, and David Wroe, "Champions of Democracy, or People With Bloodied Hands?" *Sydney Morning Herald,* July 31, 2010.

The US can pressure Amazon.com and other companies to stop hosting WikiLeaks servers, but there are many other people out there who would. Then what?

What about the major papers (*New York Times, Guardian, Der Spiegel, El Pais* and *Le Monde*) that willingly received the documents from WikiLeaks and treated them as genuine news sources? What action will Washington take against them?

WikiLeaks has merely shown us how far technology and the thirst for information can take us. And don't let anyone lie to you that the diplomatic cables are mere gossip.

I believe the fallout will be slow, but is it coming, in waves. Diplomacy is two way traffic. The Iron Curtain collapsed decades ago, but in its place came a more sinister replacement, the Internet Cloud.

Maybe the cable leaks is exactly what the US needed. It should now stop the pretensions and just show us its teeth and claws.

2.9

ASSANGE NO DO-GOODER: WIKILEAKS ISN'T WHISTLEBLOWING, IT'S ESPIONAGE

Ezra Levant

Julian Assange, the boss of WikiLeaks, gave himself the online nickname Mendax. It means liar in Latin. It's a good fit for him.

Take the word WikiLeaks itself. Wiki is a Hawaiian word that means quick. But its meaning on the Internet is different. A wiki is a web-site that allows many people to collaborate on something quickly—like Wikipedia, the encyclopedia anyone in the world can edit.

So it doesn't just mean quick. It means quick and democratic.

Which is the opposite of WikiLeaks.

Only Assange, the unelected boss of WikiLeaks, gets to decide what's published.

WikiLeaks' original mandate was to expose repressive countries such as China, Russia and Iran. But Assange vetoed that. He's all about being anti-American.

But wiki is only half the name. The other half is leaks. A leak implies someone on the inside of an institution voluntarily releases information.

The thousands of classified military and diplomatic documents WikiLeaks has published were not leaked by someone with lawful access to them. They were stolen. One of the alleged thieves, a U.S. soldier named Bradley Manning, told a fellow hacker he was feeling sad and conflicted because of his sexuality, and "no one took any notice of me," and his theft might change that. He was about to be kicked out of the Army for assault, so he had to act fast.

That's not a leak on principle. That's an act of sabotage by an emotional infant.

Source: Ezra Levant, "Assange No Do-Gooder: WikiLeaks Isn't Whistleblowing, It's Espionage," *The Toronto Sun,* December 7, 2010.

Does WikiLeaks distance itself from Manning's alleged theft? The opposite: Its logo now has the words "Free Bradley" added to it.

Is stealing secret information justifiable if it blows the whistle on wrongdoing? Perhaps. But that's not what WikiLeaks does. It doesn't embarrass wrongdoers. It exposes and endangers real whistleblowers.

WikiLeaks published a document that named an Algerian activist covertly aiding the democracy movement there. It identified a Venezuelan reporter secretly exposing the appalling conditions of hospitals for the poor. Both are real whistleblowers. Both were outed by Assange.

Assange admits WikiLeaks will probably end up with "blood on our hands." But he's not too worried.

Vladimir Putin and Mahmoud Ahmadinejad can't believe their good luck.

So it's not wiki. It's not leaks. It's not whistleblowing. It's not even journalism. Assange got his hands on e-mails sent by Venezuela's ambassador to Argentina. He tried to auction them to the highest bidder—presumably to Chavez, too. That's not journalism. That's a shakedown. Maybe even a willingness to keep secrets, for the right price.

Then there's Assange's threat that if he's treated improperly—say, if he's forced to stand trial for rape in Sweden—he'll release another batch of secrets, he has labelled "insurance."

If a real journalist had real news, he'd publish it for its own sake. But by using his "news" as a bargaining chip, he gives away his game. It's not journalism. It's espionage. It's a weapon of war. And if police try to hold him accountable to the law, he'll use his weapon.

Assange revealed secret U.S. counterterrorism work in Yemen. That will likely end now, and Yemen may fall to al Qaeda.

Do you doubt if WikiLeaks was around in the 1940s it would have tipped off the Nazis to D-Day or leaked Anne Frank's hiding place too?

2.10

NEW TECHNOLOGIES STRENGTHENING AFRICA'S ECONOMY

Megan Neff

Economic development is increasingly affected by accessibility to information and communication technologies. The next selection examines the importance of technology in Africa's attempt to integrate itself in global markets and accelerate its efforts to develop economically. What is true of Africa is equally true of other less developed countries in Asia and Latin America.

Source: Megan Neff, "New Technologies Strengthening Africa's Economy," U.S. Department of State, Bureau of International Information Programs, June 29, 2009.

Washington—Across Africa, new technologies are being joined with local customs to strengthen the continent's infrastructure and economy.

Using information and communication technologies (ICTs), such as mobile phones and the Internet, Africans are finding business and trade to be easier and more afford-able, said Sala Patterson, a policy analyst at the Paris-based Organisation for Economic Co-operation and Development (OECD).

Patterson, along with representatives of the U.S. Agency for International Development (USAID), the African Development Bank and Africare, spoke with Congressmen Donald Payne and Charles Rangel and the European Commission's Ambassador John Bruton June 18 on Capitol Hill. The panel discussed the annual "African Economic Outlook," a study that examines Africa's economic development over the past year and makes pro-jections for the coming year.

In Africa, where communications networks have been limited, things are beginning to change, according to Payne. New ICTs, such as text messaging, are surpassing old com-munication networks in Africa, which have been handicapped by geography and politics.

These new ICTs are enabling Africans to access information on health and agriculture and services such as online banking, and to connect more effectively with the rest of the world. European companies, such as the United Kingdom's Vodafone and France's Vivendi and Orange, are turning their attention to the African market, where only 40 percent of Africans own a cell phone. By contrast, cell phone usage in Europe is at nearly 100 percent, said Laura Recuero-Virto, an economist for the OECD. Nokia, Intel and Microsoft are also investing in the African ICTs.

Projected economic growth for Africa in 2009 is 3 percent, down from 6 percent last year, said Leonce Ndikumana, research director for the African Development Bank. A report cited by the African Economic Outlook study shows that increased use of ICTs in Africa is helping to sustain parts of the African economy during this time of economic turbulence.

For example, mobile phones in Niger, one of the poorest countries in Africa, are being used as marketing tools. Farmers are able to text and use the Internet to communicate with markets around their farm and find the best prices for their goods. This has helped to reduce prices and it allows farmers to bring goods where they are most needed and where they will get the highest profit.

Online banking has also helped to sustain African communities through the recession, and there have been significant strides in increasing the affordability of money transfers. Where a Western Union transfer of 1,000 Kenyan shillings (about $13) would cost the user a 500 shilling transaction fee, Patterson said, with M-Pesa, a new money-transfer service available between cell phones, Kenyans can send the same amount with a transac-tion fee of 30 shillings to 75 shillings (about 39 cents to 97 cents). The lower transaction fees offered by M-Pesa have attracted 5 million users to the service in the past two years. M-Pesa is seeking to expand in East Africa and Afghanistan.

Africa still faces challenges with Internet accessibility and technical infrastructure. According to the panel, less than 7 percent of Africans have Internet access, and the Internet that is available is inconvenient and expensive, accessible only along the fiber optic lines laid along the west coast of Africa or through satellites. Limited Internet resources and lack of competition among Internet providers have led to exorbitant costs, the panel said.

But, Patterson said, broadband connections should be more widely available in Africa as the infrastructure expands. It is hoped that a web of fiber optic cables will be able to connect all of the main metropolitan areas in Africa by 2012.

For this expansion to take place, the African Economic Outlook study found, local government involvement will be extremely important to ensure that price drops are passed on to the consumers, and that ICTs are properly integrated into overall infrastructure development.

Chapter 3

ECONOMIC GLOBALIZATION

In this chapter, we focus on the economic dimension of globalization, perhaps the most controversial and most widely discussed of all the aspects of globalization. We will examine several of the most important economic consequences of globalization, especially the roots and consequences of the neoliberal principles on which the current global economic system is built.

The end of the Cold War witnessed the global spread of free market or neoliberal capitalism as the economic ideology of globalization. Russia, Eastern Europe, and the developing world joined the West and Japan in embracing policies of reduced government intervention in markets, deregulation and privatization, free trade, and free movement of investment. The spread of neoliberal economics has been accompanied by the global expansion of transnational corporations (with integrated global production, management, and distribution networks), the shifting of jobs and industries "off shore," the proliferation of global networks of production and distribution, the emergence of "world cities" such as New York, London, and Shanghai, and the emergence of an urbanized economic elite. Markets stretch beyond the boundaries of states, making it difficult for countries to determine their own economic destinies or protect themselves from the vagaries of global supply and demand or economic crises outside their borders.

Globalization enthusiasts point to free market capitalism as largely responsible for driving and sustaining economic globalization and increasing global wealth. Free trade, they argue, stimulates technological innovation and encourages states to produce what they do best, that is, most efficiently, thereby reducing inflation and providing consumers with an unprecedented variety of inexpensive but high-quality products. Support for economic globalization in developing countries rests on a belief that took hold in the 1980s and 1990s that market capitalism spurred economic growth while reducing poverty.

By contrast, critics of globalization argue that neoliberal policies have increased the gap between rich and poor, resulted in exploitation of developing societies, despoiled the environment, reduced wages, and forced a reduction in welfare costs in countries trying to compete economically with one another. Thus, they contend that competition compels states to outsource tasks that they once performed for citizens to private actors and firms. Domestically, states are slashing expensive social welfare programs and selling off inefficient state-owned companies and are sending their citizens to the marketplace to find new suppliers for health care, pensions, and utilities.

Demonizing Neoliberal Economics

3.1

NEOLIBERALISM AS CREATIVE DESTRUCTION

David Harvey

The first selection in the chapter is an article by the distinguished British anthropologist and critic of capitalism, David Harvey. Harvey begins by enumerating the elements of economic neoliberalism and goes on to explain how neoliberal economic principles, which he vigorously criticizes, spread and came to dominate globalized economic practice. Part of neoliberalism's attraction, he suggests, lies in its emphasis on individual freedom, themes that were effectively used by the American president Ronald Reagan and British prime minister Margaret Thatcher in the 1980s. Harvey observes that the widespread adoption of neoliberalism has produced the "destruction" of a variety of older and, in his view, more humane institutions and practices and that from an economic point of view it has not lived up to the claims of its enthusiasts.

America's invasion of Iraq in 2003, Harvey argues, was in part an effort to extend neoliberal principles, as was its involvement in overthrowing Chile's president Salvador Allende three decades earlier. In this effort, Britain and America have been aided by international economic institutions like the International Monetary Fund and World Trade Organization and by sympathetic, like-minded elites in countries such as China and India, and they have since continued to pressure countries to accept the neoliberal model.

At the heart of Harvey's argument is his explanation of the motivation of the purveyors of neoliberalism as a highly successful effort to restore the power and wealth of the upper classes and roll back policies that in previous decades had fostered economic equality and increased states' efforts to provide citizens with welfare and social security. This effort, in his view, climaxed with the "Washington Consensus," in favor of neoliberal policies that evolved between 1980 and 2000, an effort that gained strength with the Republican congressional triumph in 1994 and the success of the Republicans in using social and cultural issues to attract voters whose economic interests should have made them oppose neoliberal economics. America's fiscal crisis, the growing influence of conservative Republicans in the media, and the

Source: Excerpted from David Harvey, "Neoliberalism as Creative Destruction," *Annals of the American Academy of Political and Social Science* 610 (March 2007), 22–44. Notes appearing in the original have been deleted.

willingness of American and British leaders to act against labor unions also fostered the neoliberal agenda.

The result of all of this, according to Harvey, is "accumulation by dispossession" by the upper classes, characterized by privatization of public assets, financial speculation, manipulation of international economic crises to impose neoliberal policies, and redistribution of wealth upward. Harvey, nevertheless, envisions alternatives to neoliberal economics, which he reviews at the end of his essay, especially those put forward by antiglobalizers, social democrats, and civil society.

Neoliberalism is a theory of political economic practices proposing that human well-being can best be advanced by the maximization of entrepreneurial freedoms within an institutional framework characterized by private property rights, individual liberty, unencumbered markets, and free trade. The role of the state is to create and preserve an institutional framework appropriate to such practices. The state has to be concerned, for example, with the quality and integrity of money. It must also set up military, defense, police, and juridical functions required to secure private property rights and to support freely functioning markets. Furthermore, if markets do not exist (in areas such as education, health care, social security, or environmental pollution), then they must be created, by state action if necessary. But beyond these tasks the state should not venture. State interventions in markets (once created) must be kept to a bare minimum because the state cannot possibly possess enough information to second-guess market signals (prices) and because powerful interests will inevitably distort and bias state interventions (particularly in democracies) for their own benefit.

For a variety of reasons, the actual practices of neoliberalism frequently diverge from this template. Nevertheless, there has everywhere been an emphatic turn, ostensibly led by the Thatcher/Reagan revolutions in Britain and the United States, in political-economic practices and thinking since the 1970s. State after state, from the new ones that emerged from the collapse of the Soviet Union to old-style social democracies and welfare states such as New Zealand and Sweden, have embraced, sometimes voluntarily and sometimes in response to coercive pressures, some version of neoliberal theory and adjusted at least some of their policies and practices accordingly. Postapartheid South Africa quickly adopted the neoliberal frame and even contemporary China appears to be headed in that direction. Furthermore, advocates of the neoliberal mindset now occupy positions of considerable influence in education (universities and many "think tanks"), in the media, in corporate board rooms and financial institutions, in key state institutions (treasury departments, central banks), and also in those international institutions such as the International Monetary Fund (IMF) and the World Trade Organization (WTO) that regulate global finance and commerce. Neoliberalism has, in short, become hegemonic as a mode of discourse and has pervasive effects on ways of thought and political-economic practices to the point where it has become incorporated into the commonsense way we interpret, live in, and understand the world.

Neoliberalization has in effect swept across the world like a vast tidal wave of institutional reform and discursive adjustment. While plenty of evidence shows its uneven geographical development, no place can claim total immunity (with the exception of a few states such as North Korea). Furthermore, the rules of engagement now established through the WTO (governing international trade) and by the IMF (governing international finance) instantiate neoliberalism as a global set of rules. All states that sign on to the WTO and the IMF (and who can afford not to?) agree to abide (albeit with a "grace period" to permit smooth adjustment) by these rules or face severe penalties.

The creation of this neoliberal system has entailed much destruction, not only of prior institutional frameworks and powers (such as the supposed prior state sovereignty over political-economic affairs) but also of divisions of labor, social relations, welfare provisions, technological mixes, ways of life, attachments to the land, habits of the heart, ways of thought, and the like. Some assessment of the positives and negatives of this neoliberal revolution is called for. In what follows, therefore, I will sketch in some preliminary arguments as to how to both understand and evaluate this transformation in the way global capitalism is working. This requires that we come to terms with the underlying forces, interests, and agents that have propelled the neoliberal revolution forward with such relentless intensity. To turn the neoliberal rhetoric against itself, we may reasonably ask, In whose particular interests is it that the state take a neoliberal stance and in what ways have those interests used neoliberalism to benefit themselves rather than, as is claimed, everyone, everywhere?

The "Naturalization" of Neoliberalism

For any system of thought to become dominant, it requires the articulation of fundamental concepts that become so deeply embedded in commonsense understandings that they are taken for granted and beyond question. For this to occur, not any old concepts will do. A conceptual apparatus has to be constructed that appeals almost naturally to our intuitions and instincts, to our values and our desires, as well as to the possibilities that seem to inhere in the social world we inhabit. The founding figures of neoliberal thought took political ideals of individual liberty and freedom as sacrosanct—as the central values of civilization. And in so doing they chose wisely and well, for these are indeed compelling and greatly appealing concepts. Such values were threatened, they argued, not only by fascism, dictatorships, and communism, but also by all forms of state intervention that substituted collective judgments for those of individuals set free to choose. They then concluded that without "the diffused power and initiative associated with (private property and the competitive market) it is difficult to imagine a society in which freedom may be effectively preserved."

Setting aside the question of whether the final part of the argument necessarily follows from the first, there can be no doubt that the concepts of individual liberty and freedom are powerful in their own right, even beyond those terrains where the liberal tradition has had a strong historical presence. Such ideals empowered the dissident movements in Eastern Europe and the Soviet Union before the end of the Cold War as well as the students in Tiananmen Square. The student movement that swept the world in 1968—from Paris and Chicago to Bangkok and Mexico City—was in part animated by the quest for greater freedoms of speech and individual choice. These ideals have proven again and again to be a mighty historical force for change.

It is not surprising, therefore, that appeals to freedom and liberty surround the United States rhetorically at every turn and populate all manner of contemporary political manifestos. This has been particularly true of the United States in recent years. On the first anniversary of the attacks now known as 9/11, President Bush wrote an op-ed piece for the *New York Times* that extracted ideas from a U.S. National Defense Strategy document issued shortly thereafter. "A peaceful world of growing freedom," he wrote, even as his cabinet geared up to go to war with Iraq, "serves American long-term interests, reflects enduring American ideals and unites America's allies." ...

What the United States evidently sought to impose upon Iraq was a full-fledged neoliberal state apparatus whose fundamental mission was and is to facilitate conditions for profitable capital accumulation for all comers, Iraqis and foreigners alike. The Iraqis were, in short, expected to ride their horse of freedom straight into the corral of neoliberalism. ...

It is useful to recall, however, that the first great experiment with neoliberal state formation was Chile after Augusto Pinochet's coup ..., on the "little September 11th" of 1973. The coup, against the democratically elected and leftist social demo-cratic government of Salvador Allende, was strongly backed by the CIA and supported by U.S. Secretary of State Henry Kissinger. It violently repressed all left-of-center social movements and political organizations and dismantled all forms of popular organization, such as community health centers in poorer neighborhoods. The labor market was "freed" from regulatory or institutional restraints—trade union power, for example. But by 1973, the policies of import substitution that had formerly dominated in Latin American attempts at economic regeneration ... had fallen into disrepute. With the world economy in the midst of a serious reces-sion, something new was plainly called for. A group of U.S. economists known as "the Chicago boys," because of their attachment to the neoliberal theories of Milton Friedman, then teaching at the University of Chicago, were summoned to help reconstruct the Chilean economy. They did so along free-market lines, priva-tizing public assets, opening up natural resources to private exploitation, and facilitating foreign direct investment and free trade. The right of foreign companies to repatriate profits from their Chilean operations was guaranteed. Export-led growth was favored over import substitution. The subsequent revival of the Chilean economy in terms of growth, capital accumulation, and high rates of return on foreign investments provided evidence upon which the subsequent turn to more open neoliberal policies in both Britain (under Thatcher) and the United States (under Reagan) could be modeled. ...

The fact that two such obviously similar restructurings of the state apparatus occurred at such different times in quite different parts of the world under the coercive influence of the United States might be taken as indicative that the grim reach of U.S. imperial power might lie behind the rapid proliferation of neoliberal state forms throughout the world from the mid-1970s onward. But U.S. power and recklessness do not constitute the whole story. It was not the United States, after all, that forced Margaret Thatcher to take the neoliberal path in 1979. And during the early 1980s, Thatcher was a far more consistent advocate of neoliberalism than Reagan ever proved to be. Nor was it the United States that forced China in 1978 to follow the path that has over time brought it closer and closer to the embrace of neoliberalism. It would be hard to attribute the moves toward neoliberalism in India and Sweden in 1992 to the imperial reach of the United States. . . . So why, then, did the neoliberal turn occur, and what were the forces compelling it onward to the point where it has now become a hegemonic system within global capitalism?

Why the Neoliberal Turn?

Toward the end of the 1960s, global capitalism was falling into disarray. A significant recession occurred in early 1973—the first since the great slump of the 1930s. The oil embargo and oil price hike that followed later that year in the wake of the Arab-Israeli war exacerbated critical problems. The embedded capitalism of the postwar period, with its heavy emphasis on an uneasy compact between capital and labor brokered by an interventionist state that paid great attention to the social (i.e., welfare programs) and individual wage, was no longer working. The Bretton Woods accord set up to regulate international trade and finance was finally abandoned in favor of floating exchange rates in 1973. That system had delivered high rates of growth in the advanced capitalist countries and generated some spillover benefits—most obviously to Japan but also unevenly across South America and to some other countries of South East Asia—during the "golden age" of capitalism in the 1950s and early 1960s. By the next decade, however, the preexisting arrangements were exhausted and a new alternative was urgently needed to restart the process of capital accumulation. How and why neoliberalism emerged victorious as an answer to that quandary is a complex story. In retrospect, it may seem as if neoliberalism had been inevitable, but at the time no one really knew or understood with any certainty what kind of response would work and how.

The world stumbled toward neoliberalism through a series of gyrations and chaotic motions that eventually converged on the so-called "Washington Consensus" in the 1990s. . . .

There is, however, one element within this transition that deserves concerted attention. The crisis of capital accumulation of the 1970s affected everyone through the combination of rising unemployment and accelerating inflation. Discontent was widespread, and the conjoining of labor and urban social movements throughout much of the advanced capitalist world augured a socialist alternative to the social compromise between capital and labor that had grounded capital accumulation so successfully in the postwar period. Communist and socialist parties were gaining ground across much of

Europe, and even in the United States popular forces were agitating for widespread reforms and state interventions in everything ranging from environmental protection to occupational safety and health and consumer protection from corporate malfeasance. There was, in this, a clear *political* threat to ruling classes everywhere, both in advanced capitalist countries, like Italy and France, and in many developing countries, like Mexico and Argentina.

Beyond political changes, the *economic* threat to the position of ruling classes was now becoming palpable. One condition of the postwar settlement in almost all countries was to restrain the economic power of the upper classes and for labor to be accorded a much larger share of the economic pie. In the United States, for example, the share of the national income taken by the top 1 percent of earners fell from a prewar high of 16 percent to less than 8 percent by the end of the Second World War and stayed close to that level for nearly three decades. While growth was strong such restraints seemed not to matter, but when growth collapsed in the 1970s, even as real interest rates went negative and dividends and profits shrunk, ruling classes felt threatened. They had to move decisively if they were to protect their power from political and economic annihilation.

The coup d'etat in Chile and the military takeover in Argentina . . . provided one kind of solution. But the Chilean experiment with neoliberalism demonstrated that the benefits of revived capital accumulation were highly skewed. The country and its ruling elites along with foreign investors did well enough while the people in general fared poorly. This has been such a persistent effect of neoliberal policies over time as to be regarded a structural component of the whole project. . . . [D]ata show that the top 0.1 percent of income earners increased their share of the national income from 2 percent in 1978 to more than 6 percent by 1999. Yet another measure shows that the ratio of the median compensation of workers to the salaries of chief executive officers increased from just over thirty to one in 1970 to more than four hundred to one by 2000. . . .

And the United States is not alone in this: the top 1 percent of income earners in Britain doubled their share of the national income from 6.5 percent to 13 percent over the past twenty years. When we look further afield, we see extraordinary concentrations of wealth and power within a small oligarchy after the application of neoliberal shock therapy in Russia and a staggering surge in income inequalities and wealth in China as it adopts neoliberal practices. While there are exceptions to this trend—several East and Southeast Asian countries have contained income inequalities within modest bounds, as have France and the Scandinavian countries—the evidence suggests that the neoliberal turn is in some way and to some degree associated with attempts to restore or reconstruct upper-class power.

We can, therefore, examine the history of neoliberalism either as a utopian project providing a theoretical template for the reorganization of international capitalism or as a political scheme aimed at reestablishing the conditions for capital accumulation and the restoration of class power. In what follows, I shall argue that the last of these objectives has dominated. Neoliberalism has not proven effective at revitalizing global capital accumulation, but it has succeeded in restoring class power. As a consequence, the theoretical utopianism of the neoliberal argument has worked more as a system of justification and legitimization. The principles of neoliberalism are quickly abandoned whenever they conflict with this class project.

Toward the Restoration of Class Power

If there were movements to restore class power within global capitalism, then how were they enacted and by whom? The answer to that question in countries such as Chile and Argentina was simple: a swift, brutal, and self-assured military coup backed by the upper classes and the subsequent fierce repression of all solidarities created within the labor and urban social movements that had so threatened their power. Elsewhere, as in Britain and Mexico in 1976, it took the gentle prodding of a not yet fiercely neoliberal International Monetary Fund to push countries toward practices—although by no means policy commitment—to cut back on social expenditures and welfare programs to reestablish fiscal probity. In Britain, of course, Margaret Thatcher later took up the neoliberal cudgel with a vengeance in 1979 and wielded it to great effect. . . . The process of neoliberalization has been halting, geographically uneven, and heavily influenced by class structures and other social forces moving for or against its central propositions within particular state formations and even within particular sectors, for example, health or education.

It is informative to look more closely at how the process unfolded in the United States, since this case was pivotal as an influence on other and more recent transformations. Various threads of power intertwined to create a transition that culminated in the mid-1990s with the takeover of Congress by the Republican Party. That feat represented in fact a neoliberal "Contract with America" as a program for domestic action. Before that dramatic denouement, however, many steps were taken, each building upon and reinforcing the other.

To begin with, by 1970 or so, there was a growing sense among the U.S. upper classes that the anti-business and anti-imperialist climate that had emerged toward the end of the 1960s had gone too far. In a celebrated memo, Lewis Powell (about to be elevated to the Supreme Court by Richard Nixon) urged the American Chamber of Commerce in 1971 to mount a *collective* campaign to demonstrate that what was good for business was good for America. Shortly thereafter, a shadowy but influential Business Round Table was formed that still exists and plays a significant strategic role in Republican Party politics. Corporate political action committees, legalized under the post-Watergate campaign finance laws of 1974, proliferated like wildfire. With their activities protected under the First Amendment as a form of free speech in a 1976 Supreme Court decision, the systematic capture of the Republican Party as a class instrument of *collective* (rather than particular or individual) corporate and financial power began. But the Republican Party needed a popular base, and that proved more problematic to achieve. The incorporation of leaders of the Christian right, depicted as a moral majority, together with the Business Round Table provided the solution to that problem. A large segment of a disaffected, insecure, and largely white working class was persuaded to vote consistently against its own material interests on cultural (antiliberal, antiblack, antifeminist and antigay), nationalist and religious grounds. By the mid-1990s, the Republican Party had lost almost all of its liberal elements and become a homogeneous right-wing machine connecting the financial resources of large corporate capital with a populist base, the Moral Majority, that was particularly strong in the U.S. South.

The second element in the U.S. transition concerned fiscal discipline. The recession of 1973 to 1975 diminished tax revenues at all levels at a time of rising demand for social expenditures. Deficits emerged everywhere as a key problem. Something had to be done about the fiscal crisis of the state; the restoration of monetary discipline was essential. That conviction empowered financial institutions that controlled the lines of credit to government. In 1975, they refused to roll over New York's debt and forced that city to the edge of bankruptcy. A powerful cabal of bankers joined together with the state to tighten control over the city. This meant curbing the aspirations of municipal unions, layoffs in public employment, wage freezes, cutbacks in social provision (education, public health, and transport services), and the imposition of user fees (tuition was introduced in the CUNY university system for the first time). The bailout entailed the construction of new institutions that had first rights to city tax revenues in order to pay off bond holders: whatever was left went into the city budget for essential services. . . .

The management of New York's fiscal crisis paved the way for neoliberal practices both domestically under Ronald Reagan and internationally through the International Monetary Fund throughout the 1980s. It established a principle that, in the event of a conflict between the integrity of financial institutions and bondholders on one hand and the well-being of the citizens on the other, the former would be given preference. It hammered home the view that the role of government was to create a good business climate rather than look to the needs and well-being of the population at large. Fiscal redistributions to benefit the upper classes resulted in the midst of a general fiscal crisis. . . .

The third element in the U.S. transition entailed an ideological assault upon the media and upon educational institutions. Independent "think tanks" financed by wealthy individuals and corporate donors proliferated—the Heritage Foundation in the lead—to prepare an ideological onslaught aimed at persuading the public of the commonsense character of neoliberal propositions. A flood of policy papers and proposals and a veritable army of well-paid hired lieutenants trained to promote neoliberal ideas coupled with the corporate acquisition of media channels effectively transformed the discursive climate in the United States by the mid-1980s. The project to "get government off the backs of the people" and to shrink government to the point where it could be "drowned in a bathtub" was loudly proclaimed. With respect to this, the promoters of the new gospel found a ready audience in that wing of the 1968 movement whose goal was greater individual liberty and freedom from state power and the manipulations of monopoly capital. The libertarian argument for neoliberalism proved a powerful force for change. To the degree that capitalism reorganized to both open a space for individual entrepreneurship and switch its efforts to satisfy innumerable niche markets, particularly those defined by sexual liberation, that were spawned out of an increasingly individualized consumerism, so it could match words with deeds.

This carrot of individualized entrepreneurship and consumerism was backed by the big stick wielded by the state and financial institutions against that other wing of the 1968 movement whose members had sought social justice through collective negotiation and social solidarities. Reagan's destruction of the air traffic controllers (PATCO) in 1980 and Margaret Thatcher's defeat of the British miners in 1984 were crucial moments in the global turn toward neoliberalism. The assault upon institutions, such as trade unions and welfare rights organizations, that sought to protect and further working-class interests, was as broad as it was deep. The savage cutbacks in social expenditures and the welfare state, and the passing of all responsibility for their well-being to individuals and their families, proceeded apace. But these practices did not and could not stop at national borders. After 1980, the United States, now firmly committed to neoliberalization and clearly backed by Britain, sought, through a mix of leadership, persuasion—the economics departments of U.S. research universities played a major role in training many of the economists from around the world in neoliberal principles—and coercion to export neoliberalization far and wide. The purge of Keynesian economists and their replacement by neoliberal monetarists in the International Monetary Fund in 1982 transformed the U.S.-dominated IMF into a prime agent of neoliberalization through its structural adjustment programs visited upon any state (and there were many in the 1980s and 1990s) that required its help with debt repayments. The Washington Consensus that was forged in the 1990s and the negotiating rules set up under the World Trade Organization in 1998 confirmed the global turn toward neoliberal practices.

The new international compact also depended upon the reanimation and reconfiguration of the U.S. imperial tradition. That tradition had been forged in Central America in the 1920s, as a form of domination without colonies. Independent republics could be kept under the thumb of the United States and effectively act, in the best of cases, as proxies for U.S. interests through the support of strongmen—like Somoza in Nicaragua, the Shah in Iran, and Pinochet in Chile—and a coterie of followers backed by military assistance and financial aid. Covert aid was available to promote the rise to power of such leaders, but by the 1970s it became clear that something else was needed: the opening of markets, of new spaces for investment, and clear fields where financial powers could operate securely. This entailed a much closer integration of the global economy with a well-defined financial architecture. The creation of new institutional practices, such as those set out by the IMF and the WTO, provided convenient vehicles through which financial and market power could be exercised. The model required collaboration among the top capitalist powers and the Group of Seven (G7), bringing Europe and Japan into alignment with the United States to shape the global financial and trading system in ways that effectively forced all other nations to submit. "Rogue nations," defined as those that failed to conform to these global rules, could then be dealt with by sanctions or coercive and even military force if necessary. In this way, U.S. neoliberal imperialist strategies were articulated through a global network of power relations, one effect of which was to permit the U.S. upper classes to exact financial tribute and command rents from the rest of the world as a means to augment their already hegemonic control.

Neoliberalism as Creative Destruction

In what ways has neoliberalization resolved the problems of flagging capital accumulation? Its actual record in stimulating economic growth is dismal. Aggregate growth rates stood at 3.5 percent or so in the 1960s and even during the troubled 1970s fell to only 2.4 percent. The subsequent global growth rates of 1.4 percent and 1.1 percent for the 1980s and 1990s, and a rate that barely touches 1 percent since 2000, indicate that neoliberalism has broadly failed to stimulate worldwide growth. Even if we exclude from this calculation the catastrophic effects of the collapse of the Russian and some Central European economies in the wake of the neoliberal shock therapy treatment of the 1990s, global economic performance from the standpoint of restoring the conditions of general capital accumulation has been weak.

Despite their rhetoric about curing sick economies, neither Britain nor the United States achieved high economic performance in the 1980s. That decade belonged to Japan, the East Asian "Tigers," and West Germany as powerhouses of the global economy. Such countries were very successful, but their radically different institutional arrangements make it difficult to pin their achievements on neoliberalism. . . .

It was only in the 1990s that neoliberalization began to pay off for both the United States and Britain. This happened in the midst of a long-drawn-out period of deflation in Japan and relative stagnation in a newly unified Germany. . . .

So why, then, in the face of this patchy if not dismal record, have so many been persuaded that neoliberalization is a successful solution? Over and beyond the persistent stream of propaganda emanating from the neoliberal think tanks and suffusing the media, two material reasons stand out. First, neoliberalization has been accompanied by increasing volatility within global capitalism. That success was to materialize somewhere obscured the reality that neoliberalism was generally failing. Periodic episodes of growth interspersed with phases of creative destruction, usually registered as severe financial crises. Argentina was opened up to foreign capital and privatization in the 1990s and for several years was the darling of Wall Street, only to collapse into disaster as international capital withdrew at the end of the decade. . . . Financial turmoil proliferated all over the developing world, and in some instances, such as Brazil and Mexico, repeated waves of structural adjustment and austerity led to economic paralysis.

On the other hand, neoliberalism has been a huge success from the standpoint of the upper classes. It has either restored class position to ruling elites, as in the United States and Britain, or created conditions for capitalist class formation, as in China, India, Russia, and elsewhere. Even countries that have suffered extensively from neoliberalization have seen the massive reordering of class structures internally. The wave of privatization that came to Mexico with the Salinas de Gortari administration in 1992 spawned unprecedented concentrations of wealth in the hands of a few people. . . .

With the media dominated by upper-class interests, the myth could be propagated that certain sectors failed because they were not competitive enough, thereby setting the stage for even more neoliberal reforms. Increased social inequality was necessary to encourage entrepreneurial risk and innovation, and these, in turn, conferred competitive advantage and stimulated growth. If conditions among the lower classes deteriorated, it was because they failed for personal and cultural reasons to enhance their own human capital through education, the acquisition of a protestant work ethic, and submission to work discipline and flexibility. In short, problems arose because of the lack of competitive strength or because of personal, cultural, and political failings. . . .

If the main effect of neoliberalism has been redistributive rather than generative, then ways had to be found to transfer assets and channel wealth and income either from the mass of the population toward the upper classes or from vulnerable to richer countries. I have elsewhere provided an account of these processes under the rubric of *accumulation by dispossession*. By this, I mean the continuation and proliferation of accretion practices. . . . These include (1) the commodification and privatization of land and the forceful expulsion of peasant populations (as in Mexico and India in recent times); (2) conversion of various forms of property rights (common, collective, state, etc.) into exclusively private property rights; (3) suppression of rights to the commons; (4) commodification of labor power and the suppression of alternative (indigenous) forms of production and consumption; (5) colonial, neocolonial, and imperial processes of appropriation of assets (including natural resources); (6) monetization of exchange and taxation, particularly of land; (7) the slave trade (which continues, particularly in the sex industry); and (8) usury, the national debt, and, most devastating of all, the use of the credit system as radical means of primitive accumulation.

The state, with its monopoly of violence and definitions of legality, plays a crucial role in backing and promoting these processes. To this list of mechanisms, we may now add a raft of additional techniques, such as the extraction of rents from patents and intellectual property rights and the diminution or erasure of various forms of communal property rights-such as state pensions, paid vacations, access to education, and health care—won through a generation or more of social democratic struggles. . . .

[T]he practices that restored class power to capitalist elites in the United States and elsewhere are best described as an ongoing process of accumulation by dispossession that grew rapidly under neoliberalism. In what follows, I isolate four main elements.

1. Privatization

The corporatization, commodification, and privatization of hitherto public assets have been signal features of the neoliberal project. Its primary aim has been to open up new fields for capital accumulation in domains formerly regarded off-limits to the calculus of profitability. Public utilities of all kinds (water, telecommunications, transportation), social welfare provision (public housing, education, health care, pensions), public institutions (such as universities, research laboratories, prisons), and even warfare (as illustrated by the "army" of private contractors operating alongside the armed forces in Iraq) have all been privatized to some degree throughout the capitalist world.

Intellectual property rights established through the so-called TRIPS (Trade-Related Aspects of Intellectual Property Rights) agreement within the WTO defines genetic materials, seed plasmas, and all manner of other products as private property. Rents for use can then be extracted from populations whose practices had played a crucial role in the development of such genetic materials. Bio-piracy is rampant, and the pillaging of the world's stockpile of genetic resources is well under way to the benefit of a few large pharmaceutical companies. The escalating depletion of the global environmental commons (land, air, water) and proliferating habitat degradations that preclude anything but capital-intensive modes of agricultural production have likewise resulted from the wholesale commodification of nature in all its forms. The commodification (through tourism) of cultural forms, histories, and intellectual creativity entails wholesale dispossessions (the music industry is notorious for the appropriation and exploitation of grassroots culture and creativity). As in the past, the power of the state is frequently used to force such processes through even against popular will. The rolling back of regulatory frameworks designed to protect labor and the environment from degradation has entailed the loss of rights. The reversion of common property rights won through years of hard class struggle (the right to a state pension, to welfare, to national health care) into the private domain has been one of the most egregious of all policies of dispossession pursued in the name of neoliberal orthodoxy.

All of these processes amount to the transfer of assets from the public and popular realms to the private and class-privileged domains. Privatization, Arundhati Roy argued with respect to the Indian case, entails "the transfer of productive public assets from the state to private companies. Productive assets include natural resources: earth, forest, water, air. These are the assets that the state holds in trust for the people it represents. . . . To snatch these away and sell them as stock to private companies is a process of barbaric dispossession on a scale that has no parallel in history."

2. Financialization

The strong financial wave that set in after 1980 has been marked by its speculative and predatory style. The total daily turnover of financial transactions in international markets that stood at $2.3 billion in 1983 had risen to $130 billion by 2001. This $40 trillion annual turnover in 2001 compares to the estimated $800 billion that would be required to support international trade and productive investment flows. Deregulation allowed the financial system to become one of the main centers of redistributive activity through speculation, predation, fraud, and thievery. Stock promotions; Ponzi schemes; structured asset destruction through inflation; asset stripping through mergers and acquisitions; and the promotion of debt incumbency that reduced whole populations, even in the advanced capitalist countries, to debt peonage—to say nothing of corporate fraud and dispossession of assets, such as the raiding of pension funds and their decimation by stock and corporate collapses through credit and stock manipulations—are all features of the capitalist financial system.

The emphasis on stock values, which arose after bringing together the interests of owners and managers of capital through the remuneration of the latter in stock options, led, as we now know, to manipulations in the market that created immense wealth for a few at the expense of the many. The spectacular collapse of Enron was emblematic of a general process that deprived many of their livelihoods and pension rights. Beyond this, we also must look at the speculative raiding carried out by hedge funds and other major instruments of finance capital that formed the real cutting edge of accumulation by dispossession on the global stage, even as they supposedly conferred the positive benefit to the capitalist class of "spreading risks."

3. The Management and Manipulation of Crises

Beyond the speculative and often fraudulent froth that characterizes much of neoliberal financial manipulation, there lies a deeper process that entails the springing of the debt trap as a primary means of accumulation by dispossession. Crisis creation, management, and manipulation on the world stage has evolved into the fine art of deliberative redistribution of wealth from poor countries to the rich. By suddenly raising interest rates in 1979, Paul Volcker, then chairman of the U.S. Federal Reserve, raised the proportion of foreign earnings that borrowing countries had to put to debt-interest payments. Forced into bankruptcy, countries like Mexico had to agree to structural adjustment. While proclaiming its role as a noble leader organizing bailouts to keep global capital accumulation stable and on track, the United States could also open the way to pillage the Mexican economy through deployment of its superior financial power under conditions of local crisis. This was what the U.S. Treasury/Wall Street/IMF complex became expert at doing everywhere. Volcker's successor, Alan Greenspan, resorted to similar tactics several times in the 1990s. Debt crises in individual countries, uncommon in the 1960s, became frequent during the 1980s and 1990s. Hardly any developing country remained untouched and in some cases, as in Latin America, such crises were frequent enough to be considered endemic. These debt crises were orchestrated, managed, and controlled both to rationalize the system and to redistribute assets during the 1980s and 1990s. . . .

The analogy to the deliberate creation of unemployment to produce a pool of low-wage surplus labor convenient for further accumulation is precise. Valuable assets are thrown out of use and lose their value. They lie fallow and dormant until capitalists possessed of liquidity choose to seize upon them and breathe new life into them. The danger, however, is that crises can spin out of control and become generalized, or that revolts will arise against the system that creates them. One of the prime functions of state interventions and of international institutions is to orchestrate crises and devaluations in ways that permit accumulation by dispossession to occur without sparking a general collapse or popular revolt. The structural adjustment program administered by the Wall Street/Treasury/IMF complex takes care of the first function. It is the job of the comprador neoliberal state apparatus . . . to ensure that insurrections do not occur in whichever country has been raided. Yet signs of popular revolt have emerged, first with the Zapatista uprising in Mexico in 1994 and later in the generalized discontent that informed antiglobalization movements such as the one that culminated in Seattle in 1999.

4. State Redistributions

The state, once transformed into a neoliberal set of institutions, becomes a prime agent of redistributive policies, reversing the flow from upper to lower classes that had been implemented during the preceding social democratic era. It does this in the first instance through privatization schemes and cutbacks in government expenditures meant to support the social wage. Even when privatization appears as beneficial to the lower classes, the long-term effects can be negative. At first blush, for example, Thatcher's program for the privatization of social housing in Britain appeared as a gift to the lower classes whose members could now convert from rental to ownership at a relatively low cost, gain control over a valuable asset, and augment their wealth. But once the transfer was accomplished, housing speculation took over particularly in prime central locations, eventually bribing or forcing low-income populations out to the periphery in cities like London and turning erstwhile working-class housing estates into centers of intense gentrification. The loss of affordable housing in central areas produced homelessness for many and extraordinarily long commutes for those who did have low-paying service jobs. . . . The Chinese state has taken a whole series of draconian measures through which assets have been conferred upon a small elite to the detriment of the masses.

The neoliberal state also seeks redistributions through a variety of other means such as revisions in the tax code to benefit returns on investment rather than incomes and wages, promotion of regressive elements in the tax code (such as sales taxes), displacement of state expenditures and free access to all by user fees (e.g., on higher education), and the provision of a vast array of subsidies and tax breaks to corporations. The welfare programs that now exist in the United States at federal, state, and local levels amount to a vast redirection of public moneys for corporate benefit (directly as in the case of subsidies to agribusiness and indirectly as in the case of the military-industrial sector), in much the same way that the mortgage interest rate tax deduction operates in the United States as a massive subsidy to upper-income home owners and the construction of industry. . . .

In effect, reported Roy, "India's rural economy, which supports seven hundred million people, is being garroted. Farmers who produce too much are in distress, farmers who produce too little are in distress, and landless agricultural laborers are out of work as big estates and farms lay off their workers. They're all flocking to the cities in search of employment." In China, the estimate is that at least half a billion people will have to be absorbed by urbanization over the next ten years if rural mayhem and revolt is to be avoided. What those migrants will do in the cities remains unclear, though the vast physical infrastructural plans now in the works will go some way to absorbing the labor surpluses released by primitive accumulation.

The redistributive tactics of neoliberalism are wide-ranging, sophisticated, frequently masked by ideological gambits, but devastating for the dignity and social well-being of vulnerable populations and territories. The wave of creative destruction neoliberalization has visited across the globe is unparalleled in the history of capitalism. Understandably, it has spawned resistance and a search for viable alternatives.

Alternatives

Neoliberalism has spawned a swath of oppositional movements both within and outside of its compass. . . . Traditional worker-based movements are by no means dead even in the advanced capitalist countries where they have been much weakened by the neoliberal onslaught. . . .

But struggles against accumulation by dispossession are fomenting quite different lines of social and political struggle. Partly because of the distinctive conditions that give rise to such movements, their political orientation and modes of organization depart markedly from those typical in social democratic politics.

The Zapatista rebellion, for example, did not seek to take over state power or accomplish a political revolution. It sought instead a more inclusive politics to work through the whole of civil society in an open and fluid search for alternatives that would consider the specific needs of different social groups and allow them to improve their lot. . . .

The effect of such movements has been to shift the terrain of political organization away from traditional political parties and labor organizing into a less focused political dynamic of social action across the whole spectrum of civil society. But what they lost in focus they gained in relevance. They drew their strengths from embeddedness in the nitty-gritty of daily life and struggle but in so doing often found it hard to extract themselves from the local and the particular to understand the macro-politics of what neoliberal accumulation by dispossession was and is all about. The variety of such struggles was and is simply stunning. It is hard to even imagine connections between them. They were and are all part of a volatile mix of protest movements that swept the world and increasingly grabbed the headlines during and after the 1980s. . . .

The movements themselves have produced an abundance of ideas regarding alternatives. Some seek to de-link wholly or partially from the overwhelming powers of neoliberalism and neoconservatism. Others seek global social and environmental justice by reform or dissolution of powerful institutions such as the IMF, the WTO, and the World Bank. Still others emphasize a reclaiming of the commons, thereby signaling deep continuities with struggles of long ago as well as with struggles waged throughout the bitter history of colonialism and imperialism. Some envisage a multitude in motion, or a movement within global civil society, to confront the dispersed and de-centered powers of the neoliberal order, while others more modestly look to local experiments with new production and consumption systems animated by different kinds of social relations and ecological practices. There are also those who put their faith in more conventional political party structures with the aim of gaining state power as one step toward global reform of the economic order. Many of these diverse currents now come together at the World Social Forum in an attempt to define their shared mission and build an organizational structure capable of confronting the many variants of neoliberalism and of neoconservatism. There is much here to admire and to inspire.

But what sorts of conclusions can be derived from an analysis of the sort here constructed? To begin with, the whole history of the social democratic compromise and the subsequent turn to neoliberalism indicates the crucial role played by class struggle in either checking or restoring class power. Though it has been effectively disguised, we have lived through a whole generation of sophisticated class struggle on the part of the upper strata to restore or, as in China and Russia, construct class dominance. This occurred in decades when many progressives were theoretically persuaded that class was a meaningless category and when those institutions from which struggle had hitherto been waged on behalf of the working classes were under fierce assault. The first lesson we must learn, therefore, is that if it looks like class struggle and acts like class struggle, then we have to name it for what it is. The mass of the population has either to resign itself to the historical and geographical trajectory defined by this overwhelming class power or respond to it in class terms. . . .

Analysis also points up exploitable contradictions within the neoliberal agenda. The gap between rhetoric (for the benefit of all) and realization (for the benefit of a small ruling class) increases over space and time, and social movements have done much to focus on that gap. The idea that the market is about fair competition is increasingly negated by the facts of extraordinary monopoly, centralization, and internationalization on the part of corporate and financial powers. The startling increase in class and regional inequalities both within states . . . as well as internationally poses a serious political problem that can no longer be swept under the rug as something transitional on the way to a perfected neoliberal world. . . .The more neoliberalism is recognized as a failed if not disingenuous and utopian project masking the restoration of class power, the more it lays the basis for a resurgence of mass movements voicing egalitarian political demands, seeking economic justice, fair trade, and greater economic security and democratization.

But it is the profoundly antidemocratic nature of neoliberalism that should surely be the main focus of political struggle. Institutions with enormous leverage, like the Federal Reserve, are outside any democratic control. Internationally, the lack of elementary accountability let alone democratic control over institutions such as the IMF, the WTO, and the World Bank, to say nothing of the great private power of financial institutions, makes a mockery of any credible concern about democratization. . . .

The more clearly oppositional movements recognize that their central objective must be to confront the class power that has been so effectively restored under neoliberalization, the more they will be likely to cohere. Tearing aside the neoliberal mask and exposing its seductive rhetoric, used so aptly to justify and legitimate the restoration of that power, has a significant role to play in contemporary struggles. It took neoliberals many years to set up and accomplish their march through the institutions of contemporary capitalism. We can expect no less of a struggle when pushing in the opposite direction.

3.2

TOP 10 REASONS TO OPPOSE THE WTO

from *National Post*

Although the following selection was not explicitly written in response to David Harvey's critique of neoliberal capitalism in the previous article, its defense of the World Trade Organization (WTO) effectively responds to many of his claims. Thus, the author denies that the institutions of globalization are

In Praise of Economic Globalization

Source: "Top 10 Reasons to Oppose the WTO: The World Trade Organization's Ministerial Conference Opens in Seattle Tomorrow, and Everyone From Farmers to Left-Wing Activists Have Protests in the Works. Yet the Association of 134 Countries Says the Most Common Arguments Against It Are Dead Wrong," *National Post*, November 29, 1999.

any less democratic than their member states, noting that the WTO even requires unanimity to act. Governments, moreover, must and do take account of the myriad interest groups that constitute civil society and, in the name of fairness, must treat them all equally. Dispute panels are virtually always selected with the agreement of those involved in the dispute. Far from limiting national sovereignty, WTO rules encourage states to take account of the public interest.

The author notes that the WTO takes account of labor and environmental standards but must first decide whether or not trade law has been broken, and it recognizes that raising environmental, labor, and safety standards may impede economic growth in developing countries. Its rules do not favor rich countries but are applied equally to all. Nor does the WTO defend intellectual property rights to the detriment of citizens or take the side of corporations against governments, which it could not do in any event since its members *are* governments. Finally, free trade increases overall wealth. Both rich and poor benefit from the growing pie. Whether inequality has been growing is a highly debatable issue.

With opposition coming from all fronts in the impending Battle at Seattle, a beleaguered World Trade Organization is taking on its critics by answering what it says are the top 10 reasons to oppose the WTO.

1. The WTO only serves the interests of multinational corporations, who have inside access to the negotiations and who write the rules to suit themselves.

Reality: The WTO is as democratic as its member governments; and among the members it is ultra-democratic because all members must agree. Member governments alone have access to the negotiations. WTO rules and agreements are approved by all national parliaments before they take effect.

2. The WTO keeps the public in the dark, ignoring citizen input by consumer, environmental, human rights and labour organizations, and holding proceedings in secret.

Reality: Democratically elected governments—regularly citing pressure from consumer, environmental, human rights and labour organizations, as well as business—take into account the views of various groups in their societies.

The WTO Web site currently contains over 60,000 official documents, publicly available in the three official languages (English, French and Spanish). Most official documents are published immediately. Few remain restricted, and even then for a maximum of about six months. Some 200,000 visitors per month download the equivalent of 80 million pages each month.

3. The WTO is a stacked court. Its dispute panels, which rule on whether domestic laws are 'barriers to trade,' consist of three trade bureaucrats subject to conflict of

interests. For example, in Mexico's tuna/dolphin case, the United States was forced to repeal its law barring tuna from being caught by mile-long nets that kill hundreds of thousands of dolphins each year. This case involved a judge from a corporate front group that lobbied on behalf of the Mexican government for NAFTA.

Reality: Dispute panels rule on whether countries break their WTO agreements—not on 'whether domestic laws are barriers to trade.' All three panelists are normally agreed to by both sides in a dispute. In the few exceptions (15 out of almost 200 cases), the WTO director-general selects the panelists. Without these independent panels, countries could be tempted to settle trade conflicts by force.

All member governments agree to the WTO's dispute settlement procedures. They were not imposed on anyone. . . .

4. The WTO tramples over labour and human rights, ignoring the fact that countries that actively enforce labour rights are disadvantaged by those that don't. Many developing countries, such as Mexico, contend that labour standards constitute a 'barrier to free trade' for countries whose competitive advantage in the global economy is cheap labour. The WTO blocked potential solutions by ruling it illegal for a government to ban a product based on its method of production (i.e., with child labour) or for a government to judge the behaviour of companies that do business with vicious dictatorships such as Burma.

Reality: At their first ministerial meeting (Singapore, 1996), WTO members reaffirmed their commitment to core labour standards.

The WTO's developing-country members resist including labour standards, which they see as a guise for protectionism in developed-country markets and a smokescreen for undermining the comparative advantage of lower-wage developing countries. They argue that better working conditions and improved labour rights arise through economic growth, and that sanctions imposed against countries with lower labour standards would merely perpetuate poverty and delay improvements in workplace standards.

To suggest that developed countries that enforce labour standards are handicapped ignores the developed countries' success in exporting—they have by far the largest share of export markets.

No one has argued in the WTO that "labour standards constitute a 'barrier to free trade'."

The issue of child labour has never come up for a ruling, countries' efforts to deal with child labour problems have never been challenged in the WTO, and the WTO made no such ruling over trade with Myanmar (Burma). The WTO agreements (GATT article 21) allow countries to follow United Nations decisions, as when sanctions were imposed against South Africa under apartheid.

5. The WTO is destroying the environment by letting corporations use the WTO to dismantle hard-won environmental protections, calling them barriers to trade. Recently, the WTO declared illegal an Endangered Species Act provision requiring shrimp sold in the U.S. to be caught with an inexpensive device that allows endangered sea turtles to escape. The WTO is currently negotiating an agreement to eliminate tariffs on wood products, which would increase the demand for timber and escalate deforestation.

Reality: The WTO 'shrimp-turtle' panel and the appeals body stated clearly that the United States can protect endangered turtles. They did not rule that the provision of the Endangered Species Act is illegal. They ruled, among other things, that the U.S. government discriminated against Asian suppliers and in favour of Caribbean suppliers.

The proposal to lower tariffs on wood products, as with other proposals, includes environmental conservation issues. The outcome depends entirely on what governments are willing to do.

6. The WTO is killing people. Its fierce defence of intellectual property rights—patents, copyrights and trademarks—empowers pharmaceutical companies against governments seeking to protect their people's health. In sub-Saharan Africa, where 80% of the world's new AIDS cases are found, the U.S. government, on behalf of U.S. drug companies, is trying to block developing countries' access to less expensive, generic, life-saving drugs.

Reality: The need to protect health and human life is built into the WTO agreement on intellectual property rights. The WTO cannot support pharmaceutical companies against governments because governments run the WTO, and decisions require consensus among those governments. Nothing in the WTO intellectual property agreement discriminates against generic drugs.

7. The WTO undermines local development and penalizes poor countries. Its 'most-favoured nation' provisions require WTO member countries to treat each other equally and to treat all corporations from these countries equally, regardless of their track record. Rewarding companies who hire local residents, use domestic materials, or adopt environmentally sound practices are essentially illegal under the WTO, whose rules prohibit developing countries from following the same polices that developed countries pursued, such as protecting nascent, domestic industries until they can be internationally competitive.

Reality: Most-favoured-nation treatment means non-discrimination among countries, not among corporations. Equal country treatment is an overwhelmingly important and useful principle for both fairness and efficiency.

A government can reward or penalize corporations—by hiring local staff, using domestic materials or encouraging sound environmental practices—but its criteria must normally apply to all foreign companies.

Developing countries may adopt longer timetables for implementing many important provisions and commitments to allow them to protect nascent industries.

8. The WTO is increasing inequality. While global trade and investment grew rapidly from 1960 to 1998, inequality worsened both internationally and within countries—the richest 20% of the world's population consumes 86% of the world's resources, while the poorest 80% consumes just 14%. WTO rules have hastened these trends by opening up countries to foreign investment and letting production go where the labour is cheapest and environmental costs are low.

Reality: This is an analytical question, unlike the previous points, which are factual errors, except that no one pretends the present WTO system is 'free trade.'

Trade contributes to increasing standards of living and to lifting people out of poverty. Without trade liberalization and international trade rules, the majority would almost certainly be poorer. Whether trade worsened inequality is debatable—inequality can rise and fall as countries go through different levels of development. However, even if the world were more equal without trade, it would almost certainly be poorer, and most of the poor would almost certainly be poorer.

Arguing against investment creating jobs in poor countries amounts to arguing that the poorest people in the world should be kept poor. Trade, by raising incomes, helps poor countries find the resources to protect their environment.

9. The WTO undermines national sovereignty. By creating a supranational court system with the power to economically sanction countries to force them to comply with its rulings, the WTO has essentially replaced national governments with an unelected, unaccountable corporate-backed government. For the past nine years, the European Union has banned beef raised with artificial growth hormones. The WTO recently ruled this public health law a barrier to trade. The EU must roll back its ban or pay stiff penalties. Under the WTO, governments can no longer act in the public interest.

Reality: All parties in a dispute have agreed to the WTO dispute-settlement system.

The winning country—not the WTO—imposes sanctions. The United States voluntarily imposed sanctions on the EU, within WTO rules and procedures. The WTO does not have the power to initiate a case.

The United States first imposed $100 million (US) in annual sanctions against the EU for the beef-hormone ban in 1989, six years before the WTO came into being.

The WTO did not say the law should be abolished. The ruling said the ban (not the law) violated WTO agreements that the EU itself negotiated and signed. The EU had the option of providing sufficient evidence of health risk to support the ban, or of removing the ban. It chose to supply the evidence, but within the agreed time limit it was unable to do so and U.S. sanctions were imposed. The EU still says it will supply the evidence. Meanwhile, the ban has not been lifted. No one has been forced to do anything.

WTO agreements include countless provisions allowing governments to take public interest into account. The agreements are also the result of negotiations in which all governments pursued what they saw as the interests of their public. If their view of the public interest changes, they are completely free to seek to amend the agreements. That has already happened in eight successive trade rounds under GATT, with the ninth approaching after the Seattle Ministerial Conference.

10.   The tide is turning against free trade and the WTO There is a growing international backlash against the WTO and the process of corporate globalization over which it presides. Movement-building by coalitions such as People's Global Action against the WTO in Europe and the Citizen's Trade Campaign in the United States are growing fast, as public support for corporate-managed free trade dwindles. This is why tens of thousands of people from all walks of life will converge in Seattle Nov. 29 to Dec. 4 to confront the World Trade Organization head on at its ministerial meeting.

Reality: The countries queuing up to join the WTO, from the most populous (China) and the largest physically (Russia) to tiny Andorra, are proof that a significant part of the world believes that its economic future lies in the WTO system. And opinion polls suggest that the public in the United States and elsewhere are in favour of freer trade, even if they have reservations about some aspects.

3.3

THE PROPHET OF PROGRESS

Marcus Gee

> The next selection reflects optimism regarding the future of economic globalization and its role in ending economic stagnation brought on by the global economic recession of 2007–2009. It describes an interview with a leading Indian entrepreneur, who describes how his corporation developed into a global leader and why maintaining an open trading system promises universal benefits.

Capitalism is done like dinner. The free market is over. Globalization is dead. The great recession has finished them all. So say the prophets of doom.

Nandan Nilekani has a different view. Mr. Nilekani is a prophet of a different kind: a prophet of progress. The co-founder of Infosys Technologies Ltd., a leading Indian IT and offshoring firm, believes that globalization is here to stay, despite the biggest economic slump since the Second World War. In fact, the way to beat the crisis is to embrace globalization, not reject it.

"I personally believe that one of the fastest ways we can recover from this global crisis is increasing trade among nations and not by putting up barricades," he said this week while on a visit to Toronto.

Mr. Nilekani has the credentials to back that assertion. Perhaps more than any other developing world business figure, he has become associated with the phenomenon of globalization. And all because of one phrase: The world is flat.

During a conversation with *New York Times* columnist Thomas Friedman he made a remark that would make him famous and Mr. Friedman rich. "Tom," he said, "the playing field is being levelled."

What he meant was that the huge rise in computing power and the huge drop in the cost of transmitting data globally were allowing companies in developing countries such as India to compete on the same footing as their rich-world rivals. A company like Infosys, based in Bangalore, southern India, could run the payroll of a huge corporation in New York as effectively—and for far less—than a U.S. payroll firm down the street in Manhattan.

Out of that insight came Mr. Friedman's best-selling paean to globalization, 2005's *The World Is Flat,* still a standard in airport bookshops from Tokyo to Istanbul. In it, Mr. Nilekani and others like him argued that globalization helped countries in both rich

Source: Marcus Gee, "The Prophet of Progress," *The Globe and Mail,* May 6, 2009.

world and poor, allowing rich ones to lower their business costs by outsourcing low-end back office work and letting poor ones leverage the advantage of their young, eager and increasingly well-educated work forces.

Today, the whole process of globalization is under attack. It is precisely because the world is flat that the credit crisis born in the United States travelled around the world so quickly, infecting just about every corner of the globe.

"This is clearly a checkpoint in the globalization journey," said Mr. Nilekani, acknowledging that the global crisis has created "apprehension and trepidation" about the phenomenon.

It has proved, for example, that financial markets need strong, streamlined regulation—a point that most of globalization's champions never really challenged.

Still, "I think globalization is going to happen. It's been happening for thousands of years and it will happen for many more years. The current episode in some sense is just a point of introspection and pause," he said.

The Indian IT sector is a case in point. Since Infosys was founded in 1981 by "seven skinny kids"—Mr. Nilekani was one of them—it has become the most dynamic and globalized part of the trillion-dollar Indian economy. Its revenue grew from $50 million (U.S.) in 1991, when Indian's era of economic reform began, to $50 billion today. Infosys alone has more than 100,000 employees spread around 22 countries, including Canada. And Mr. Nilekani, the son of a manager in a textile mill, was listed in Forbes magazine last year as having a net worth of $1.1 billion.

Like so many other companies, Infosys has been suffering of late. Growth slowed to 11 per cent in the fiscal year ended March 31 and Mr. Nilekani, the company's co-chairman, said it expects the business to actually shrink by 3 to 6 per cent this year, an unheard of thing in a sector used to year after year of gains.

But he argued that, even as countries and companies suffer, the world continues to flatten. Computers are becoming smarter, smaller, faster and more wireless. Telecom charges keep falling.

In fact, the global crisis has made it more important than ever for companies to transform themselves into smarter, more efficient organizations—just the thing companies like Infosys can help them do.

"This global crisis is going to fundamentally change companies," Mr. Nilekani said. "They will have to reinvent themselves hugely; their supply chains, what they sell, how they sell—all that is going to change and that is going to drive the business transformation of the kind that we do."

To keep up, Infosys has invested heavily in educating its work force and seeking out the "best practices" from around the world. Before long, he said, the company will start growing again. That will be good not only for India, which has seen its economy take off in the past two decades because of entrepreneurs such as Mr. Nilekani, but for the rest of the world.

"When countries like India and China grow, they create huge markets," he argued. Already, he says of India, "We are buying more from the world than we're selling to the world."

The way Mr. Nilekani sees it, the story of globalization is far from over. Crisis or no crisis, the world is flat.

3.4

CHINA ECONOMY WILL SURPASS US, BUT WHEN?

Ron Scherer

China has become an economic superpower, overtaking Japan to become the second largest economy in the world and Germany to become the world's leading exporter. The next selection asks when China will surpass the United States in terms of economic clout and what the consequences of this are likely to be.

The Chinese economy has sprinted right past Japan's to become the No. 2 economy in the world.

So, how long will it be before China overtakes the United States?

America doesn't need to worry about the China economy leaving the US in the dust anytime soon, economists say.

"We don't have to look over our shoulder at all," says Jay Bryson, international economist at Wells Fargo Economics in Charlotte, N.C. "They probably will not surpass us for 20 years under current growth rates. But even when they do, they won't be anywhere close to our standard of living."

The numbers illustrate the vast gulf. The Chinese economy, the International Monetary Fund estimates, will total about $5.4 trillion this year, while the US one will be about $14.8 trillion—almost three times the size of the Chinese economy. To catch the US, China will have to grow extremely fast while the US economy dawdles.

The US economy will grow by 3.8 percent this year, while the Chinese economy grows by 9.3 percent, the IMF estimates.

For China to catch the US in 10 years, its economy would have to grow at more than 12 percent per annum, for example, while the US grows at 2 percent, Mr. Bryson estimates. However, most economists say, it is unlikely that China will have sustained growth that high and the US will be that low.

"It would be safe to say they will catch us sometime in the next generation," Bryson says.

In an analysis this past January, John Hawksworth, an economist at PricewaterhouseCoopers, projected that China will surpass the US by 2020 and "is likely to be some way ahead of the US by 2030."

However, Mr. Hawksworth, who is based in London, also makes the point that Chinese growth begins to slow after 2020 because of its rapidly aging population (due in part to its one-child policy). In fact in two years, he projects, India will become the third-largest economy, racing past Japan. After 2020, he thinks, India will grow more quickly than China because it will have a younger and faster-growing population.

Source: Ron Scherer, "China Economy Will Surpass US, but When?" *The Christian Science Monitor,* August 16, 2010.

Even when China's gross domestic product moves past America's, China, with a population of 1.3 billion people, will still be far behind the US, with its 307 million people, in terms of the standard of living.

"The average Chinese will not live as good as the average American for at least a century," Bryson estimates.

When the Chinese economy does become No. 1, there might be some "psychological implications," says Todd Lee, group director of global economics at IHS Global Insight in Lexington, Mass.

For example, the Chinese will have more money for defense and space exploration. "At that point, what China does with its political system could have some import. If they have reforms and turn towards democracy, we may feel less threatened than if it stays the same as today," he says.

One improbable way China could catch the US: if the US economy suffers a meltdown while the Chinese economy continues to grow. If the US economy shrank by two-thirds, the Chinese economy would be larger than America's.

"To put that into perspective," says Bryson, "during the Great Depression the economy shrank by one-third. So the US economy would have to decline by two times the Great Depression. That maybe could happen, but it's very unlikely."

China could also catch up to the US economy sooner if it were to allow its currency to appreciate faster, since its GDP is measured in terms of dollars, after inflation. "It all depends on how they view the global recovery is going," Mr. Lee says. "Once they feel it is sustainable, they could allow their currency to appreciate at a relatively steady pace."

The US economy probably became top dog in the early 20th century, when it surpassed Britain, Bryson says. But that was an era when it would have been difficult, if not impossible, to have accurate economic measurements.

"The US was the first to dominate during the Industrial Revolution," he says. Now, China is becoming dominant. "So, it's only a matter of time until they catch us."

3.5

GLOBAL OUTSOURCING NOT A ONE-WAY STREET FROM U.S.

Rob Preston

> The movement or "outsourcing" of industries and jobs from developed to less developed countries has been a sore point for many Americans. This movement has, however, also led to foreign investment in the United States that has created jobs. To illustrate the point, the next selection describes a large investment in the United States by a major Indian corporation, as well as other international investments beneficial to Americans.

Source: Rob Preston, "Global Outsourcing Not a One-Way Street From U.S.," *InformationWeek*, August 13, 2007.

Several outsourcing industry deals last week show that the world of business technology is indeed getting flatter—but also that tech globalization is a multidimensional thoroughfare, not a one-way street out of the United States.

The biggest deal is Wipro Technologies' $600 million acquisition of Leonia, N.J.-based Infocrossing, planting the huge Indian outsourcer firmly on U.S. soil, complete with expansion and hiring plans. Infocrossing operates five data centers in the United States, providing hosted and managed IT services. As Wipro extends its U.S. footprint, including opening software development centers in Atlanta and three other cities, the company says it's looking to hire hundreds of Americans with associate's degrees in tech-related fields, train them, and pay for the best to earn bachelor's degrees in technology—much like it does with tens of thousands of locals back home.

It's by no means a U.S. hiring spree for Wipro, whose employees in the States are mostly Indian nationals, notes senior writer Marianne Kolbasuk McGee in our cover story this week. But it's at least a sign of long-term investment in the domestic market.

And those expansion and hiring plans aren't just opportunistic PR for an offshore company (and industry) that strikes fear into the hearts and minds of the American IT rank and file. They're also smart business, as Wipro appeals to U.S. customers as a full-service IT outsourcer rather than a bit player that merely picks off low-hanging business and ships it back to India. Before it had U.S. data center and development operations, Wipro was probably a legitimate option for two in 10 U.S. companies, says Dean Davison of consulting firm NeoIT, while now it'll be an option for seven of 10 companies.

The tech globalization road also is leading to China, as evidenced by two other outsourcing industry deals last week. Under one, private equity firm Francisco Partners is investing $48 million in DarwinSuzsoft, a U.S. company that specializes in outsourcing to China. DarwinSuzsoft, which employs 800 of its 1,000 people in China, does both business process and IT outsourcing, mainly for financial, insurance, technology, and health care customers. CEO Dan Ross says companies are looking to China to access tech talent that's up to 40% cheaper than in India, with less turnover. "It's a massive phenomenon," Ross told editor at large Mary Hayes Weier. "I don't know any large company that is not considering China at this point."

Also last week, Sierra Atlantic, an IT services provider with operations mainly in India, said it's acquiring ArrAy, a Boston-based company with 200 engineers in Guangzhou and Shanghai. The biggest tech vendors have their sights on China as well: IBM, Oracle, Tata Consultancy Services, and others plan to hire thousands more engineers and developers in that country.

None of these moves is evidence of a kinder, gentler technology industry. Disruption will define the tech profession for many years to come. But what these moves do show is a tech industry that's becoming more global rather than merely international, the difference being the level of commitment—not just "presence"—that offshore-based employers must prove locally.

In the United States, despite the often painful upheaval of tech globalization, especially as jobs and competencies are scattered worldwide, services exports still exceed imports. In the category of "professional, technical, and other private services," U.S. exports (which include IT work done in the States for offshore companies) rose $2.2 billion between May 2006 and May 2007, while imports increased only $1.1 billion.

Granted, there's a dozen ways to slice and dice trade figures to make them look good or bad, depending on your world view. What's fact is that tech globalization isn't slowing down. The enormous challenge is to anticipate and adapt, or get left behind.

3.6

ASK WHAT YOUR COUNTRY CAN DO FOR YOUR CORPORATION

Kuseni Dlamini

> In the final selection of the chapter, a South African author describes the necessity of cooperation between governments and corporations for both to prosper in a globalized economy. Governments, he believes, should place the interests of corporations, most have which have national identities, at the forefront of foreign policy concerns. Corporate well-being is in the national interest and affects South Africa's domestic prosperity in a major way.

The relationship between foreign policy and business is key to the mutual success of the economy and the government. However, Yale scholar Jeffrey Garten rightly observes that "the connection between business and foreign policy is poorly thought out and mismanaged, on both sides."

The end of the Cold War settled the ideological contest between East and West or, put differently, between capitalism and communism.

However, it unleashed a new form of economic rivalry among nations. Today, no country can effectively deal with the twin challenges of globalisation and rising international competition without effectively managing the relationship between its foreign policy and business. It is imperative to have appropriate alignment between foreign policy and the commercial strategies of the country's flagship companies.

This is key to the national interest, not least because a country is as good as its companies and companies can be as good or as successful as their countries. One of the best ways of attaining domestic socioeconomic objectives such as job creation, education, health, poverty alleviation and growth is through wealth creation at home and abroad.

There is no country in the world that has managed to be self-sufficient without having to access foreign markets, raw materials, capital and services. That is why foreign policy,

Source: Kuseni Dlamini, "Ask What Your Country Can Do for Your Corporation," *Sunday Times,* May 29, 2005.

in most successful countries, has increasingly shifted away from traditional political and cultural issues to focus more on commercial and economic issues.

In the 21st century, foreign policy should, above all else, be informed by the strategic imperative of positioning South Africa in the mainstream, if not at the forefront, of the global economy.

Simply put, the business of foreign policy should be business first and other things later; and the business of business should be the national interest in its broadest terms.

National interest is increasingly defined in economic terms and issues of sovereignty and ideology are not as key as they were during the Cold War. Economic strength is more important and more respected than ideological purity or military might in our era of deepening globalisation and increasing international competition. No business is successful without a sense of national identity and pride.

All the successful global giants on Wall Street and in the City of London have very clear national identities that they assert as and when necessary. This tells us that it is possible for companies from developing country economies to be globally competitive and to assume dominant and leadership positions in their market segments.

Developing country economies such as South Korea, Malaysia, Singapore, India and Brazil have successfully nurtured the growth of global giants that have become national flagships in the global economy. The international success of local companies which have gone offshore is indicative of the potential that exists to nurture the growth of global giants with firm roots in the domestic economy.

The end of apartheid opened the doors of the global economy to local companies. Until then, isolation either bred arrogance and splendid ignorance or low self-esteem—none of which is helpful in ensuring success in the globally competitive economic landscape of our time. However, a number of local companies, such as BHP Billiton, Anglo American, SABMiller, Old Mutual, De Beers and others have successfully diversified and globalised their production and operation bases in geographic terms.

The question to ask is: to what extent has the government assisted local companies to prosper internationally? Are our diplomatic missions geared to work with and assist local companies to penetrate foreign markets and access investment opportunities abroad? How often does President Thabo Mbeki visit the operations of local companies as part of his trips abroad?

When US President George W. Bush was last in South Africa, one of the least-reported parts of his itinerary was his visit to the Ford plant outside Pretoria. He made the visit because US companies are not totally detached from US foreign policy and the national interest. They are part of it. The war in Iraq is, in its broadest terms, about US economic security, which cannot be assured without a reliable supply of energy resources such as petroleum.

It is encouraging that international visits by Mbeki increasingly include local business people as part of the delegation. This is indicative of the increasing appreciation of the link between foreign policy and business, which cannot be overemphasised. There is more that can and must be done to ensure that the connection between the two is effectively managed on both sides in pursuit of the national interest.

The challenge that lies ahead is to consolidate existing relationships, learn from past mistakes and improve the communication and clarification of foreign policy choices.

Chapter 4

POLITICAL GLOBALIZATION

Traditionally, international relations has been viewed as an anarchic realm, in which "anarchy" refers to the fact that there is no authority above that of sovereign states. All decisions in this anarchic system are those made by states individually or in agreement with one another, and all other institutions, such as international organizations (IGOs) and nongovernmental organizations (NGOs), are viewed as the instruments of states and their policymakers.

Globalization has begun to alter this rigid view of the way in which decisions are made in world affairs. While the governments of major states like the United States and China remain the leading players in global politics, decisions increasingly involve a diverse cast of actors. IGOs like the World Trade Organization, NGOs including political parties, transnational corporations like IBM, and advocacy groups like Amnesty International participate in decision making. Thus, the term *governance*, meaning decision making that involves nongovernmental actors, lacking sovereignty, was coined to describe how political life is evolving in the era of globalization. The growing participation and interconnectedness of nongovernmental actors is referred to as global civil society. "Global governance" and "global civil society," then, reflect the reality of authority at different levels and in different locations and suggest that "world order" exists on many levels, public and private, and not merely at that of sovereign states. Governance includes government actions but also encompasses other groups with the authority to participate in making decisions and formulating policies. In this sense, global governance and civil society may be viewed as reducing the degree of anarchy in global politics.

4.1

THE IDEA OF GLOBAL CIVIL SOCIETY

Mary Kaldor

The first selection of the chapter on political globalization, written by Mary Kaldor, professor of global governance at the London School of Economics, was originally a memorial lecture in honor of the political scientist

Source: Mary Kaldor, "The Idea of Global Civil Society," *International Affairs* 79:3 (May 2003), 583–93. Notes appearing in the original have been deleted.

Global Civil Society

Martin Wight. The article defines the idea of global civil society. The author begins by suggesting the degree to which globalization has altered world affairs, especially the emergence of global civil society, which is central to "global governance," that is, the expanding participation of nonstate actors in wielding authority. These changes, she continues, raise questions about the traditional primacy of states. The author proceeds to review the sources and evolution of the concept of civil society and assesses its impact on transforming international or interstate relations into global politics. She views the realm of civil society as that site where private individuals have the greatest scope for political participation and self-realization and traces its modern revival to the regime opponents in Eastern Europe and Latin America during the final decades of the Cold War. With the emergence of global civil society, she argues, global governance became possible, "a system in which states are increasingly hemmed in by a set of agreements, treaties and rules of a transnational character." Although global civil society was set back by 9/11 and the subsequent Iraq war, the author believes that these events will not reverse the trends she describes.

I would probably be put in the category 'soft revolutionist' or possibly 'cosmopolitan.' I certainly would not object to being called a Kantian. But what I want to argue here is that this tradition is much more realistic than it was three decades ago, when Martin Wight was writing, because of the profound changes that have occurred in the world in the interim—changes we lump together under the rubric of 'globalization.' Martin Wight argued that one cannot talk properly about international relations before the advent of the state. What I think is happening today is that the growing interconnectedness of states, the emergence of a system of global governance, and the explosion of the movements, groups, networks and organizations that engage in a global or transnational public debate, have called into question the primacy of states.

This does not mean the demise of states. On the contrary, I think that states will continue to be the juridical repository of sovereignty, although sovereignty will be much more conditional than before—increasingly dependent on both domestic consent and international respect. Rather, it means that the global system (and I use the term 'global system' rather than 'international relations') is increasingly composed of layers of political institutions, individuals, groups and even companies, as well as states and international institutions.

The term 'global civil society' has only really come into use in the past ten years—although Kant had referred to the possibility of a universal civil society. My aim in this article is to explore the evolution of that idea and how it challenges the concept of international relations. I will start with a thumbnail sketch of the changing meaning of civil society. I will describe the reinvention of civil society simultaneously in Latin America and Eastern Europe, and how its meaning at this juncture differed from earlier meanings. I then want to say something about how the idea has changed again in the 1990s and the competing versions of it that now exist. Finally, I will ask whether September 11 and the war in Iraq represent a defeat for the idea—a reversion to international relations.

Changing Meanings of Civil Society

Civil society is a modem concept although, like all great political ideas, it can be traced back to Aristotle. . . . For early modem thinkers, there was no distinction between civil society and the state. Civil society was a type of state characterized by a social contract. Civil society was a society governed by laws, based on the principle of equality before the law, in which everyone (including the ruler—at least in the Lockean conception) was subject to the law; in other words, a social contract agreed among the individual members of society. It was not until the nineteenth century that civil society became understood as something distinct from the state. It was Hegel who defined civil society as the intermediate realm between the family and the state, where the individual becomes a public person and, through membership in various institutions, is able to reconcile the particular and the universal. For Hegel, civil society was 'the achievement of the modern world—the territory of mediation where there is free play for every idiosyncrasy, every talent, every accident of birth and fortune and where waves of passion gust forth, regulated only by reason glinting through them'. . . .

The definition narrowed again in the twentieth century, when civil society came to be understood as the realm not just between the state and the family but occupying the space outside the market, state and family—in other words, the realm of culture, ideology and political debate. The Italian Marxist Antonio Gramsci is the thinker most associated with this definition. He was preoccupied with the question of why it was so much easier to have a communist revolution in Russia than in Italy. His answer was civil society. In Italy, he said, 'there was a proper relation between state and society and, when the state trembled, a sturdy structure of civil society was at once revealed.' . . .

Despite the changing of the content of the term, I want to suggest that all these different definitions had a common core meaning. They were about a rule-governed society based on the consent of individuals; or, if you like, a society based on a social contract among individuals. The changing definitions of civil society expressed the different ways in which consent was generated in different periods, and the different issues that were important at different times. In other words, civil society, according to my definition, is the process through which individuals negotiate, argue, struggle against or agree with each other and with the centres of political and economic authority. Through voluntary associations, movements, parties, unions, the individual is able to act publicly. Thus, in the early modern period, the main concern was civil rights—freedom from fear. Hence civil society was a society where laws replace physical coercion, arbitrary arrest, etc. In the nineteenth century, the issue was political rights, and the actors in civil society were the emerging bourgeoisie. In the twentieth century, it was the workers' movement that was challenging the state, and the issue was economic and social emancipation—hence the further narrowing of the term.

Not only did all these definitions have this common core of meaning, but also they all conceived of civil society as territorially tied. Civil society was inextricably linked up with the territorial state. It was contrasted with other states characterized by coercion—the empires of the East. It was also contrasted with premodern societies, which lacked a state and lacked the concept of individualism—Highlanders, or American Indians. And, above all, it was contrasted with international relations, which was equated with the state of nature because it lacked a single authority. Many civil society theorists believed that civil society at home was linked to war abroad. It was the ability to unite against an external enemy that made civil society possible. . . .

The Reinvention of Civil Society

The revival of the idea of civil society in the 1970s and 1980s, I believe, broke that link with the state. Interestingly, the idea was rediscovered simultaneously in Latin America and eastern Europe. I was deeply involved in the east Europeans' discussions and always thought it was they who reinvented the term. However, subsequently I discovered that it had been used earlier by the Latin Americans, notable among them Cardoso (until recently the president of Brazil). It is a fascinating task in the history of ideas to explore the way in which this concept proved useful in two different continents at the same time, but (so far as I am aware) with no communication between them—indeed, there seems on the contrary to have been widespread mutual mistrust, since by and large the Latin Americans were Marxists and the east Europeans were anti-Marxists.

In both cases, the term 'civil society' proved a useful concept in opposing militarized regimes. Latin Americans were opposing military dictatorships; east Europeans were opposing totalitarianism—a sort of war society. Both came to the conclusion that the overthrow of their regimes 'from above' was not feasible; rather, it was necessary to change society. Michnik, in his classic article first published in 1978, 'The new evolutionism,' argued that attempts to bring change from above (as in Hungary in 1956 or Czechoslovakia in 1968) had failed, and that the only possible strategy was change from below, changing the relationship between state and society. What he meant by civil society was autonomy and self-organization. Thus the emphasis (and this was shared by the Latin Americans) was on withdrawal from the state. They talked about creating islands of civic engagement—a concept shared by both east Europeans and Latin Americans. East Europeans also used terms like 'anti-politics' and 'living in truth'—the notion of refusing the lies of the regime or 'parallel polis,' of creating their own Aristotelian community based on the 'good', i.e., moral, life. (Martin Wight would have loved the east European dissidents. Forced into inactivity, especially in Czechoslovakia where they had to become stokers and window cleaners, they spent their time reading classical political thinkers and discussing them, which is why, I think, they were able to articulate the ideas of a generation. I remember a friend saying when I visited Prague in the early 1990s in the throes of revolutionary fervour: 'What I really miss are those evenings where understanding a passage from Plato's *Republic* seemed the most important thing in the world.')

As well as the emphasis on autonomy and civil organization, civil society also acquired a global meaning. This was a period of growing interconnectedness, increased travel and communication, even before the advent of the internet. The emergence of 'islands of civic engagement' was made possible by two things:

1 Links with like-minded groups in other countries. The Latin Americans were supported by North American human rights groups. The east Europeans forged links

with west European peace and human rights groups, which supported them materially and publicized their cases, and put pressure on governments and institutions.

2 The existence of international human rights legislation to which their governments subscribed and which could be used as a form of pressure. For Latin America, it was the human rights legislation that was important. For eastern Europe, the Helsinki agreement of 1975, in which east European governments signed up to human rights norms, provided a platform for new groups like Charter 77 and KOR.

In other words, through international links and appeals to international authorities, these groups were able to create political space. Keck and Sikkink, in their book on transnational activism, talk about the 'boomerang effect,' whereby instead of directly addressing your government, appeals to the international community bounce back, as it were, and put pressure on governments to tolerate certain activities.

This transnational or global aspect of the new understanding of civil society has been widely neglected by Western commentaries on the period, perhaps because they understood civil society within their own traditions of thought. Yet it was stressed by the new thinkers themselves, certainly in eastern Europe. George Konrad, the Hungarian writer, and my favourite of these thinkers, used the word 'globalization' in his book *Anti-Politics* written in 1982. Vaclav Havel talked about the 'global technological civilisation.' 'The post-totalitarian system,' wrote Havel,

> is only one aspect—a particularly drastic aspect and thus all the more revealing of its real origins—of the general inability of modern humanity to be master of its own situation. The automatism of the post-totalitarian system is merely an extreme version of the global automatism of technological civilisation. The human failure that it mirrors is only one variant of the general failure of humanity. . . . It would appear that the traditional parliamentary democracies can offer no fundamental opposition to the automatism of technological civilisation and the industrial-consumer society, for they, too, are being dragged helplessly along. People are manipulated in ways that are infinitely more subtle and refined than the brutal methods used in post-totalitarian societies. . . . In a democracy, human beings may enjoy personal freedoms and securities that are unknown to us, but in the end they do them no good, for they too are ultimately victims of the same automatism, and are incapable of defending their concerns about their own identity or preventing their superficialisation or transcending concerns about their own personal survival to become proud and responsible members of the polis, making a genuine contribution to the creation of its destiny.

Thus the new understanding of civil society represented both a withdrawal from the state and a move towards global rules and institutions. The groups who pioneered these ideas were central to the pressures for democratization in Latin America and the 1989 revolutions in eastern Europe. It is sometimes said that there were no new ideas in the 1989 revolutions—that the revolutionaries just wanted to be like the West. But I think this new understanding of civil society was the big new idea, an idea that was to contribute to a new set of global arrangements in the 1990s.

Global Civil Society in the 1990s

In the aftermath of 1989, the idea of global civil society changed its meaning and was understood in very different ways. In good Wightian tradition, let me describe three main meanings—paradigms, if you like.

1 First of all, the term was taken up all over the world by the so-called 'new social movements'—the movements that developed after 1968 concerned with new issues, like peace, women, human rights, the environment, and new forms of protest. The language of civil society seemed to express very well their brand of non-party politics. The concept was enthusiastically taken up in South Asia, Africa—especially South Africa—and western Europe. During the 1990s, a new phenomenon of great importance was the emergence of transnational networks of activists who came together on particular issues—landmines, human rights, climate change, dams, AIDS/HIV, corporate responsibility. I believe they had a significant impact on strengthening processes of global governance, especially in the humanitarian field. Notions of humanitarian norms that override sovereignty, the establishment of the International Criminal Court, the strengthening of human rights awareness—all of these factors were very important in the construction of a new set of multilateral rules: what we might call a humanitarian regime. Towards the end of the 1990s, the emergence of a so-called anti-globalization movement—concerned with global social justice—used the concept of civil society in the same way. I call this understanding the 'activist version.'

2 Second, the term was taken up by the global institutions and by Western governments. It became part of the so-called 'new policy agenda.' Civil society was understood as what the West has; it is seen as a mechanism for facilitating market reform and the introduction of parliamentary democracy. I call this the 'neoliberal version.' The key agents are not social movements but NGOs. I regard NGOs as tamed social movements. Social movements always rise and fall. And as they fall, they are either 'tamed'—institutionalized and professionalized—or they become marginal and disappear or turn to violence. Becoming 'tamed' means that you become the respectable opposition—the partner in negotiations. Historically, social movements were tamed within a national framework. Campaigners for the suffrage or against slavery in the nineteenth century became absorbed into liberal parties. Labour movements were originally universalist and internationalist but became transformed into official trade unions and Labour and Social Democratic parties. What was significant in the 1990s was that the new social movements became tamed within a global framework. There have always been international NGOs like the Anti-Slavery Society or the International Committee of the Red Cross, but their numbers increased dramatically in the 1990s, often as a result of official funding. Indeed, NGOs increasingly look both like quasi-governmental institutions, because of the way they substitute for state functions, and at the same time like a market, because of the way they compete with one another. The dominance of NGOs

has led some activists to become disillusioned with the concept of civil society. Thus Neera Chandhoke, a civil society theorist from Delhi University, says civil society has become a 'hurrah word' and 'flattened out.' 'Witness the tragedy that has visited proponents of the concept: people struggling against authoritarian regimes demanded civil society, what they got were NGOs. If everyone from trade unions, social movements, the UN, the IMF, lending agencies, to states both chauvinistic and democratic hail civil society as the most recent elixir to the ills of the contemporary world, there must be something gone wrong.' And Mahmoud Mamdami, a brilliant African political scientist, says 'NGOs are killing civil society.'

3 Yet a third concept of global civil society is what I call the 'postmodern version.' Social anthropologists criticize the concept of society as Euro-centric, something born of the Western cultural context (according to this argument, Latin America and eastern Europe are both culturally part of Europe). They suggest that non-Western societies experience or have the potential to experience something similar to civil society, but not based on individualism. They argue, for example, that in Islamic societies, institutions like religious orders, the bazaar or religious foundations represent a check on state power.

Thus for postmodernists, new religions and ethnic movements that have also grown dramatically over the last decade are also part of global civil society. Global civil society cannot be just the 'nice, good movements.'

Civil society has always had both a normative and a descriptive content. The definition that I gave at the beginning of this article was a normative definition. I said that civil society is the process through which consent is generated, the arena where the individual negotiates, struggles against, or debates with the centres of political and economic authority. Today, those centres include global institutions, both international bodies and companies. I think that all three versions have to be included in the concept. The neoliberal version makes the term respectable, providing a platform via which more radical groups can gain access to power (both 'insiders' like NGOs and 'outsiders' like social movements). In normative terms, it might be argued that service-providing NGOs, especially those funded by states, should be excluded because they are not engaged in public debate and are not autonomous from the state. Likewise, it could also be argued that communalist groups should be excluded because central to the concept of civil society is individual emancipation; if communalist groups are compulsory, then they cannot be viewed as vehicles for individual emancipation. But in practice, in actually existing civil society, it is almost impossible to draw boundaries between who is included and who is excluded.

What has happened in the 1990s, I would argue, is that a system of global governance has emerged which involves both states and international institutions. It is not a single world state, but a system in which states are increasingly hemmed in by a set of agreements, treaties and rules of a transnational character. Increasingly, these rules are based not just on agreement between states but on public support, generated through global civil society. Of particular importance, in my view, is a growing body of cosmopolitan law, by which I mean the combination of humanitarian law (laws of war) and human rights law, brilliantly analysed by Geoffrey Best in his Martin Wight lecture delivered at the London School of Economics on 9 March 1995. Cosmopolitan law is international law that applies not just to states but to individuals—something Martin Wight thought was impossibly utopian. This broadening and strengthening of cosmopolitan law, both immediately after the Second World War and in the 1990s, was largely a consequence of pressure from global civil society.

In other words, global civil society is a platform inhabited by activists (or post-Marxists), NGOs and neoliberals, as well as national and religious groups, where they argue about, campaign for (or against), negotiate about, or lobby for the arrangements that shape global developments. There is not one global civil society but many, affecting a range of issues—human rights, environment and so on. It is not democratic; there are no processes of election, nor could there be at a global level, since that would require a world state. And such a state, even if democratically elected, would be totalitarian. It is also uneven and Northern-dominated. Nevertheless, the emergence of this phenomenon does offer a potential for individuals—a potential for emancipation. It opens up closed societies, as happened in eastern Europe and Latin America, and it offers the possibility to participate in debates about global issues. And it is my view that the emergence of this phenomenon—this new global system—makes the term 'international relations' much less appropriate.

After September 11

How have these trends, this activity, been affected by September 11 and the war on Iraq? Do terror and war on terror mark a reversal of the developments I describe? Both terror and war on terror are profoundly inimical to global civil society. Terror can be regarded as a direct attack on global civil society, a way of creating fear and insecurity that are the opposite of civil society. President Bush's response, I would argue, has been an attempt to re-impose international relations; that is to say, to put the threat of terrorism within a state framework. The United States is the only country not hemmed in by globalization, the only state able to continue to act as an autonomous nation-state: a 'global unilateralist,' as Javier Solana puts it, or the last nation-state. Bush declared the destruction of the World Trade Center towers as an attack on the United States, using the analogy of Pearl Harbor, and he identified the enemies as states that sponsor terrorism or possess weapons of mass destruction-whether Afghanistan or Iraq or the 'axis of evil.' The term 'war' implies a traditional state conflagration. The language of war and war on terrorism closes down debate and narrows the space for different political positions. And the American determination to go to war with Iraq unilaterally has caused a profound crisis in the institutions of global governance.

But I do not think Bush can reverse the process of globalization. The consequences of trying to do so will be a still more uneven, anarchic, wild globalization. If you like, it will be a situation in which the 'outside' of international relations, at least in a realist conception, comes 'inside'; in which we can no longer insulate civil society from what goes on outside. The distinction between war and domestic peace made by the classical theorists of civil society no longer holds. Global civil society offers the promise of bringing the 'inside' outside. The war on terror offers the opposite. The polarizing effect of war is likely to increase rather than reduce terrorist attacks. It is the nature of war to discriminate among groups of human beings; however much the coalition forces insist on saving civilian lives, in practice their own lives are privileged over the lives of Iraqis, both military and civilian. The war has already generated tremendous anger and resentment, especially in the Middle East. Moreover, the extreme ideologies are likely to be reproduced for the foreseeable future. Moreover, the difficulty of stabilizing the region in the aftermath means that the kinds of conditions that nurture terrorism—repression, sporadic violence, inequality, extreme ideologies—are likely to be reproduced for the foreseeable future.

Is there an alternative? Could we imagine domestic politics on the global scene—something else Wight thought impossibly utopian? What I have been trying to say here is that this is exactly what has been happening over the last decade. Moreover, global civil society, especially the activist strand, has not gone away. The anti-globalization movement is very active, especially in Latin America. There are new synergies between the anti-globalization movement, the peace movement and Muslim communities, which have burst forth in a global anti-war movement, historically unprecedented in size and geographical spread. Many states, notably Germany and France, have followed public opinion and not the United States. On the one hand, this is the reason for the crisis in multilateral institutions. On the other hand, a new responsiveness to global civil society offers the possibility of a system of global institutions which act on the basis of deliberation, rather than, as in the past, on the basis of consent for American hegemony.

What happens depends on politics, on the agency of people who make history. The idea of global civil society is an emancipatory idea, which allows every individual the potential to engage in this debate. I do think we are living through a very dangerous moment: the war in the Middle East could spread, there could be a new war in South Asia, including the possible use of weapons of mass destruction, and we are likely to witness an increase in global terrorism. To what extent can global civil society convince states to adopt an alternative multilateralist framework for dealing with dictators, terrorism and weapons of mass destruction, not to mention poverty, AIDS/HIV, the environment and other desperately important issues? Many commentators pointed out that the attacks of September 11 should have been dealt with in the framework of international law. They should have been treated as a crime against humanity; a war crimes tribunal should have been established by the Security Council; and efforts to catch and destroy terrorists, even if they involve the use of military means, should be considered not war but law enforcement. And the same argument can be made about the situation in Iraq. There were ways of dealing with Iraq, which might have been gleaned from the experience of eastern Europe in the 1980s; United Nations Security Council resolutions, especially 687, emphasized human rights and democracy as well as weapons of mass destruction and could have been used in the same way as the Helsinki Agreement to put pressure on the regime; weapons inspectors could have been accompanied by human rights monitors; and the international community could have made it clear that it would protect Iraqis from Saddam Hussein's forces in the event of an uprising, as it did in northern Iraq in 1991 and failed to do in the case of the Shiite uprising.

I do not see any other way out of the current dangerous impasse than trying to establish a set of global rules based on consent. We have to find ways to minimize violence at a global level, in the same way that early modem thinkers envisaged civil society as a way of minimizing violence at domestic levels. And this means opening up the conversation about what might be done. . . .

4.2

RESOLVING KEY GLOBAL TENSIONS

from *Chinadaily.com.cn*

> The next selection reveals Asia's interest in increasing the extent of global governance to ease the global tensions that have accompanied globalization. These tensions are between (a) the desire for sovereignty and the imperatives of globalization that transcend national boundaries, (b) the wealthy Western states and the rapidly rising emerging powers in Asia and elsewhere that are underrepresented in major international institutions, and (3) the requirements of the great powers and the interests of a majority of the world's population.

The need to reform global governance has never been greater. Paradoxically, at a time when the world urgently needs new thinking in global governance, old thinking dominates. *The Economist's* cover story on global governance in July 2008 brilliantly used the image of the Tower of Babel to capture the contradictions and confusion surrounding the global governance debate. Sadly, the essay itself was full of conventional wisdom to the effect that we only need to reform existing global governance institutions.

Tinkering will not work. The world has changed fundamentally since 1945 and will change even more radically in the coming decades. We need new thinking, not new tinkering. To arrive at the new thinking, we need to focus on three tensions that have arisen in global governance.

The first tension is between the desire to cling to sovereignty and the need to respond to globalization. Globalization has changed the world fundamentally. Most new challenges respect no borders. Neither terrorism nor epidemics, financial crises or environmental challenges respect borders. None can be solved by any country working alone. At a time when the global village needs to convene global village councils to address these

---

Source: "Resolving Key Global Tensions," *Chinadaily.com.cn,* November 12, 2008.

issues, these very institutions are being weakened. Sadly, the most powerful country in the world, the United States, is allergic to global governance. Strobe Talbott explains this allergy well: "It is not surprising that talk of global governance should elicit more skepticism, suspicion and sometimes bilious opposition in the United States than elsewhere. The more powerful a state is, the more likely its people are to regard the pooling of national authority as an unnatural act." Paradoxically, the US has the most to gain from good global governance because the richest home in any village has the most to lose from global disorder and instability. Good global governance also puts less pressure on the world's sole sheriff to intervene unilaterally.

The second tension in global governance is between the old and new rising powers. We are coming to the end of two centuries of Western domination of world history. All the new emerging powers are non-Western. Yet, the West continues to be over-represented in existing global institutions. In an effort to avoid the fate of the League of Nations, the UN's founding fathers wisely created the veto to anchor the great powers in the UN. Sadly, they did not anticipate that the great powers of the day could become the great powers of yesterday. Similarly, the G8 represents the great powers of yesterday. It maintains a charade of addressing global challenges. This charade is sustained by the Western media, which legitimizes the G8 as a global village council, even though it only represents 13.5 percent of the world population.

Persuading great powers to give up privileged positions will not be easy, unless a new social contract can be created that also serves their own long-term national interests in global order. The rich Western powers stand to lose the most from global disorder. Hence, it should be in their interest to support a new principle that all new powers and old powers who want to occupy privileged positions in global organizations like the UN Security Council (UNSC) or G8, International Monetary Fund or Bank for International Settlements should take on responsibilities commensurate with their privileges. Hence, if a financial crisis arises in Asia, if an epidemic emerges in Africa or if global warming worsens, the great powers must assume the responsibility to address these challenges. Today, many countries are vying for privileged positions in global organizations because these privileges come with no responsibilities. However, if veto power in, say, the UNSC is combined with significant financial and military responsibilities, the new claimants will pause. Equally important, the rest of the world, which would otherwise see no reason to confer privileges to a few great powers, will also find it in everyone's interest to see that all great powers assume greater responsibilities to bring about a stable global order.

This approach will also help to resolve the third tension between great power imperatives and the need to reflect the views and interests of the majority of the world's population in global governance. Great powers can no longer dominate global politics as they did in the 19th and 20th centuries. The majority of the world's population has gone from being an object of world history to becoming the subject. People want to take greater control of their destinies and not have their views or interests ignored. The views and interests of those who are currently in the margin of the global system must also be heeded. Hence, any reform of global governance should pay attention to both institutions that respond to great power interests (like the UNSC and G8) and institutions that respond to the universal interests of humanity (the UN General Assembly and comprehensive conferences such as the Copenhagen Conference).

It will not be easy to resolve these three tensions. However, if we are unable to do so, both rich and poor countries will become losers, and our global village might be destroyed. Therefore, there is an urgent and pressing need to convince key policy-makers and elites that we need to discard old thinking on global governance and prepare new perspectives. Every villager understands the wisdom of this phrase: "To protect our home, we must protect the village." Hence, we should say, "To protect our country, we must protect the planet."

4.3

INTERNET: GLOBALISING GOVERNANCE

from *The Guardian*

> The following article, published in a leading British newspaper, argues that the Internet, which has remained largely free of government interference, needs improved governance. At present, a nongovernmental American group, Icann, which reports to the U.S. Department of Commerce, manages domain names and root servers. The article argues that this link should be gradually loosened and the Internet should be managed by a nongovernmental organization representing users globally.

The question "Who should run the internet" ought to be a no-brainer. It is, despite its US provenance, a global phenomenon and its governance should reflect that. Nothing previously devised has put people and communities around the world in touch with each other to such an extent. This week's purchase by Google of YouTube, which claims 100m downloads of its videos each day, will expedite that process. The internet has, happily, been almost free of governmental interference. Indeed the burgeoning army of bloggers, video creators and web communities has proved a brake on some of the more nefarious activities of governments. But at its heart the internet needs strong rule over the issuing of domain names such as .co.uk and .com and control of the root servers critical to the net's infrastructure with its tens of millions of pathways and intersections. The body that does this, the International Corporation for Assigned Names and Numbers (Icann) is an "independent" not-for-profit organisation based in California that reports to the US department of commerce.

Source: "Internet: Globalising Governance," *The Guardian*, October 11, 2006.

Clearly this ought to be changed and the recent loosening of the reins by the commerce department is a step in the right direction. The concessions—such as replacing a duty to report to the department every six months with an annual report to the internet community—may not seem much but they are significant, not least because they have been conceded by an administration not famous for handing power to international organisations.

There is a strong case for gradualism because even critics admit that despite past problems, Icann has not made a bad fist of a highly sensitive job. And, even more importantly, it is vital that the organisation is future-proofed before becoming fully independent. The easy bit should be rectifying the past pattern of insufficient transparency. More difficult will be ensuring that Icann fully reflects its global role without becoming too bureaucratic; the need to safeguard itself against hijack by political or corporate special interests is another big challenge.

It is easy to say that the body should report to the whole net community but making that a reality is likely to be a formidable task. It would be nice, but idealistic, to think the UN could ensure this happens, as some countries are urging. Icann now has an opportunity. If it can devise a non-governmental institution for international governance it might create a model that could be applied elsewhere, to tackle other problems posed by globalisation.

4.4

THE CHALLENGES OF GLOBAL GOVERNANCE

Alia McMullen

The next selection deals with the role of international economic institutions in providing governance for the international economic system. The article recounts an interview with Kenneth Rogoff, a leading American economist, which appeared in a Canadian newspaper. In the interview, the economist argues that national authorities should cede a greater role to international institutions in managing the global economy, especially the global financial system, and that this would contribute to global governance. However, the International Monetary Fund (IMF) is, in his view, not the right institution to govern the financial system because, like the World Trade Organization (WTO), it is too willing to assist countries that do not merit such assistance.

Source: Alia McMullen, "The Challenges of Global Governance; IMF Isn't the Right Body to Become Regulator," *National Post,* October 13, 2009.

International Institutions and
Economic Governance

National governments need to make way for international authorities to play a greater role in governance, particularly when it comes to finance and trade, says Kenneth Rogoff, a Harvard University professor and former chief economist at the International Monetary Fund.

"We probably need to strike a different balance between roles for national authorities, with international authorities taking more of a role," Prof. Rogoff said in an interview with the Financial Post at a recent governance conference held at the Centre for International Governance Innovation in Kitchener-Waterloo, Ont.

He said the financial sector was a prime example where global governance was needed, with the inadequacies of the present system highlighted by the financial crisis.

"I agree that we should have a global financial regulator," he said. "My main reason is that I think a financial regulator needs to be insulated from political pressures and it is very hard to do that with a domestic financial regulator."

He said the financial crisis was a watershed for the Groups of 20 nations, with developed countries recognizing the need for developing and emerging-market economies to have a seat at the table in international talks. At the same time, he said he was concerned that the multitude of interests in the G20 would result in more talk than action.

The IMF, a global financial authority, has also increased in importance as a result of the crisis, with a number of countries approaching the body for financial aid. But Prof. Rogoff said the IMF was not the right institution to become a global financial regulator.

"I think it's great that it's been given much more of a role in supervision and regulation and it's really had a rebirth from the crisis, but at the same time, I'm against having a super-sized IMF," he said.

He said a larger IMF would raise huge questions of moral hazard—that is, creating a governance system where the players in it did not fear failure and took imprudent risks.

"People think the IMF is tough. The truth is it finds it almost impossible to say no," he said. "The IMF is lending in places like the Ukraine and Eastern Europe and over time it's just going to let them dig a deeper hole before they have their financial crisis."

Other institutions, such as the World Trade Organization, have also been faced with challenges as globalization brings countries closer together. Prof. Rogoff said the WTO had run into a brick wall regarding such countries as China, India and Brazil.

"For all their complaining about the WTO, they are the world's biggest beneficiaries of it," he said of the three countries. "They're allowed to export goods with virtually no restrictions and they are still allowed to place heavy import quotas."

He said import barriers in China were extremely unfair and the WTO needed to provide more leadership to encourage developing and emerging-market countries such as China to open their markets because of their growing role in world trade.

"The big problem with the WTO is that the fast-growing countries that are taking over an ever-larger share of world trade are operating as if they're small African countries," Prof. Rogoff said.

He said the WTO was one of many international organizations in a transition of rebalancing power.

4.5

MONTREAL JOINS MICROFINANCE NETWORK TO COMBAT GLOBAL POVERTY

Peter Hadekel

> Nongovernmental organizations (NGOs) play a key role in global governance and constitute the core of an emerging global civil society. The following article describes the NGO PlaNet Finance, which provides small loans ("microfinance") to individuals, especially women, to start or maintain small business enterprises, thereby reducing global poverty. Such NGOs and the loans they provide constitute an increasingly important avenue for impoverished individuals to escape their poverty.

Microfinance is one of the most popular ways currently being used to fight global inequality and poverty.

The idea involves making small loans to entrepreneurs or merchants in the developing world who want to start a business but who do not have access to capital.

Now, one of the world's leading microfinance organizations, PlaNet Finance, is opening an office in Montreal, its president Jacques Attali said in an interview.

Attali, who was in town recently to deliver a talk on globalization, is a French economist, author and public intellectual who founded the European Bank for Reconstruction and Development. It funneled loans into eastern Europe following the collapse of the Iron Curtain.

He set up PlaNet Finance in Paris 10 years ago as a non-profit organization to aid microfinance efforts around the world. The organization employs 700 people full time.

"We have offices in all the G8 countries except Canada," Attali said. The Montreal office will work with Canadian authorities, engage in fundraising and coordinate Canadian technical assistance to microfinance projects around the globe.

Source: Peter Hadekel, "Montreal Joins Microfinance Network to Combat Global Poverty," *Montreal Gazette*, October 21, 2009.

Nongovernmental Organizations

"We are present in 80 countries" with credit, insurance and consulting services, he said. "We want to use the expertise that's available in Canada."

The former senior adviser to French President François Mitterrand sees PlaNet Finance as a key player in efforts to make economic globalization more equitable.

"I am convinced that microfinance is the most effective way to fight poverty," Attali said.

He hopes to make it easier for individual Canadians who want to invest in microfinance projects to do so.

Typically, such investments involve a loan of a few hundred dollars, often made to women starting a home-based business. Repayment rates have been excellent, which has helped fuel success of the initiative.

The concept was developed by Bangladeshi economist Mohammad Yunus, winner of the 2006 Nobel Peace Prize. Yunus founded the Grameen Bank and Grameen Foundation, which have built a network of financial institutions making loans in two dozen countries.

The global spread of microfinance has been rapid. About 10,000 institutions offer such loans to more than 150 million people. Several are active raising money from Canadians.

One of PlaNet Finance's initiatives, Attali said, is setting up a ratings agency, known as Planet Rating, to provide more information on the credit quality of microfinance institutions active in the field.

Its role in reducing global poverty is a subject of some debate among economists. But at the very least microfinance has helped reduce the dependence of the poor on money lenders charging high interest rates and has allowed entrepreneurs without collateral to build private property and assets.

Attali said the rapid and sweeping globalization of markets urgently requires a system of global governance and regulation, otherwise the protection of consumers and investors will be compromised.

"The fundamental cause of the global financial crisis was the absence of global rule of law. Global markets cannot function properly without it."

Excessive risks were taken without proper scrutiny by authorities and those risks spread across the world because of securitization, he noted.

"The message to banks from governments has been: don't worry about your losses, they are ours. But profits are yours." That kind of policy simply encourages banks to take on too much risk.

While some are skeptical about systems of global governance, Attali said precedents already exist, including the World Trade Organization, which adjudicates disputes among trading nations. Another example is international co-operation on air-traffic control.

The global community has shown it can act together when required. He cited the example of piracy off the shores of Somalia, which resulted in a "police force" of international warships to protect maritime traffic.

Action on financial regulation is just as urgently required, he argued, because technology is rapidly creating a single global market. "We are on a bus moving really fast. And we're realizing there's no driver and no steering wheel."

4.6

BRICS PROVIDING FUTURE GROWTH

Simona Stankovska

The following selection describes the growing role of the "emerging economies" in the global economy. These countries, especially the "Brics" (Brazil, Russia, India, and China), with the later addition of South Africa, are also becoming key players in economic governance. They are, for example, the core countries in what is called the G-20 (Group of 20) emerging economies, a group that is replacing the older G-7 (Group of 7), which consisted of wealthy Western countries plus Japan and until recent years provided global economic leadership. Finally, they are advocates of "state capitalism," a form of capitalism in which the state plays a much larger role than in the neoliberal capitalist model of the West. Thus, the Brics have simultaneously become engines of global economic growth and governance.

Turbulent global markets have made it difficult to make money in the past year, with investors left with few places to shelter from the storm.

As western economic growth stagnates, it is the east, and emerging markets in particular, that are going to provide growth in future.

Goldman Sachs predicted that this would be the case eight years ago, when in 2001, economist Jim O'Neill created the acronym Bric for the four nations of Brazil, Russia, India and China. He predicted these economies would become the world's largest by 2050, as a result of their growing population and wealth.

According to Nick Smith, managing director of Allianz Global Investors Europe, a lot of industry professionals and economists scoffed at Mr. O'Neill's concept at the time, thinking it was an extraordinary prediction.

"It didn't seem obvious at that point that those four countries would embark on such sustainable growth paths, but as the past 10 years have proved, it looks like it's coming true," said Mr Smith. "In fact, the latest data suggests those four economies could become larger even quicker than Goldman Sachs initially thought. You could see countries like China, which is the world's second largest economy, catching up with the US and overtaking it faster than 2050."

Will Landers, portfolio manager of the BlackRock Latin American Investment Trust adds: "Brazil's inclusion in Bric at the time was puzzling to many market players, given its history of failed economic plans, hyperinflation, and its inability to grow at a consistent and sustainable pace.

Source: Simona Stankovska, "Brics Providing Future Growth," *Financial Times,* October 6, 2011.

"The past decade has proved that Brazil's potential justified its inclusion, as the country has managed to control its inflation demon, seen a significant expansion of its domestic economy, benefited from the commodities boom in both hard as well as soft commodities, and solidified its democratic institutions to guarantee economic stability and consistency."

Data shows the Brics have lower debt-to-GDP ratios than the developed world, as well as solid growth and earnings potential.

According to Allianz Global Investors, the average earnings per share (EPS) for the four Bric countries in 2011 is 20.4 per cent, compared with an average price-to-earnings ratio (p/e) of 9.1, meaning that valuations are low and earnings are strong.

Mr Smith says: "The valuations in the short term are incredibly compelling. The Bric markets are trading at levels we haven't seen since the Lehman crash, especially Brazil and China. If you're looking for an entry point, this certainly has to be a great one. Especially as inflation is trending down—if interest rates fall it will stimulate equity markets."

In spite of their fundamentals, however, Bric markets sold off indiscriminately in the past year, with global investors battening down the hatches in unpredictable market conditions.

"Brics are the largest and most liquid of emerging markets, so when markets are under stress or there's questions about global growth, as there has been in recent months, global investors tend to pull out of them before they pull out of other smaller emerging markets. Also there were inflationary concerns in some of the Bric markets over the past year," explains Mr Smith.

Bric funds made an average loss of 10.7 per cent in the year to September 16 2011, according to Morningstar, with the worst performing fund—Allianz RCM Bric Equity— losing 12.94 per cent.

"Most equity funds have made a loss year-to-date, as equity markets in general are down," argues Ross Mcfarlane, portfolio manager for global equities at Ignis Asset Management.

Year-to-date (September 22) equities are down, with the FTSE All-Share and FTSE 100 recording losses of 7.82 per cent and 8.02 per cent respectively. The FTSE All-World Bric index and the MSCI Bric suffered even more, recording a loss of 19.52 per cent and 20 per cent respectively.

"Brics in particular became too overpriced, but there has slowly been a correction. As the prices become more attractive you'll see people coming back in to buy them," adds Mr Mcfarlane.

"They have underperformed but the world economy is under stress at the moment and one shouldn't lose sight of the big picture, which is this amazing transformation that's happened with these four countries over time," states Mr Smith.

According to Allianz, in the past 10 years, Brics have been the winning asset class, outperforming both other emerging markets and the developed world with returns of 350 per cent compared with 165 per cent and 10 per cent respectively.

In the five years to September 16 the average return for Bric funds was 54.64 per cent, according to Morningstar, showing that Brics are a long-term trend rather than a short-term phenomenon.

"There's this major transformation going on. A majority of these people are becoming affluent and that really is unleashing a range of investment themes, whether it's commodities, agriculture, energy demand, infrastructure or domestic demand," says Mr Smith.

"What's interesting is, because they are large, companies can establish themselves and grow significantly domestically, as there is a large population to serve."

According to Mr Mcfarlane, Ignis has started to add to its positions in Brics after being underweight in the first half of 2011.

"We've moved to neutral weighting in Brazil, we are slightly underweight China, having been quite heavily underweight before, and we've started to put some money into India as valuations get more reasonable," adds Mr Mcfarlane.

In July, Ignis' James Smith told Investment Adviser that Russia was the only Bric market the company found attractive, claiming it was a "screaming buy" based on a p/e of around 7–8x earnings.

"There's greater volatility and more risk in Bric markets. However, where are returns going to come from if you don't look to the emerging markets, Brics in particular?" questions Mr Smith.

"By holding cash you're losing money—the developed markets are suffering from low or no growth and it's unlikely the equity markets are going to deliver great returns. Even a cautious investor should look at the bigger picture and how they can diversify their portfolio, as emerging markets will be driving the growth going forward.

"The world that we now know will be very different in 10–15 years' time," he concludes.

4.7

DEATH BY ECO DIALOGUE

Peter Foster

Among the most influential of transnational nongovernmental organizations involved in global civil society are those that lobby against environmental degradation and for international cooperation to solve environmental threats like global warming. One of the best known of these groups is Greenpeace, which regularly takes highly visible and controversial actions against those it believes are responsible for harming the environment. The next selection describes how Greenpeace was denounced by a prominent British politician for acting against globalization and how the organization's leadership denied this allegation. The article's author agrees with the charge leveled against Greenpeace and relates how the group's opposition to exploiting Canada's oil sands threatens economic growth.

Source: Peter Foster, "Death by Eco Dialogue," *National Post,* May 15, 2009.

Environmental Governance:
Greenpeace

Just as Greenpeace was gearing up to take its anti-oils and rottweiler-and-pony show to next week's annual meeting of Norwegian oil giant Statoil-Hydro, the radical environmental group got a nip in the rump from an unlikely source. British peer Lord May, former chief science adviser to the U.K. government and himself no slouch as an environmental alarmist, declared that Greenpeace and the whole environmental movement had been hijacked by a political agenda, and now operated like "multinational corporations."

Has ground control at last got through to Major Tom? Has Lord May finally cottoned on to the fact that environmentalism is both into twisting arms and making money?

Speaking at a U.K. parliamentary event, Lord May also fingered Greenpeace for having "transmogrified" into primarily a force for anti-globalization. "Maybe they are right," he said, "but I wish they would wear the uniform of the army they are fighting [with]." Battle analogies are appropriate. Still, I guess they'd pull in much less cash if they were called "Redwar."

Lord May is an old Greenpeace-nik himself, so his criticism stung. In response, Greenpeace U.K.'s chairman John Sauven, ignoring the multi-national corporation bit, said "I don't know who he is talking about. As far as I know, no mainstream environmental organization has been anti-globalization per se."

But surely anti-globalization is part of Greenpeace's very raison d'etre: that trade and industry—per se—lead to environmental destruction. And although it wasn't prominent at the Seattle riots that saw the birth of the anti-globalization movement in 1999, it soon got with the program. Greenpeace's diplomatic gunboat, the Rainbow Warrior, has been regularly sighted on the waters around G8 and WTO meetings, and its trademark assault dinghies have more than once attempted to breech the security perimeters of such events. A couple of years ago, authorities forced down a Greenpeace hot air balloon trying to penetrate the airspace above a G8 meeting in Germany.

But they're not anti-globalizers "per se."

Another British peer, Lord Krebs, former chairman of the U.K.'s Food Standards Agency, took up the theme that Greenpeace was "a multinational corporation just like Monsanto or Tesco. They have very effective marketing departments. . . . Their product is worry because worry is what recruits members."

The political perversion of Greenpeace has been chronicled by one of its founders, Patrick Moore, who has outlined how an organization rooted in pacifism and science-based environmental concerns was gradually taken over by environmental entrepreneurs and grandstanding eco-warriors. Greenpeace pressures corporations—and governments—to make decisions that make no sense from a consumer-protection point of view.

In response to his poor "peer review," Greenpeace's Mr. Sauven declared that Greenpeace was tiny compared with Monsanto or Tesco. Certainly, Greenpeace's reported income is "only" around US $300 million, but it is a world-scale anti-marketer.

Mr. Sauven claimed that Greenpeace only campaigned against "unsustainable trade, such as transporting bottled water between continents." But Greenpeace obviously feels that it has the right to stand in judgment on all aspects of trade and industry, from what sort of paper is used in toilet rolls to how and where oil is produced: wherever there's a consumer to alarm, or a corporation to shake down for the public good.

Greenpeace's latest move is to pressure Statoil to abandon the oil sands, into which it bought its way two years ago. As reported yesterday by the Post's Claudia Cattaneo, Greenpeace plans to use Statoil's annual meeting to publicize its opposition to "dirty" oil. Like most such initiatives, this one has no chance of success. After all, the Norwegian government owns two-thirds of Statoil's shares and has made clear that it has no plans to overrule the judgment of the company's board.

The head of Statoil's Canadian operations, Bob Skinner, told the Post that the company was "absolutely not" considering Greenpeace's demands, and that "the oil sands constitute a significant base for our long-term growth."

The oil sands may appear to have much bigger problems than opposition from green groups at the moment. First and foremost, there is the collapse in oil prices. But there is also the uncertainty surrounding global warming legislation, which has a great deal to do with the astonishing clout of green activists.

Greenpeace has had some success in turning at least one Norwegian pension fund, KPA, off the oil sands. KPA's "environmental manager" declared boldly but vaguely this week that "We feel that if Statoil cannot protect the environment, it should withdraw from Alberta—this goes with our criteria for environmental investments." Another Statoil investor that has felt the hot breath of Greenpeace, Danske Bank, waffled meekly that it was "checking whether the oil sands engagement breached its responsible investment rules." Its head of "socially responsible investments" burbled that "if it should violate international norms, we will seek dialogue with the company."

Death of a thousand green dialogues. And if dialogue doesn't work, there's always a rubber dinghy at the ready, or a banner to be unfurled or a campaign of disinformation to be launched.

4.8

JAMAICA'S ASSERTIVE GANGS SYMPTOM OF DEEPER CRISIS

Jorge Heine

> Criminals have also profited from globalization and are involved in global governance. Transnational criminal groups, especially those involved in drug trafficking, enjoy enormous political influence in a number of countries. The final article in the chapter describes how the country of Jamaica and its political leaders have ceded political power to the country's drug gangs. It also explains why the Caribbean region has become vulnerable to the influence of criminal groups.

Source: Jorge Heine, "Jamaica's Assertive Gangs Symptom of Deeper Crisis; Effects of Globalization Have Left Caribbean Region Vulnerable to Organized Crime," *The Toronto Star,* May 28, 2010.

Governance by Criminal Syndicates

Urban warfare in downtown Kingston has led some to refer to Jamaica as the next narco-state (we already have one, Guinea-Bissau). Christopher ("Dudus") Coke, the don whose requested extradition by the United States has triggered this furore, is being compared to Pablo Escobar, the Colombian drug cartel boss. The unofficial figure of 60 dead in four days (including two policemen and one soldier), and the pictures of pitched gun-battles in the barricaded streets of Tivoli Gardens between the Jamaican Defence Force and reputed members of the Posse led by Coke are not reassuring.

Jamaican Prime Minister Bruce Golding's refusal for nine months to extradite Coke to the United States, where he is wanted for drug trafficking and gun running, is at the root of this crisis. Sixteen months into the Obama administration, there is no U.S. ambassador to Jamaica. Golding's hiring of a California law firm to lobby the U.S. government to lay off raised a ruckus in parliament and forced his hand. He then announced the extradition order would be signed after all. This in itself raises many questions—extraditions should be executed rather than "announced."

Yet, Golding, whom I have met, does not fit the picture of the corrupt politician he is portrayed to be. With a business background and a low-key, self-effacing style, he served honourably as construction minister in the government of Edward Seaga in the eighties. Although the leader of the right-wing Labour party (JLP), he is independent-minded enough to have refused (twice) invitations to visit the White House in the dying months of the George W. Bush administration and to have advocated publicly the lifting of the U.S. embargo on Cuba. His predicament is a function of the clientelistic nature of Jamaican politics, and of the link between street gangs, organized crime and political parties in a country with one of the highest murder rates—60 per 100,000—in the hemisphere, slightly below Colombia's.

It is no coincidence that Seaga, like Golding, also was an MP for West Kingston, where Tivoli Gardens is located. He had such a close relationship with Coke's father, Lester Coke, also a crime boss, that he attended his funeral upon the latter's death in a prison cell in 1992. The notion that the current PM should represent the same gang-infested area as his party's predecessor and that he has to deal with the son, who inherited his lordship over it, reflects how the JLP machine operates. Under the circumstances, what is remarkable is that Golding has gone so far as to give the go-ahead to the extradition order.

The problem goes deeper than Golding's attitude toward one don. The control exercised by the latter over West Kingston—where he is reputed to have even built medical centres—reflects the deep crisis of the Jamaican state, and that of the Caribbean more generally.

The lands of the Caribbean archipelago are in crisis, perhaps their worst ever, a condition that stands in stark contrast to thriving South America. The Caribbean economies have been unable to find a niche in a globalized world economy. Jamaica's debt-to-GDP ratio is 130 per cent, one of the highest, and its unemployment rate is 14.5 per cent. Even Puerto Rico, once the most prosperous of all islands, is bankrupt.

Since its inception, the Caribbean has been the most globalized region in the developing world—in terms of the powers that made it, the populations that formed it and its integration into the world economy as "King Sugar" financed several European empires.

After independence, the islands latched onto special access and privileges in the markets of the old and new colonial powers.

Yet with globalization and liberalization, these privileges evaporated (the banana regime with the EU comes to mind; tax havens may be next), and Caribbean nations have been left holding the bag. Even tourism, hailed as the region's last best hope, is succumbing to global trends. As the airfare share of a travel package gets lower, a Thai vacation can be cheaper than a Jamaican one.

Globalization embraces some and tosses out others. The Caribbean is being tossed out. The dark side of globalization then takes over. Organized crime, drug trafficking and gun running step into the vacuum. Jamaican gangs ("posses"), spread throughout North America, are among the fiercest, most effective and most difficult to infiltrate by the police. Variously defined as the United States' "third border" or its "front yard," the Caribbean is becoming something else entirely—a convenient drug hub to North America, its last remaining comparative advantage.

The English-speaking Caribbean is one area of the developing world with which Canada has strong bonds. Some 200,000 West Indians live in Canada, many of them in Toronto. Urban warfare in Kingston is not an odd anomaly. It may well be a harbinger of things to come as the crisis unfolds throughout the archipelago.

Chapter 5

SECURITY GLOBALIZATION

The two world wars and the Cold War, all of which involved the world's major regions, globalized security issues for the first time. Indeed, historically warfare has been a principal source of globalization as armies were dispatched far from home and soldiers and warriors interacted with those politically and culturally different. To date, however, there has been relatively little written that links globalization and security. Instead, the study of globalization has tended to emphasize its economic and cultural dimensions. In the chapter's first selection, Victor Cha, former Director for Asian Affairs on the National Security Council, examines how the processes of globalization have altered how we think about security. Cha contends that nonphysical security, a diversity of threats ranging from disease and crime to illegal arms sales and human rights abuses, and the growing importance of collective identities are among the major consequences of globalization with implications for security. Among the most important of these are proliferation of weapons of mass destruction to rogue states and, potentially, to terrorists; transnational and intrastate military and nonmilitary threats to well-being and survival; and irregular warfare waged by nonstate groups ranging from armed militias to terrorists. New forms of violence involving different types of actors make it difficult to compare adversaries' capabilities.

5.1

GLOBALIZATION AND THE STUDY OF INTERNATIONAL SECURITY

Victor D. Cha

Introduction

At the threshold of the 21st century, two topics have dominated the study of international relations in the USA: globalization and the 'new' security environment after the end of the Cold War. The latter has been the object of intense debate, largely

Source: Victor D. Cha, "Globalization and the Study of International Security," *Journal of Peace Research* 37:3 (May 2000), 391–403. Notes appearing in the original have been deleted.

dominated by those arguing about the relative importance of structural, institutional, and cultural variables for explaining the likelihood of global or regional peace. The former dynamic has been discussed so widely in scholarly and popular circles that it has reached the ignoble status of 'buzzword,' familiarly used by many to refer to some fuzzy phenomenon or trend in the world, but hardly understood by any.

This essay explores how the processes of globalization have fundamentally changed the way we think about security. In spite of the plethora of literature on security and globalization, there is relatively little work written by US security specialists that interconnects the two. . . . In the case of the globalization literature, this has stemmed from a relatively stronger focus on the social and economic processes of globalization. The 'new' security environment in the 21st century will operate increasingly in the space defined by the interpenetration between two spheres: globalization and national identity.

Security and Globalization

Globalization is best understood as a spatial phenomenon. It is not an 'event,' but a gradual and ongoing expansion of interaction processes, forms of organization, and forms of cooperation outside the traditional spaces defined by sovereignty. Activity takes place in a less localized, less insulated way as transcontinental and interregional patterns criss-cross and overlap one another.

The process of globalization is analytically distinct from interdependence. The latter . . . denotes growth in connections and linkages between sovereign entities. Interdependence complicates external sovereignty in that sovereign choices have to be made to accommodate these interdependent ties. Globalization processes are not just about linkages but about interpenetration. . . . It affects not only external sovereignty choices but also internal sovereignty in terms of relations between the public and private sectors.

Contrary to popular notions of globalization, this does not mean that sovereignty ceases to exist in the traditional Weberian sense (i.e., monopoly of legitimate authority over citizen and subjects within a given territory). Instead, globalization is a spatial reorganization of production, industry, finance, and other areas which causes local decisions to have global repercussions and daily life to be affected by global events.

Comparisons are often made between globalization at the end of the 20th century and the period before World War I when the developed world witnessed unprecedented high volumes of trade across borders and movements of capital that led to the dissolution of empires and traditional structures of governance. However, these analogies are not accurate because the process of change at the turn of the 20th century was driven by, and had as its final outcome, nationalism and the consolidation of statehood. A century later, statehood and notions of sovereignty are not so much under attack by so-called 'globalization forces' as empires were, but are being modified and re-oriented by them. In short, the nation-state does not end; it is just less in control. Activity and decisions for the state increasingly take place in a post-sovereign space. In this sense, globalization is both a boundary-broadening process and a boundary-weakening one.

Much of the literature on globalization has focused on its economic rather than security implications. In part, this is because the security effects of globalization often get conflated with changes to the international security agenda with the end of Cold War Superpower competition. It is also because, unlike economics where globalization's effects are manifested and measured everyday in terms of things like international capital flows and Internet use, in security, the effects are inherently harder to conceptualize and measure. To the extent possible, the ensuing analysis tries to differentiate globalization from post–Cold War effects on security. As a first-cut, one can envision a 'globalization-security' spectrum along which certain dialogues in security studies would fall. For example, the notion of selective engagement, pre-emptive withdrawal, democratic enlargement, or preventive defense as viable US grand strategies for the coming century would sit at the far end of this spectrum because they are predominantly security effects deriving from the end of bipolar competition rather than from globalization. Progressively closer to the middle would be arguments about the 'debellicization' of security or the obsolescence of war which do not have globalization as their primary cause, but are clearly related to some of these processes. Also in this middle range would be discussions on 'rogue' or 'pariah' states as this term is a function of the end of the Cold War; at the same time, however, the spread of information and technology exponentially raises the danger of these threats. Similarly, the end of the Cold War provides the permissive condition for the salience of weapons of mass destruction as the Soviet collapse directly affected the subsequent accessibility of formerly controlled substances such as plutonium or enriched uranium. But an equally important driver is globalization because the technologies for creating these weapons have become easily accessible. Finally, at the far end of the 'globalization-security' spectrum might be the salience of substate extremist groups or fundamentalist groups because their ability to organize transnationally, meet virtually, and utilize terrorist tactics has been substantially enhanced by the globalization of technology and information. While the US security studies field has made reference to many of these issues, a more systematic understanding of globalization's security effects is lacking.

Agency and Scope of Threats

The most far-reaching security effect of globalization is its complication of the basic concept of 'threat' in international relations. This is in terms of both agency and scope. Agents of threat can be states but can also be non-state groups or individuals. While the vocabulary of conflict in international security traditionally centered on interstate war (e.g., between large set-piece battalions and national armed forces), with globalization, terms such as global violence and human security become common parlance, where the fight is between irregular substate units such as ethnic militias, paramilitary guerrillas, cults and religious organizations, organized crime, and terrorists. Increasingly, targets are not exclusively opposing force structures or even cities, but local groups and individuals. Similarly, security constituencies, while nominally defined by traditional sovereign borders increasingly are defined at every level from the global to the regional to the individual. . . . Thus the providers of security are still nationally defined in terms of capabilities and resources; however, increasingly they apply these in a post-sovereign space whose spectrum ranges from nonstate to substate to transstate arrangements. For this reason, security threats become inherently more difficult to measure, locate, monitor, and contain.

Globalization widens the scope of security as well. As the Copenhagen school has noted, how states conceive of security and how they determine what it means to be secure in the post–Cold War era expand beyond military security at the national level. Globalization's effects on security scope are distinct from those of the post–Cold War in that the basic transaction processes engendered by globalization—instantaneous communication and transportation, exchanges of information and technology, flow of capital—catalyze certain dangerous phenomena or empower certain groups in ways unimagined previously. In the former category are things such as viruses and pollution. Because of human mobility, disease has become much more of a transnational security concern. Global warming, ozone depletion, acid rain, biodiversity loss, and radioactive contamination are health and environmental problems that have intensified as transnational security concerns precisely because of increased human mobility and interaction.

Globalization also has given rise to a 'skill revolution' that enhances the capabilities of groups such as drug smugglers, political terrorists, criminal organizations, and ethnic insurgents to carry out their agenda more effectively than ever before. It is important to note that the widening scope of security to these transnational issues is not simply a short-term fixation with the end of bipolar Cold War competition as the defining axis for security. The threat posed by drugs, terrorism, transnational crime, and environmental degradation has been intensified precisely because of globalization. Moreover, the security solutions to these problems in terms of enforcement or containment increasingly are ineffective through national or unilateral means.

Globalization has ignited identity as a source of conflict. The elevation of regional and ethnic conflict as a top-tier security issue has generally been treated as a function of the end of the Cold War. However, it is also a function of globalization. The process of globalization carries implicit homogenization tendencies and messages, which in combination with the 'borderlessness' of the globalization phenomenon elicits a cultural pluralist response.

At the same time, globalization has made us both more aware and less decisive about our motivations to intervene in such ethnic conflicts. Real-time visual images of horror and bloodshed in far-off places transmitted through CNN make the conflicts impossible to ignore, creating pressures for intervention. On the other hand, the hesitancy to act is palpable, as standard measures by which to determine intervention (i.e., bipolar competition in the periphery) are no longer appropriate, forcing us to grope with fuzzy motivations such as humanitarian intervention.

Non-Physical Security

Globalization has anointed the concept of non-physical security. Traditional definitions of security in terms of protection of territory and sovereignty, while certainly not irrelevant in a globalized era, expand to protection of information and technology assets. . . . In a similar vein, the revolution in military affairs highlights not greater firepower but greater information technology and 'smartness' of weapons as the defining advantage for future warfare.

These non-physical security aspects have always been a part of the traditional national defense agenda. Indeed, concerns about the unauthorized transfer of sensitive technologies gave rise to such techno-nationalist institutions as COCOM during the Cold War. However, the challenge posed by globalization is that the nation-state can no longer control the movement of technology and information. Strategic alliances form in the private sector among leading corporations that are not fettered by notions of techno-nationalism and driven instead by competitive, cost-cutting, or cutting-edge innovative needs. The result is a transnationalization of defense production that further reduces the state's control over these activities.

More and more private companies, individuals, and other non-state groups are the producers, consumers, and merchants of a US$50 billion per year global arms market. The end of the Cold War has certainly been a permissive condition for the indiscriminate, profit-based incentives to sell weapons or dual-use technologies to anybody. But globalization of information and technology has made barriers to non-state entry low and detection costs high. Moreover, while enforcement authorities still have the benefit of these technologies, two critical developments have altered the equation: (1) Absence of discrimination: over the past two decades, the private sector, rather than the government, has become the primary creator of new technologies, which in essence has removed any relative advantages state agencies formerly possessed in terms of exclusive access to eavesdropping technology, surveillance, and encryption. Governments once in the position of holding monopolies on cutting edge technologies that could later be 'spun off' in the national commercial sector are now consumers of 'spin-on' technologies. (2) Volume and variety: the sheer growth in volume and variety of communications has overwhelmed any attempts at monitoring or control. As noted earlier, these phenomena of globalization most dangerously manifest themselves as the threat posed by substate actors with violent intentions. Through the Internet and the privatization of formerly secured national assets (e.g., plutonium or highly enriched uranium), these groups are now able to start substantially higher on the learning curve for building a weapon of mass destruction. Building an inefficient fission weapon capable of killing 100,000 in an urban center or cultivating cultures for biological use is child's play relative to the past. Thus in a globalized world, information and technology increasingly are the currency of non-physical security.

Propositions for Security Behavior

If non-physical security, diversification of threats, and the salience of identity are key effects of globalization in the security realm, then how might this translate in terms of a state's foreign policy? The literature on globalization in both Europe and the USA remains conspicuously silent on this question. Globalization authors might argue that this criticism is inappropriate because it suggests an ideal endstate at which a 'globalized' country should arrive. However, the point here is not to suggest that there will be a single uniform model, but that as globalization processes permeate a state's security agenda, this might be manifested in certain general inclinations and contours of behavior. Put another way, we should observe globalization processes altering in some cases, and creating in other cases, new sets of security interests for states.

Intermestic Security

First, the globalization and security literature asserts but does not elaborate how security decisions increasingly take place outside the traditional purview of sovereignty. Globalization creates an interpenetration of foreign and domestic issues that national governments must recognize in developing policy. One example of this 'intermestic' approach to security policy might be an acceptance that the transnationalization of threats has blurred traditional divisions between internal and external security. The obverse would be the frequency with which a state adheres to 'delimiting' security, formulating and justifying policy on the basis of 'national security' interests rather than universal/global interests. Examples of the former are European institutions such as Interpol, TREVI, and the Schengen Accord, which represent an acknowledgment that domestic issues such as crime, drug-trafficking, terrorism, and immigration increasingly require transnational cooperation. TREVI was composed of ministers of the interior and justice of EC member-states whose purpose was to coordinate policy on terrorism (at Germany's initiative in 1975) and international crime. The Schengen Accords also represented a convergence of internal and external security with regard to common standards border controls, pursuit of criminals across borders, asylum procedures, and refugees. In Asia, one might see environmental pollution and transnational crime as issues where international and domestic security converge. However, in the near future, maritime piracy is the most likely focal point. These are cases where substate actors armed with sophisticated weapons, satellite-tracking technology, and cutting-edge document-forging equipment hijack vessels in the South and East China seas with millions of dollars worth of cargo. These groups operate transnationally; planning may occur at one destination, tracking of the ship at another, the attack launched from another port, and the cargo off-loaded at yet another port. These acts fall under the purview of local law enforcement, but they are clearly 'intermestic' security issues. The attacks occur in overlapping sovereign waters or international waters, and sometimes receive the tacit consent of governments where the pirated vessels are clandestinely ported. Moreover, if targeted cargos move beyond luxury autos and video cassette recorders to strategic goods such as plutonium, then distinctions between external and internal security and criminal and strategic threats disappear.

Multilateralism

Second, the globalization literature acknowledges that security is increasingly conceived of in post-sovereign, globalized terms, but does not delineate how the modes of obtaining security should change. As noted above, globalization means that both the agency and scope of threats have become more diverse and non-state in form. This also suggests that the payoffs lessen for obtaining security through traditional means. Controlling pollution, disease, technology, and information transfer cannot be easily dealt with through national, unilateral means but can only be effectively dealt with through the application of national resources in multilateral fora or through encouragement of transnational cooperation. As UN Secretary-General Kofi Annan intimated, US bombing of targets in Sudan in retaliation for terrorist bombings of two US embassies in Africa is a unilateral piecemeal approach far inferior to concerted global efforts at denying terrorists sanctuaries, financing, and technology and encouraging their extradition and prosecution.

Thus one would expect globalized security processes reflected in a state's striving for regional coordination and cooperative security. It should emphasize not exclusivity and bilateralism in relations but inclusivity and multilateralism as the best way to solve security problems. At the extreme end of the spectrum, globalization might downplay the importance of eternal iron-clad alliances and encourage the growth of select trans-national 'policy coalitions' among national governments, nongovernmental organizations (NGOs), and individuals specific to each problem.

In conjunction with multilateralism, globalized conceptions of security should be reflected in norms of diffuse reciprocity and international responsibility. This is admittedly more amorphous and harder to operationalize. While some self-serving instrumental motives lie behind most diplomacy, there must be a strong sense of global responsibility and obligation that compels the state to act. Actions taken in the national interest must be balanced with a basic principle that contributes to a universal, globalized value system underpinning one's own values.

Bureaucratic Innovation

The globalization literature has not done justice to the role bureaucratic innovation plays in response to the new challenges of globalization. On this point, indeed, the literature has not kept pace with the empirics. For example, in the USA, the Clinton Administration created the position of Undersecretary for Global Affairs, whose portfolio included environmental issues, promotion of democracy and human rights, population and migration issues, and law enforcement. In a similar vein, the US State Department's Foreign Service Institute now has a new core course for FSOs on narcotics-trafficking, refugee flows, and environmental technologies. In May 1998, the Clinton Administration put forward its first comprehensive plan to combat world crime, identifying drug-trafficking, transfer of sensitive technology and WMD, and trafficking of women and children as threats to the USA. One might also expect to see foreign service bureaucracies placing greater emphasis on international organizations and NGOs in terms of representation, placement, and leadership if these are recognized as the key vehicles of security and politics in a globalized world.

Implicit in each of these examples is the trend toward greater specialization in the pursuit of security. As globalization makes security problems more complex and diverse, national security structures need to be re-oriented, sometimes through elimination of anachronistic bureaucracies or through rationalization of wasteful and overlapping ones. In the US system, for example, while combating the spread of weapons of mass destruction is widely acknowledged as a key security objective in the 21st century, various branches of the government operate autonomously in dealing with these threats. Hence, there are greater calls for renovation and coordination to eliminate the overlap, inefficiency, and lack of organization among State, Defense, Commerce, Energy, CIA, and FBI in combating proliferation.

Another trend engendered by the security challenges of globalization is greater cross-fertilization between domestic law enforcement and foreign policy agencies. This relationship, at least in the USA (less the case in Europe), is at worst non-existent because domestic law enforcement has operated traditionally in isolation from national security and diplomatic concerns, or at best is a mutually frustrating relationship because the two have neither inclination nor interest in cooperating. States that understand the challenges of globalization, particularly on issues of drug-trafficking, environmental crimes, and technology transfer, will seek to bridge this gap, creating and capitalizing on synergies that develop between the two groups. Foreign policy agencies will seek out greater interaction with domestic agencies, not only on a pragmatic short-term basis employing law enforcement's skills to deal with a particular problem, but also on a longer-term and regular basis cultivating familiarity, transparency, and common knowledge. On the domestic side, agencies such as the FBI, Customs, and police departments (of major cities) would find themselves engaged in foreign policy dialogues, again not only at the practitioner's level, but also in academia and think-tank forums.

One of the longer-term effects of specialization and cross-fertilization is that security also becomes more 'porous.' Specialization will often require changes not just at the sovereign national level, but across borders and with substate actors. 'Boilerplate' security (e.g., dealt with by 'hardshell' nation-states with national resources) becomes increasingly replaced by cooperation and coordination that may still be initiated by the national government but with indispensable partners (depending on the issue) such as NGOs, transnational groups, and the media. The obverse of this dynamic also obtains. With globalization, specialized 'communities of choice' (e.g., landmine ban) are empowered to organize transnationally and penetrate the national security agendas with issues that might not otherwise have been paid attention to.

Aggregating Capabilities

The globalization literature remains relatively silent on how globalization processes substantially alter the way in which states calculate relative capabilities. The single most important variable in this process is the diffusion of technology (both old and new). In the past, measuring relative capabilities was largely a linear process. Higher technology generally meant qualitatively better weapons and hence stronger capabilities. States could be assessed along a ship-for-ship, tank-for-tank, jet-for-jet comparison in terms of the threat posed and their relative strength based on such linear measurements. However, the diffusion of technology has had distorting effects. While states at the higher end technologically still retain advantages, globalization has enabled wider access to technology such that the measurement process is more dynamic. First, shifts in relative capabilities are more frequent and have occurred in certain cases much earlier than anticipated. Second, and more significant, the measurement process is no longer one-dimensional in the sense that one cannot readily draw linear associations between technology, capabilities, and power. For example, what gives local, economically backward states regional and even global influence in the 21st century is their ability to threaten across longer distances. Globalization facilitates access to select technologies related to force projection and weapons of mass destruction, which in turn enable states to pose threats that are asymmetric and disproportionate to their size. Moreover, these threats emanate not from acquisition of state-of-the-art but *old and outdated* technology. Thus countries like North Korea, which along most traditional measurements of power could not compare, can with old technology (SCUD and rudimentary nuclear technology) pose threats and affect behavior in ways unforeseen in the past.

Strategies and Operational Considerations

Finally, the literature on globalization is notably silent on the long-term impact of globalization processes on time-tested modes of strategic thinking and fighting. In the former vein, the widening scope of security engendered by globalization means that the definition of security and the fight for it will occur not on battlefields but in unconventional places against non-traditional security adversaries. As noted above, when states cannot deal with these threats through sovereign means, they will encourage multilateralism and cooperation at the national, transnational, and international levels. However, the nature of these conflicts may also require new ways of fighting, i.e., the ability to engage militarily with a high degree of lethality against combatants, but low levels of collateral damage. As a result, globalization's widening security scope dictates not only new strategies (discussed below) but also new forms of combat. Examples include incapacitating crowd control munitions such as blunt projectiles (rubber balls), non-lethal crowd dispersal cartridges, 'stick 'em' and 'slick 'em' traction modifiers, or 'stink' bombs. 'Smart' non-lethal warfare that incapacitates equipment will also be favored, including rigid foam substances, and radio frequency and microwave technologies to disable electronics and communications.

Regarding strategy, as the agency and scope of threats diversifies in a globalized world, traditional modes of deterrence become less relevant. Nuclear deterrence throughout the Cold War and post–Cold War eras, for example, was based on certain assumptions. First, the target of the strategy was another nation-state. Second, this deterred state was assumed to have a degree of centralization in the decision making process over nuclear weapons use. Third, and most important, the opponent possessed both counterforce and countervalue targets that would be the object of a second strike. While this sort of rationally based, existential deterrence will still apply to interstate security, the proliferation of weaponized non-state and substate actors increasingly renders this sort of strategic thinking obsolete. They do not occupy sovereign territorial space and therefore cannot be targeted with the threat of retaliation. They also may operate as self-contained cells rather than an organic whole which makes decapitating strikes at a central decision making structure ineffective. In short, you cannot deter with the threat of retaliation that which you cannot target.

Governments may respond to this in a variety of ways. One method would be, as noted above, greater emphasis on the specialized utilization of whatever state, substate, and multilateral methods are necessary to defend against such threats. A second likely response would be greater attention and resources directed at civil defense preparation and 'consequence' management to minimize widespread panic and pain in the event of an attack. A third possible response is unilateral in nature. Governments may increasingly employ pre-emptive or preventive strategies if rational deterrence does not apply against non-state entities. Hence one might envision two tiers of security in which stable rational deterrence applies at the state-state level but unstable pre-emptive/preventive strategies apply at the state–non-state level.

Conclusion

What then is the 'new' security environment in the 21st century that the globalization/ security literature must strive to understand? It is most likely one that sits at the intersection of globalization and national identity. In other words, as globalization processes complicate the nature of security (i.e., in terms of agency and scope), this effects a transformation in the interests that inform security policy. Globalization's imperatives permeate the domestic level and should be manifested in some very broad behavioral trends or styles of security policy. Manifestations of this transformation are inclinations toward intermestic security, multilateralism, and bureaucratic innovation and specialization.

However, it would be short-sighted to expect that all states will respond similarly. In some cases, policies will emerge that directly meet or adjust to the imperatives of globalization, but in other cases the policy that emerges will not be what one might expect to linearly follow from globalization pressures. The latter outcomes are the types of anomalies that offer the most clear indications of the causal role of domestic factors in the 'new' security environment; however, these alone only highlight national identity as a residual variable (i.e., capable of explaining only aberrations) in the 'new' security environment. One would expect, therefore, that the former outcomes would be as important to process trace: If policy adjustments appear outwardly consistent with globalization but the underlying rationale for such action is not, then this illustrates that the domestic-ideational mediation process is an ever-present one. The new security environment would therefore be one in which globalization pressures on security policy and grand strategy are continually refracted through the prism of national identity.

5.2

CYBER WAR AND INSTITUTIONAL VULNERABILITY

Richard W. Mansbach

> One prominent feature of a globalized security environment is the growing prospect of cyber war among major states and between such states and nonstate entities. Using trained computer hackers, it may be possible to launch cyber attacks that could rapidly bring an enemy society to its knees. The next selection describes the relatively short history of cyber warfare and what it threatens in an era of advanced but vulnerable microelectronic technologies.

Technological change has always affected national security. In the 1950s, John Herz concluded that nuclear weapons and their delivery systems were making territorial states obsolete because they enabled penetration of the state's "hard shell" of "impenetrability.[1]

The development of continent-spanning missiles confirmed the belief that territory no longer afforded military security.

Today, distance and topography are devalued when real-time contemporary knowledge of a field of battle allows precision-guided drones to locate and destroy targets such as individual houses or automobiles in the remote mountains of Waziristan in Pakistan or the desert outside Misrata in northwestern Libya. A powerful combination of satellites, computers, and microelectronic technologies provide unprecedented command, control, and communication across entire battlefields. This capacity has influenced American military thinking in the Persian Gulf War of 1991, Kosovo in 1999, Iraq in 2003, and Afghanistan since 2001.

Cyberspace is becoming a site of growing conflict. Governments are vulnerable to the manipulation or destruction of information, the disruption of communication and economic transactions, and the theft of proprietary and classified information. Telecommunications, air control, immigration, electric power grids, gas and oil storage, banking, transportation, water supply, and emergency and government (including military) services are all potential targets for official and unofficial computer hackers. Disruption of interdependent computers in such systems would quickly spread to other computers, producing chaos across a country. As a result, "information assurance" has become a growth field.

Estonia was the first country to come under a sustained Internet attack, and it was especially vulnerable because of its reliance on Internet connectivity; most Estonians use mobile phones and online banking and bank cards to pay for almost anything they purchase. A Russia-originated cyber attack began in the evening of April 26, 2007, apparently in retaliation for the removal of the "Bronze Soldier," a Soviet war memorial, from central Tallinn. The attackers had taken control of upward of a million computers around the world and infected them with malware, and as a result, Estonians could neither pay their bills nor phone one another. As Sergei Markov, a Duma deputy from Vladimir Putin's United Russia party, put it, "About the cyberattack on Estonia . . . don't worry, that attack was carried out by my assistant. I won't tell you his name, because then he might not be able to get visas."[2] During its brief war with Russia in 2008, Georgia too became a victim of a Russian cyber attack.

Chinese hackers have also been deeply involved in cyber warfare as part of a strategy of asymmetric warfare. Chinese hacking of American facilities routinely increases during moments of tension between the two governments. A vast Chinese espionage operation on the Internet was revealed in 2009 to have stolen confidential material from government and corporate offices in many countries. The attackers were able to take control of infected computers, download files, and covertly attach devices such as microphones and web cameras. Chinese officials also hacked into a contractor for the U.S. Department of Defense and Google's computer system, leading the company to leave the country.

The technologies needed for hacking are inexpensive and accessible and provide an excellent source of intelligence at a low cost. For instance, insurgents in Iraq and Afghanistan using off-the-shelf software costing $26 have hacked into unmanned American drones.[3] In one case, a single Chinese hacker with a junior high school education created chaos within China in 2006 and 2007.

The United States and other economically developed societies are especially vulnerable to cyber attack owing to their dependence on the Internet and on networked computerized information and communications systems in virtually all their key industries and services. Moreover, they have largely failed to develop reliable cyber defenses—in the American case, especially in the private sector. In 2007 alone, some 44,000 malicious cyber attacks were carried out against American targets by foreign governments and individual hackers, and the following year, it was discovered that cyber spies had penetrated America's electrical grid and had planted software that could be used to degrade the system.

Evidence of a growing threat led the Obama administration to create a cyber security office in the White House, and the U.S. Defense Department has created a new Cyber Command. The threat of cyber war has led the United States and Russia to hold talks about trying to reduce its likelihood by improving Internet security.

In a recent book, Richard Clarke—formerly Special Assistant to the President for Global Affairs, National Coordinator for Security and Counterterrorism, and Special Advisor to the President for Cyber Security—and Andrew Knake paint a frightening picture of the results of a cyber attack on the United States.

> It's now 8:15 p.m. Within a quarter of an hour, 157 major metropolitan areas have been thrown into knots by a nationwide power blackout hitting during rush hour. Poison gas clouds are wafting toward Wilmington and Houston. Refineries are burning up oil supplies in several cities. Subways have crashed in New York, Oakland, Washington, and Los Angeles. Freight trains have derailed outside major junctions and marshaling yards on four major railroads. Aircraft are literally falling out of the sky as a result of midair collisions across the country. Pipelines carrying natural gas to the Northeast have exploded, leaving millions in the cold. The financial system has also frozen because of the terabytes of information at data centers being wiped out. Weather, navigation, and communications satellites are spinning out of their orbits into space. And the U.S. military is a series of isolated units, struggling to communicate with each other.[4]

Although some observers take issue with Clarke and Knake about the dangers of cyber war, the United States as well as other major states are taking the potential consequences of cyber war seriously and are making intensive efforts to reduce their vulnerability to cyber attack.

Notes

1   John H. Herz, *International Politics in the Atomic Age* (New York: Columbia University Press, 1959).

2   Cited in Radio Free Europe/Radio Liberty, "Behind The Estonia Cyberattacks," March 6, 2009, http://www.rferl.org/content/Behind_The_Estonia_Cyberattacks/1505613.html.

3   Siobhan Gorman, Yochi J. Dreazen, and August Cole, "Insurgents Hack U.S. Drones," *Wall Street Journal,* December 17, 2009, A1, A21.

4   Richard A. Clarke and Andrew K. Knake, *Cyber War* (New York: HarperCollins, 2010), 67. For a contrasting view of the dangers of cyber-war, see Thomas Rid, "Think Again: Cyber-war," *Foreign Policy* 192 (March/April 2012), 80–84.

5.3

CYBER WAR: ONE STRIKE, AND YOU'RE OUT

Grace Chng

> Although some observers fear that terrorists could launch a cyber attack, the following selection, based on a cybersecurity conference in Singapore, suggests that this is less likely than a preemptive first-strike cyber war initiated by one state against another.

Terrorists aim for horror—they want the visual and visceral impact best expressed by images of crumbling buildings and bloody corpses. But cyber terrorism does not create that kind of widespread emotional impact, said Dr Irving Lachow of the National Defence University (NDU), an American institution which trains the military's infocommunications professionals.

Also, cyber terrorists do not have technical skills that are up to the mark when it comes to executing a digital attack with an impact equivalent to 9/11.

It would take at least US $1 million (S $1.4 million) to plan and require at least 18 to 24 months to get ready, by which time, he said, intelligence agencies would have gotten wind of it.

That is why cyber terrorism is not a likely scenario, he said in a workshop that was part of a conference held at the Shangri-La Hotel last Tuesday and Wednesday.

Billed as The Regional Collaboration On Cybersecurity, this was the first time the conference was organised here for cyber-security professionals to learn how the military prepares for cyber warfare.

The two-day conference saw about 200 participants from 10 countries representing the public and private sectors, national security agencies and the military. It was organised by the Institute of Systems Science (ISS) of the National University of Singapore and the NDU.

If cyber terrorism is unlikely in the immediate future, cyber war, on the other hand, is a distinct possibility. As NDU professor Dan Kuehl pointed out, hackers could bring down military logistics networks and communications systems so that troops do not get food, arms or medicine and officers do not get their instructions. 'Such attacks can go on for days or be over in nanoseconds,' he said at his workshop.

In a traditional war, you can lose the first battles but win the larger war, just as the United States lost Pearl Harbour but recovered to win World War II. 'In cyber war, the first battle may be over and lost even before you know it,' he said.

Cyber wars, he said, can be a pre-emptive strike to soften the ground of the opponent. Computer bugs sent into the networks will, among other things, crash electrical grids

Source: Grace Chng, "Cyber War: One Strike, and You're Out," *The Straits Times,* July 18, 2010.

and bring down the stock markets. This will disrupt public services, thus creating confusion before the tanks roll in and the soldiers march into a capital city.

The conference participants agreed that hackers, who were motivated by the geek street cred they gained when they broke into a network in the early days of the Internet, are now becoming politically motivated.

While the conference did not identify who the hackers may be today, previous news reports have identified them as digital vigilantes with political affiliations or state-sponsored groups.

The threat of cyber war has been raised because of the exponential growth of the Internet. As of the end of last December, there were over 234 million websites and nearly 1.9 billion Internet users. In this vast landscape of criss-crossing networks, there are likely to be weak links hackers can exploit since no software or network is foolproof.

Dr James Heath, technical director of the US Forces Korea, special adviser for cyber operations, said that from the US Department of Defence (DoD) perspective, the cyber threats faced by the military are no different from those faced by a financial institution or corporate entity.

One difference between the two is that businesses accept a 2 per cent to 3 per cent risk of hacking.

'The DoD cannot accept this high risk,' he stressed.

While he did not elaborate on the US cyber defence capabilities, he said a big step forward was the setting up in 2008 of the Comprehensive National Cybersecurity Initiative (CNCI). This provided a framework for how the federal government protects sensitive information from hackers and nations trying to break into agency networks.

Among the CNCI's tasks are identifying the features of cyber attacks, using technology to indicate and warn of possible attacks, and creating awareness of cyber security.

Dr Heath said the US Cyber Command set up in May this year will look closely at the way national security agencies exchange sensitive information with other domestic organisations.

To prepare against cyber attacks on the battlefield, military commanders must be supported by network defenders and officers who can make sense of the information collected on network traffic.

In Singapore, the military's philosophy is to assume that the networks will be compromised, said Brigadier-General David Koh, director of military intelligence at the Ministry of Defence.

Since the military does not have the First World resources to build its own cyber defences, the Singapore Armed Forces have, for the last 10 years, built a closed network not linked to the Internet for its sensitive information like battlefield command and control systems.

It is a recognition that the SAF's cyber defenders cannot guard everything since 'we know that security breaches will happen; it's only when they will occur,' said BG Koh.

'It is not a '1' or '0' decision. In the cyber realm, we want to have our cake and eat it. By separating the sensitive information from the general communication, we can get control,' he added.

At the end of the conference, the consensus was that more collaboration is needed for information exchange.

There are pockets of ongoing country-to-country collaboration. Many countries such as the US, Australia and Singapore have set up computer emergency response teams to monitor cyber attacks and cooperate with one another. For Asean, the regional teams participate in a yearly drill where they learn to respond to a cyber attack.

On a global level, the International Telecommunication Union has set up the International Multilateral Partnership Against Cyber Threats that brings together governments, industry and the academia to discuss cyber-security initiatives.

Certainly, more needs to be done. Said ISS chief executive officer Lim Swee Cheang: 'Cyber war is a complex challenge. There is a need for coordination which may lead to the creation of a national cyber security command and control authority and the establishment of a legal framework to let law enforcement agencies trace and prosecute cyber criminals across countries.'

Also needed is a common set of reference that defines a cyber war, such as when a cyber attack turns into a war and the use of force against a cyber attack or cyber war.

Going forward, Dr Heath emphasised international engagement and diplomacy with foreign governments and law enforcement agencies.

5.4

SON OF STUXNET?

Mark Clayton

In September 2010, Iranian nuclear facilities were attacked by a worm called Stuxnet. The worm was designed to attack a particular Iranian nuclear facility with software provided by the German firm Siemans, involving knowledge of both the company's production processes and control system and the nuclear facility's blueprints. The attack sent nuclear centrifuges at Iran's Natanz uranium enrichment facility out of control. The attack significantly delayed

Source: Mark Clayton, "Son of Stuxnet? Variants of the cyberweapon likely, senators told," *The Christian Science Monitor*, November 17, 2010.

Stuxnet

Iran's apparent effort to acquire a nuclear weapon and illustrated what a highly sophisticated cyber attack can accomplish. As the next selection indicates, the cyberworm, which may have been developed with American expertise, could be utilized against the United States in the future.

Stuxnet, the first known weaponized software designed to destroy a specific industrial process, could soon be modified to target an array of industrial systems in the US and abroad, cyber experts told US senators Wednesday.

The Stuxnet malware, discovered this summer, was apparently designed to strike one target—Iran's nuclear-fuel centrifuge facilities, researchers now say. But Stuxnet's "digital warhead," they caution, could be copied and altered by others to wreak havoc on a much grander scale.

Variants of Stuxnet could target a host of critical infrastructure, from the power grid and water supplies to transportation systems, four cybersecurity experts told the Senate Committee on Homeland Security and Governmental Affairs.

"The concern for the future of Stuxnet is that the underlying code could be adapted to target a broader range of control systems in any number of critical infrastructure sectors," said Sean McGurk, acting director of the National Cyber-security and Communications Integration Center at the US Department of Homeland Security.

Stuxnet infiltrated and targeted an industrial control system software that is widely used in US infrastructure and industry, meaning the nation is vulnerable to future Stuxnet-like attacks, he said. "While we do not know which process was the intended target [of Stuxnet], it is important to note that the combination of Windows operating software and Siemens hardware can be used in control systems across critical infrastructure sectors—from automobile assembly lines to mixing baby formula to processing chemicals," said Mr. McGurk.

As of last week, 44,000 computers worldwide were still infected with the Stuxnet worm—including 1,600 in the US, said Dean Turner, head of global intelligence for Symantec Corp., the computer security firm that detailed Stuxnet's inner workings. Fifty of those US infections had worked their way from Windows operating systems into industrial control systems. It's not publicly known who created Stuxnet.

"Our level of preparedness . . . in the private sector is better than it ever has been, but still has a long way to go," said Mr. Turner. "It's a cliché, but we don't know what we don't know."

Perhaps the sharpest alarm was sounded by Michael Assante, president of the National Board of Information Security Examiners. He's seen the threat up close, having held key posts in industrial control system security research at the Idaho National Laboratory and then as chief security officer of the North American Electric Reliability Corp., which is charged with power grid reliability.

"Stuxnet is, at the very least, an important wake-up call for digitally enhanced and reliant countries—at its worst, a blueprint for future attackers," he said. It is a "good example of a cyberthreat thought to be hypothetically possible, but not considered probable by many." Its sophistication "should disturb security professionals, engineers, businessmen, and government leaders alike."

Citing his research at the national lab, Mr. Assante noted that his team there had explored a similar avenue earlier—alluding apparently to a 2007 test that used Internet-delivered commands to destroy a diesel generator—prompting black smoke and bolts flying off the machine. "I have participated in research that demonstrated this capability in a controlled environment to understand how it could be done," he said. "I believe that the analysis to date has indicated that Stuxnet may be such a weapon."

Concern about vulnerability of the power grid has led to warnings and new standards. Yet the grid remains vulnerable to a Stuxnet-style threat, Assante asserted. New government standards have become a "glass ceiling" for companies to perfunctorily meet, he said, but not to exceed.

The Department of Homeland Security (DHS) and a team at the national lab have reverse-engineered and decoded Stuxnet, McGurk said. But DHS is worried that attackers "could use publicly available information about the code" to develop variants targeted at broader installations of programmable equipment in control systems, he said.

That statement may well be a slap at Symantec, which published detailed reports on precisely how Stuxnet works. Bulletins from DHS, on the other hand, omitted key details, said several cybersecurity researchers interviewed by the Monitor.

Still, lack of information-sharing is preventing readiness to combat advanced cyberthreats like Stuxnet, said other witnesses at the hearing.

"A significant cause for concern is that much of the information about cybersecurity-related threats remains classified in the homeland security, defense, and intelligence communities, with restricted opportunity to share information with security researchers, technology providers, and affected private-sector asset owners," Assante said. Restricted use of newly gained knowledge about advanced cyberthreats, he added, places "our nation's critical infrastructure . . . at significant risk."

The witnesses gave varying assessments about how prepared the private sector is to deal with a threat of Stuxnet's sophistication.

Mark Gandy, global cybersecurity chief for Dow Corning Corp. and chairman of the American Chemistry Council's cybersecurity steering committee, said industry is working hard and is up to the task.

"The chemical sector understands this evolving threat," he said. "The ACC and its members have been working for years across the sector to prepare and share information about these issues. . . . We continue to comprehensively improve control system security."

Assante, sounding much less enthusiastic about industry preparedness, cited technology trends that make it easier for attackers to strike control systems.

"I believe we're extremely susceptible," he said. "In fact, I believe our susceptibility grows every day. If you just look at the very trends in the technology that we deploy, we're doing things that would allow an attacker more freedom of action within these environments. . . . Stuxnet is an important harbinger of things that may come if we do not use this opportunity to learn about this threat and apply it."

5.5

HOW WILL THE WORLD CHANGE IN 2010s?

Park Sang-Seek

> Our next reading, from a Korean newspaper, identifies four key issues in the era of globalization: (1) whether American military hegemony is necessary for peace in a globalizing world, (2) whether the spread of democracy will bring peace in its train, (3) whether the key consequences of globalization can be managed unilaterally or require multilateral action, and (4) what security strategy countries should follow. It describes the erosion of U.S. hegemony and the growing military power of China, India, and Russia and the problems that this poses for U.S. President Barack Obama.

Recently the BBC Magazine selected 9/11 as the world's most frequently mentioned and significant word in the first decade of the 21st century. What has happened in the world in the first decade of the 21st century shows that 9/11 is a sign for the emergence of a new international order.

The euphoria of the Western world following the collapse of the Soviet bloc lasted for only a decade. Political leaders and pundits in the West predicted that the world would be safer and more prosperous in the post–Cold War era because democracy would become the universally accepted form of state governance and liberal internationalism would promote free economic exchange and co-prosperity among nations.

Contrary to such predictions, in the non-Western world a disguised form of democracy has become prevalent and the international economic order based on the Washington consensus has aggravated the wealth disparity between rich and poor nations and within nations in the non-Western world, although it has accelerated economic growth globally.

In the first decade of the 21st century the problems of good governance and wealth distribution have become more serious and additional issues have emerged.

The first issue is whether the unipolar world order led by the United States is necessary for world peace and prosperity. Not only the non-Western world but also some Western nations question the desirability and even feasibility of U.S. hegemony.

The second is whether democracy should be practiced at the international level and whether the spread of democracy can guarantee peace among nations. The non-Western world supports the former view, while the Western world has strong reservations. On the latter, the Western world, particularly the United States, believes it, while the non-Western world questions it. The United States under the George W. Bush administration strongly

Source: Park Sang-Seek, "How Will the World Change in 2010s?" *The Korea Herald,* December 31, 2009.

championed democratic peace theory and made efforts to transform non-democratic states into democracies.

The third issue concerns whether global issues created by globalization, including wealth disparity, resources depletion, environmental degradation, international terrorism/crimes and religious/ideological clashes, can and should be handled by states alone or multilaterally, particularly through international organizations. Most nations agree that unilateral solutions may be desirable but multilateral solutions are more effective. The irony is that nations, particularly great powers and developing countries, have no intention to compromise on their national sovereignty for multilateral solutions.

What kind of national security strategy nations should pursue is the fourth issue. This issue is related to the question of how to deal with nontraditional security issues such as terrorism and international crimes which cannot be solved by hard power alone. In the rapidly globalizing world, a nuclear power can kill a million people instantly but can hardly subjugate a person's mind, as Zbigniew Brzezinski pointed out. Ordinary people in the age of globalization are intellectually and ideologically well armed to resist foreign domination and suppression.

In the first decade the United States has made all efforts to preserve the unipolar moment through informal as well as formal alliances and solution of security issues mainly through traditional military means unilaterally or through alliances rather than multilateral mechanisms. It also has used the international financial institutions to maintain its economic supremacy. In other words, the United States has created an imagined hostile bloc with the cold war mindset. This imagined bloc includes any countries or group of countries which oppose U.S. leadership and American ideology.

Meanwhile, China has been building up its national power and economy. Some wonder whether China will assume the position of the Soviet Union in the cold war era and become another superpower challenging U.S. hegemony. This view has become particularly popular since the October 2009 international financial crisis.

Obama presented his political philosophy at the award-giving ceremony for his Noble Peace Prize in Oslo on Dec. 10. He supports just war and defends American hegemony in the cold war and the two decades of the post-cold war period. Based on this conviction, he supports war in self-defense and humanitarian intervention.

The problem with his philosophy is that it is very difficult, if not impossible, to define acts of self-defense and humanitarian intervention. In order to avoid this pitfall, many world-renowned scholars and pundits advocate multilateral intervention, collective security and cooperative security. He emphasizes multilateral actions, but only when led by the United States His philosophy reflects the traditional view of American hegemony, albeit an enlightened one.

In the second decade, it will become more difficult for the United States to maintain its hegemony. First of all, in the security field the United States can hardly deal with nontraditional issues alone. Even in the case of traditional security issues, the United States can defeat a nation but can hardly subjugate its people. Moreover, international public opinion will strongly oppose it.

Secondly, China and other great powers including India and Russia will make stronger efforts to transform the unipolar political and economic order into a new one. This new international order is already emerging and is likely to coexist with the existing one at least in the second decade.

Third, nations will have no choice but to deal with the consequences of globalization jointly. Henceforth, the United Nations will play a more proactive role and international civil society organizations will become more influential. They will closely cooperate to nurture new global common goods and preserve the existing ones.

Fourth, despite globalization, nation-states will continue to remain the main actors and this will make international relations more complicated, and domestic, regional and global disputes and conflicts of all kinds will increase.

Finally, as U.S. hegemony weakens, the world is likely to split into three security and economic complexes: Asian, European and Asia-Pacific. The United States will try to stay between the three, Russia between the European and Asia-Pacific complexes and China between the Asian and Asia-Pacific complexes.

In view of this future development and its geopolitical and economic necessity, South Korea in the second decade needs to navigate very cautiously between the Asian continent and the Pacific Ocean.

5.6

RELATIVITY OF MILITARY TRANSPARENCY

Lu Yin

A major concern of American military planners is the rapidly increasing military power of China and its growing capability to project this power throughout Asia. As the next reading, written by a Chinese researcher at Beijing's National Defense Institute, suggests, China sees its policies in a very different light. It argues that China's military efforts are transparent and that China actively seeks to increase Sino-American mutual trust.

In recent years, military transparency has been mentioned repeatedly in military contacts between China and other countries, especially the United States. On the issue of military transparency, three observations and three comments may be made from a Chinese military officer's perspective.

Military transparency has a role in enhancing mutual understanding and mutual confidence. Following the trend of globalization, international communications and exchanges gave birth to common practices and arrangements of military transparency,

Source: Lu Yin, "Relativity of Military Transparency," *Chinadaily.com.cn,* October 29, 2009.

which became recognized gradually by more and more countries in the world. However, transparency has also become an instrument of the strong to exert pressure on the weak. Obviously, transparency is in favor of the strong, as deterrence. For the weak, transparency means revealing weaknesses and becoming more vulnerable. Consequently, the stronger countries tend to make full use of military transparency as an instrument to exert pressure on or even bully weak countries, which cast a shadow on the positive trend of military transparency.

First, transparency is a relative concept without a uniform standard. Military transparency involves revealing military information concerning national security. Hence, the degree of transparency is based on the precondition of national security interest being safeguarded. Every country has special laws and regulations for keeping military secrets and even the developed countries like the US are no exception. So, in general, there exists only relative transparency instead of absolute transparency. Different countries and people have different understandings of and different approaches to transparency due to their own circumstances, such as different domestic conditions and experience, different levels of strength of military power and different cultural and traditional backgrounds.

Second, building mutual trust is the foundation for achieving mutual transparency. A higher level of military transparency can only be achieved by deepening mutual trust. That is the reason why allied countries enjoy the highest level of military transparency. Moreover, the weaker countries feel insecure if they maintain the same level of transparency as the stronger countries, especially when they are facing the pressure from a country with which there is no deep mutual trust.

We can take the issue of military transparency between China and the US as an example. China is a responsible country pursuing a national defense policy that is defensive in nature and adamantly takes on the path of peaceful development. And, China has no intention to challenge the interests of the US in this region. And China is still a developing country. In terms of its national strength, especially military strength, China is no match for the US.

However, the US government, in official reports, mentions China again and again as a competitor that poses the biggest potential threat to the US. There are similar expressions in the Quadrennial Defense Review 2006, the annual reports on the Military Power of China and some other official documents. Not long ago, on Sept 15, the newly-released National Intelligence Strategy 2009 includes China among a number of nation-states that have the ability to challenge US interests in traditional (e.g., military force and espionage) and emerging (e.g., cyber operations) ways.

Apart from that, in spite of China's strong opposition, the US has been selling advanced weapons to Taiwan, challenging China's core interest. US military aircraft and naval vessels have been conducting frequent and intense reconnaissance activities in the EEZ of China. All those factors have negatively affected mutual trust between China and US, and subsequently, negatively affected military transparency between China and the US. It should be pointed out that while the US often accuses China of lacking transparency, the US military also has imposed restrictions on Chinese delegations visiting US military facilities.

Therefore, to thoroughly resolve the question of military transparency between China and the US, the US should take concrete action to enhance mutual trust and show its sincerity in advancing bilateral relations. Otherwise it would be difficult to achieve a high level of mutual military transparency. The Nuclear Posture Review 2002 is another example that may be cited here. While there is a lack of mutual trust between China and the US, and while China is named as one of seven target countries of nuclear attack in the review, how can China, as a country being listed as a target for nuclear attack, comfortably engage in nuclear dialogue and exchange with the US?

Third, China has been actively pursuing military transparency in recent years. China has published six editions of the Defense White Paper, revealing plenty of information of China's military development.

China actively participates in the international negotiations in the field of arms control, disarmament and non-proliferation. China has taken concrete measures to faithfully fulfill its relevant obligations designated in such international treaties as NPT and CTBT. China has also participated in the UN Military Expenditure Transparency System and resumed the UN Conventional Weapons Registration System. The spokesmen system of the Ministry of National Defense was introduced last year and the official website of the Ministry of National Defense was released last month.

Moreover, China has been trying to enhance its military transparency by increasing and enlarging military contacts and cooperation with other countries and attempts to create a security environment featuring mutual trust and mutual benefit. What is also worth mentioning is that many of China's military facilities and assets, such as the headquarters of Guangzhou and Nanjing military regions, the headquarters of the Second Artillery, China's strategic missile force, the type 99 tank, which is the best main battle tank in China, the FB 7 military aircraft, and some other newest types of destroyers and frigates of the Chinese navy, were first shown to US military delegations in recent years.

With the improvement of mutual trust, a higher level of military transparency can be achieved. As a result, military-to-military relations and even state-to-state relations can be greatly improved. In terms of military transparency between China and the US, given the wide range of shared interests of the two countries and with the joint efforts of both sides, this problem will be eventually solved and mutual trust established.

5.7

TIME TO CORRECT THOSE WESTERN MISCONCEPTIONS

Yang Wenchang

> The next reading, by the president of the Chinese People's Institute of Foreign Affairs, is China's response to Western fears that its "rise" is dangerous. The article seeks to correct what its author regards as Western "misconceptions" of China.

Source: Yang Wenchang, "Time to Correct Those Western Misconceptions," *Chinadaily.com.cn,* July 9, 2007.

In less than two decades since the end of the Cold War, Western media and academic circles have misread China three times.

An objective review and analysis of these misconceptions will help us better appreciate China's way of building socialism with Chinese characteristics, and reinforce our commitment to peace, development and cooperation, and to building a harmonious world.

The first misreading was "the coming collapse of China."

The late 1980s and early 1990s saw political turmoil in Eastern Europe and the disintegration of the Soviet Union. And the June 4th incident occurred in Beijing in late spring and early summer in 1989. Western media and many China watchers came to the conclusion that following the Soviet Union's collapse, it would only be a matter of time before Communist-led China met the same destiny. The US government then imposed sanctions against China, followed by many other Western countries. Despite enormous international pressure, the Chinese government did not fall like the former Soviet Union, as many had predicted in the West. On the contrary, China maintained political stability and robust economic growth and was increasingly assuming a solid position in the international arena. To explain this, I would cite the following three factors.

First, Western scholars failed to grasp the fact that the June 4th incident was not in keeping with the fundamental interests of the Chinese people. Adhering to the path of developing socialism with Chinese characteristics best suited China's national conditions. Eleven years of reform and opening-up had led most of the people in China to understand that their nation could only succeed by advancing reforms in the political, economic and other areas in an environment of stability and national unity. It was on the basis of this understanding that most Chinese did not support acts that would destabilize the nation.

Second, Western scholars, obsessed with an ideological perspective, confused the Chinese model with that of the Soviet Union and failed to appreciate the strategy of reform and opening-up initiated by Deng Xiaoping. It was based on no other than a negation of the over-centralized Soviet model of planned economy.

Third, in a globalized world, countries are increasingly interdependent. Business communities and consumers in these countries do not see it in their own interests to bring about the collapse of China with sanctions or even the curtailing of its growth. Thus political leaders in these countries often voiced doubt themselves about whether sanctions would work at all.

In less than three years, Western sanctions came to nothing. China defied Western pressure and predictions of its demise.

The second misreading was the "China threat" theory.

This theory that emerged in countries like the United States and Japan in the late 1990s persisted into the early 21st century. The main arguments of the theory were: first, China's economy had seen fast growth in two decades and would soon catch up with the United States, Japan and Germany, and China's rapid development and its growing national strength would pose a serious threat to the international status of developed Western countries; second, China had turned itself into a "world factory" with inexhaustible labor and cheap land and was exporting cheap consumer goods, which put the squeeze on manufacturing industries in the West; third, China was running a huge trade surplus, undercutting developed countries' dominance of the world market; fourth, China was faced with bottlenecks in energy and resources and would inevitably compete for resources worldwide with developed countries; and fifth, China's national strength was growing with the rapid economic development but its defense expenditure remained "non-transparent."

Influenced by the above arguments, governments of major Western countries, with the US taking the lead, formulated their two-sided China strategies featuring "containment plus engagement." In the military field, "containment" was mainly exercised through the setting-up of an "Asian version of NATO" with military alliance among the United States, Japan and Australia at the center to guard against enhanced military power of China; in the economic field, "containment" was mainly about limiting imports from China, pressuring China to revalue the RMB, not recognizing China's market economy status and restricting high-tech exports to China. "Engagement" in the political field means maintaining normal state-to-state relations with China and trying to incorporate China into the international order dominated by US-led Western countries. In the economic field, "engagement" requires active investment in China and trading with China.

The two-sided China policy of US-led Western countries could not possibly achieve its aim. There are five reasons.

First, China has always valued its independence since ancient times and the Chinese nation will not change the direction of its development according to the will of others. China sticks to the path of socialism with Chinese characteristics. This is determined by China's national conditions.

Second, in terms of the economic system, China has gradually introduced market mechanisms. All imports and exports of Chinese enterprises follow the basic rules of the game of a market economy. Therefore, the West's economic "containment" of China is groundless.

Third, though China has become a trading power in the world, over 60 percent of its high-value-added exports come from foreign-funded companies. Western investors generally ship large quantities of parts and components into China to finish the final assembly here with cheap labor and preferential taxation policy and then export these products with a "Made in China" label on them.

Fourth, Western analysts tend to emphasize the threat of competition by Chinese commodities but overlook the fact that China is the largest importer in Asia. China's fast economic development is greatly enhancing the consumption capacity of 1.3 billion people, which is not a threat but a rare opportunity to the economies of Europe, the US and Japan.

Fifth, many Western observers have doubts about China's much-reiterated commitment to peaceful development, leading to confusion in Western public opinion on China. China has resolved to pursue a peaceful development consistent with its national condition, history and tradition, and the basic characteristics of the times. The third misreading is that "China should assume more responsibilities."

In 2005, US Deputy Secretary of State Robert Zoelick put forward the now well-known idea that China should become a "responsible stakeholder." A closer look at this term shows that on the one hand, it recognizes the economic achievements made by

China in the past 30 years or so and the fact that China has become an important member of the international community, which is a big step forward. Yet on the other hand, it implies doubts about whether China will fulfill the international responsibilities they think China should undertake. Some talked about guiding China in exercising its responsibilities. Others criticized China's "irresponsible behavior" in many areas, and still others pointed an accusing finger at China's Africa policy, saying it failed to meet Western standards. This is obviously unfair. We should approach the issue from the following aspects:

First, in political and security areas, as a permanent member of the UN Security Council, China has faithfully observed the basic principles of the UN Charter and honored its responsibility toward world peace. In its foreign policy, China always maintains that international conflicts and disputes should be resolved through peaceful negotiation, and opposes the use or threat of force. China has settled historical border disputes with most of its neighbors through peaceful negotiation. On the Korean Peninsula nuclear issue, the Iranian nuclear issue and other hot issues, China stands for upholding the integrity of relevant international treaties and is firmly opposed to nuclear proliferation, and has been working for their resolution through peaceful negotiation. On issues such as countering terrorism and containing spread of diseases, China has taken an active part in international cooperation with the US and other Western countries. Another fact worth mentioning is that China is a major contributor to UN peacekeeping forces.

Second, in the economic field, although some Western countries still do not recognize China as a market economy, China, as a WTO member, has always acted in compliance with prevailing international market rules. China launched financial and monetary reforms and introduced a floating RMB exchange rate regime in line with its stage of economic development.

In the energy field, the Chinese government has not only included in its 11th Five-Year Plan a mandatory target of lowering energy consumption per unit of GDP, but also expressed on many occasions its willingness to cooperate with other countries, in energy saving, developing alternative energy and strengthening environmental protection.

Third, China follows a scientific thinking on development. China has indeed encountered severe constraints on its development in the areas of energy, resources and environment. But China will be able to transform its inefficient growth pattern into an efficient and environment-friendly model of economic development. China will not shift its problems to other countries. Even less will China seek development by plundering others.

Fourth, China's assistance to Africa and China-Africa trade keeps expanding every year as China's economy grows. This is quite normal in South-South cooperation. However, some European scholars have made irresponsible comments on China-Africa relations. In those people's minds, China would be responsible only when it dealt with its relations with Africa in line with Western values, and non-interference in Africa's internal affairs would be equal to irresponsibility. China is not against development of democracy in African countries. However, more important than the specific forms of democracy is whether real benefits can be brought to 800 million people in Africa as a result. Once Africa attains fast development, democracy on that continent will be greatly promoted.

5.8

Piracy

COMMERCIAL SHIP STRIKES BACK IN DEADLY SHOOTOUT WITH SOMALI PIRATES

Scott Baldauf

Piracy has become a widespread danger off the Horn of East Africa in the Arabian Sea and the Indian Ocean owing to state failure in Somalia, where, in the absence of a functioning government since 1992, many former fishermen, with fishing stocks exhausted and confronting toxic wastes in coastal waters, have taken to hijacking and holding ships for ransom. The next article describes an incident in which guards on a commercial vessel killed one such pirate and why such events may increase violence at sea.

Private security guards protecting a commercial ship shot dead a Somali pirate Tuesday, the first recorded incident of its kind.

The pirate attack on the Panamanian-flagged MV Almezaan occurred off the coast of Somalia, and comes at a time when increasing numbers of commercial ships are hiring private armed security units to protect them during their passage through the Indian Ocean to the Red Sea. While US and French Navy crews have killed Somali pirates before during hostage rescues on the high seas, today's shooting shows that the Somali piracy problem is potentially growing more violent.

"This could be the beginning of a violent period," says E.J. Hogendoorn, head of the Horn of Africa program at the International Crisis Group's office in Nairobi. "If [the pirates] see guys with shiny barrels pointing at them, they might fire first."

The waters off Somalia are among the most dangerous sea lanes in the world, but Somali pirates have begun venturing far afield—to the Seychelles Islands and the waters of India—as a 20-ship combined force of European Union and United States Navy ships patrol the Somali coast. For every pirate attack that is repelled, and every pirate crew arrested and pirate ship destroyed, there are estimated to be hundreds more that continue to operate freely.

Somalia has had a piracy problem almost from the day that its last functioning government, that of President Siad Barre, was overthrown in 1991, beginning two decades of near anarchy. The inability of Somali authorities to control their own territory, including fishing seaport towns, gives criminal syndicates a haven to launch attacks on shipping lanes and to hold captured ships hostage for months. Ransoms for large cargo vessels can

Source: Scott Baldauf, "Commercial Ship Strikes Back in Deadly Shootout With Somali Pirates," *The Christian Science Monitor*, March 24, 2010.

range up to $4 million, a tidy profit for what is essentially the investment of a Somali small entrepreneur.

Pirates want to kidnap, not kill.

European Union Navy ships received a distress call from the MV Almezaan on Tuesday, and responded quickly. On arrival, the Spanish-flagged naval vessel ESPS Navarra found and captured one pirate mother-ship and two small skiffs that were apparently used during the attack on the Almezaan. Six suspected pirates were arrested. Bullet holes were found in one of the skiffs, along with the body of an apparent pirate. The private security company aboard the Almezaan, armed with small arms, was greatly outgunned by the pirates, who were discovered with AK-47s and rocket-propelled grenade launchers.

"Piracy itself is violent," says J. Peter Pham, director of the Africa Project at the National Committee on American Foreign Policy in New York City. "They are firing guns, and they are not missing intentionally. They're just bad shots."

Unlike pirates in the Strait of Malacca, who often kill the shipping crews and offload the goods at any number of container ports in Malaysia or Indonesia, the pirates of Somalia don't have the option of taking ships for the goods aboard. That's because there are no ports in Somalia—other than the government-controlled ports of Berbera and Mogadishu—where pirates can offload large shipping containers. So the only thing of value to the Somali pirates are the crews and the ships themselves.

"The pirates don't have an incentive to have dead sailors on their hands," says Mr. Pham, the piracy expert. "The only thing they have of value is the crew, to kidnap for ransom, and the ship itself. If the crew is dead, they lose."

5.9

'HEAD OFFICE HAS GONE MISSING'

Michael Valpy

The final selection in the chapter deals with the changing threat posed by al-Qaeda. Written from a Canadian perspective before the death of Osama bin Laden, the article describes how al-Qaeda can no longer directly manage global terrorism. Instead, although bin Laden remains a symbol of Islamic extremism, the terrorist network has divided and become ever more localized, a development that in some respects makes it more difficult to defend against. The author illustrates this localization by describing some of the differences in the manner in which several "local" al-Qaedas operate.

Source: Michael Valpy, "'Head Office Has Gone Missing,'" *The Globe and Mail,* January 9, 2010.

Global Terrorism

In December, 2001, Richard Reid—also known as Abdul Raheem—paid cash for a one-way airfare from Paris to Miami. He boarded American Airlines Flight 63 with the explosive PETN in his shoe, which he tried unsuccessfully to ignite until being subdued by fellow passengers.

That was then. Here is now: In December, 2009, Umar Farouk Abdulmutallab paid cash for a one-way airfare from Amsterdam to Detroit. He boarded Northwestern Airline Flight 253 with PETN sewn into his underpants, which he tried to ignite. Until he was subdued by fellow passengers.

What that says about the dreaded global terrorist organization al-Qaeda—which has claimed responsibility for the actions of both men—is a great deal.

It says there appears to be no learning curve. No brains in the executive suite calling the plays. No intelligence atop al-Qaeda's hierarchy comparable to the luminous planning behind the events of Sept. 11, 2001, or the well-orchestrated East Africa bombings in 1998. Indeed, many experts who've studied al-Qaeda believe that the whole metaphor of head office and branch plants is wrong.

"Head office has gone missing," says Janice Stein, director of University of Toronto's Munk Centre for International Studies.

And, paradoxically, that may speak to an even more dangerous foe confronted by U.S. President Barack Obama this week with his words of war: Instead of an enemy whose behaviours were relatively familiar, there are now a multitude of unpredictable and even unknown al-Qaedas.

The image of the organization that's been emblazoned in the media since 9/11 was that of a bureaucratically multilayered organization run by fiat by Osama bin Laden and his clever, highly educated, tactical and theological privy council headquartered in the mountainous badlands between Pakistan and Afghanistan.

It had its iron fingers of control on everything. It had a penchant for paperwork, budgets and titles. It had a shura, a war council. It had a finance committee, a religious committee, even a human-resources committee that monitored who was where in the hierarchy and the state of well-being and engagement of recruits.

Its word was law, and its singular voice of command spoke from every corner of its domain. And as far as anyone on the outside knew, that is how al-Qaeda worked.

In fact, information about it has been thin since its founding by Mr. bin Laden and a dozen or so others in 1988—a fact readily acknowledged by scholars. University of Toronto's Wesley Wark, a specialist in security issues, describes its operational dynamics as "mysteries."

Today—especially with the rise of a powerful faction in Yemen, making the country a sort of third global front after Pakistan-Afghanistan and Iraq in the war against al-Qaeda—its structure is the subject of heated debate.

Most, although not all, terrorism experts believe that there is now no al-Qaeda "central," the pre-9/11 organization. The bin Laden cadre has been isolated militarily and many of its original leaders have been killed or captured.

What has replaced the pre-9/11 structure is an al-Qaeda brand, a spreading syndicate of autonomous al-Qaeda franchises and affiliates and a stunningly powerful media unit (as-Sahab, "The Clouds") creating high-quality documentary films, iPod files, cellphone videos and websites—a six-fold production output since 2005, all of it aimed at radicalizing young Muslims.

The autonomous franchises and affiliates can be found in Iraq (al-Qaeda in Mesopotamia), Yemen and Saudi Arabia (al-Qaeda in the Arabian Peninsula), North Africa (al-Qaeda in the Islamic Maghreb), Somalia (the affiliated al-Shabaab), Indonesia (Jemaah Islamiyah), Sudan, Egypt, Turkey and South Asia as well as Pakistan-Afghanistan and elsewhere.

They are not linked by shura—or by anything else operationally. In a world of cell-phones, satellite phones, e-mail and Skype, all of which can be monitored by high-tech snoopers, communication between Mr. bin Laden's inner circle and the rest of al-Qaeda—when it takes place—is mainly reliant on couriers, a means as old as humanity's two legs.

Mokhtar Lamani, a research fellow at the Centre for International Governance Innovation in Waterloo, Ont., and a former Moroccan diplomat and senior officer with the League of Arab States, says that as far as anyone knows, franchise operational decisions are completely local, exemplified by the Yemini assignment handed out to Mr. Abdulmutallab.

There is no hint of prior consultation with the bin Laden circle or the other dominions. In the Abdulmutallab case, the nature of the operation was the main tie-in to the al-Qaeda brand: an attack against the "Far Enemy," the United States, and a readiness to incur mass casualties, by blowing up an airliner.

Yet at the same time, operational techniques vary.

If you're kidnapped by al-Qaeda in Iraq, said Mr. Lamani, the likelihood is you'll be killed without even a claim of responsibility being made for your death. If you're kidnapped by al-Qaeda in the Maghreb—like Canadian diplomats Robert Fowler and Louis Guay—the likelihood is greater that your release will be negotiated for a ransom.

Why? It may be because the cultures are different, possibly because al-Qaeda in the Maghreb—or, more accurately, its predecessor, the Salafist Group for Preaching and Combat—was founded in 1998 by Hassan Hattab, a former Armed Islamic Group regional commander who broke with the group in 1998 in protest against its slaughter of civilians. In contrast, al-Qaeda in Iraq has been notorious for ruthless tactics since the onset of its presence in the Iraqi insurgency.

But whereas the operational reach and effectiveness of al-Qaeda in Iraq and Pakistan is currently seen as limited, the operational capability of al-Qaeda in the Maghreb is "scary," says Prof. Max Taylor, director of the Centre for the Study of Terrorism and Political Violence at Scotland's St. Andrew's University.

It can do long-range reconnaissance and logistics and move around at ease, and plan an operation in Morocco that can be executed in Mali. No other al-Qaeda franchise has that capability. No one for sure knows why. No one for certain knows how numerically strong it is. It could be like al-Qaeda in Yemen—"which has either 50 or hundreds of members," said Prof. Taylor.

Over and over, that same answer comes up: No one knows.

For now, says the University of Toronto's Prof. Wark, the ideological bonds that bind al-Qaeda are tight—a cohesiveness wrought by a consistent fundamentalist ideology: the objective of re-establishing the Islamist caliphate as the religious and political authority over all the peoples of the Muslim world and purifying it from Western, mainly American, contamination.

But that's hardly a complex theology needing centralized doctrinal control comparable, say, to Roman Catholicism's muscular Vatican vigilance. It's simple religious fundamentalism for simple folk.

By far the most significant bond, the essential glue that's made al-Qaeda the world's first global transnational terrorist organization, is the work of as-Sahab and the use of the Internet and other media for propaganda, proselytizing, for spreading the inspirational words and images of Osama bin Laden.

It is why fear of al-Qaeda remains, despite the demise of any clean, recognizable structure of hierarchy, such as that which characterized the Irish Republican Army. What's replaced it is dark anarchy without identity or borders.

It's those incredibly sophisticated media vehicles—Internet-posted or couriered out of Pakistan's wild country—that entice a seemingly endless stream of global wannabe jihadists into making a compact with violence. It is why the Americans keep hunting for Mr. bin Laden even though his hands no longer appear on the levers of operational power.

His idol power on the Internet and on television, his ability to ignite so-called homegrown radicalization, makes him a continuing threat.

It's a virtual seduction of young minds that scholars understand only imperfectly, says Dr. Taylor—a complex menu of ideology, religion, hero-worship and the serpentine attraction of the forbidden and appealing. Dr. Taylor, a psychologist, suggests the dynamic has parallels to images of child sexual abuse on the Internet: dangerous, doubtful, taboo and therefore enticing.

It is this threat that President Obama has declared war on—and it is this threat, says Dr. Taylor, that social scientists have far too little knowledge about how to combat.

* * * * * *

Many Faces of al-Qaeda

Al-Qaeda in the Arabian Peninsula

Formed in January 2009 by a merger between al-Qaeda in Saudi Arabia and Yemen, it's now based in eastern Yemen. It aims to topple the Saudi monarchy and Yemeni government. Prominent attacks include the Riyadh bombings in 2003 and a 2008 attack on the U.S. embassy in Yemen.

Al-Qaeda in the Islamic Maghreb

Based in Algeria, it emerged in early 2007 and is notorious for bombing government targets and kidnapping Westerners (including Canadians Robert Fowler and Louis Guay).

Harakat al-Shabaab Mujahideen

Spread across pockets of Somalia, its members enforce harsh interpretation of Islamic law in areas of their control. Most of their attacks are aimed at warlords, African Union peacekeepers and Somali government soldiers.

Al-Qaeda in Iraq

Aiming to push foreign troops out of Iraq and replace the U.S.-backed Iraqi government with Islamic rule, the Iraqi arm of al-Qaeda comprises various extremist groups that opposed the American invasion.

Jemaah Islamiyah

The Indonesian-based arm of al-Qaeda, its most notorious strike was the Bali nightclub bombings of 2002. With links to militants in Malaysia and the Philippines, it aims to bring Islamic rule to a broad swath of Asia.

Chapter 6

CULTURAL GLOBALIZATION

One of the most important features of globalization is the spread of norms, values, meanings, and ideas more generally. Technology, notably the Internet and the mobile phone, has been especially powerful in this regard. Information and communication technologies have not simply reduced the significance of geographic distance but have eroded the capacity of states and other political or social institutions to filter or block the transnational flow of ideas, while narrowing the divide between the elites and the masses in terms of access to ideas and information. The culture of "modernity," for example, now is transmitted across boundaries and class lines and includes the spread of neoliberal ideas about what individual qualities are needed in a globalizing world. Other frequently noted attributes of global culture include secularism, democracy, consumerism, human rights, and pornography. The spread of such values has at once inspired educated young people, especially middle-class professionals, to demand a voice in politics, while simultaneously stirring a backlash among local elites whose status is being undermined and among those who fear that traditional values and national identity are under attack. Thus, the spread of ideas via the technologies of globalization has played a significant role in spreading unrest throughout the Arabic Middle East and North Africa, even while China's government erects high-tech impediments to the free use of the Internet and Muslim fundamentalists like Afghanistan's Taliban react, sometimes violently, to the resulting secularism, women's rights, and democratic aspirations.

6.1

GLOBALISATION AND CULTURE: THREE PARADIGMS

Jan Nederveen Pieterse

We introduce the chapter with an essay by the sociologist Jan Nederveen Pieterse, in which he compares three paradigms or models of cultural dynamics in a globalized world. The first was that propounded by the Harvard

Source: Excerpted from Jan Nederveen Pieterse, "Globalisation and Culture: Three Paradigms," *Economic and Political Weekly* 31:23 (June 8, 1996), 1389–93. Notes appearing in the original have been deleted.

political scientist Samuel Huntington. In a controversial article titled "The Clash of Civilizations?", Huntington described a paradigm of world politics in which the principal patterns of conflict and cooperation were shaped by culture and, ultimately, by civilizations. He argued that the civilizations that would determine the future of global politics were the "Western, Confucian, Japanese, Islamic, Hindu, Slavic-Orthodox, Latin American, and possibly African." For Huntington, the clash among civilizations is a historic development. Previously, the history of the international system had been about the struggle among states within Western civilization. The end of the Cold War, in his view, began a new era involving the relative decline of the West, the rise of Asia, a resurgence of Islam, and an expansion of transnational flows of ideas and people. In Huntington's paradigm, culture is anchored in territory and migration produces conflict. Pieterse regards this first paradigm as simply a continuation of Cold War politics.

A second paradigm he terms "McDonaldization"—the spread of a single dominant culture based on individualism, secularism, democracy, and free market economics that results in cultural convergence. Pieterse believes that it takes inadequate account of the local. McDonaldization assumes cultural homogenization owing to diffusion from a dominant Western or American culture.

Pieterse prefers a third model, "hybridization," that sees a mixing of cultural elements that resolves the tension between the local and the global. Cultural complexity results owing to the exchange of ideas and styles in cyberspace and in the course of travel and migration and the creation of diasporas. Cultural mixing erodes nationalism because it relies on border crossing and subverts claims to cultural purity and authenticity because it starts out from the fuzziness of boundaries.

Each paradigm views globalization differently. "Clash of civilizations" regards globalization as a surface phenomenon. Instead, the real dynamic is the formation of regional blocs, which reflect civilizations. As a result, globalization produces interregional rivalry. McDonaldization equates globalization with the triumph of a hegemonic culture. In contrast, hybridization is an open-ended consequence of globalization that reflects Easternization as well as Westernization and the simultaneous presence of globalizing and localizing elements.

Globalisation or the trend of growing worldwide interconnectedness is presently accompanied by several coinciding and clashing notions of cultural change. A growing sensitivity to cultural difference coincides with an awareness of the world 'becoming smaller' and the idea of cultural difference receding. . . . Modernisation has been advancing like a steamroller denying and erasing cultural differences in its way and now not only the gains (rationalisation, standardisation, control) but also the losses (alienation, displacement, disenchantment) are becoming apparent. Stamping out cultural variety has been a form of 'disenchantment of the world.'

It is interesting to note how the notion of cultural difference itself has changed form. It used to take the form of national differences, as in the familiar discussions of national character. Now different forms of difference have come to the foreground, for instance in relation to identity politics, gender, minorities rights, indigenous peoples, and ethnic and religious movements. A recent argument is that we are presently experiencing a 'clash of civilisations.' In this thesis cultural difference is regarded as immutable and generating rivalry and conflict. At the same time there is a widespread understanding that growing global interdependence and interconnectedness may lead toward increasing cultural standardisation and uniformisation, as in the global sweep of consumerism. A shorthand version of this momentum is 'McDonaldisation.' A third position, altogether different from both these models of intercultural relations, is that what is taking place is a process of translocal cultural mixing or hybridisation.

Cultural differentialism or lasting difference, cultural convergence or growing sameness, cultural hybridisation or ongoing mixing: while these are not the only perspectives on intercultural relations it is probably fair to say that they are the main ones. Each of these positions involves particular theoretical precepts and as such they are paradigms. Each represents a particular politics of difference—as lasting and immutable; as erasable and being erased; and as mixing and in the process generating new, translocal forms of difference. Each involves different subjectivities and larger perspectives. The first two, civilisational clash and McDonaldisation, may be considered forms of modernism, respectively in its Romantic and Enlightenment versions, while hybridisation refers to a postmodern sensibility of travelling culture. I will discuss the claims of these three perspectives, their wider theoretical implications, and ask what kind of futures they evoke.

Clash of Civilisations

In 1993 Samuel Huntington, as president of the Institute for Strategic Studies at Harvard University, published a controversial paper in which he argued that a crucial, indeed a central, aspect of what global politics is likely to be in the coming years . . . will be the clash of civilizations . . . With the end of the cold war, international politics moves out of its Western phase, and its centre piece becomes the interaction between the West and non-Western civilisations and among non-Western civilisations.

The imagery is that of civilisational spheres as tectonic plates at whose fault lines conflict, no longer subsumed under ideology, is increasingly likely. The fault lines include Islam's borders in Europe (as in former Yugoslavia), Africa (animist or Christian cultures to the south and west), Asia (India, China). The argument centres on Islam: the "centuries-old military interaction between the West and Islam is unlikely to decline." "Islam has bloody borders." Huntington warns against a "Confucian-Islamic military connection" that has come into being in the form of arms flows between east Asia and west Asia. Thus "the paramount axis of world politics will be the relations between 'the West and the Rest'" and "a central focus of conflict for the immediate future will be between the West and several Islamic-Confucian states." He therefore recommends greater cooperation and unity in the West, particularly between Europe and North America; the inclusion of eastern Europe and Latin America in the west; co-operative relations with

Russia and Japan; exploiting differences and conflicts among Confucian and Islamic states; and for the west to maintain its economic and military power so as to protect its interests.

The principle of dividing the world into civilisational spheres has a long lineage. Toynbee adopted this approach in his world history. . . . It is the blatant admixture of security interests with a crude rendition of civilisational difference that makes Huntington's position stand out for its demagogic character. Obviously it belongs to the genre of 'new enemy' discourse. In fact it merges two existing enemy discourses, the 'fundamentalist threat' of Islam and the 'yellow peril,' and its novelty lies in combining them.

It recycles the cold war: "The fault lines between civilisations are replacing the political and ideological boundaries of the cold war as the flash points for crisis and bloodshed." "The Velvet Curtain of culture has replaced the Iron Curtain of ideology as the most significant dividing line in Europe." Hence there will be no 'peace dividend.' The cold war is over but war is everlasting. This has rightly been referred to as a new politics of containment. More precisely, it refers to a new round of intercore rivalry which is now translated from an ideological into a civilisational idiom.

Huntington constructs the west as a 'universal civilisation,' "directly at odds with the particularism of most Asian societies and their emphasis on what distinguishes one people from another." The charge against 'the Rest' is that they attempt modernization without westernisation. This may be what constitutes the actual danger: the spectre of different modernities. Japan does not quite belong here since it occupies a unique position "as an associate member of the west". . . .

What is overlooked in this geopolitical construction are the dialectics of the cold war and the role the US has been playing in these relations. It is not so much a matter of civilisational conflict as the unravelling of geopolitical security games most of which have been initiated by the US in the first place and which the hegemon in its latter days can no longer control, so that it calls on 'allied states' to help channel them in a desirable direction. At the turn of the century the British Empire in its latter days of waning economic and military power did the same, calling on the US to 'police' the Pacific, the Caribbean and Latin America, on Japan to play a military and naval role in the China Sea and to contain the Russian empire, and seeking allies in the European concert of powers. Then as now the waning hegemon calls on 'civilisational' affinities: the White Man's Burden and his civilising mission, and now 'democracy' and the virtues of the free market, also known as the Free World. . . .

This shows up the oddity of Huntington's view: it is a political perspective on culture, phrased in the standardised national security language. Culture is politicised, bound in civilisational packages, which happen to coincide with geopolitical entities. Obviously there is much slippage along the way, and all along one wonders: what is national security doctrine doing in a world of globalisation and in the sphere of cultural practices?

Indeed the most remarkable element of the thesis is its surface claim, of a clash of civilisations. Why is culture being presented as the new fault line of conflict? Huntington's framework is a fine specimen of what he blames Asian societies for: "their emphasis on what distinguishes one people from another." At a general level this involves a particular kind of reading of culture. Compare Wallerstein on "culture as the ideological battle-ground of the modern world-system," note that culture and ideology are being merged in a single perspective, and that culture is defined as 'the set of characteristics which distinguish one group from another.' Anthony King uses a similar concept of culture as "collective articulations of human diversity."

If we would take this to its ultimate consequence then, for instance, bilingualism would not be 'cultural' because "it does not distinguish one group from another." Indeed any bicultural, multicultural or intercultural practices could not, according to this defini-tion, be 'cultural.' Whichever mode of communication or intercourse different groups would develop to interact with one another would not be 'cultural' for culture only refers to intergroup diversity. We have thus defined any form of intergroup or transnational culture out of existence for such per definition could not exist. Inter-cultural diffusion through trade and migration, returnees from abroad with bicultural experience, children of mixed parentage, travelers with multicultural experience, professionals interacting cross-culturally, the fields of cyberspace—all of these fall outside 'culture.' . . .

This is in fact an anomalous definition of culture. More common a definition in anthropology is that culture refers to behaviour and beliefs that are learned and shared: learned so that it is not 'instinctual,' shared so that it is not individual. The sharing refers to social sharing but there is no limitation as to the nature of this sociality. No territorial or historical boundaries are implied as part of the definition. This understanding of cul-ture is open-ended. Learning is always ongoing as a function of changing circumstances, therefore culture is always open. To sharing there are no fixed boundaries other than those of common social experience, therefore there are no territorial limitations to cul-ture. Accordingly culture refers as much to commonality as to diversity. I have referred to these fundamentally different notions of culture as territorial culture and translocal culture. That such an open definition of culture is relevant to international relations is apparent in a recent collection which adopts as a working definition of culture 'any interpersonal shared system of meanings, perceptions and values.'

Cultural relativism represents an angle on culture that may be characterised as cultur-alist differentialism. Its lineage goes back to the Romantics such as Herder who regarded language as the key to nationhood. Both nationalism and racism bear the stamp of cul-tural differentialism, one emphasising territory and language, and the other biology as destiny. Nation and race have long been tandem and at times indistinguishable dis-courses. During the era of nationalism, cultural distinction for one's own nation and inferiority for others has been claimed by all nations, usually in racial terms. 'Jewishness' 'Germanness' 'Japaneseness,' 'Englishness,' 'Turkishness,' 'Greekness,' etc—all imply an inward-looking take on culture and identity. They all share the problem of boundaries: who belongs and who does not, just where is the borderline? They are 'creation myths' of modem times.

A different, affirmative dimension of cultural differentialism is that it can serve as a position in defence of cultural diversity. This tends to be evoked by local groups resisting the steamroller of assorted 'developers,' by anthropologists, by ecological networks as well as tourist agencies promoting local authenticity. 'Culture and development' is a growing trend in development discourse. It calls to mind the familiar theme of the 'human mosaic.' The upside of this perspective is local empowerment, the downside may be a politics of nostalgia, a conservationist posture that ultimately leads to the promotion of open-air museums. Either way the fallacy is that of the reification of the local, sidelining the interplay between the local and the global. The imagery of the 'mosaic' is biased in the first place . . . because a mosaic consists of discrete pieces whereas human experience, claims and postures notwithstanding, is open-ended. Accordingly what has been on the rise in critical anthropology are de-territorialised notions such as cultural flows and 'travelling culture.'

Huntington's thesis is at odds with the usual self-understanding of east and south-East Asian societies which is that of east-west fusion—as in 'western technology, eastern values.' The Confucian ethic hypothesis does carry overtones of east Asian chauvinism, but it too represents an east-west nexus of a kind because the form of Confucianism it refers to owes its status to its interpretation as an 'Asian Protestant ethic.' Confucianism used to figure as a reason why east Asian countries were stagnating, while in the late-20th century it is presented as the reason why the 'Tigers' have been progressing. In the process Confucianism has been reinterpreted, recoded. Part of this recoding owes to a cross-cultural translation of the Weberian thesis of the Protestant ethic as the 'spirit of modern capitalism.' The Confucian hypothesis carries some weight in the 'Sinic' circle of Singapore, Taiwan, China, Korea. It carries less weight in Japan. It carries no weight among precisely those who advocate an 'Asian way' such as prime minister Mahathir Mohamad of Malaysia and his 'Look East' programme. Given the tensions between the ethnic Chinese and the 'bumiputra' Malays in Malaysia, just as in Indonesia, here an Islamic-Confucian alliance is indeed the least likely of all options.

While Huntington reproduces standard enemy images of 'the rest' he also rehearses a standard self-image of the west. 'The West' is a notion conditioned by and emerging from two historical polarities: the north-south polarity of imperialism and the colonising and colonised world; and the east-west polarity of capitalism-communism and the cold war. These were such overriding fields of tension that differences within the west/north, among imperialist countries and within capitalism faded into the background, subsided in relation to the bigger issue, i.e., the seeming, but to a considerable extent effective, unity of imperialist or neo-colonial countries and of the 'free world' led by the US. In view of this expansionist history we may well turn the tables and say: the west has bloody borders. . . .

In his usual capacity as comparative political scientist Huntington observes a worldwide 'third wave' of democratisation. Apparently at this level of discourse civilisational differences are receding. In this mode Huntington adheres to the familiar thesis of convergence, i.e., the usual modernisation paradigm of growing worldwide standardisation around the model of the 'most advanced country.' His position matches Fukuyama's argument of the universal triumph of the idea of liberal democracy.

McDonaldisation

The McDonaldisation thesis is a version of the idea of the worldwide homogenisation of cultures through the impact of multi-national corporations. McDonaldisation, according to George Ritzer, is "the process whereby the principles of the fast-food restaurant are coming to dominate more and more sectors of American society as well as the rest of the world." The expression 'the rest of the world' bears contemplating. The process through which this takes place is . . . through formal rationality laid down in rules and regulations. McDonald's formula is successful because it is efficient (rapid service), calculable (fast and inexpensive), predictable (no surprises), and controls labour and customers.

McDonaldisation is a variation on a theme. First, on the theme of modernisation. An instance of the global spread of capitalist culture. Since the 1950s this has been held to take the form of Americanisation. Since the 1960s multinational corporations have been viewed as harbingers of American modernisation. It is also a variation on the theme of cultural imperialism. In the 1970s in Latin America this was known as Coca-colonisation.

Modernisation and Americanisation are the latest versions of westernisation. If Colonialism delivered westernisation neo-colonialism under US hegemony delivers Americanisation. Common to both is the modernisation thesis, of which Marx and Weber have been the most influential proponents. Marx's thesis was the worldwide spread of capitalism. World-system theory is the latest version of this perspective. With Weber the emphasis is on rationalisation, in the form of bureaucratisation and other rational social technologies. Both perspectives fall within the general framework of 19th century evolutionism, or the idea of a single-track universal process of evolution through which all societies, some faster than others, are progressing. A vision of universal progress such as befits an imperial world.

Shannon Peters Talbott examines the McDonaldisation thesis through an ethnography of the fast food formula in the case of McDonald's in Moscow and finds the argument highly inaccurate on every score. Instead of efficiency, queueing (up to several hours) and lingering are commonplace. Instead of being inexpensive an average McDonald's meal costs more than one-third of a Russian worker's average daily wage. Instead of predictability, it is difference and uniqueness that attract Russian customers while many standard menu items are not served in Moscow. Instead of uniform corporate control, McDonald's Moscow introduces variations in labour control ('extra fun motivations,' fast service competitions, special hours for workers to bring their families to eat in the restaurant) and in customer control by allowing customers to linger—often for more than an hour on a cup of tea, to 'soak up the atmosphere.'

She concludes that the introduction of McDonald's in Moscow does not represent cultural homogenisation but should rather be understood along the lines of global localisation: corporations, also when they seek to represent 'world products,' only succeed if and to the extent that they adapt themselves to local cultures and markets. This principle is also known as 'insiderisation,' for which Sony chairman Akio Morita coined the phrase 'glocalisation,' or 'looking in both directions.'

So far, this only considers the angle of the corporation. The other side of global localisation is the attitude of customers. The McDonald's Moscow experience compares with adaptations of American fast food principles elsewhere, for instance in China, south-east Asia, India. Here fast food restaurants, though outwardly the same as their American models, serve quite different tastes and needs. They are not downmarket junkfood but cater to middle class tastes, they are sought out for their 'modern' aesthetics, are appreciated for food variation rather than uniformity, and generate 'mixed' offspring, such as 'Chinglish' or 'Chamerican' restaurants in China. They offer a public space, a meeting place—in one sense culturally neutral on account of its novelty—for new types of consumers, such as the consumer market of the young, working women and middle class families. They function in similar ways in southern Europe and the west Asia. In wintry Tokyo, upstairs in Wendy's, young students spend hours—doing their home-work, smoking and chatting with friends.

Thus rather than cultural homogenisation McDonald's and others in the family of western fast food restaurants (Burger King, KFC, Pizza Hut, Wendy's, Wimpy) usher in difference, variety, giving rise to and reflecting new, mixed social forms. Where they are imported they serve different social, cultural and economic functions than in their place of origin, and their formula accordingly tends to be adapted to local conditions. In Manhattan, London and other western metropolises we now see oriental fast food restaurants and chains. Considered more closely, the fast food format might have origi-nated outside the west. . . . American fast food restaurants serve German food (ham-burgers, frankfurters) with French (French fries, dressing) and Italian (pizza) elements in American style. The American contribution, besides ketchup, may be mainly assem-bly-line mechanisation and standardization. . . . Thus it would be more appropriate to consider McDonaldisation as a form of intercultural hybridisation, partly in its origins and certainly in its present globally localising variety of forms.

Hybridisation

This perspective differs fundamentally from the previous two paradigms. It does not build on an older theorem but opens a new avenue. It springs from the taboo zone of racism because it refers to that which the doctrines of racial purity and integrism could not even bear to acknowledge the existence of: the half-caste, mixed-breed, metis. If it was acknowledged at all it was in diabolical terms. Nineteenth century race thinking abhorred mixing because, according to Comte de Gobineau and many others, in any mixture the 'lower' element would predominate. It goes against all the doctrines of purity as strength and sanctity, ancient and classical, of which 'race science' and racism have been modern, biologised versions.

Hybridisation offers an antidote to the cultural differentialism of racial and national-ist doctrines because it takes as its point of departure precisely those experiences that have been banished, marginalised, tabooed in cultural differentialism. It subverts nationalism because it privileges border crossing. It subverts identity politics such as ethnicity or other claims to purity and authenticity because it starts out from the fuzzi-ness of boundaries, from boundary crossing. If modernity stands for an ethos of order, the neat separation by tight boundaries, hybridisation reflects a postmodern sensibility cut'n'mix, transgression, subversion. . . .

Related notions are global ecumene, global localisation and local globalization. . . .

Hybridisation occurs of course also among cultural elements and spheres within soci-eties. In Japan, "grandmothers in kimonos bow in gratitude to their automated banking machines. Young couples bring hand-held computer games along for romantic evenings out." Is the hybridisation of cultural styles then typically an urban phenomenon, a consequence of urbanisation and industrialisation? If we would look into the countryside virtually anywhere in the world we would also find traces of cultural mixing: the crops planted, planting methods and agricultural techniques, implements and inputs used (seeds, fertiliser, irrigation methods, credit) are usually of translocal origin. Besides farmers and peasants throughout the world are wired, directly or indirectly, to the fluctuations of global commodity prices which affect their economies and decision-making. The ecologies of agriculture are local, the cultural resources are translocal.

An interesting objection that can be made to the hybridisation argument is that what is actually being mixed is cultural languages rather than cultural grammars. The distinction runs between surface and deep-seated elements of culture. It is, then, the folkloric, superficial elements of culture—foods, costumes, fashions, consumption habits, arts and crafts, entertainments, healing methods—that 'travel' while deeper attitudes and values, the way elements hang together, the structural ensemble of culture, remain contextually bound. There are several implications to this argument. It would imply that contemporary 'planetarisation' is a surface phenomenon only because 'deep down' humanity remains divided in historically formed cultural clusters. Does this also imply that the new social technologies of translocal communication—from transport to electronic media— are surface phenomena only that do not affect deep-seated attitudes? If so, the implications would be profoundly conservative. A mid-way position may be that probably the new social technologies are profound in themselves while at the same time each historically framed culture provides its own 'take' on the new space of commonality.

Another issue is that of immigrant and settler societies where, over time, intermingling itself represents a historical momentum, profound enough to engage cultural grammar and not merely language. The prime example is North America. Probably part of the profound and peculiar appeal of American popular culture is precisely its mixed and 'traveling' character, its 'foot-loose' lightness, unhinged from the feudal past. This is a culture where the grammars of multiple cultures mix and this intercultural density may constitute part of the subliminal attraction of American popular media, music, film, television: the encounter, and often enough the clash, but an intimate clash, of ethnicities, cultures, histories. In other words, it is the clash and intermingling of cultural grammars that makes up the deeply human appeal of American narratives.

Intercultural mingling itself is a deeply creative process and indeed not only at the present phase of accelerated globalisation but far back in time. This is acknowledged by one of the proponents of the cultural homogenisation thesis, Hamelink, who notes: "the richest cultural traditions emerged at the actual meeting point of markedly different cultures, such as Sudan, Athens, the Indus Valley, and Mexico". . . .

Futures

The futures evoked by these three paradigms are dramatically different. McDonaldisation evokes both a triumphalist Americanism and a gloomy picture of a global 'iron cage.' The clash of civilisations likewise offers the horizon of a world of iron: a deeply pessimistic politics of cultural difference as a curse which dooms humanity to lasting conflict and rivalry. The human dialogue as a dialogue of war, the global ecumene as a battlefield. Benjamin Barber's book Jihad vs McWorld discusses the clash between these two perspectives without giving a sense of the third option, mixing. Hybridisation is open-ended in terms of experience as well as in a theoretical sense. Its newness means that the ramifications over time are not predictable because it does not fit an existing matrix or established paradigm but itself signifies paradigm shift.

Each paradigm represents a different politics of multiculturalism. Cultural differentialism translates into a policy of closure and apartheid. If outsiders are let in at all they are preferably kept at arm's length in ghettoes, concentration zones or reservations. Cultural communities are best kept separate, as in colonial 'plural society' in which communities are not supposed to not mix except in the market-place. Cultural convergence translates into a politics of assimilation. Cultural mixing refers to a politics of integration without the need to give up identity, while cohabitation is expected to result in new crosscultural patterns of difference.

In the end it turns out that the two coinciding and clashing trends noted at the beginning, growing awareness of cultural difference and globalisation, are not simply contradictory but interdependent. Growing awareness of cultural difference is a function of globalisation. Increasing crosscultural communication, mobility, migration, trade, investment, tourism, all generate awareness of cultural difference. The other side of the politics of difference is that the very striving for recognition implies a claim to equality, equal rights, same treatment: in other words, a common universe of difference. Accordingly the clash between cultural diversity and globalisation may well be considered a creative clash.

6.2

'WOULD YOU LIKE FRIES WITH YOUR JIHAD?'

Stephen Humphries

> The second selection is a review of Thomas Friedman's influential book praising globalization, in which he describes the relationship between what is global ("the lexus") and what is local and traditional ("the olive tree"). The review takes special note of Friedman's emphasis on technology and its implications for spreading a globalized culture.

THE LEXUS AND THE OLIVE TREE: UNDERSTANDING GLOBALIZATION By Thomas Friedman (Farrar, Straus & Giroux), 394 pp., $ 27.50

Source: Stephen Humphries, "'Would You Like Fries With Your Jihad?'" *The Christian Science Monitor*, April 29, 1999.

The buzz term "global village" has been bandied about a lot in the '90s, but no one gives a better explanation of this radical concept than *New York Times* correspondent Thomas Friedman.

In "The Lexus and the Olive Tree," Friedman observes, "We understand as much about how today's system of globalization is going to work as we understood about how the Cold War system was going to work in 1946."

Globalization began with the tearing down of the Berlin Wall, a fittingly symbolic event to herald in an age when old barriers—both economic and cultural—are being systematically dismantled by gigantic leaps in information technology. The author's primer on how this technology has raised living standards worldwide is required reading for anyone who still thinks of the Internet as little more than a gimmick for computer nerds.

The borderless Internet has begun to usurp traditional entry barriers to all sorts of markets. It has also helped to democratize capital investment, swelling the number of investors to include a vast swath of citizenry of every demographic description. In one of his many telling examples, Friedman describes a bare-footed Bangkok cigarette vender watching the stock market to see how her investments are performing. The competition for these increasingly liquid funds not only among nearby geographic neighbors, but also countries on distant continents, has placed each country's economic policies under scrutiny by this "electronic herd."

Contrary to the efforts of central planners, every nation is being forced to don the free market "golden straitjacket" to avoid "trampling by the herd." But, to use the author's analogy, some nations have chosen to wear a looser fitting straitjacket with the costly padding of social-welfare systems.

The worldwide spread of American commodities and highly visible products, such as McDonald's or Hollywood icons, has in effect given globalization an American face. Many people (especially older generations) have viewed America's success with a mixture of envy and suspicion—perceiving that their cultures are under threat. The author is quick to observe that, even though the globalization train has no driver, America has been scapegoated for these accelerated and irreversible changes. Friedman hopes that globalization doesn't lead to a wholesale Americanization of the globe at the expense of other cultures. However, like Nobel Prize-winning economist Friedrich Hayek, he realizes that cultures, social orders, and traditions draw from one another in a competitive, spontaneous, and undesigned process. In Friedman's words, "As with species, cultures spawning, evolving and dying is part of evolution.". . .

Friedman's years of extensive globe trotting and his reporter's eye for a good story enable him to draw upon a rich array of fascinating characters and highly readable anecdotal experiences to illustrate his worldview.

We meet the son of a PLO terrorist who leads an entrepreneurial lifestyle; a Brazilian lumberjack who is just beginning to understand the impact conservation policies will have on his community's economy; and a veiled Muslim woman who runs an Internet cafe in Kuwait City. We get to listen in to the campaign pledges of more technology from a candidate for village chief in a remote China hamlet where there is only one telephone.

The author also describes a half-comical incident in which fearsome gun-toting muggers in a Mexican taxi suddenly implore Friedman not to report the incident in his newspaper because it might dent Mexico's national pride. More so than ever, no man, woman, or nation is an island.

Ultimately, Friedman deftly accomplishes the impressive task of encapsulating the complex economic, cultural, and environmental challenges of globalization with the sort of hindsight that future historians will bring to bear upon the subject.

6.3

JUST HOW GLOBAL ARE SOUTH KOREANS?

Luz T. Suplico

> Has South Korea become globalized? The following selection examines that question. It suggests that Korean nationalism and globalization do not contradict each other and that the country has consciously sought to globalize since the 1990s, especially for economic reasons. It then reports on a poll of Korean university students that showed that they welcomed both economic and cultural globalization, that Koreans were becoming world travelers, and that they enjoyed the infusion of cultural imports. Not surprisingly, young people were the most eager to embrace elements of cultural globalization.

Have you ever noticed a group of young teenagers, in Nike or North Face tracksuits, watching breaking news on a laptop? This scene takes place in Starbucks cafes in Tokyo, New York, London, Zurich, Toronto—and Seoul. Young Koreans are now embracing the world's largest coffee retailer, which has been labeled as the new symbol of globalization. Starbucks is not the only brand enjoying brisk sales: luxury lines like Louis Vuitton, Gucci, Rolex, Fendi and Ferragamo became exceeding popular with Koreans in 2007.

Does acceptance of international products show that Koreans are becoming global? Ranked the 29th most global economy out of 62 countries in 2006 by the A.T. Kearney Globalization Index, Koreans' affinity to fashionable global brands is most visible in young, 20-something shoppers.

However, an AC Nielsen global online survey on consumer attitudes toward globalization showed that one-fifth of Koreans did not agree that global companies allow consumers to gain access to the same quality of goods and services available to anyone else in the world. This validates a Pew Research Center report on global attitudes that showed that only 54 percent of Koreans think that foreign companies have a positive

Source: Luz T. Suplico, "Just How Global Are South Koreans?" *The Korea Herald,* April 30, 2008.

impact on their country. This attitude reflects a concern that globalization may threaten the viability of Korean-made products.

Gi-Wook Shin, a sociology professor at Stanford University and author of an article titled "The Paradox of Korean Globalization," stressed that Koreans' strong nationalist tendencies do not contradict globalization. On the contrary, this nationalism is a strong feature of Korean globalization. According to Shin, Koreans view globalization as a means to achieve a competitive edge for the nation. As an example, Shin cites the Korean attitude toward the English language. He pointed out that Koreans would support making English their second official language since it could enhance their national interests but they would not support it as an official language replacing Korean. Further, Shin noted that nationalism and globalization could coexist in Korea.

The Korean government adopted a "segyehwa," or globalization, policy in late 1994. As part of segyehwa, the government encouraged greater competition, privatization, and deregulation within the booming Korean economy. To develop a competent workforce able to think and work globally, the government has recently announced that it may shorten the length of compulsory military duty for young men who volunteer for foreign-aid services.

To gain an empirical basis of Korean attitudes toward globalization, the author conducted a study involving college students. In this study, attitudes toward globalization were classified into two major groups: 1) attitudes toward economic globalization; and 2) attitudes toward cultural globalization. Economic globalization referred to the trade, investment and labor flows that integrated countries into the world economy. On the other hand, cultural globalization referred to the continuous flow of ideas, information, commitment and values across the world, mediated via mobile individuals, symbols and electronic simulations.

Attempts to measure attitudes on economic globalization included questions on the effect of globalization on standards of living, the local economy and the world economy. There were also questions on whether South Korea should promote international trade, foreign investments, World Trade Organization membership and restrictions on imports. Attempts to measure cultural globalization included questions on foreign travel, news media, foreign stores and foreign popular culture. The survey instrument, which used a five-point Likert scale, used questions from the U.S.-based Program on International Policy Attitudes study.

The study's results showed that the respondents held favorable attitudes toward both economic and cultural globalization. In terms of economic globalization, they were most enthusiastic about their belief that globalization is good for the economy and that Korea should promote international trade. This is justifiable since the local economy relies heavily on foreign trade. Authors York Bradshaw, Young-Jeong Kim and Bruce London, who wrote a study titled "Transnational Economic Linkages, the State and Dependent Development in South Korea," describe the South Korean economy as a form of "dependent development" which relies heavily on international trade, especially exports, a strong national state, and local business. They argued that this contrasts with Latin American dependent development, which places a heavy emphasis on direct foreign investment.

The respondents were most fearful about the effects of globalization on the environment. In this regard, male and female respondents demonstrated statistically significant attitudes: Women were more cautious about the effects of globalization on the environment than their male counterparts. This finding validates previous studies that show that women tend to be less enthusiastic toward globalization than do men. It has been observed that globalization may reinforce gender inequality especially in times of economic downturn, because women are the first to be laid off in a global economy.

The 1997 financial crisis led some local firms to close their operations. While both men and women were laid off, the women were encouraged to resign first since they had husbands, fathers and brothers to rely on. Women were called on to donate or sell their jewelry to help ease the financial crisis. This may explain why women are more skeptical about globalization.

When asked if they support Korea's membership in the World Trade Organization, most respondents said they did. This shows that they do not oppose the trade body despite its adverse rulings on the local shipbuilding and semiconductor industries.

The students surveyed had favorable attitudes toward cultural globalization. They were most enthusiastic about traveling around the world. This confirms the national trend for foreign travel. With the deregulation of outbound travel in 1989, and the national obsession for globalization, overseas travel increased at an annual average growth rate of 21.3 percent prior to the Asian economic downturn, based on government records. Koreans rate the United States their No. 1 choice for their first trip abroad. In 1994, Koreans became the third-largest national group, behind Japan and Hong Kong, in the number of incoming tourists to the United States.

Koreans also like to travel to other Asian countries. The number of Korean tourists to Japan exceeded the number of Japanese tourists to Korea for the first time in about 40 years in 2007. Some 1.96 million South Koreans were estimated to have visited Japan between January and September 2007, an increase of 24.9 percent from 2006.

Korea is one of Thailand's most rapidly growing tourist markets. Thailand has become the third most popular destination for Korean tourists, following China and Japan. After the Japanese, Korean tourists number the second-highest in China.

Korean tourist numbers in the Philippines were the highest as of 2007. Government records show that there has been a 51 percent increase in Korean tourist arrivals, from 378,602 in 2003 to 572,133 in 2006. Likewise, Korean tourist numbers are the highest in Vietnam as of 2007 based on records from the Vietnam National Administration of Tourism, which show that 422,000 Koreans visited Vietnam last year, a 29.4 percent on-year increase.

Data from the Korea National Tourism Organization shows that over 13 million Koreans traveled to foreign countries in 2007. As the number of Koreans traveling overseas exceeded the expenditure of foreigners who visited Korea in 2007, the country's tourism deficit hit a record high of $10.1 billion.

The students surveyed were enthusiastic about foreign cultures and pop culture. American TV shows such as "Sex in the City" and "Prison Break" and Japanese dramas like "Nodame Cantabile" are popular. Young Koreans are also becoming interested in imported things such as rock and roll, pop music, McDonalds, Pizza Hut, the Back Street Boys, Britney Spears and Christina Aguilera.

Exposure to foreign cultures has become easier with the popularity of Korean films, TV dramas and pop music. This phenomenon, known as the Korean Wave, has exposed Koreans to foreign cultures in their own country. The Korean Wave contributed to the increase of incoming tourists to Korea, from 2.8 million in 2003 to 3.7 million in 2004. The bulk of these tourists were Korean Wave-loving Asian women.

Most students surveyed were glad to have more foreign stores opening. This is in sharp contrast to the reception of foreign products years ago: When Coca Cola started selling in 1951 and McDonalds opened its first location in 1988, there was lukewarm reception. Now, global brands enjoy patronage from Koreans, especially the youth.

In terms of cultural globalization, gender seems to have no impact on the responses of students who were surveyed. They also find cultural globalization an easier concept to embrace than economic globalization.

This implies that young Koreans belong to the "global teenager" market, which consists of 500 million consumers in Europe, North and South America and industrialized Asian nations. An article in *The Economist* explains that these "global teenagers" share the same intense exposure to MTV, movies, travel, the internet and global advertising such that their similarities are greater than their differences.

The article reveals that a global study of teenagers' rooms in 25 industrialized countries indicated that it was difficult to tell whether the rooms were in Los Angeles, Mexico City, Tokyo, Rio de Janeiro, Sydney, Seoul or Paris because the rooms had a common gallery of products. Teens are estimated to spend an average of $100 billion annually on global brands such as Sony video games, Tommy Hilfiger shirts, Levi's blue jeans, Nike trainers, Swatch watches and Clearasil lotion. The "global teenager" market appreciates fashionable clothes, popular music, international food and coffee such as Starbucks.

Howard Schultz, Starbucks' chief global strategist, was right in setting up stores in Korea. This is one market where the youth are as global as their peers in other parts of the world.

6.4

WHEN SOCCER NUTS MINGLE

Marcus Gee

> Sports, especially soccer, vividly reveal how globalization and localization coexist. On the one hand, soccer has become highly globalized. On the other hand, sports fans, and especially soccer fans, remain passionate nationalists. Thus, people do not have to make an invidious choice between globalization and localization.

Global Sport

Source: Marcus Gee, "When Soccer Nuts Mingle," *The Globe and Mail,* June 21, 2006.

I love the World Cup, and I say this as someone who has never watched a complete game. The thrill of seeing men in short pants chase a ball aimlessly across a vast field—then kick the ball 20 feet wide—has always eluded me. Globe sportswriter Stephen Brunt once explained that soccer (sorry, football) is like jazz: creative, improvised, non-linear.

That made things clearer to me.

I can't stand jazz.

Soccer leaves me cold. But, in my neighbourhood, that makes me a distinct minority. West-end Toronto is Canada's capital of soccer mania. When Portugal or Brazil win, the horns blare and flags wave well into the night. Italy's victories fill College Street with revellers, and South Korea's turn Bloor into an all-day party. Then, from time to time, a car with an unfamiliar flag tears by. Who was that? Oh, Trinidad and Tobago just won a game. Life in Toronto during World Cup is a full-time festival of nationalism and globalization.

Those are usually seen as opposing forces. Globalization means free trade, melting borders, mingling cultures, migrating people and everything international. Nationalism means devotion to home, flag, soil and everything local. Yet, in the World Cup, nationalism and globalization are happily married.

Except in war, nationalism reaches its highest pitch in international sports. The frenzy is wildest in soccer, the world's most popular sport and the closest thing these days to a universal faith. We've all seen the hordes of fans draped in national colours screaming themselves hoarse and drinking themselves senseless. Human beings are social animals, and we cling to our group identities even in (perhaps especially in) this age of mass communication and global consciousness.

But soccer is also the most globalized of sports, with players moving freely from country to country. The trade in soccer talent is so open and so intense that every player on Ivory Coast's World Cup squad plays professionally outside the country. Partly by importing foreign stars, clubs such as Manchester United have become global brands with fans around the world. When he isn't playing for England, David Beckham roves the pitch for Spain's Real Madrid. Brazil's Ronaldinho plays for FC Barcelona.

Foes of globalization have always claimed that this type of marauding cross-border capitalism exploits small countries and homogenizes the world, undermining local culture and chipping away at national identity. The story of the World Cup suggests otherwise. Small countries such as Togo (population: six million) made it into the event, while giants such as China (1.3 billion) did not. Playing abroad hones their players' skills and makes the national squad more competitive.

Though Ivory Coast's best players may go to France to ply their trade, its citizens are every bit as proud of their national team. There is nothing homogenized about a World Cup, a joyous celebration of national identity through international sport. In fact, cheering for a home team is one way that people cling to their local, group identity in the face of a rapidly changing, globalizing world. The same holds true in other cultural fields. People in Brazil may flock to the latest Tom Cruise picture, but what they really love watching is their local soap operas. People in Chengdu, China, may love dining at McDonald's, but they still eat spicy Sichuan food at home. In this World Cup, which is all the rage in China, many people are cheering for Brazil.

The wonder of the modern world is that people need not choose between a blinkered provincialism on the one hand and a rootless cosmopolitanism on the other.

They can celebrate their national achievements and keep their local ways, yet still be open to the world outside.

That's how it works in Canada. In my part of town, they cheer their lungs out for Brazil, Portugal and Italy (and Croatia and Angola and, yes, even England), but does anyone think they are less Canadian as a result? My guess is that a lot of those soccer nuts took a break on Monday night to watch the seventh game of the Stanley Cup.

The mixing and mingling of a globalized world need not stamp out national identity. If the World Cup is any sign, they may even make it stronger.

6.5

JAPAN DEBATES EARLY ENGLISH STUDY

from *The Nikkei Weekly*

English has become the language of globalization. A country like India, in which English is spoken by elites, enjoys a variety of advantages. By contrast, countries in which English is not spoken or is spoken poorly are at a global disadvantage. The following selection describes the lively debate in Japan about how to teach English effectively, to whom it should be taught, and whether teaching English to young children is at the expense of their knowledge of Japanese. Put differently, does the acquisition of a nonindigenous cultural asset erode an indigenous culture?

It is really a discussion about globalization. And it has been hotly argued in Japan for decades. But now the debate over how to make English-language education more effective is taking on a more urgent tone. The debate was reignited earlier this year by a report from a government council.

Japanese already study English for six years from middle school through high school, and another four years for many who go on to university. Yet many complain that, even after 10 years of English study, they still cannot hold a conversation with a foreigner.

So what is the solution? According to the Central Council for Education, which filed its report in March, it is two more years of English classes, which would begin for fifth graders in elementary school with at least one lesson per week. The Ministry of Education, Culture, Sports, Science and Technology now plans to change its guidelines for schools in 2006 to put the proposal into practice.

Source: "Japan Debates Early English Study," *The Nikkei Weekly,* August 14, 2006.

English: The Global Language

However, many politicians and teachers have quite different views, saying it is non-sense to teach English to young children before giving them enough training in their own language, Japanese. They also argue that the nation does not have enough teachers to teach English at elementary schools.

Lack of Confidence

Consider the plight of one 52-year-old second-grade teacher at a public school. She said she is uncomfortable going to work once a week to teach a subject she did not like during her own school days and that she purposely avoided by attending a private university, where she did not have to write an English-language exam. Her worry, she said, is that because of her low English level, "there is no way I can teach English."

She became anxious when nearby schools began holding English-language activities several years ago, and especially when a similar program started at her school this year.

She was so distressed that she became ill and had to take time off in the spring. For now, she leaves the English classes to a foreign teaching assistant. But after they become mandatory, her role as a qualified teacher will expand.

A 24-year-old teacher who likes English has a different reaction. She enjoyed traveling abroad during her university days and still goes to English conversation school, paying for the lessons out of her own pocket. "English-language activities seem to make children express more about themselves," she said.

While the public debates the matter, the Education Ministry is more concerned with the increasing importance of cross-border communication abilities in a world that is being brought ever closer together by information technology and globalization.

In fiscal 2005, about 1.5 million Japanese took the TOEIC (Test of English for International Communication). That is 2.7 times more than 10 years ago—an indication that English-language skills have become more crucial in business.

Japan is already part of a worldwide trend in which schools in non-English-speaking countries are starting to teach the language to younger pupils. Some 90% of elementary schools incorporate some form of English lessons into their curriculum. Yet, as far as the public is concerned, contentious issues abound.

Bone of Contention

Just what should these mandatory lessons include? There is no consensus on this matter.

How will teachers be trained? Those in favor of the proposal say it is necessary to start young so tomorrow's Japanese will be able to speak correct English. But those opposed to the idea say Japan simply does not have enough qualified English teachers.

The Education Ministry is responding with a program that will give all general teachers 30 hours of in-school training over two years. It will also require self-paced learning via DVDs. The preparations are moving forward with the help of experts.

"The problem is that we have not been teaching English at the elementary school level," said Kensaku Yoshida, dean of the faculty of foreign studies at Sophia University and a member of the Central Council for Education, which first recommended mandatory

English lessons in elementary schools. However, Japan was already behind the curve. Other Asian countries have been making early English-language classes mandatory since the 1990s. Thailand did so in 1996, South Korea followed in 1997 and China jumped on the bandwagon in 2001.

Japan, and Indonesia, have been left on the curb. "Those are about the only countries left behind," Yoshida said.

An Education Ministry survey shows that 68% of parents approve of mandatory English classes in elementary school. Even English conversation classes for toddlers have been surging in popularity.

But there are critics who argue against the proposal. Some well-known scholars and politicians have expressed strong opposition, saying it is important to teach the Japanese language at an early stage. They maintain that English lessons may impede young children's reading comprehension of Japanese.

When the Education Ministry invited the public to express opinions in April and early May, it received about 400 responses. Usually when a ministry asks for public input it receives about 10 replies. Officials were caught off-guard not only by the volume but also by the length of the submissions. Some even included long, pedagogical arguments based on individual beliefs about English-language education.

6.6

RWANDA: AMERICANISATION OR GLOBALISATION?

Allan Brian Ssenyonga

The next article reflects an African view of globalization as equivalent to the spread of American influence around the world. Globalization in the author's view is a form of cultural imperialism in which ever more people are "Americanized." This is a highly contested claim. Unlike the author, others believe that, while the origins of globalization owe much to the global spread of American economic, political, and cultural customs following World War II, it is more accurate to say that contemporary globalization reflects modernity in general.

Global socio-political issues never cease to fascinate any interested soul. From the times of civilization came the era of colonialism then independence. This was followed by the

Source: Allan Brian Ssenyonga, "Rwanda: Americanisation or Globalisation?" *Africa News,* August 9, 2006. Originally published in *The New Times.*

cold war era where the Soviets were slowly but surely out-smarted by the more versatile capitalists of the day.

The post cold war era led to the increasing influence of what some people these days call quasi-governments (such as the International Monetary Fund and the World Bank).

The IMF and World Bank consequently took on the role of the world's economic 'police' telling particularly poorer nations how to spend their money. In order to receive more aid, these Bretton Woods institutions demanded that countries open up their economies to liberalization under Structural Adjustment Programmes that encouraged governments to fund privatization programmes, ahead of welfare and public services. Concurrently we had the influence of multinational civilizations like the United Nations Organisation also greatly formatting global issues.

Fast-forward to the new millennium things took a different path. All of a sudden we were being pumped with rhetoric titled globalization. Globalization is an umbrella term for a complex series of economic, social, technological, and political changes seen as increasing interdependence and interaction between people and companies in disparate locations. In general use within the field of economics and political economy, it refers to the increasing integration of economies around the world, particularly through trade and financial flows. The term sometimes also refers to the movement of people (labour) and knowledge (technology) across international borders. There are also broader cultural, political and environmental dimensions of globalization. For the common man it was always argued that the world had become like a global village of sorts.

At its most basic, there is nothing mysterious about globalization. But not so first, some people are now arguing that globalization has mainly benefited the already strong economies of the world and it has given them leverage to not only trade with the rest of the world but to also influence their general lifestyles and politics. Proponents of the school of thought contend that countries like U.S.A. are using the globalization as an engine of "corporate imperialism"; one which tramples over the human rights of developing societies, claims to bring prosperity, yet often simply amounts to plundering and profiteering.

Another negative effect of globalization has been cultural assimilation via cultural imperialism. This can be further explained as a situation of exporting of artificial wants, and the destruction or inhibition of authentic local cultures. This brings me to the gist of my submission. At a closer look, globalization is slowly shifting towards Americanization. Have you heard the word "Americanization"? Well in the early 1900's Americanization meant taking new immigrants and turning them into Americans ... whether they wanted to give up their traditional ways or not. This process often involved learning English and adjusting to American culture, customs, and dress.

Critics now say globalization is nothing more than the imposition of American culture on the entire world. In fact, the most visible sign of globalization seems to be the spread of American hamburgers and cola (Pepsi and Coca Cola products) to nearly every country on earth. The song Amerika by the German rock band Rammstein is often seen as a satire of Americanization. It has received mixed reviews: some perceive it as anti-American, others as being opposed to globalization. The band views it as a satirical commentary on "cocacolonization."

According to information from Globalisation.about.com even globalization champions like Thomas Friedman see it. In a recent column describing why terrorists hate the

United States, Friedman wrote: ". . . globalization is in so many ways Americanization: globalization wears Mickey Mouse ears, it drinks Pepsi and Coke, eats Big Macs, does its computing on an IBM laptop with Windows 98. Many societies around the world can't get enough of it, but others see it as a fundamental threat."

The rest of the world seems to be following Uncle Sam (U.S.A.) and leaving behind its authentic ways of life. This has not spared even the 'air tight' Chinese society. Americanization is the contemporary term used for the influence the United States of America has on the culture of other countries, substituting their culture with American culture. When encountered unwillingly, it has a negative connotation; when sought voluntarily, it has a positive connotation.

How Are We Being Americanised?

U.S.A., which has the world's biggest economy and strongest known army, has taken gigantic steps in persuading the rest of the world to think and act like them. Many people especially the Europeans have often despised Americans saying they have no culture. But as any sociologist will tell you, even having no culture is a culture in itself. So for many years, the land of immigrants has been on a process of creating an identity and hence a culture. Now they seem to be selling their culture to the rest of the world as a new and improved product of what we all have as culture.

As far as fashion is concerned, the casual 'American' style of wearing jeans, T-Shirts and sports shoes is now common and acceptable in many places. For the office it is not rare to see someone wearing tight jeans with a long sleeved shirt plus a tie. His defence is of course that it is the American style (read modern). Cowboy hats, boots and large silver belt buckles are also a common imitation of the dress style of Americans especially those from Texas and Arizona. The American music industry has also gone a long way in influencing the dress culture of other people around the world. What about the example youths have picked up from famous American rap artists like 50-cent, Eminem, Tupac Shakur (R.I.P) and Snoop Dogg with their flashy fashions characterized by what is commonly known as "bling bling" (expensive shiny jewellery and watches). Look at the music played in the Nyamirambo bound taxis and you will be amazed at how it matches with the dress style of the passengers!

Around the world the United States is perhaps best known for it's numerous and successful fast food franchises. Such chains, including McDonald's, Burger King, and Kentucky Fried Chicken are known for selling simple, pre-prepared meals of foods such as hamburgers, French fries (chips), soft drinks, fried chicken, and ice cream. Though undeniably popular, such food, with its emphasis on deep-frying, has been criticized by dietitians in recent decades for being unhealthy and a cause of obesity. It has thus become somewhat of a stereotype to associate American cuisine with obesity and junk food. The whole world now is full of similar eating joints. In Africa many are referred to as take-aways.

Popular Culture

This transmission of American culture has been mainly through several conduits with the number one medium being the electronic media. Television in particular has done a lot in Americanizing those who view images especially from Hollywood. The guys in

Hollywood have made us to adore the tough cigar-smoking guys in the Casinos, the thin shapely long legged women, and to dream about rags-to-riches stories that are a common tag line of the movies. We now adore jazz, hip-hop, rap music, country music as well as gospel music all of which were pioneered by the United States.

And trust us in following the Uncle Sam; many countries now have equivalents of the American awards of Oscars for the movies and Grammy's for the music. Just check out the PAM awards in Uganda or the Kisima awards in Kenya, not forgetting the continental Kora awards held annually in South Africa. Many countries have also gone ahead to construct theme parks based on the American Disney World model. Americanization has also led to the popularity and acceptability of what is known as American English. I have seen many posters here in Rwanda of schools claiming to teach American English. Many youths are now using this type of English considering it 'modern.'

We ought not to ignore the heavy influence that the United States has demonstrated in the development of the Internet and its subsequent control. Remember the conference that was held at the beginning of this year in Tunisia where nations were complaining about the control the US has over the Internet. They were proposing that instead an international body should take over but the conference ended in defeat of this line of argument. The iPod, the most popular gadget for portable digital music, is also an American invention.

American sports especially basketball have now become famous worldwide especially among college students. However other games like baseball and American football have not been easily adopted by other people in the world, as has been the case with basketball. Soccer, which is known to be the world's most popular sport, is not so popular in the US. However the US women's soccer team is one the of the world's premier women's sides.

War on Terrorism

Americans have also been known to spearhead the spread of the Pentecostal, Charismatic, Evangelical or born again religious movements worldwide. American preachers are always globetrotting all in the name of spreading the word of 'God.' We should not ignore the fact that the United States Constitution enshrined individual freedom of religious practice, which courts have since interpreted to mean that the government is a secular institution, an idea called "separation of church and state." This notion of separating religion from the state is one of the controversial aspects of exporting American culture. This is embedded in the Bush administration's "War on terror" which some have gone ahead to read as a war on Islam. This controversial American policy is what inspired Prof. Mamdani to write a book titled, "Bad Muslim good Muslim."

America, which has thousands of military servicemen around the world, has of late been preoccupied with fighting terror in Afghanistan, Iraq and it is getting ready to deal with the Iran problem soon. Actually some people are already speculating that the current crisis between Israel and Hezbollah is a precursor to America's war with Iran. That US is supporting the Olmert government to keep bombing Lebanon until Iran which is said to be the Godfather of Hezbollah gets angry enough to join the war. At this point it is argued that the US will join hands with Israel and fight the Iran government because "they have weapons of mass destruction." At the end of the war as usual US will be expected by many viewers to have conquered another oil producing country.

Many see the War on terror as a veil for acquiring cheap oil to run the US economy. Returning to the Israeli conflict with Hezbollah, one can not fail to see an American tone in the whole conflict. Do you remember the first people to use the word "collateral damage"? This was what Americans first used to describe the death of innocent civilians and destruction of infrastructure by 'precision' missiles during the Afghan war after the 9/11. This was an excuse used for having bombed the Chinese Embassy and a Red Cross facility during the war. Now compare it with the death of thousand of Lebanese civilians and the destruction of hundreds of buildings. The death of UN officers and the recent Qana massacre can be accurately referred to as collateral damage by the Israeli government.

The apparent determination by the US to appoint itself "Mr. Fix it all" is a somewhat naive but optimistic belief among Americans that all problems can be fixed with enough commitment and effort. This sometimes leads America into problematic situations such as Vietnam and Iraq. In some cases though, American fix it all attitude has positively led to large outpouring of humanitarianism. This is clearly evidenced by the enormous aid that Americans especially at the individual level, are sending to poor nations. Americans like Bill Gates and CNN's Ted Turner are some of the world's biggest donors.

In conclusion, therefore, the global stage is at a period of American conquest in many different ways than you can imagine. Globalization seems to be hijacked by the Americans. The world also seems to be clamouring for more of the Yankee lifestyle. However simply dismissing—or demonizing—globalization as mere Americanization is misleading. Globalization has the ability to alter much more than just the movies or food consumed by a society. And the results can be powerfully positive, devastatingly negative, or (more often) something in between.

6.7

21ST CENTURY TASTE

Jarrett Paschel

> The final selection in the chapter is taken from a publication on America's retail food industry. It describes a focus group of young American consumers who when asked where they wished to have lunch all chose "foreign" restaurants. The author sees this as reflecting acceptance of culinary globalization in the United States, which he believes will be permanent and will reduce the demand for traditional foods in grocery stores.

Source: Jarrett Paschel, "21st Century Taste," *Progressive Grocer,* May 2007.

Recently I posed what I thought was a pretty basic question to several focus groups of young consumers in their late teens and early 20s: "You and a friend decide to go out for lunch tomorrow, and it's your turn to pick. Where are you going to go?" Without hesitation, the answers rolled off their tongues "Thai, Chinese, bento, Mexican, pho, Indian, teriyaki, taco truck. . . ." All 15 of them mentioned a cuisine or a preparation, and in each case their answers reflected an international selection. As a follow-up, I asked about McDonald's, Taco Bell, Burger King, Wendy's, KFC, and the like. While several admitted occasionally dining at these restaurants, the consensus was pretty clear.

As one unusually articulate young consumer put it: "American food sucks." While we're surely aware of the danger of reading too much into the responses of a few consumers in a focus group setting, what we do know is that the general pattern of their responses matches a consistent finding in the Hartman Group's ongoing research. Namely, Americans—especially young Americans—have become completely comfortable, if not enchanted, with the foods, cuisines, and menus of foreign lands. To be certain, the comfort level varies—generally the older and more rural are somewhat less open to foreign or "ethnic" cuisines—but the big picture is clear: We are rapidly evolving into a culture marked by truly global food preferences. Moreover, we believe this is a permanent development, the inevitable consequence of the inexorable march of globalization. These developments have important implications for the retail food industry. We will witness the slow demise of a common understanding of an American way of eating. To be certain, families and other institutions will always have their own food traditions and preferences, and certain food items (e.g., hot dogs or hamburgers) may continue to enjoy long-standing popularity within our culture. But the idea that there will be a "commonly understood" cuisine served at critical ritual occasions such as weddings, parties, or summer picnics is quickly becoming a thing of the past. One need merely consider the diversity of preparations gracing wedding menus to get a sense of what I'm referring to here. Those of us born after, say, the late 1990s will feel little, if any, inclination not to pick freely from a truly global buffet. As part and parcel of our ongoing consumer research, we routinely interview families whose young children may opt for scones for breakfast, yakisoba for lunch, and an evening meal of papadums and curried chicken. This isn't a blip on the trend map—it's a permanent feature of globalization. Conversely, as a reaction to the spread of globalization, there will be also be a permanent and growing interest in all things regional, local, and authentic in the world of food. Organizations such as the "slow food" movement—which stands for "good, clean, and fair food" that's produced without harm to the environment or animals—will continue to expand, as will artisan products and heirloom fruits and vegetables. But the important thing for people in the food business to remember here is that "authenticity" isn't an objective status, but instead a designation referring to a product, process, or "way of doing" to which food critics, experts, artisans, craftspeople, and the food industry have lent their support, resulting in product narratives that are deemed "the real deal." The end of brands? In other words, while the consumer interest in authenticity may seem, at first glance, to limit marketplace opportunities (how many authentic cheeses are there from Vermont?), the reality is exactly the opposite. It's possible for there to be thousands of authentic cheeses from Vermont. All that's necessary is a horde of interested artisans, a network of cooperative actors (critics, writers, and the like), and a slew of impressive narratives. At the end of the day, however, you can't fake authenticity. Most troubling of all, I believe we're going to witness a long, steady decline of consumer interest in many of the legacy brands that dominated the American commercial landscape of the past century. In one sense we're already witnessing this phenomenon in the shape of declining center store sales and the rise of private label brands such as Trader Joe's, but a more fundamental problem is that the consumer of tomorrow is going to be thinking in terms of preparations, flavors, and ingredients, rather than branded food products. Oreos, Kraft Macaroni & Cheese, and Campbell's soups may one day be replaced by desires for biscotti, fettuccini Alfredo, chicken molé, or rasam soup. True, consumers may not always have the interest or time necessary to create those preparations themselves, but that won't be a problem, because the successful grocery store of the future's perimeter area will resemble an international food court. In fact, many of the most successful grocers are already adapting this model. To put things bluntly, if your prepared food case is currently stocked with potato salad, cole slaw, fried chicken, and the like, you had better rethink your model, and do so with the utmost urgency. While these foods are surely familiar, and may provide comfort by evoking nostalgia, they're not the foods capturing the imagination of existing and future Americans.

Chapter 7

GLOBALIZATION AND MIGRATION

This chapter examines the movement of "persons" that is integral to globalization. The most important of these trends is the migration of persons—legally and illegally—from poor or unstable countries to wealthy and stable ones in search of jobs and security and the impact this has on both the society gaining these individuals and the society "losing" them, including the economic impact of the remittances these individuals return to their homelands.

A major problem associated with such movement is the assimilation of "aliens" into the dominant culture or society, a problem observable, inter alia, in the movement of Latinos into the United States, of individuals from Eastern Europe and Islamic societies into Western Europe, of Central Asians and individuals from the Caucasus region to Russia, and of Zimbabweans to South Africa.

Although it has been economically beneficial for the developed world and its aging populations, immigration—both legal and illegal—has produced resentment and opposition in Europe and the United States, especially following the economic recession that began in 2007–2008. Europe has historically been Caucasian and Christian, but after World War II, Muslims began to arrive in order to fill the poorly paid jobs that Europeans avoided. Europe's Muslim population continued to grow as families followed the workers; it reached between 15 million and 20 million by 2005 (between 4% and 5% of the total population) and is expected to double by 2015. Today, many of the children and grandchildren of the first generation of Muslim migrants to Europe are alienated both from their parents' home countries and from Western culture and define themselves by their religious affiliation. Large majorities of European Muslims regard themselves as Muslims first and only secondarily as citizens of their country. Muslims from Pakistan, Turkey, and North Africa live in British, German, and French cities, and many consider Europeans to be hostile toward them. In sum, Islam is now Europe's second largest religion, and the growing European concern about this has been translated into increased votes for anti-immigrant political parties.

America's hostility to immigration is focused on the movement of illegal immigrants from Mexico and Central America. It is encapsulated in a book written by Harvard's Samuel P. Huntington, in which he declared that Hispanic immigrants were not assimilating into American society. These migrants, he claimed, failed to learn English and had low levels of education and income. Hispanics, he argued, were concentrated in insulated cultural islands in areas such as Southern California, and their sheer number constituted a threat to American culture. The challenge posed by Hispanic migrants, according to Huntington, is greater than that posed by earlier migrants who struggled to learn

English, because of the inability or unwillingness of Hispanics to assimilate, thus producing "a culturally bifurcated Anglo-Hispanic society with two national languages."[1]

Note

1 Samuel P. Huntington, *Who Are We? The Challenges to America's National Identity* (New York: Simon & Schuster, 2004), 221.

7.1

DETERMINANTS OF EMIGRATION: COMPARING MIGRANTS' SELECTIVITY FROM PERU AND MEXICO

Ayumi Takenaka and Karen A. Pren

> The first two articles in the chapter reveal as mistaken a number of assumptions about Hispanic migrants to the United States. The first suggests that Hispanic immigrants are not typically poor and uneducated and that there are significant differences among Hispanic migrants. Peruvians, for example tend to be better educated and professionally more advanced than Mexican migrants and, therefore, assimilate more easily. Moreover, patterns of Hispanic immigration are related to migrant networks in the United States. Education matters more when such networks are not well developed, and as they develop, migrants reflect more accurately the society from which they come.

As the volume of Latin American migration has grown, so has its diversity. In the context of heated immigration debates, "Latinos" are typically portrayed as uneducated, unskilled, and sometimes unassimilable migrants with persistently low earnings, few mobility prospects, limited English proficiency, and a low economic status relative to other immigrants. In reality, however, Latin American immigrants are quite heterogeneous and increasingly so. Whereas Mexico has sent a large number of unskilled and usually undocumented migrants to the United States, more recently arrived Latin American migrants from more distant countries, such as Peru, are disproportionately well educated.

Source: Excerpted from Ayumi Takenaka and Karen A. Pren, "Determinants of Emigration: Comparing Migrants' Selectivity From Peru and Mexico," *The Annals of the American Academy of Political and Social Science* 630 (July 2010), 178–93. Notes appearing in the original have been deleted.

The relatively high education of South American emigrants has been noted elsewhere. According to the 2000 U.S. Census, 53 percent of persons in the United States born in Peru had some college education, about the same rate as in the United States generally (52 percent) and much greater than the rate among those born in Mexico (14 percent), the Dominican Republic (28 percent), Ecuador (37 percent), or Colombia (46 percent). Among Latinos, only those born in Argentina displayed a higher rate of college attendance (59 percent). Peruvians are also more likely to engage in professional and managerial occupations and to earn more than other Latin American immigrants, with the exception of Colombians. In 2000, some 24 percent of Peruvians in the United States worked in professional or managerial jobs, compared with just 8 percent of Mexicans, 15 percent of Dominicans, and 16 percent of Ecuadorians. (Similar to the case of Peruvians, 24 percent of Colombians in the U.S. worked in professional or managerial jobs.)

Among respondents surveyed . . . , Peruvians stand out for their high education levels, with particularly striking contrast to Mexicans. . . . Peruvian migrants are twice as educated as Mexican migrants, with average schooling of 14.8 years versus 6.2 years for Mexican migrants. . . . Peruvian migrants are also more *selected* than Mexican migrants in terms of education, as indicated by the higher ratio between the schooling of migrants and nonmigrants.

The selectivity of migration is important partly because it affects how migrants fare and adapt within the receiving society, but also because of its consequences for development in sending countries, either through brain drain or capital gain. What accounts for the educational selectivity of migration, however, remains unclear. We also do not fully understand why it varies so much across countries in Latin America and particularly why there is such a large difference between Peruvians and Mexicans. We seek to account for this difference by focusing on the nature and development of migrant networks in each setting. Though largely neglected in studies of migrant selectivity, networks play a critical role in determining who leaves and who does not. We demonstrate this situation by measuring how access to social networks influences the educational profile of migrants departing from two Latin American nations that lie at opposite ends of the continuum of educational selectivity—Peru and Mexico.

Past Studies of Migrant Selectivity

Studies of migrant selectivity across countries generally consider the influence of macroeconomic characteristics such as gross domestic product (GDP) per capita and income inequality. According to these studies, richer countries with more equitable income distributions generally send more educated migrants. These results, however, do not quite explain the difference in educational selectivity between Peru and Mexico. Although Peruvian migrants are more educated, Peru is actually poorer than Mexico (with GDP per capita of $6,039 versus $10,751 in Mexico) and characterized both by greater income inequality . . . and a higher poverty rate. . . . In unequal societies such as Peru, the returns on education are presumably greater, and thus, the educated elite should have greater incentive to stay in the country rather then emigrating; however, this does not seem to be the case for Peru.

Studies of Latin American emigration have also considered the influence of several other factors in explaining migrant selectivity. These include distance, which is assumed to be a proxy for the costs—real and psychic—of international movement. . . .

In general, long-distance migration requires more financial capital, human capital, and information than short-distance migration. Consequently, migrants coming from afar are more selected with respect to variables such as education. Those with greater schooling are better equipped to satisfy the requirements of immigration bureaucracies and to gain access to credit markets to meet travel costs.

Another factor that has often been mentioned as influencing Latin American migration is the region's extended economic crisis. Studies have linked the out-flow of skilled workers to the end of import substitution industrialization and the subsequent "erosion of living standards for the middle-income sectors." These studies focus mainly on the issue of brain drain and argue that educated individuals emigrate because of political and economic instability as well as lack of career opportunities at home.

In sum, the relatively high levels of education that prevail among emigrants from South America are most commonly attributed to push and pull factors within the framework of human capital theory. Individuals respond to positive and negative incentives and move when they perceive greater net returns to human capital abroad than at home. When costs of migration are high and job opportunities at home are scarce, those endowed with human capital (skills and education) are more likely to migrate because they have the means to overcome the barrier of distance and because they feel relatively more deprived of the kinds of jobs they think they deserve given their education. Such an individually focused human capital account nevertheless tells us little about how individual decisions are constrained or enhanced by other factors, in part because the paradigm treats migrants as autonomous economic agents who independently respond to market forces.

This account is problematic, however, as networks have been identified as central to understanding migration dynamics. In their classic study of migration from four Mexican communities to the United States, for example, Massey et al. found that migration was fundamentally a social process and that "once networks have developed to the point where a foreign job is within easy reach, international migration becomes a preferred strategy among poor families seeking to alleviate pressing economic needs." As networks develop, migration becomes increasingly diffuse and selectivity diminishes over time. Networks, then, should disproportionately benefit poorer individuals with lower levels of education. Once networks are in place and expanding, the costs of migration should matter less.

Perhaps, then, Peruvian migrants are more positively selected owing to their relative lack of access to social capital, and Mexican migrants are negatively selected because of their access to well-developed and widely diffused social networks. Several studies have found an inverse relationship between human and social capital, with educated migrants relying less on social capital and the less educated relying more on social networks. Others have found that the networks used by well educated migrants are qualitatively different from those used by migrants with less education. According to

Wong and Salaff, skilled migrants from Hong Kong use more extensive networks of weak ties than unskilled migrants, who typically rely on stronger kin networks.

The question of how social capital operates to influence the movement of skilled migrants, or how it affects migrant selectivity, has not been well explored. As a result, we know little about the role played by social capital in Peruvian versus Mexican migration, or how educated migrants from Peru use and rely on personal networks. To analyze how social networks matter in explaining migrant selectivity—determining who migrates and who does not—we draw on data from Peru and Mexico to examine the development of migrant networks over time and how they shape the characteristics of those who elect to move internationally.

Characteristics of Peruvian and Mexican Migrants

The migrant flows emanating from Peru and Mexico are quite different in several key respects. First, whereas Mexico sends virtually all of its migrants to one destination, the United States, Peruvian migrants are dispersed widely across the globe. Among those Peruvians surveyed by the LAMP, for example, migrants went to thirty-five different countries, including places as far away as Japan and Australia. According to estimates developed by the Peruvian government, nearly half of all emigrants are in the United States, with 30 percent located elsewhere in South America (principally Chile, Argentina, and Bolivia), 20 percent in Europe (mainly Spain and Italy), and 10 percent in Asia (mostly Japan) or Oceania (mainly Australia).

This geographic dispersion is partly attributable to immigration policies in receiving countries, which facilitate the entry of Peruvians on the basis of colonial and ethnic ties. It also reflects the absence of targeted recruitment programs, such as the U.S.–Mexico Bracero Program, which explicitly worked to promote migration solely to the United States. In contrast, in response to a series of economic crises beginning in the 1980s, downwardly mobile Peruvians resorted to whatever means were available to leave for whichever countries they could enter.

In addition, whereas Mexican migration to the United States dates back to World War I, when the first labor recruitment programs began, Peruvian emigration has emerged only in the past few decades. Prior to 1970, relatively few emigrants left Peru, and most of them were members of the elite who went abroad for education. The lower educational selectivity observed among Mexican migrants, therefore, may be simply a function of their longer history of migration. Since average levels of education have risen over the past two decades throughout Latin America, those who migrated earlier will naturally have fewer years of education than those who left more recently.

Educational differences between Peruvians and Mexicans appear to be correlated with differences in other social and demographic characteristics. Today's mass migration from Mexico to the United States originated in guest-worker programs that deliberately targeted young males for recruitment, yielding a flow disproportionately made up of men of prime working age who moved back and forth seasonally. In contrast, in the absence of deliberate recruitment, Peruvian emigration includes women as well as men of diverse ages and varying motivations for migration. Although a majority (54 percent) of Peruvian emigrants surveyed by the International Organization for Migration (2006) said they migrated for economic reasons, 15 percent reported leaving for family reasons, and another 8.4 percent for educational reasons. Such differences with respect to age, gender, and motivations for migration are correlated with levels of education.

Although the share of urban-origin migrants has increased recently among Mexicans, the Bracero Program was designed explicitly to recruit farmworkers, yielding a flow that continues to originate largely in rural areas In contrast, Peruvian emigrants are typically from urban areas, most notably metropolitan Lima, and they are rarely employed in agriculture. Rural migrants generally move first to the capital city, which has the country's only international airport, and then relocate abroad after spending several years in the city accumulating capital. The urban origin of Peruvian migrants also implies higher average levels of education, as urban residents have access to more and better schools than rural residents. In addition, migrant farmworkers tend to have lower educations than those employed in other sectors.

Legal status constitutes another salient difference between Mexican and Peruvian migrants. Given the relative ease of crossing a land border and the shorter distances involved, a much larger percentage of Mexicans enter the United States without legal documents. Whereas 70 percent of U.S. migrants . . . were undocumented, the figure was only 5 percent among Peruvians. . . . Studies have consistently shown legal migrants to be more educated than illegal migrants, in part because immigration policies favor skilled and educated migrants in the absence of a kinship tie. . . .

Migrant Selectivity in Mexico and Peru

. . . Once they migrate, Mexicans tend to stay for a shorter time and are much more likely to remit money home than Peruvian migrants. The general demographic characteristics, apart from the high percentage of males among Mexican migrants, are more or less comparable for both countries.

The most striking difference here, once again, is education. The difference remains significant even after limiting our Mexican data to urban communities surveyed in recent years. It is particularly salient not only among migrants (15.1 mean years of education for Peruvian migrants versus 6.7 years for Mexican migrants) but also among nonmigrants (13.5 mean years of education for nonmigrants in Peru compared to 7.5 years for nonmigrants in Mexico) . . .

In terms of occupation, a much higher proportion of Peruvian migrants (44 percent) and nonmigrants (29.3 percent) alike held professional occupations at the time of the survey, compared with their counterparts from Mexico (7.6 percent and 13.8 percent, respectively). . . . To explain the mechanisms behind this selection, we undertook an event history analysis of the determinants of first migration from Peru and Mexico between 1970 and 2001.

. . . The independent variables included various measures of human and social capital. Human capital is measured by education (years of schooling) and occupational skill (professional-managerial, skilled, services, and unskilled manual work). Social

capital is measured based on (1) whether the household head had a spouse, an immediate family member (siblings, parents, or children), some other relative (extended
family), or a close friend abroad during the person-year in question and (2) the prevalence of migration in the community of origin. . . .

The Peruvian models . . . show that education is indeed quite robust in predicting
migration. That is, education increases the likelihood of migration from Peru, regardless of demographic characteristics, physical capital, and social capital. . . .

Human capital, however, is not the sole determinant; social capital also matters in
predicting migration from Peru. Those who have a spouse, immediate family member, or
other relative with migratory experience are significantly more likely to migrate than
those without such ties, regardless of education. Living in a community with a higher
migration prevalence ratio also increases the odds of out-migration. Even though human
capital effects (specifically education) are robust, they operate not at the expense of, but
in tandem with, social capital effects, possibly because long-distance migration requires
both human *and* social capital to overcome greater barriers to migration. . . .

[I]n Peru the highly educated (college graduates) tend to have more migrant network
ties and are more likely to use them in migrating compared with people in the medium
(nine to fifteen years) and lowest (less than nine years) educational categories. In other
words, among those who have migrant networks, a higher proportion of the highly
educated actually migrated.

The data for Mexico show the opposite pattern. Those in the lowest educational
category have more network ties than the highly educated, and they are slightly more
likely to use them in migrating. This pattern suggests that migrant networks may
develop in class-specific ways. When migrants are dominated by the highly educated,
as in Peru, migrant networks proliferate among the highly educated. However, there
is little difference in the type of personal network educated people use in migrating.
Regardless of their level of education, migrants are more likely to rely on close family
ties than on other relatives or friends. Wong and Salaff suggest, however, that Peruvian
migrants rely more on other types of networks, such as employers, than Mexicans do
when it comes to housing after arriving in the host country.

The results of the Mexican models . . . indicate the very strong effect of network-
based social capital in predicting migration. As documented by past studies, Mexican
migration is strongly driven by social networks, even from urban communities. Moreover,
while social capital matters, human capital does not. . . . Education may have little
effect because widespread access to social networks has lowered the costs of migration.

Conclusion: Explaining Migrant Selectivity

Our results show that the Mexican–Peruvian difference in migrant selectivity is not
attributable to legal status, urban versus rural origins, or demographic background;
neither is it due to the mere presence or absence of migrant networks; and although
distance is frequently cited to explain migrant selectivity, this factor by itself also does
not account for differential selection. Indeed, the average education of Peruvian
migrants does not vary much by how far they traveled: 13.8 years among those moving
within South America, 15.1 years among those going to North America, 14.9 years

among those going to Europe, and 15.1 years among those going to Asia. Among Mexicans, those migrating to border states such as Texas, Arizona, and California had an average education of 6 years, compared with 4.8 years among those going to more distant states such as Illinois. Our results suggest that three factors, all related to social capital, largely account for migrant selectivity.

The first factor is how widespread networks are. In the initial stages of migration, where migrant networks are not well developed, education matters more and migrants tend to be more highly selected. As networks expand and become more diffuse and widespread, however, education matters less and migrants become more representative of the population in general. It is for this reason that Peruvian migrants are more educationally selected than their Mexican counterparts, as migrant networks in Peru have not developed as well or spread as widely. Just as others have found, we also discovered that once migration becomes accessible to many through diffuse social networks, it becomes a common economic strategy for lower-income and less educated people, though migrants are typically not the poorest of the poor.

The second factor determining selectivity is who has access to migrant networks, which tend to replicate the characteristics of the original participants, yielding class-specific processes of network expansion. Because the first migrants from Peru were well educated, those connected to them were also well educated, and network growth occurred disproportionately among the upper classes, yielding social capital that was not accessible to the less educated. Because educated Peruvian migrants had ties with other educated Peruvians, the networks that developed in Peru reinforced, rather than diluted, the salience of education. Self-replicating selectivity is particularly likely in a country with high rates of poverty and income inequality, such as Peru. These profound class divisions, along with stark geographical divides between mountainous hinterlands and more developed coastal regions, yield migrant networks that are inaccessible to most of the population. . . .

Finally, selectivity is reinforced in Peru by a greater mismatch between education and occupation. As noted above, Peruvians are better educated than Mexicans, on average, yet the economy produces fewer jobs for people with advanced education. The combination of a relatively high average education with a poor economy means that many well-educated Peruvians cannot find an occupation commensurate with their training. This mismatch is reflected in the results of our event history analysis, which shows that whereas education was quite important in predicting first migration from Peru, occupation mattered little. Even though highly educated people are more likely to migrate, those in skilled occupations are not necessarily more likely to leave the country. Indeed, among the highly educated in Peru, only 50 percent were in a professional occupation, compared with 59 percent in Mexico. . . . Moreover, Abler, Rodríguez, and Robles and the World Bank found that the rate of return on education is lower in Peru than in Mexico, indicating that having a good education does not yield as much of an economic bonus in Peru as in Mexico. This mismatch between education and occupation is an important reason why highly educated individuals are more likely to migrate from Peru than from Mexico.

In summary, our analysis of the determinants of migration from Peru and Mexico reveals very different patterns and processes of international migration. Mexican migrants are more likely to be males of prime working age with lower education and a stronger orientation toward home. They are less likely to migrate if they already own property in Mexico and are motivated to finance home acquisition and send more remittances to family members left behind. In contrast, Peruvian migrants generally possess high levels of human capital compared to nonmigrants and tend to hail from middle-class communities. Once they emigrate, they remit less money to family members in Peru, return home less often, and experience more upward mobility than Mexicans do. In short, Mexicans seem to emigrate to advance economically at home, whereas Peruvians emigrate for better career prospects abroad.

An important lesson suggested by our analysis is that the salience of education varies depending on how social capital develops over time and the degree to which migrant networks rise in prevalence and become diffused widely in sending societies. To date, studies of skilled migration have focused largely on individual characteristics rather than social context. But our work suggests the relevance of both human and social capital in determining long-distance migration. In examining migrant selectivity, therefore, we need to pay more attention to the nature of networks and their stage of development.

Latin American emigration is growing in volume and diversity. BBC Mundo (a Spanish-language radio program) recently reported the results of a Web-based survey indicating that Mexican migration is becoming more selective, with as many as 82 percent of postsecondary graduates aspiring to migrate to the United States (June 4, 2008). Growing concern over a potential brain drain from Latin America was expressed at a June 2008 meeting convened in Colombia by the Instituto Internacional para la Educación Superior en la America Latino y el Caribe of the United Nations Educational, Social, and Cultural Organization. In addressing this complex issue, understanding the mechanisms of migrant selectivity—who migrates and under what circumstances—is critical. It makes little sense to lump all Latin American emigrants together, treating them as uneducated migrants who constitute a threat to the receiving society.

7.2

MIGRATION AND IMPERIALISM: THE MEXICAN WORKFORCE IN THE CONTEXT OF NAFTA

Raul Delgado Wise

The second selection, written from a Mexican perspective, views Mexican immigration to the United States as benefiting the host country while harming Mexico. Neoliberal economics, the author argues, moves Mexican workers northward, where they help restructure the American economy. Most are in

Source: Excerpted from Raul Delgado Wise, "Migration and Imperialism: The Mexican Workforce in the Context of NAFTA," trans. Mariana Ortega Breiia, *Latin American Perspectives* 33:2 (March 2006), 33–45. Notes from the original have been deleted.

industry, not in agriculture, and are better educated than is commonly believed. Many remit funds back home to support their families. The resulting brain drain impedes Mexican economic development. Moreover, the industries built along the Mexican–U.S. border as a result of the North American Free Trade Agreement (NAFTA), called "maquiladoras," send profits northward and distort investment in Mexico, and Mexico also subsidizes the jobs in these industries. To compete in a globalized world, Mexico has had to limit public investment and sell government enterprises, thereby limiting economic growth. Although the remittances benefit Mexico and emigration reduces unemployment, migration means a hemorrhaging of skills and talent that benefit the United States, not Mexico.

Since the imposition of neoliberal politics and the North American Free Trade Agreement (NAFTA), Mexico's economic integration with the United States has undergone significant changes. The intensification of commercial ties between the two nations as part of a new strategy of imperialist domination controlled by financial capital and the large U.S. multinational corporations has restructured binational work processes and strongly affected the labor force. I shall argue here that the reigning model of economic integration is sustained by the role that the Mexican workforce—both in Mexico and outside its borders—has played in the industrial restructuring of the United States. This process has elements that can be characterized as a kind of transnationalism "from the top," a strategy that responds to the interests of U.S. capital. At the same time it has elements that some writers see as a transnationalism "from below," embodied in the practices of migrant workers and their organizations and their counterparts in Mexico. Transnationalism from below not only creates opportunities for resistance but also outlines avenues for an alternative kind of development. The interplay between the two perspectives presents a number of possibilities.

Starting with these premises, the essay is subdivided into four sections. The first describes the Mexican export model in the context of Mexico–U.S. integration under neoliberalism and NAFTA. The second presents some revealing data on the consequences of the new migratory dynamics. The third addresses the dialectic between Mexico's export growth and international migration, and the final section reviews the responses of the migrant community.

The Mexican Export Model and the Dynamics of Integration

Mexico is typically considered a case of successful economic integration because it exports manufactured goods: it is Latin America's number-one exporter and occupies thirteenth place worldwide. The rigorous, even fundamentalist application of neoliberal recipes backed up by NAFTA has helped to make the economy one of the world's most open even though its export platform is focused primarily on the United States. The fact that 90 percent of its exports consist of manufactured goods is purportedly a sign of the country's advanced export profile. Of that 90 percent, the so-called disseminators of technical progress make up 39.4 percent.

The optimistic assessment of this integration, which is related to the notion of open regionalism . . . is mainly a distorted view of reality. In fact, an analysis of Mexico's new export profile indicates the importance of the maquiladoras, whose exports multiplied 26 times between 1982 and 2004, eventually amounting to more than half . . . total manufactured exports. Additionally, we observe a process of "disguised assembly" in other areas of manufactured exports such as the automotive industry. Between 1993 and 2000, the proportion of temporary imports in the export total was almost 80 percent. Another component of this dynamic is the disproportionate interfirm commerce, estimated at between 65 and 75 percent. The shared production scheme that is essential to interfirm commerce does not carry equally shared profits, and export prices are artificially established by the same firms without declaring earnings. Net profits are transferred out of the country while the jobs created are subsidized at the expense of the Mexican economy. The facts regarding the Mexican export model contradict the notion of free interplay among market forces proclaimed by neoliberal orthodoxy. What is worse, the model plunders investment resources that might otherwise revitalize the Mexican economy.

Needless to say, the fragility and the structural volatility of the export sector are subject to the ebbs and flows of the U.S. economy and, above all, the phases of a static and short-term comparative advantage, as in the case of a cheap workforce. Recently Mexico experienced an important decrease in the growth of manufactured exports because of the U.S. economy's loss of dynamism and China's entry into the World Trade Organization. Although the maquiladora has since 1990 been the center of the Mexican export model, it has experienced a decline since the end of 2000 because of reduced demand in the United States and the competition of regions with lower wages than Mexico such as China and Central America. This has propelled the relocation of maquiladoras and affected relative wage increases for those operating in Mexico.

In order to understand Mexico's integration with the United States it is necessary to consider what it is that the country really exports and demystify the notion that it possesses a buoyant export manufacturing sector. What the nation exports is in fact labor inputs that do not leave the country. The purported growth in the export manufacturing sector is nothing more than a smokescreen, serving to obscure the contraction of part of the Mexican economy, which is compelled to serve as a labor reserve for foreign capital. The kind of specialization that takes place in this kind of integration is clearly linked to the direct export of Mexican labor to the United States. The result is an incalculable loss for the country. The maquiladora implies the net transfer of profits abroad. For its part, migration forces Mexico to absorb the costs of the reproduction and training of the workforce and deprives the Mexican economy of the chief force required for the accumulation of capital.

The New U.S.-Mexico Migratory Dynamic

We must not lose sight of the fact that, in general terms, international migration has its historical roots in economic, political, social, and cultural factors. Although Mexican labor migration to the United States dates back to the nineteenth century, it now exhibits unprecedented vigor. One need only point out that in the past 34 years

(1970–2004) the Mexican-born population in the United States has multiplied thirteen-fold. This figure calls into question the alleged benevolence of the integration process in which the country is immersed . . .

The contemporary proportions of this phenomenon may be summarized as follows: The United States has the highest immigration rate in the world, and Mexicans constitute the largest group.

The Mexican-descended population residing in the United States in 2004 was estimated at 26.6 million people, 10 million of whom were Mexican-born migrants (legal or not). There is no other diaspora of equal magnitude in the world.

The annual average number of Mexicans who left their country and established residence in the United States in 2004 was estimated at 400,000. According to UN estimates for the 2000–2005 period, this makes Mexico the main source of migration in the world, followed by China (390,000) and India (280,000). Remittances received by Mexico in 2004 amounted to US$16.6 billion. This is the highest rate worldwide, followed by India (27 percent less) and the Philippines (36 percent less).

This quantifiable growth is accompanied by some significant qualitative transformations: Practically every place in Mexico registers some international migration; 96.2 percent of municipalities have some kind of connection with migration. At the same time, and despite the fact that it remains concentrated in a handful of states, the Mexican population in the United States is now distributed across most of the country. There is an expansion of migratory circuits toward the eastern and central-northern parts of the country, where some of the most dynamic centers of industrial restructuring are located.

There has been a steady increase in the educational level of Mexican migrants over the past decade. In 2003, 34.9 percent of Mexican-born U.S. residents 15 and older had more than a high-school education. This rate increases to 49 percent when the whole population of Mexican origin is taken into account. In contrast, the Mexican average in 2000 was 27.8 percent, which means that, in general terms and contrary to common assumptions, the number of qualified workers leaving the country is larger than the number that remains. It must be pointed out, however, that compared with other groups of immigrants in the United States the Mexican contingent has the least schooling. This illustrates the serious educational deficit that persists in the country and is accentuated by the implementation of neoliberal policies.

The higher-education figures for U.S. residents in 2004 included 385,000 Mexican-born individuals and 1.4 million people of Mexican origin. Eighty-six thousand of the former had graduate degrees, while the figure for the latter was 327,000. This suggests that the loss of qualified professionals has become an important problem. The country has little need for a qualified workforce, and there are practically no requirements regarding scientific and technological knowledge under the prevailing assembly model.

In the United States 36.2 percent of Mexican workers are in the secondary sector (i.e., manufacturing) compared with 27.8 percent in Mexico. These numbers challenge the stereotypical view of the migrant as an agricultural worker and highlight the fundamental changes in the trans-border labor market. Only 13.3 percent of migrants work in the primary sector (raw materials). Also, Mexicans are the U.S. immigrant group with the greatest industrial participation and the lowest average income.

Finally, these changes have transformed the pattern of migration: what was once a circular flow is now characterized by the preeminence of the established immigrant and includes variants such as larger female and family-member participation.

The Dialectics of Export Growth and International Migration

. . . The export thrust of the Mexican economy requires certain macro-economic conditions that are achieved through the constriction of internal accumulation, particularly the shrinking of public investment spending, the state's abandonment of strictly productive activities, the sale of public enterprises and control of the fiscal deficit, and attractive interest rates for foreign capital, which result in a reduction of the economy's domestic activity. Social inequality deepens, generating an ever-increasing mass of workers who have no place in the country's formal job market. This is why a third of Mexico's population belongs to the informal economy, which ultimately feeds the vigorous migratory process.

The contradictory migration and growth dynamic generated by this context can be synthesized as follows: First, international migration is accompanied by certain "positive" elements that benefit the Mexican economy. On the one hand, migrants' remittances are a source of currency for the nation. With the decline of other sources of external financing (foreign debt and direct foreign investment) and the loss of dynamism for the maquila industry's exports, remittances become a crucial foundation for the fragile macro economic balance that characterizes the contemporary neoliberal model. On the other hand, by reducing the pressures on the labor market and social conflict, migration functions as a sort of escape valve given the diminished job-generating structural capacity of the economy. In this sense, the family and, above all, remittances help to cover the social costs and minimal infrastructure previously supported by public investment, aiding in the subsistence of many Mexican households. They tend to moderate the distributive conflict between the state and the society's most vulnerable groups, to some extent alleviating poverty and marginalization. All of this ultimately constitutes a paradox: migration unintentionally operates as a crucial support for the neoliberal system, providing it with a certain "stability" and a "human face."

Second and more important, migration constitutes a loss of valuable economic resources and the export of potential wealth. The exporting of a work-force implies transferring to the receiving country a wealth whose reproduction and training costs are absorbed by all Mexicans.

Third, in contrast to the case of the labor force that is exported indirectly (via maquilas), emigrants who establish themselves in the United States spend a very significant part of their wages there, with consequent benefits for the U.S. economy. Mexican consumers residing in the United States in 2003 contributed US$395 billion to the U.S. economy. This amount significantly contrasts with the remittances sent to Mexico, which amounted to US$13.4 billion.

Fourth, from a fiscal point of view, Mexican migrants' contributions to the U.S. economy exceed the benefits and public services they receive in exchange and thus contribute to the social security of U.S. workers.

Fifth, although it is difficult to measure their precise impact, the pressure exerted on the labor market by migrants negatively affects wage rates in the U.S. economy, particularly in the fields or sectors in which they work. A recent study reveals that the gap between Mexican migrants' average income and the established minimum wage in the United States has decreased in the last 25 years. Measured in constant 2000 prices, migrants' average income declined 38 percent during that period, from US$11.70 to US$7.20 per hour. The paradox lies in the fact that this situation parallels the changes in migrants' profiles previously described—that is, their higher educational levels and increased presence in the manufacturing sector. Still, despite Mexican migrants' contribution to the reduction of production costs in the U.S. economy, their impact is limited to certain areas of the labor market and does not affect the majority of U.S. workers. In fact, there is no correlation between the flow of Mexican migration and the unemployment rate in the United States, which suggests that the migrant workforce has instead helped to satisfy the existing demand in certain areas of the U.S. labor market.

Finally, there is a new trend that calls into question the medium- and long-term viability of this pattern in the present integration model (along with its beneficial impact on the U.S. economy and its role in Mexico's macroeconomic and social "stability"): depopulation. In the last half of the 1990s, 755 of Mexico's 2,435 municipalities (31 percent) had a negative growth rate, and there are also signs of an abandonment of productive activities and a diminution of remittances per family. This new scenario undermines the basis for future migration and thus its socioeconomic function. This shows the perverse relationship between the Mexican export sector and international migration. Thus, Mexico is responsible for the reproduction and training of the workforce, and the United States exploits this resource to restructure its industry and reduce its production costs. This process is sustained by wage differences and the accompanying sources of resource transfer. Overall, the resulting dynamic can hardly be perpetuated in the face of one-sided migration and depopulation. This calls attention to the competitive limitations of a short-term strategy that depends for restructuring on a cheap workforce.

The Migrant Community and the Challenges of Neoliberal Globalism

To conclude, it is important to point out that the migrant community is increasingly less isolated, dispersed, and disorganized. As a contradictory by-product of historical development and the maturation of migratory networks, individual migrants are becoming what Miguel Moctezuma describes as a collective binational and transterritorial agent. This process is taking shape through a broad network of clubs (more than 700 at present), associations, and federations operating in several states of the United States and a multiplicity of alliances and coalitions with a national and binational perspective. In this sense, the migrant community shows an incipient development toward superior organizational schemes. Among their characteristics are relatively permanent formal organizations, the strengthening of cultural identity, belonging, and acts of solidarity involving home communities, the establishment of lines of communication with various public and private institutions both in Mexico and in the United States, and substantial financial potential (made up of collective funds that transcend the characteristic limit of individual or family remittances) devoted to social work and, eventually, local and regional development projects.

One of the most significant demands made by migrant communities has been full exercise of the rights of Mexican citizens abroad, particularly the right to vote, which the Mexican Congress approved on June 28, 2005. This demand was a direct consequence of 1998 constitutional reform regarding the maintenance of Mexican nationality and incorporates three issues that counter the ideology and practices of neoliberal globalism: the strengthening of national identity, contrary to the disintegrative and disarticulating tendencies inherent in globalism; a collective impulse toward local and regional development that opposes the destructive impact of the internal market and the neoliberal basis of production; and democracy from below that decries the breach between the political class and civil society exacerbated by neoliberal "democracy."

At another level, the demands of the migrants in the United States include the regularization of their legal status, full citizen rights, and the shaping of a multicultural society that rejects political exclusion, socioeconomic marginalization, and the formation of permanent ethnic minorities. The demand for open borders is also important, since it takes aim at one of the vital points of the present strategy of imperialist domination characteristic of Mexico–U.S. interaction.

7.3

KYRGYZSTAN FEARS FINANCIAL CRISIS TO HIT MIGRANT WORKERS

from *BBC Monitoring Central Asia Unit/Interfax*

The global economic downturn following America's subprime mortgage crisis produced widespread unemployment. As a result, countries began to send guest workers home, even as those who remained saw their jobs disappear or their wages reduced. One result was a dramatic reduction in remittances from migrant workers to their home countries.

Text of report by corporate-owned Russian news agency Interfax:

Bishkek, 28 October: The chairperson of the Kyrgyz State Committee for Migration and Employment considers that money transfers arriving from Kyrgyz migrant workers from abroad may be reduced as a result of the global financial crisis.

Source: "Kyrgyzstan Fears Financial Crisis to Hit Migrant Workers," BBC Monitoring Central Asia Unit, October 28, 2008. Original text from Interfax.

Economic Recession and Migration

"The global financial crisis will certainly affect the Kyrgyz migrant workers abroad," Aygul Ryskulova said at a news conference today.

She predicted that money transfers arriving from migrants, which "total millions of soms every year," would probably be reduced, which would "also affect the republic's economy, as a result of the crisis.

"The crisis may affect in two directions: the first, migrant workers' wages will be reduced and the second, work places will be reduced, which will lead to an outflow of migrants from one place to another," Ryskulova said.

She, however, noted that "there has been no information on a reduction in money transfers from migrant workers so far."

According to the chairperson of the state committee, Kyrgyz migrant workers have sent over 800m dollars to their homes in 2008.

"Given that our migrants are also buying real property and sending cash through their acquaintances, this sum is over a billion dollars," Ryskulova added.

According to the Kyrgyz State Committee for Migration and Employment, from 500,000 to 800,000 Kyrgyz citizens work abroad.

7.4

IMMIGRATION IS FALLING BECAUSE OF THE ECONOMY

Tim Finch

With fewer jobs during the economic downturn, migration also slowed, and consequently, the pool of young workers able to pay for the growing ranks of elderly retired people in developed countries began to shrink.

More than a decade of growth, then in 2008, sudden decline. Sound familiar? Yes, the latest figures on migration seem to be mirroring the economy. The statistics show that the net migration rate in 2008 was down to 118,000—a 44 per cent drop on the previous year. Dramatic though it is, this decline is not surprising. Migration responds to economic conditions—people come when jobs are plentiful, go when jobs are scarce.

A large part of this new trend in migration to the UK is explained by rapidly-increasing emigration of non-British citizens—up 50 per cent in 2008. This trend is marked in Eastern Europeans—largely Poles—who arrived in such numbers when their countries joined the EU in 2004. The migration rate from these countries was 14,000 in 2008—the peak was 80,000 in 2007.

Source: Tim Finch, "Immigration Is Falling Because of the Economy: Analysis," *The Independent,* August 28, 2009.

At the same time these figures demonstrate that our population is growing, partly because of recent strong levels of immigration. This is good in many ways. Immigrants are mostly young so their arrival helps avert negative effects of an ageing population. Some migrants have integrated and started families. Since this takes a few years, it is unsurprising that the population figures show growth when the migration figures show a drop.

Because overall migration to the UK is now declining, those who use high levels of immigration to scaremonger about population growth may have to revise their predictions. They have falsely assumed that migrants want to stay forever. An Institute for Public Policy Research study published last month showed that increasing numbers of migrants are only staying for short periods. Young, skilled, hard working migrants have lots of countries that want them—so the UK may have to work harder to attract and retain such people.

7.5

IMMIGRATION: EU TO PENALISE EMPLOYERS OF ILLEGAL IMMIGRANTS

Nathalie Vandystadt

> American and European employers have an incentive to hire illegal immigrants, to whom they pay lower wages and who enjoy little job security. During economic hard times, however, domestic workers and politicians seeking to maintain political support at home step up efforts to reduce illegal immigration. The following selection describes the effort of the European Union to impose penalties on employers who hire illegal immigrants.

Over the past two years, the European Union has considerably stepped up its arsenal of instruments to combat illegal immigration. In the wake of the very controversial directive on the return of illegal immigrants to their country of origin (Return Directive), it is now preparing to take on common rules to penalise the employers of undocumented workers, including penal sanctions in the most serious cases. Meeting in Strasbourg, the European Parliament (EP) is due to adopt, on 4 February, a compromise worked out with the Council on a proposal for a directive to combat illegal immigration by tackling bad bosses.

Rapporteur Claudio Fava (PES, Italy) had to bring all his negotiating skills into play to reverse the proposal's logic of punitive action. Originally, the idea was to fight against the illegal immigrants alone, but now the aim is also to protect them, he said during the

---

Source: Nathalie Vandystadt, "Immigration: EU to Penalise Employers of Illegal Immigrants," *Europolitics,* Issue No. 3686, February 4, 2009.

EP debate on the eve of the vote. "Otherwise, they were being punished twice, first by being exploited and second by being sent back home," he observed.

Protection of Minors

It is especially on the case of children employed illegally that the EP has managed to obtain a more socially progressive approach. The member states would grant temporary residence permits to such children and to adults subjected to particularly abusive working conditions (human trafficking) who cooperate on the criminal prosecution against their employer. Fava had hoped to expand such a right to all immigrants, but had to take the Return Directive into account.

Employers acting illegally will be subject to financial and administrative penalties: fines, obligation to pay back wages at legal conditions and up to five years' ineligibility for public tenders in their home country and at EU level. Criminal sanctions will even be imposed on repeat offenders, employers of minors or of large numbers of illegal immigrants, those imposing slave-like conditions or employers knowingly employing victims of human trafficking.

The EP also succeeded in "introducing the definition of pay owed to illegal workers, under the pay conditions of the country of origin," said Fava. He also welcomed the fact that unions will be able to defend these workers without being prosecuted for aiding illegal immigrants.

Subcontracting

Although employers approve of the objective, which they see as slowing the "unfair competition" of undeclared labour, they reject the concept of subsidiary liability. Indeed, the Council and EP have also agreed to hold responsible employers who subcontract work to temporary employment agencies that employ illegal residents. They will even be held wholly liable if it can be demonstrated that they were aware of the unlawful practices of the subcontractor. This was a necessity, argues the European Trade Union Confederation (ETUC), because "most illegal workers are not hired directly by the big employers, but by temporary agencies or subcontractors."

For European employers, represented by BusinessEurope, this represents "intolerable pressure on the employer." "It is impossible for employers to check the compliance of their subcontractors," explains Marcus Schwenke, adviser at BusinessEurope, who denounces "a heavy administrative burden for companies and overly severe penalties."

The EP is determined to move forward, however, and has called for a declaration to be attached to the directive stating that the new text does not exclude a future initiative on subcontracting.

Priority on Inspections

The Commission finds that the compromise creates an "effective, common and dissuasive instrument." The EU executive will nonetheless remain "vigilant on inspections," said Justice, Freedom and Security Commissioner Jacques Barrot. "It remains to be seen in the coming years whether qualitative and better targeted inspections are effective, whether the criteria we have selected have been applied," he explained. The Commission will make this its "priority" in its reports on application of the new legislation.

On the whole, "this is the first significant step in combating illegal immigration, while protecting legal immigrants," concluded the commissioner, who recognises that undocumented immigrants are "very often victims".

This is also the first text that tackles the "incentive nature" of illegal immigration, notes Maltese Conservative Simon Busuttil.

The Union has between 4.5 and eight million undocumented residents. In addition to the Return Directive, which has been denounced by NGOs and the African and South American countries of origin, the EU is in the process of adopting other texts on "selective immigration," sought by the former French EU Presidency, such as the Blue Card Directive on highly qualified immigrants.

MEPs are divided over the question of legalisation of residence. The Conservative side (EPP-ED) maintains that "it is essential to point out that this new directive is an instrument to fight illegal immigration and not to legalise the residence of those without papers," insisted Busuttil. At the opposite end, Greek Socialist Stavros Lambrinidis called for rules on legal immigration, "because others who are in a legal situation are also being exploited." For now, in the absence of the Lisbon Treaty, the EP is simply consulted on legal immigration matters.

For Italian Communist Giusto Catania, this legislation maintains the punitive logic of the Return Directive: "We need something that encourages legality [...] this directive increases the illegal nature of workers and their exploitation by unscrupulous employers," he commented.

After formal adoption in Council, the member states will have two years to bring the new rules into force.

7.6

OUR WAY OF LIFE IS ENRICHED BY MIGRANTS

Peter Cosgrove

> Australia is a land of immigrants. During much of its history, however, it has been a Caucasian society with migrants largely from Europe. As the next article suggests, the challenge of becoming a multicultural society has posed difficulties for many Australians. Nevertheless, the newer groups of immigrants made the effort and succeeded in assimilating themselves into the country's mainstream. Once all-white Australia began to absorb Asian migrants, its

Source: Peter Cosgrove, "Our Way of Life Is Enriched by Migrants," *Weekend Australian,* December 5, 2009.

culture was enriched. Although there has been friction with recent Muslim migrants, the author believes that Australia can and should assimilate this group as successfully as it has previous groups.

The record shows Australian society can absorb new people and influences and evolve in unity.

If a younger Australian were transported back to the 1950s and could listen to the casual language used by ordinary people about, and sometimes to, some of our recent migrants, they would faint in shock.

By the standards of today, it just wouldn't do; today, all that would be termed racism and there would be hell to pay.

Looking back, it may have been confronting and even offensive for those new Australians who found themselves typecast with patronising verbal tags.

But if racism it was, then it seemed to me at the time that it was pretty superficial.

Because in the shadow of the war it was very obvious that all of these migrants had come from a poor and damaged place to this shining new place, Australia, looking to work hard, to pitch in and to make a go of it.

They had made the most profound social commitment: they had volunteered to become Australians whereas the rest of us had had no say in the matter.

Put simply, it was obvious to all of us that they had devoted themselves to assimilating into Australian society, our values and culture, even while cherishing and displaying their own.

The heavy accents and broken English of those mums and dads are now only faint echoes in the dry and arid tones of their kids and grandkids who are now indistinguishably part of our social fabric.

I wonder why what seemed so easy and unremarkable back then—the assimilation of hundreds of thousands of people for whom English was a second language or an unknown one—is now so fraught, so front of mind. For most of my lifetime attitudes towards ethnic minorities have been irreverent but have seemed to be without malice.

I mentioned the term assimilation. It's an interesting word and in an immigration context it is meant to imply the absorption of individuals and family groups into mainstream Australian society. There is an implicit understanding that this process of absorption will entail the assumption of a broad range of Australian obligations, loyalties, values and characteristics.

There is nothing inherently flawed or evil in that understanding, as far as it goes. For example, whether a migrant came here in 1947 or in 2009, whether the migrant stepped off a passenger liner or a sinking fishing boat near Christmas Island, all must be prepared to obey the laws of their new home. All should predispose themselves to a loyalty for and liking of our home. But that is about as far as you can go. Loyalty in its fullest sense must be earned. Our values and characteristics are not proprietal: no section of society, no generation past or present owns or dictates those values and characteristics.

Even though pundits and would-be pundits like me occasionally attempt to list our values and our national characteristics, Australian society is really best at defining them in the negative: by that I mean we all intuitively understand when some action has deeply offended our values or when some person has displayed an "un-Australian" characteristic. Generally and uselessly we tend to think of our values and our characteristics as all that is good.

Occasionally some stirrer will hand us a characteristic they reckon we have that is straight-out bad and of course we all reject that out of hand. Germaine Greer sometimes fills that role for us.

In reflecting back to that great wave of immigration in the 50s, 60s and 70s, I think assimilation was not as useful a word as merge. For sure, most of those immigrants were absorbed seamlessly into our society within one or at most two generations.

But I think that it was more of a merger than perhaps we give it credit for: just as so many of those immigrants now so obviously love this place as their home, the flag as their own and regard the old country as being just that, we have also absorbed much from them. Because it crept up on us, I think to a great degree we haven't noticed how extensively we have been enriched by their cultures and previous lifestyles.

The 70s also saw the final dismantling of the White Australia policy and a theoretical opening of Australia's doors to neighbours from Asia and Africa. With the vast majority of new immigrants coming from Asia, a great new potpourri of cultural influences entered our broader society. Apart from a relatively few casual affronts from a white society still coming to terms with a new social pluralism, this new wave of immigration, particularly from the 70s until the present day, has gone very well, with some exceptions. Leaping into the present day, I'll bet a great number of you are uneasy about a seam of friction between some of our ethnic minorities and elements of the amorphous majority.

Not to beat about the bush, I refer to an ongoing estrangement between broader society and elements of our Muslim community. Our extended history way back to early colonial days shows that from time to time there have been episodes of bad blood between sections of the community based on ethnicity or very occasionally, on religion. Yet they have almost invariably been quite limited in scope and duration.

Over a very long period, Muslim families have been migrating to this country. By and large they have merged into society as seamlessly as any other grouping. Let me just mention what an outstanding role model rugby league footballer Hazem El Masri has been.

Mosques have been respected places of worship around Australia for many years. It is easy to point to an estrangement between parts of the global Muslim community and all non-Muslims but especially Christians over the past 20 years or so, and obviously since the Al-Qa'ida attacks on September 11, 2001.

I think in hindsight it could be claimed that these events and the reactions to them were simply catalysts of our further failure.

By that I mean that some of our Islamic community already felt alienated and isolated from the mainstream in Australia. It is a volatile mix when especially younger people are told that they are surrounded by corrupt and impious behaviour.

It is unsurprising that some of them then perform in ways that stigmatise the whole Islamic community. All of this is exacerbated by the ongoing wider confrontation between jihadists and their range of perceived enemies around the world.

In the elevated temperature and polarised views that characterise this problem, it is hard to have a neat and persuasive prescription on how we move past this.

However, a few observations: first, we must not be panicked into somehow changing or restricting our immigration patterns because of these sorts of issues.

Second, we should be very careful before assigning blame for the problem to our broad Australian way of life, as if the estrangement was all somehow our fault and we should change accordingly. The Australian people know that is not true and wouldn't wear it anyway.

Third, we should continue the many and various ways we engage with the broader Islamic community and especially those who have turned away from us, to bring them back.

Last, we should remember that even over our short history we have dealt with and survived and moved on from some pretty big problems and remained as a society intact and remarkably unified.

7.7

WELCOME NEIGHBOURS

Paul Syvret

> Australia has been settled by successive waves of refugees who have enriched the country economically and culturally. The following article briefly recounts the Australian experience and describes the harrowing experience of some of the country's newest refugees, those fleeing violence and poverty in Afghanistan. These refugees are victims who are like global neighbors, unlike those who profit from human trafficking and smuggling, who are "villains." The author concludes by denouncing right-wing opponents of immigration, whom he labels xenophobes with a "white-bread view of the world."

We are a nation of refugees.

From the day the First Fleet sailed into Sydney Cove in 1788, and over more than two centuries of history, this sunburnt land has been a receptacle for the world's downtrodden, the desperate and the dispossessed.

Our Irish Catholic heritage owes much to those who came to Australia in the period after 1845 fleeing the Potato Famine.

In more recent times our nation has been further enriched by waves of refugees fleeing the deprivations of Europe after World War II (including my natural mother), and then

---

Source: Paul Syvret, "Welcome Neighbours," *The Courier Mail,* April 21, 2009.

from Indochina in the wake of years of bloody conflict in countries such as Korea, Vietnam and Cambodia.

The story is the same today, as ordinary people—people like you and I who just want peace, the opportunity to work, to contribute to a community and to raise a family without the threat of starvation and repression—seek refuge on our shores.

These are people from countries in Africa torn apart by famine and riven by ethnic cleansing; from the ravages of civil war in Sri Lanka; and from the seemingly endless bloodshed and religious and tribal persecution in parts of the Middle East.

They come here because, like us, they dare to hope.

As the mainly Afghan victims of the maritime tragedy off the northern coast last week recover in the burns and intensive care units of hospitals, take a moment to consider their journey, what they sacrificed and what they risked.

And, please, take a moment to offer a prayer for their wellbeing and a chance to settle among us.

These men, women and children left a land their families had called home long before Australia even existed on a map. They travelled halfway around the world in appalling conditions and at constant risk of capture and detention (or worse) in search of a better life.

The final leg of their flight was on an overcrowded timber vessel across the open ocean, organised by people smugglers motivated only by the fees they could gouge, and not any humanitarian considerations.

The people smugglers are the villains of this story, not the fearful refugees seeking shelter and safety. They are the parasites who seek to profit from human suffering, not the asylum seekers who are victims of circumstances beyond their control.

The other villains in this tragedy are those who seek to make political capital out of the plight of others, and also those whose blinkered and xenophobic delusions of self or national interest pollute internet blogs with often bigoted calls to "send them back" from whence they came.

A quick question: Were one of your neighbours to arrive on your doorstep in the middle of the night, distressed, hungry and terrified and asking for help, would you turn them away? Or would you consider it not your problem?

For these asylum seekers are our neighbours in the global village and they deserve our compassion and assistance.

They are not queue jumpers, for in many cases they have fled a land where the said queues, basic freedoms and "proper processes" that we take for granted simply don't exist.

If you live in a remote area in Kurdistan, you don't just pop down to the local consulate office to fill out some forms or fire off a few emails. When there are no straightforward processes for seeking to emigrate, and the lives of you and your family are in peril, you flee.

As for the politics of this latest disaster, the Government should be applauded for putting humanitarian considerations first, and not speculating on the exact circumstances of the boat's sinking before investigations are complete.

The last thing we need now is a repeat of the shamefully cynical half-truths, lies and dog-whistle politics that surrounded the "children overboard" episode a few years ago.

Right-wing columnists like Andrew Bolt who foment unrest with cheap populism only add to the static by accusing the Government of "withholding the facts."

What "facts" are these? Let the investigation run its course, and in the meantime hope (or pray depending on your spiritual bent) for the wellbeing of the victims.

These are human lives—and human lives lost—that we are talking about, not an opportunity to generate a few more lowest-common-denominator posts on a cheaply populist blog. And to those whose self-interested, white-bread view of the world spawns concern of allegedly soft border protection and immigration encouraging waves of ocean-going asylum seekers bound for Australia consider this:

Less than 5 per cent of the nearly 5000 people who applied for asylum on reaching Australian shores last year came by boat.

In Europe nations such as Greece and Italy—countries far smaller and more densely populated than Australia—process refugee applications by the hundreds of thousands. Australia and New Zealand combined account for less than 1 per cent of the world's refugee applications.

As it is, Australia spends hundreds of millions of dollars a year on border protection—in a continent with a population less than that of California but with a coastline larger than that of the United States.

Perhaps some of that money would be better spent on assisting genuine asylum seekers to reach our shores and settle here via better-funded processing of applicants overseas. Population growth equals economic growth.

And here it should be noted—despite popular misconceptions—that recent arrivals are not entitled to the range of social security and care benefits that we are. They do it tough, often relying solely on family, community and church organisations for support.

And in terms of community and assimilation, I'm proud to live next door to a family of Middle-Eastern extraction.

So a short memo to my neighbour Abdul and his family: If the rest of us shared the work ethic and family values of you and your wife we would truly be a richer nation.

Welcome mate. It's good to have you here, and that offer of a cuppa or a home-cooked meal still stands. My door is open.

7.8

GADDAFI'S £4BN MIGRANT DEMAND

Macer Hall

Recent years have witnessed a rising tide of West and North African refugees, many of whom are Muslim, driven by poverty, unemployment, violence, population pressure, and environmental degradation to seek entry into Europe. Southern European countries such as Italy, Spain, and Greece have

Source: Macer Hall, "Gaddafi's £4bn Migrant Demand," *The Express,* September 1, 2010.

been favored destinations for these migrants, and these countries have sought to curb the flow. The following selection describes deceased Libyan dictator Muammar Gaddafi's offer of help—for a price.

Maverick Libyan leader Muammar Gaddafi provoked outrage last night by demanding £4.1billion a year from the EU to stop illegal immigration "turning Europe black."

Colonel Gaddafi, in a speech in Italy, claimed his country needed the money for security measures to stop thousands of Africans heading across the Mediterranean.

Gaddafi's remarks, dismissed as blackmail last night, came on the last day of a two-day visit to Italy which had already sparked controversy when he urged all Europeans to convert to Islam and lectured 200 models and actresses on the Muslim faith.

In his farewell speech in Rome, the 67-year-old dictator said: "Italy needs to convince her European allies to accept this Libyan proposal: five billion euros to Libya to stop illegal immigration. Europe runs the risk of turning black from illegal immigration, it could turn into Africa.

"We need support from the European Union to stop this army trying to get across from Libya, which is their entry point.

"At the moment there is a dangerous level of immigration from Africa into Europe and we don't know what will happen.

"What will be the reaction of the white Christian Europeans to this mass of hungry uneducated Africans?

"We don't know if Europe will remain an advanced and cohesive continent or if it will be destroyed by this barbarian invasion.

"We have to imagine that this could happen but before it does we need to work together."

In Britain, Conservative MP Daniel Kawczynski said: "Specific targeted measures from Europe to assist North African countries to tackle migration would be a good thing. But there should be no blank cheques. I would be appalled if the British Government started handing out ludicrously large sums of money like this."

Sir Andrew Green, of the pressure group Migrationwatch, said: "Cooperation with Libya over illegal immigration to Europe is clearly very important but £4billion sounds a bit steep."

And UK Independence Party Euro MP Nigel Farage said: "This is blackmail from a delusional dictator.

"It is outrageous that after calling for us all to convert to Islam, he is now threatening to send us Africa's poor benighted masses."

Libya and Italy have already agreed on a deal that allows the Italian navy to intercept illegal immigrants and return them to Libya.

But the measure triggered criticism from the United Nations' Refugee Agency and others.

Many illegal immigrants die in their attempts to cross the Mediterranean, and those who are caught are taken back to camps in Libya where conditions are appalling.

7.9

PARADISE LOST—WHERE MIGRANTS OUTNUMBER ISLANDERS BY 27 TO 1

Nick Fagge

> The first European territories that many African migrants reach are small islands like Italian-owned Lampedusa near Libya and the Spanish Canaries off West Africa. Still another is the tiny Greek island of Agathonísi, located at the northernmost point of the Dodecanese Islands near Turkey in the Aegean Sea, which found itself overwhelmed by refugees from Asia, Africa, and the Middle East.

A tiny island has become Europe's frontline in the war on illegal immigration.

Newcomers outnumber native Greeks by 27 to one on Agathonisi, five miles from the Turkish coast.

It has been overwhelmed by migrants from Asia, Africa and the Middle East passing through on their way to Britain and other rich European countries.

The island's 150-strong population was bewildered when bedraggled men, women and children began arriving in rickety boats. Now the number of migrants has passed 4,000, the islanders can no longer cope.

Last month alone 700 migrants from countries including Afghanistan, Iraq and Nigeria arrived.

Community leader Evangelos Kottoros said: "We're a warm-hearted people and at first we welcomed them.

"We gave them food, we gave them clothes, but we just don't have the infrastructure—some days 180 arrive here." The crisis yesterday prompted Greek Premier Costas Karamanlis to call on European Union leaders for help to combat the influx, which has grown by more than 90 per cent in under five years.

He claims Greece is being forced to shoulder the burden of illegal immigration alone because its location makes it the gateway to Western Europe.

With 10,000 miles of coastline, Greece has the largest sea border of any EU state.

Mr Karamanlis said: "Illegal immigration is one of Europe's most serious problems but for us it is even more pressing." Official figures state that more than 112,000 migrants entered the EU through Greece last year. The estimated total for 2008 is more than 120,000, many pushed out of traffickers' boats and forced to swim for the shore.

Source: Nick Fagge, "Paradise Lost—Where Migrants Outnumber Islanders by 27 to 1," *The Express,* October 18, 2008.

A Greek government insider said: "Hundreds of thousands of migrants arrive on our shores every year.

"The majority come without papers because they claim to be political refugees. They are not—they are just poor people looking for a better life.

Most of them do not want to stay in Greece—they want to go to Britain and other rich European countries." At first the illegals on Agathonisi were transferred to the neighbouring island of Patmos, but when the number of migrants exceeded that island's 3,000 population last month officials there closed docks to new arrivals.

Patmos's union of hoteliers said: "Our island cannot be promoted as a destination for high-end tourism on the one hand and on the other allow hundreds of illegal immigrants to wander around hungry and dirty." Last night Sir Andrew Green of MigrationWatchUK warned: "Until those who seek asylum falsely are swiftly removed, this flow is likely to continue."

7.10

WHY SWEDEN'S FAR-RIGHT, ANTI-IMMIGRANT PARTY MADE POWERFUL GAINS

Ritt Goldstein

The wave of migration into Europe following the economic recession produced a significant backlash, which is reflected in increased votes for right-wing xenophobic and anti-immigrant political parties like France's National Front. The final selection in the chapter describes the history and growing popularity of one such party, the Sweden Democrats.

Throughout much of Europe, the far right is on the rise, gaining support with a message against the political establishment, multiculturalism, and immigration that appears to be resonating with many disillusioned Europeans.

In liberal Sweden, the far-right Sweden Democrats, a party with a neo-Nazi history, won 20 seats in the Sept. 19 parliamentary vote, enough support to leave the leading center-right coalition without a governing majority. While the SD, which campaigned that it would cut immigration rates by 90 percent, is widely castigated as "racist" and "Islamaphobic," it nonetheless struck a deep chord among some in this country known for its political correctness.

Source: Ritt Goldstein, "Why Sweden's Far-Right, Anti-Immigrant Party Made Powerful Gains: Sweden Is Now Facing a Newly Powerful Political Party, the Sweden Democrats, That Has a Neo-Nazi Past and Advocates Drastically Cutting the Country's Liberal Immigration Policies," *The Christian Science Monitor,* October 7, 2010.

Europe's far-right parties comprise "an outcry of people that felt they were forgotten by the mainstream," says Cristian Norocel, a political scientist at both Stockholm University and Finland's University of Helsinki.

In Denmark, the Netherlands, Hungary, and Switzerland, far-right populist parties have similarly gained new footing, exercising their political capital to advocate anti-immigration platforms, and often focusing on Muslims, tougher stances on law and order. Their steady rise comes as much of the Continent is mired in recession, governments having made deep cuts in social programs and threatening more to come.

Though Sweden's economy is growing at more than four times the European Union average, new "economic and social reforms" here mean that many Swedes will not share in this prosperity.

Spontaneous protests in the streets followed last month's election, with thousands of Swedes railing against the SD. All seven of Sweden's major political parties have vowed to refuse cooperation with the SD. But despite all the hand-wringing among both progressives and mainstream conservatives, the SD has suddenly become a political force to be reckoned with.

The Origins of the Far-Right Sweden Democrats

The SD was founded in 1988 and its current leader, Jimmie Åkesson, joined in 1995, a period when Nazi uniforms were still seen at its meetings. With a determination to enter parliament, the party distanced itself from the Nazi imagery and adopted a public profile that appears considerably closer to the Swedish mainstream, adamantly claiming that it is a "normal party."

According to SD's website, the party rejects "multiculturalism," attributes increased crime to immigration, and calls for an end to "public support for immigrant organizations," adding that "all other activities aimed at promoting foreign cultures and identities in Sweden should be canceled."

It also wants to outlaw "religious buildings, with a non-Swedish building style, strange architecture" and forbid public workers from wearing "conspicuous religious or political symbols, such as a headscarf or turban." What's more, it calls for the government to support immigrants who want to return to their homelands.

Mr. Norocel called SD a "wolf in sheep's skin" and says that it's "very skillful at picturing a scapegoat" by targeting segments of Swedish society outside the country's traditional mainstream.

"In 2001, they suddenly got rid of all the uniforms, the swastikas, the symbolism that scared so many voters," notes Mikael Lundström, a political scientist with Lund University in Sweden. He says they have cultivated an image that adds "respectability to an issue [surrounding multiculturalism], but they still want to kick people out and they want to close the borders . . . in that they align themselves very much with the hard right."

Sweden's percentage of foreign-born residents has risen steadily, from 4 percent in 1960 to 14.3 percent today. Currently, that means 1.3 million Swedish residents were born outside the country.

Return to Sweden's Welfare State?

But while the SD is appealing to anti-immigration sentiment, it's also winning support from Swedes who are concerned about the outsourcing of jobs, particularly in manufacturing, and the erosion of the social safety nets that were once taken for granted.

The SD has "managed to fish in very murky waters on both the left and the right. The party does not have just a racist political agenda . . . it is also a matter of welfare," says Mr. Norocel.

Over the past four years, the SD and other government critics have lashed out against the current center-right governing coalition for dismantling Sweden's "welfare state" amid waves of tax cuts and efforts to privatize the public sector. Pension benefits, unemployment benefits, and a host of social programs have all taken a hit.

Agneta Börjesson, general secretary of the progressive Swedish Green Party, observed that "the major parties have not been able in addressing the negative impacts of globalization," seeing this as the dominant reason behind SD's rise. She spoke of "Big Companies" moving offshore, "schools where you have a lot of different cultures," as issues that remained unaddressed.

Political scientists Lundström and Norocel separately shared similar globalization concerns, seeing the far right's rise as rooted in globalization's negative effects. Börjesson further drew a line between SD's leadership and its voters, alluding to the latter group as people who—personally or professionally—were swayed after experiencing "something bad happen to them."

Mr. Åkesson and the SD have promised a return of the welfare state, or the "Folkhemmet" (People's Home), that was originally championed by Sweden's Social Democrats since the 1920s. But the SD wants to ensure this public welfare system includes only those it defines as "Swedish."

Norocel says that many SD supporters are drawn by the social welfare message and not the discourse that its critics call racist. Still, he says, the party's nationalism, its stance on immigration and perspective upon cultural stereotypes, plus its embrace of social programs, parallels many aspects of "very early National Socialism (Nazism) in Europe."

The SD's Newfound Political Clout

Mr. Lundström, the political scientist, observed that some Swedes have wanted to discuss immigration, but that the political establishment's down playing immigration questions has allowed SD "to rise and own that issue." But while it's still uncertain what impact the SD rise will have on Sweden's overall political tilt, their electoral success does give them more power in the country's court system.

In Swedish courts, particularly where criminal and asylum cases are handled, a traditional judge will decide a case in conjunction with two or three lay judges that are political appointees.

The SD "might use the courts as a political arena in a way that hasn't been common in Sweden," says associate law professor Eric Bylander of the University of Göteborg, Sweden. This may have a chilling effect among Sweden's foreign-born residents, especially among the country's estimated 400,000 Muslims.

In October 2009, SD leader Åkesson wrote in Scandinavia's largest paper, Aftonbladet, that "Muslims are our biggest foreign threat." The party has also released highly debated statistical reports implying that new immigrants (primarily from the Middle East) are responsible for increases in serious crimes. A local SD leader also made headlines recently by claiming that many of those from the Middle East have a "gene" that makes them more violent.

With regret obvious in her voice, the Green Party's Börjesson noted that, overall, Sweden has become "a country of more fear." Citing the fading memories of WWII and the 1930s, political scientist Lundström emphasized that if the far right could rise in Sweden, "it can happen anywhere."

Chapter 8

ENVIRONMENTAL GLOBALIZATION

Environmental issues like global warming and air and sea pollution are archetypal globalization issues inasmuch as they directly or indirectly affect all countries and require collective efforts to cope with them. The chapter addresses some of these issues and the ways in which countries have sought—successfully or unsuccessfully—to manage or control them.

Contemporary environmental threats are global in scope, a fact reflected by global warming. During the 20th century, the average global temperature warmed by 0.7° C (1.3° F), and according to the International Energy Agency, global temperature is expected to rise an additional 3.5° C (6.3° F) by 2100. The global failure to impose stringent limits on carbon emissions has led some to conclude that the failure to limit global warming reflects an absence of global governance and that the world must begin to adapt to a warmer world. Possible consequences include the melting of winter snow, causing spring floods; rising sea levels, which will flood coastal regions; coral bleaching, which will harm fish; increased rainfall in wet regions and extreme drought in arid regions; and more extreme weather conditions.

Global warming is, however, only one of many collective environmental threats. Growing populations in the developing world weigh heavily on economic growth, and poverty reduction and the growing demand for energy reflect the trade-off between ecology and economics. How do we provide sufficient energy to foster economic development and raise standards of living while coping with challenges like global warming? Other globalized environmental challenges include the loss of biodiversity, inadequate food production, disappearing forests and spreading deserts, and polluted seas and insufficient fresh water.

8.1

EXTREME NATURAL HAZARDS: POPULATION GROWTH, GLOBALIZATION AND ENVIRONMENTAL CHANGE

Herbert E. Huppert and R. Stephen J. Sparks

> The chapter opens with an analysis of the growing risk of extreme natural hazards, like the earthquake and tsunami that struck Japan in 2011 and produced the world's most dangerous nuclear crisis since the Chernobyl disaster in the Soviet Union in 1986. The authors argue that such disasters have become more probable owing to environmental factors such as global warming, which is raising sea levels and producing extreme weather; the draining of marshlands, which was linked to the damage caused in New Orleans by Hurricane Katrina; and the destruction of forests, which alters weather patterns in countries like Sri Lanka and Bangladesh. The authors argue that growing populations, especially in the developing world, combined with rapid urbanization dramatically increase the prospect of catastrophe when natural disasters like earthquakes take place. Finally, they point out that globalization and the resulting global interdependence mean that the effects of natural disasters are likely to be felt far beyond the region in which they occur.

Mankind is becoming ever more susceptible to natural disasters, largely as a consequence of population growth and globalization. It is likely that in the future, we will experience several disasters per year that kill more than 10 000 people. A calamity with a million casualties is just a matter of time. This situation is mainly a consequence of increased vulnerability. Climate change may also be affecting the frequency of extreme weather events as well as the vulnerability of coastal areas due to sea-level rise. Disastrous outcomes can only increase unless better ways are found to mitigate the effects through improved forecasting and warning, together with more community preparedness and resilience. There are particular difficulties with extreme events, which can affect several countries, while the largest events can have global consequences. The hazards of supervolcanic eruptions and asteroid impacts could cause global disaster with threats to civilization and deaths of billions of people. Although these are very rare events, they will

Source: Excerpted from Herbert E. Huppert and R. Stephen J. Sparks, "Extreme Natural Hazards: Population Growth, Globalization and Environmental Change," *Philosophical Transactions: Mathematical, Physical and Engineering Sciences* 36:1845 (August 15, 2006), 1875–88. Notes appearing in the original have been deleted.

happen and require consideration. More frequent and smaller events in the wrong place at the wrong time could have very large human, environmental and economic effects. A sustained effort is needed to identify places at risk and take steps to apply science before the events occur.

1. Introduction

The natural world can be a dramatic, dynamic and dangerous place. Life ultimately thrives on Earth because it is a dynamic planet, but the extremes of nature can threaten the survival of individuals, communities and even species. Every year television pictures and newspapers report scenes of devastation, despair and death caused by huge earthquakes, floods, droughts, cyclones, landslides and volcanic eruptions. The Asian tsunami, with around 250 000 deaths, huge economic losses and long-term damage to development programmes in the affected countries, brought home to the world the realities of the danger. We live in times of increasing vulnerability to extreme natural hazards. The Asian tsunami was a truly global disaster which affected not only many countries in the region, but also tourists from the developed world on holiday in southeast Asia. For example, the incident represented the greatest loss of life of Swedish citizens from a natural event. Again, Hurricane Katrina, which devastated New Orleans in September 2005, had global effects on oil prices and showed that even the world's most powerful and wealthy country experiences difficulties with the extremes of nature.

Science plays a critical role in understanding and mitigating the effects of extreme events. Like many individuals and organizations, the scientific community experienced a mixture of profound sympathy for the victims of the Asian tsunami and introspection on how such events could be better prepared for and faced. As a consequence, the Royal Society of London decided to hold a fast-track discussion meeting to examine the role of science and technology in ameliorating the effects of extreme natural hazards. Problems related to natural catastrophes go well beyond scientific and technological approaches. Economic, political, cultural, sociological and psychological factors are of huge importance, as is the role of governments, international agencies and NGOs in responding to crises.

2. Natural Catastrophes Are Increasing

A disturbing message from the meeting is that the frequency of major natural catastrophes is increasing. These statistics were brought alive by the Asian tsunami, Hurricane Katrina and the Kashmir earthquake in the year prior to the meeting. Although droughts were not discussed specifically, the famines in Niger, Mali and Mozambique could be added to the list of natural catastrophes for 2005. The southeast Asia tsunami and Kashmir earthquake illustrated the vulnerability of developing countries, resulting in terrible death tolls, great suffering and whole communities being destroyed. Hurricane Katrina showed that extreme events can have global economic effects as well as causing severe destruction and torment, particularly for the poor. For the foreseeable future, the world can expect several natural events per year that can kill tens of thousands of people, adversely affect millions of people and cause severe economic and social disruption.

Several speakers forecast, reluctantly, that an event that would kill more than a million people in the next few decades was likely to occur.

One possible explanation for the increasing devastation brought by natural catastrophes is that the frequency of natural events is increasing. A different and more likely explanation, however, is that there is increased influence of events due to ever increasing vulnerability arising from larger populations in high-risk locations. Human activities are also a critical issue in exacerbating vulnerability to natural hazards, ranging from anthropogenic climate change at one extreme to local deforestation and changes in land use at the other. Nevertheless, real increases in the rates of large magnitude events are worth brief consideration. The major tectonic hazards of earthquakes and volcanic eruptions are governed by plate tectonics and typically involve stochastic processes. Adjustments and changes in plate motions and arrangements are exceedingly slow, operating on time-scales of millions of years. On time-scales of decades and even the millennia relevant to human affairs, the rates of these events are relatively steady and unchanging on a global scale. Earthquakes and volcanic eruptions taken globally approximately follow a Poisson (random) distribution in time. However, there can be spatial and temporal variations in rates of events with distributions that may be clustered or more regular in time at an individual volcano or along a particular fault system, where the occurrence of events is controlled by smaller-scale, local processes and effects. There can also be issues related to rare and extreme events that are not well represented in the very short period of recorded history (ca 2000 years). Notwithstanding these possible variations, there is no evidence that the increase in devastating earthquakes, for example, represents some unexplained and indeed very unlikely increase in plate activity.

The case for increasing natural events due to environmental change, in particular of global climate, is different. Since 1960, the number of tropical cyclones that have been classified as categories 4 and 5 has doubled. This change could be due to natural variability; though a systematically warmer atmosphere and ocean could also explain the change. A warmer Earth has more energy and models of the atmosphere suggest more variability and more extreme events. For tropical cyclones, for example, warmer sea surface temperatures in sub-tropical latitudes could be a factor in increasing the rates of extreme events. The question of whether global warming can cause increases in extreme weather events is still unresolved, but is being taken very seriously by atmospheric scientists. The other less contentious effect of global warming is sea-level rise, which increases the vulnerability of coastal communities to natural hazards, including floods, storm surges and tsunamis. Wheater estimated that storm surges with a current recurrence rate of 1 in 60 years may change to 1 in 2 years by the end of the century, based on a 0.5 m rise in sea level. While quantitatively such estimates have large uncertainties, qualitatively the trend must be correct.

Consensus is definitely emerging that the major causes of increasing natural catastrophes are directly related to human activity. Obvious effects include population growth and urbanization, with spectacular growth of megacities over the last few decades, and environmental degradation and change caused by human activities. The world's population is becoming more concentrated in urban areas rather than in the less densely populated rural areas. In 2007, for the first time in human history, more people will live in urban centres than in the countryside. Taken together, these changes make communities much more vulnerable to natural hazards. Jackson gives the striking example of Iran, where villages have grown into large towns and in the case of Tehran into a megacity with 12 million inhabitants. Tehran is built on an active fault system with associated water springs, which allowed the initial habitation to develop. Tehran has been destroyed by earthquakes on four occasions over the centuries, when it was a small provincial town of no political importance. The buildings in Tehran are similar to those of other Iranian cities, which have been devastated by earthquakes with very high mortality rates (60 to 80% of the resident population being killed). Several thousand deaths 100 years ago from a population of 10 000 was a tragedy; up to a million deaths in a city of 10 million would be a momentous calamity. Many megacities around the world have developed in the last few decades in highly vulnerable sites; thus an event that dwarfs the Asian tsunami seems inevitable.

Environmental degradation and change also affect vulnerability, usually in adverse ways. For example, urban development and some agricultural practices reduce infiltration so that floods become worse even if the meteorological processes remain the same. Destruction of mangrove swamps in Sri Lanka increased the vulnerability of coastal communities to the tsunami. Deforestation can cause changes in rainfall patterns and infiltration, resulting in more devastating floods. There is, for example, evidence that environmental changes in the mountain catchment areas in the Himalayas have increased run-off and major floods, adversely affecting Bangladesh. In the SW Province of Cameroon, shanty towns have built up at the base of steep slopes, which have become unstable due to undercutting; the result has been landslides almost every rainy season with many deaths. In December 1999, flash floods in Venezuela killed more than 30 000 people, many in modern high-rise buildings, under similar circumstances of environmental degradation related to unplanned development.

3. The Influence of Extreme Events

The Asian tsunami has been described as a wake-up call for the world. This event affected 11 countries directly and there was loss of life from over 50 countries, including tourists from the affluent north. Hurricane Katrina affected oil prices for a few months, but financially the effects may not be long-lasting on a global scale. However, scientists are well aware that there are extreme natural events that can have much greater effects and consequences. Extreme events are rare, but can have an impact on humanity on a global scale. The possible consequences of extreme events include: global economic crises; many millions to tens of millions of deaths; catastrophic and irrecoverable destruction of megacities and possibly whole countries; global disruption of food supplies, transport and communications; severe climate states; and environmental pollution on a global scale. These effects may in turn lead to famine, disease, political strife, collapse of social order, failure of international and national organizations in the face of overwhelming effects and even possibly the outbreak of wars and collapse of civilization. The most extreme and rarest events (asteroid impacts and possibly the largest super-eruptions) may threaten species survival. Unfortunately, such apocalyptic visions are not science fiction and are not scare mongering. The evidence for natural events on the scale necessary for global catastrophe is robust; humanity will eventually have to face and attempt to survive them.

It is only very recently that the threat from extreme events has been recognized beyond specialist scientific circles. This recognition comes at a critical stage in human development as the world becomes increasingly interdependent and increasingly vulnerable. Globalization seems irreversible and concepts of cooperation, international agreements and global community have emerged. Many complex factors have led nations to cooperate and take collective actions in the last few decades. Response to environmental change has been one of them. The ozone problem due to chlorofluorocarbon pollution of the upper atmosphere is a strikingly successful example with the Montreal Protocol resulting in international action to prevent a very serious threat. Global warming is an even more profound threat, where international action and agreement to reduce carbon emissions is at least recognized as high on the agenda, even if the mitigation steps are proving so difficult to implement. Following the Asian earthquake, the Hyogo agreement represents the first time that the international community has recognized the need for collective and coordinated action to mitigate the effects of natural hazards. Such developments are grounds for cautious optimism that humanity can unite to reduce the effects of environmental change and natural hazards. Only international efforts can address extreme hazards; even the most powerful country on Earth has difficulties when the magnitude of the events is sufficiently large.

The first recognition that there can be global catastrophes came from the serious consideration given to asteroid impacts. This interest emerged from advances in astronomy, from observations of numerous impact craters on other planets and from research concerned with the consequences of nuclear war. In the 1970s, scientists alerted the world to the severe and catastrophic effects of nuclear war. Apart from the direct destruction and radiation, atmospheric models indicated that the Earth could be plunged into a nuclear winter with severe conditions lasting for many years and threatening human survival. These warnings from sections of the science community arguably had a major role in persuading politicians from rival power blocks, ideologies and political systems that there was an urgent need to control the proliferation of nuclear arms and reduce tensions that might lead to nuclear war. Several scientific advances coincided with the nuclear war issue to show that global disaster with similar effects could also happen by asteroid impact. The exploration of the solar system and discovery of geologically recent giant impacts on Earth made it clear that asteroid impact is a ubiquitous feature of the solar system and part of the Earth's natural environment. Sufficiently large impacts can cause mass extinctions. The US and UK Governments commissioned panels of eminent scientists to report on the threat to Earth from Near Earth object (NEOs) and this in turn led to a programme of systematic tracking of all space objects that might collide with the Earth. Asteroid impacts happen all the time; a little known but dramatic fact is that an explosion with energy equivalent to a Hiroshima-sized nuclear explosion occurs on average every year in the upper atmosphere. Fortunately, the atmosphere offers great protection to the Earth and only the largest, but also very rare, objects can get through to the Earth's surface. NEO studies, stimulated by governmental concern, have been a success.

By 2008, 90% of NEOs greater than 1 km diameter in the solar system will have been identified. Their orbits can be predicated with great accuracy. It seems likely that any object that has a chance of colliding with the Earth should be identified many years before a potential impact. It also appears that the technology may exist, at least in principle, to attempt to divert such objects from collision.

Following on from the raised awareness of NEOs and persuading governments to take the issue seriously, parallel activity is now developing for very large magnitude volcanic eruptions. As with asteroids, the effect of large eruptions has been popularized by the media in TV dramas, documentaries, movies and popular books. The dramatic, albeit scientifically poorly defined, super-volcano and super-eruption are new terms that have raised public awareness. An explosive eruption on the scale of the eruption of Toba 74 000 years ago is perhaps the only other kind of natural hazard apart from NEOs that might cause global catastrophe. However, volcanic events that could devastate large regions need not be so extreme. The Campanian eruption, which originated from the Bay of Naples ca 38 000 years ago, would be a catastrophe of apocalyptic proportions for countries in the central and eastern Mediterranean, as well as disrupting life internationally on an enormous scale and plunging the world into several years of severe anomalous weather. Such events happen globally about every 10 000 years, perhaps sufficiently frequently to be taken seriously.

For volcanic eruptions, the nature and state of the science is quite different than NEOs and it is less clear what can be done. Only ca 20% of the world's volcanoes with potential for explosive eruption have records that extend back over 10 000 years. Statistical studies of the global database suggest that for volcanism more than 2000 years ago, only 20% of large magnitude explosive eruptions have been recognized. Much work needs to be done to improve the basic record and identify high-risk areas. It is likely that several locations with potential for future super-eruptions have not yet even been recognized. A particularly thorny problem is that even if a large volcano shows signs of an impending eruption, we do not know how to recognize whether it will turn out to be a much more commonplace small eruption or a very rare super-eruption. Much more research is also needed to evaluate environmental effects and validate these assessments from geological data. Most importantly no known technology can prevent volcanic eruptions.

Although other natural hazards may not have direct global effects, a large earthquake, tsunami, giant landslide, tropical cyclone or flood in the wrong place at the wrong time can have serious global repercussions. Stein et al. illustrates this issue by an analysis of a major earthquake beneath Tokyo. This study suggests that there is a 40% chance of such an earthquake in the next 30 years and the economic losses, estimated at many billions of dollars, might plunge the world into financial crisis. Earthquakes affecting Istanbul or Tehran or an eruption of Vesuvius affecting Naples, might have a variety of political, social and economic consequences that go well beyond the borders of the directly affected nations. A large landslide of the flanks of a volcano or continental shelf may result in ocean-wide tsunamis.

A particular difficulty with extreme events is that by definition they happen infrequently. Communities tend to be better prepared to adapt to the higher frequency hazards, for which communities hold their collective memories of previous disasters.

Populations prone to frequent tropical cyclones build shelters, whereas those in earth-quake zones may design buildings that can withstand shaking. In Bangladesh, mounds and purpose-built shelters are built to protect the population from frequent floods related to storm surges. In 1970, a storm-surge flood generated by a tropical cyclone killed an estimated 300 000 people in Bangladesh. Since then, several similar events have resulted in only a few hundred deaths as a consequence of the mitigation steps of building shelters on mounds. Without wishing to underplay that loss of life still occurs, the dramatic reduction in deaths is impressive. However, in many instances designs are typically made for more frequent events of lesser magnitude or building standards fall short of design criteria. For large magnitude events that happen less frequently than once every few generations, the preparations may not be sufficient. The estimated death toll of 938 during Hurricane Katrina is large for a highly developed country and was a consequence of the effects being more severe than had been planned for.

4. Identifying Areas at Risk

A sensible approach to identifying areas at risk is to use historical information combined with scientific understanding in order to map out hazard-prone areas. . . . This works for reasonably frequent and persistent hazards, but is of limited value for rare and extreme events. The historic catalogue . . . is not long enough to be adequately representative. In some cases, areas with high risk could be missed. It is, for example, a moot point whether the threat of tsunamis on coastal Sri Lanka would have been recognized by such desk-based retrospective studies prior to 26 December 2004 and, depending on the length of the record used, the same problem may be true for other regions.

One of the most frustrating aspects of the Asian tsunami is that the science was sufficiently well-known for the tragedy to have been anticipated well before it happened. Maps of earthquake hazard published in 1987 and 1996 identified the Sumatran plate boundary as a place that had accumulated large strains over a long length. Sumatra was identified as one of the two places on Earth where a magnitude 9 earthquake might occur in the near future; Peru was the other identified locality. The basic principles of tsunami propagation and behaviour have been understood for decades and the high likelihood of tsunamis accompanying ocean floor earthquakes greater than 8.5 was also well known. Geologists . . . recognized the signs of an impending huge earthquake. They based their conclusion from the sinking of islands to the south of Sumatra due to the inexorable bending of the plate.

Hurricane Katrina is even more problematic. Such an event was foreseen in a *Scientific American* article. In this case, forecasts of the track were accurate and gave three days warning to authorities in New Orleans. In terms of storm track, the science was not only known and robust, but was communicated. However, the storm surges, intensity and resulting devastation were not well forecast.

5. Prediction, Forecasts and Warnings

The ability of scientists to predict, give good forecasts and provide timely warnings varies greatly between different hazards and in different circumstances. Here, we use prediction in the sense of quite precise statements on the time, place and size of a future event. Forecasts are more general statements about future hazardous events, which are commonly expressed probabilistically (i.e., how likely it is for an event to happen). Effective warning depends not only on science and technology but also on communication systems and on how the messages are interpreted. . . .

So-called 'false' alarms are a major problem for many hazards. For volcanic eruptions the difficulty is that it can be hard to distinguish volcanic unrest (due to underground magma movements from the signs of an impending eruption). Also, we cannot yet predict the size, duration and climax timing of an eruption. Magma movement causes earthquakes, ground deformation, release of volcanic gases and phenomena such as steam explosions. However, magma may fail to erupt. The 1976 crisis at the Soufriere Volcano, Guadeloupe, is a cause celebre, when unrest and uncertainty led to the evacuation of 70 000 people for 3 months. No significant magmatic eruption took place. This apparent failure by scientists led to skepticism among some of the local population, which will mean that a future crisis at this volcano may be even harder to manage.

Warning systems for tsunamis are now quite sophisticated and the Pacific Tsunami Warning System (PTWS) has worked well. Admittedly, there is a problem about too many false alarms, but this problem can be solved in the future. The combinations of technology, good understanding of the propagation of the waves and good communications allow timely warnings. The nature of tsunamis also means that the warnings can be given many tens of minutes, if not hours, before a tsunami arrives, except on coastlines close to the epicentre. Warnings are of no use unless the recipients are well-prepared to respond and take action. In this regard, many of the countries within the Pacific system have well-prepared communities and simple steps have been taken to make sure that there is continuous education in coastal communities. All these attributes of a warning system were tragically missing on 26th December 2004.

Extreme weather can also be forecast and effective warnings given. For Hurricane Katrina, however, while the warning came in time, the response was inadequate. A further problem was that the levees were designed for a category 3 surge and no money had been forthcoming to upgrade them. The reasons for this are complex and no doubt are currently being analysed in the aftermath of the disaster, but the essential issues are likely to relate to preparedness and education of public officials and agencies responsible for acting on warnings. Predicting accurately the intensity of extreme weather can be a problem . . .

6. Preparedness and Mitigation of Extreme Natural Events

Recent events show that nations and the international community are not well prepared for rare extreme events. The national and international mechanisms to deal with these problems have evidently not been working adequately. International organizations like the UN have envisaged that nations should take individual responsibility for developing preparedness and mitigation programmes and initiatives, albeit supported by international activities such as the International Strategy for Disaster Reduction (ISDR). For extreme natural events that affect many countries, however, this approach looks increasingly questionable. A great deal of energy is going into soul-searching and analysis following the Asian tsunami and Hurricane Katrina. The Hyogo agreement and the report of the UK Working Group on Natural Hazards are examples of the response. Suggestions for change include the formation of an International Science Panel for Natural Hazard Assessment, a wider remit for the World Meteorological Organization in distributing warnings, the creation of a global early warning system for tsunamis and a major role for the Global Earth Observing System programme . . . in assessing natural hazards. UNDP and the World Bank are also currently exploring a new programme for assessing global risks from natural hazards.

The issue then for natural hazards is: who is responsible for bringing the results of science research and technology to the communities and authorities that need this knowledge for mitigation and preparedness? Put another way, where is the demand for hazards related research? The insurance industry is perhaps the only major industry with direct interest in these issues and here the market clearly plays a central role. Until now, insurance, or the sharing of risk, is only widespread in the developed world, so that industry can only play a partial role. Politicians and civilian authorities are a major potential customer for the results of research on natural hazards for the good of their citizens. However, the costs of application, in practice, are prohibitive for many low to medium income countries and may have very low priority in comparison to poverty alleviation, economic development, education and health, for example. An important role in knowledge and technology transfer can be played by NGOs, development banks, and public private partnerships The role of individual nations is also problematic for events that affect many countries; regional and international organizations may not give natural hazards sufficiently high priority. Almost inevitably natural hazards become a priority immediately after a major disaster, with spending on disaster relief being vastly greater than spending on mitigation. The tendency for taking short-term perspectives is endemic in politics and government. The media are another potential customer who can play a positive role in education and communication about hazards and risk. Responsible journalism provides a very powerful mechanism for persuading politicians to act and communities to take notice of scientific information. Regrettably, the media can also be sensationalist and only become interested in natural hazards when death and destruction have already occurred.

Perhaps the demand that really matters is generated from the bottom by ordinary people, who are threatened by natural hazards. Education has a key role in producing citizens and specialists in the affected countries who are well-informed and part of the connected international community that understands the technical advances and how to apply them. In developing countries innovative schemes for education, self-help and access to knowledge, such as the Knowledge Centre concept in India can play a critical role. It appears that too few resources are invested in education on natural hazards in long-term educational projects that build up knowledge, understanding and ultimately demand in local communities as well as indigenous expertise that can offer effective advice to authorities.

Another psychological difficulty is that it is always much harder to justify spending money on steps that lead to loss avoidance and prevent loss of life than to spend it on the visible effects of disaster. . . .

7. Concluding Remarks

The effects of natural hazards are inexorably increasing and have to be seen in the context of an increasingly complex, interdependent and populated world. The increase is largely the consequence of growing vulnerability exacerbated by human activities, but for some hazards there may be a real increase due to climate change and associated sea-level rise. Globalization also means that the consequences of natural events are increasingly penetrating beyond the borders of the nation that is directly affected. If the disaster is in a poor country then the international community responds mostly with disaster relief. If the disaster is in a developed nation, such as the USA or Japan, then there can be adverse effects for the whole world economy, with major financial and human losses. Some disasters are on such a large scale that they affect many nations and may even have global effects and repercussions. It seems that while there have been and continue to be significant scientific advances in our understanding of natural hazards, the application of the science and the response mechanisms have been inadequate.

There is always more research to be done; this is endless and, with finite resources and many other priorities for governments, the research community cannot expect a huge increase in research funding. Responses to natural disasters are largely after the event and not enough is being done to support research to identify areas at risk, assess this risk, recommend countermeasures and strengthen resilience in communities at risk. In many areas of science, the application of scientific research is demand led, but this seems not to be the case for natural hazards. Demand is partial, short-term and typically follows a crisis. Scientists need to be more vociferous both to create demand and to make sure that robust science is prominent in policy-making. It is enormously difficult to get money to protect against a forthcoming event.

8.2

NAVIGATING THE MUDDY WATERS OF MARITIME LAW

Andy Ho

Ecoterrorism

> The following selection describes the efforts of activists of a nongovernmental group to prevent Japanese from catching whales. The Japanese regard such efforts as "ecoterrorism" and have sought to bring legal action against the group.

At the end of the whaling season last month, Japan's Antarctic whaling fleet brought home its smallest catch in years.

Source: Andy Ho, "Navigating the Muddy Waters of Maritime Law," *The Straits Times,* May 6, 2010.

The Japanese said that anti-whaling activists from the Sea Shepherd Conservation Society had harassed them for a total of 31 days. Their 'acts of piracy' and 'eco-terrorism' had imperilled the lives of whaling crews, Tokyo alleged last week. So it was putting out an arrest warrant for Mr Paul Watson, founder and leader of the United States-based group.

The group admits on its website to having sunk 10 whaling ships since 1979. Still, it says it has not purposely done so since 1998. Although ramming, scuttling, disabling or sinking ships is usually considered criminal, neither Mr Watson nor his fellow eco-activists have ever been seriously punished for their activities.

The reason, Mr Watson has opined, is that his group merely enforces international conservation law. In fact, the International Whaling Commission has had in place a global moratorium on commercial whaling since 1986.

Despite this moratorium, Japan, one of the few whaling nations left today, counters that its 'research' whaling is licit. Under the moratorium, each nation may issue scientific permits to cull whales for research purposes. The purported aim of such research is to study the health of whales so that conservation activities may be based upon hard data, not raw emotions. Leftover whale meat may be legally sold in the market.

Nevertheless, since the 1970s, whalers have had to contend with anti-whaling activism that occasionally turns violent. Clearly, this issue polarises people. Some find Japan's whaling morally repugnant. Others, notably older Japanese for whom whale meat was a cheap source of protein after World War II, support it.

Some admire Sea Shepherd's tenacity. Others revile its tactics—which include lobbing smoke bombs onto whaling ships, throwing nylon ropes into ship propellers to disable them, shuttering up drains that these ships use to disgorge whale blood into the sea and, most infamously, ramming ships, as pirates of old used to do.

Putting aside one's personal convictions on whaling, an important question is whether an individual or group can take the law into its own hands in this manner in waters that do not obviously belong to any country.

Mr Watson claims authority under the World Charter for Nature that the United Nations adopted in 1982.

The charter urges 'individuals (and) groups to safeguard and conserve nature in areas beyond national jurisdiction.' It adds that 'to the extent they are able . . . acting individually . . . each person shall strive to ensure that the (charter's) objectives and requirements are met.'

Mr Watson has indeed proven over three decades that he is able to obstruct Japanese whalers. But critics note that with no provisions for enforcement, the charter is a non-binding agreement that is merely hortatory in nature.

More recently, Australian law has become another possible refuge for Sea Shepherd. In Humane Society International versus Kyodo Senpaku Kaisha (2008), Australia held that Japan's whaling took place in what it said were Australian waters, thus violating its Environment Protection and Biodiversity Conservation Act of 1999.

But this judgment turned upon Australia's claim to sovereignty over 'its' Antarctic Territory and coastal waters. Only four countries, Japan not being one of them, recognise that claim.

At any rate, trying to enforce this injunction on the high seas would be difficult, risky and expensive. Thus, Australia is unlikely to try to physically restrain any Japanese whaling ship in the Antarctic. It certainly did not do so this season.

Moreover, Japan has publicly declared it would ignore the ruling. Its words were certainly followed up with action this season when it proceeded with its usual whaling activities in Antarctic waters.

To date, six other nations have staked claims over Antarctica and its coastal waters. However, none has secured universal recognition of its claims. This means that there is hardly any certainty as to whose laws regulate whaling in the Antarctic.

This being so, Japan would argue it is the 1982 United Nations Convention on the Law of the Sea (Unclos) that should apply. After all, Unclos covers 'all parts of the sea that are not included in the exclusive economic zone, in the territorial sea or in the internal waters of a State.'

Under Unclos, 'the high seas are open to all States' and 'reserved for peaceful purposes.' Japan charges that Sea Shepherd engages in 'acts of piracy.' This is defined under Unclos as 'any illegal acts of violence or detention, or any act of depredation committed for private ends by the crew or the passengers of a private ship . . . on the high seas, against another ship . . . or against persons or property on board such ship . . . in a place outside the jurisdiction of any State.'

Mr Watson could contend that his activities are not carried out 'for private ends,' so they cannot be construed as piracy. Still, he would have to make a watertight case that ramming, disabling or scuttling of ships make for a set of licit activities. On the high seas, in peacetime, even national navies are not ordinarily authorised to attack foreign ships, naval or civilian, in these ways.

Whaling and eco-activism on the high seas admittedly occur in a troubling situation of legal ambiguity that, in effect, translates into lawlessness on the high seas. Under Unclos, any party involved in a dispute may resort to either the International Court of Justice or the International Tribunal for the Law of the Sea. If Australia is willing to go down this route, it might help bring some calm to a cauldron of unsettled international maritime law.

8.3

OCEAN'S BOUNTY PLUNDERED: PIRATE FISHERMEN. FOOD CHAIN IN DANGER, EXPERTS WARN

Charles Mandel

Currently, fishing fleets are significantly larger than is necessary to take existing catches of fish. The result is that overfishing is depleting stocks of fish around the world. Some three-quarters of global fish stocks are depleted or on

Source: Charles Mandel, "Ocean's Bounty Plundered: Pirate Fishermen. Food Chain in Danger, Experts Warn," *Montreal Gazette,* March 17, 2006.

the verge of collapse. The next article describes how the problem has been made worse by illegal fishing "pirates" who are accelerating the exhaustion of selected species of fish despite efforts to place limits on fishing.

Mobile fleets of pirate fishermen are plundering the oceans of their fish faster than regulatory agencies can respond, a researcher at the University of Manitoba in Winnipeg says.

Fikret Berkes, Canada research chair at the university's Natural Resources Institute, says the actions of these "roving bandits" result in everything from damage to food chains and habitat to the loss of livelihood for other fishermen.

Berkes says regulatory agencies alone are too "clumsy" to deal with the fish bandits. The wide-ranging fleets "move so fast that they outstrip the ability of local authorities or regulatory agencies to react," he said in an interview yesterday.

Berkes is the lead author on an international paper titled "Globalization, roving bandits and the sequential exploitation of marine resources," published online yesterday by the journal Science. Scientists from the United States, Australia, Sweden, and the Netherlands contributed to the research.

The scientists express concern that mercenary fishermen are converging on areas, systematically fishing them out and then moving on.

"There's no transparency: who owns the boat, where the boat goes, what it does," Berkes said. "There are no systems to trace illegal catches."

If the problem is not dealt with, large-scale extinctions in the world's oceans will take place within five to 50 years, said Boris Worm, an assistant professor of biology at Halifax's Dalhousie University and one of the study's co-authors.

Worm said that as one species becomes harder to catch, the fish bandits move on to the next, always in conjunction with market demand. He gave the example of the fish known as slimeheads because of their cranial networks of mucus-filled canals.

One of the larger slimehead species became popular in recent years for its delicate flavour after it was renamed and marketed as orange roughy. To capitalize on this popularity, Worm said, fishing bandits have been going from one slimehead habitat to another, catching the species until it's fished out in each spot and leaving behind damaged deep water corals that were also home to many other species.

Other examples of piracy on the high seas Worm cited included the trade in shark fins—in which the fins are ripped off the body, which is then tossed back in the water—and the sea urchin fishery, where the entire industry off Maine collapsed after overfishing by bandits.

Worm believes greater international efforts must be placed in monitoring the trade in fish products. Most of the shark fin trade flows through Hong Kong, while much of the sea urchin trade moves through Japan, Worm said.

Berkes called for co-operation between local, national and international authorities, saying the local fishermen need to exercise stewardship, while at the higher levels agencies must provide enforcement of property rights.

Villy Christensen, an associate professor at the University of British Columbia's Fisheries Centre, called the study "old wine in new bottles." Christensen said agencies are aware of the problem, and that since the early 1990s fishermen and different layers of government have practised fisheries co-management.

8.4

WE'RE ALL TO BLAME FOR THE CURSE OF GLOBAL WARMING

Dr Neville Nicholls

In the next article, Dr. Neville Nicholls, an Australian expert on environmental science, explains what global warming is. He also discusses its causes and consequences. He describes how much the earth's temperature has risen and the sources of the "greenhouse gases" that lie behind this increase. Dr. Nicholls attributes much of the problem to the world's dependence on fossil fuels for energy and their release of carbon emissions. He also discusses the problem of ozone in the atmosphere and the hole in the ozone layer above Antarctica. He contends that sea levels are rising and that among the consequences of global warming are the need for selected animal species to adapt or perish and the growing incidence of extreme weather. Finally, Dr. Nicholls describes the Kyoto Protocol and how it was expected to work.

All nations must accept responsibility for the heating of the planet—and the consequences.

* Dr Neville Nicholls explains the facts behind the crisis.

* What is global warming?

Global warming is the heating of the atmosphere near the surface of the Earth by increases in greenhouse gases due to human activities, such as burning fossil fuels (oil, coal, gas).

The Earth's temperature has risen about 0.74C in the past 100 years, due mainly to these gas increases.

Source: Dr Neville Nicholls, "We're All to Blame for the Curse of Global Warming—Environment," *Sunday Telegraph,* January 7, 2007.

* What is the greenhouse effect and what are greenhouse gases?

Greenhouse gases include carbon dioxide, methane and water vapour. They keep the surface of the Earth warmer than if they were not present in the atmosphere.

This is the "natural" greenhouse effect. Without this effect, life on Earth would be very different.

* Are global warming and the greenhouse effect linked?

Yes, global warming is the result of strengthening of the greenhouse effect by increases in the amount of greenhouse gases.

* Is global warming a man-made phenomenon or simply the natural evolution of our planet?

Warming in the past 100 years is mainly due to increases in greenhouse gases from human activity, especially the use of fossil fuels. The climate and Earth's temperature varies naturally also, but the increases in greenhouse gases are a very strong influence on the climate.

* Why are there such divergent opinions in the scientific community about global warming?

Most atmospheric scientists agree about the reality of the greenhouse effect and that increases in greenhouse gases lead to warming. There is still uncertainty about how much warming will result from continuing greenhouse gas emissions.

This uncertainty leads to quite broad ranges of predictions about how much warming there might be by the end of the century. These range between about 1C to 4C.

* How has global warming caused a hole in the ozone layer?

The hole is caused by chemical processes linked to human activities and the release of gases used for refrigeration and in aerosol cans. These gases contribute a little to the increased greenhouse effect, but the destruction of the ozone layer is mainly a separate question to global warming.

* Why is the hole above Antarctica and why does it continually contract and expand?

The answer to this is complex, but it is due to very cold atmospheric temperatures above Antarctica in winter and the unique chemical processes related to this chilling.

* Will coastal South Australia be submerged this century by rising sea levels, as some global warming experts predict?

The ocean expands when it warms. The melting of glaciers caused by warmer temperatures also increases sea levels.

The rise in sea levels expected by the end of the century is between about a quarter and a half of a metre. This would lead to flooding in some low-lying coastal areas.

* What are the Kyoto Protocols and how are they meant to fight global warming?

The protocols were contained in a diplomatically negotiated agreement by many nations to cut future greenhouse gas emissions.

The cuts agreed to were modest, but they would slow the rate of global warming.

* Why didn't China and India sign at Kyoto?

The reductions in greenhouse gas emissions agreed to in Kyoto were to be binding for developed countries, which have produced most of the extra greenhouse gases in the atmosphere so far.

Once the developed countries had "done their bit" to reduce global warming, the developing countries, such as China and India, were expected to also start cutting emissions of greenhouse gases as their economies grew.

* Why has Prime Minister John Howard been so slow to embrace the concept of global warming?

John Howard and his government do, clearly, accept the reality and science of global warming—and that human influences are causing the Earth to warm.

* If all the world's gas-generating power stations were turned off tomorrow, how long would it take before it affected global warming?

Carbon dioxide remains in the atmosphere for a long time, so warming would continue for several decades, even if we stopped all activities creating greenhouse gases. But the rate of warming would definitely slow down.

* Has global warming increased temperatures on Earth in the past 50 years. If so, by how much?

The Earth has warmed about 0.65C in the past 50 years. Most, perhaps all, of this warming is due to increases in greenhouse gases from human activity.

* How much do temperatures have to increase before it becomes a significant issue?

Some scientists believe a warming of about 2C would cause substantial damage to the planet.

There is a great deal of evidence that warming has already affected the flowering of plants and animal breeding times.

* How much have sea levels risen due to global warming?

Sea levels, averaged across the Earth, have increased about 8cm in the past 40 years.

* Can global warming really melt icebergs and flood cities as depicted in disaster movies?

If warming continues, the ice sheet on Greenland would melt. This would raise sea levels about 6m, causing widespread coastal flooding. However, this is not expected soon. Sea levels were about 5m higher than now 125,000 years ago when the Earth was about 4C warmer.

* What effect will global warming have on plant and animal life?

If warming is not too fast, much plant and animal life would adapt to the changes in the climate.

But some species would be vulnerable, even to small temperature increases, including animals used to cold mountain temperatures. Large increases in sea levels would have a devastating effect on coastal life.

* How accurate is computer modelling of global warming?

Computer models of the climate are much better than computer models of the economy, and have improved in the past decade or so.

This is one reason why projections of warming have had such a large range. But the general understanding of the greenhouse effect was worked out in laboratory experiments many years ago.

Computer models confirm this understanding and provide more detail, such as where rainfall might change, although rainfall projections are more uncertain than temperature predictions.

Our understanding of the greenhouse effect and global warming is not dependent on models, but getting details right depends on improving the models.

* Is Australia's drought linked to global warming?

Many climate models predict that increasing greenhouse gases should lead to drying along the south coast of Australia.

However, the main cause of the very intense droughts Australia suffers, including the drought this year, is the El Nino phenomenon.

We don't know if the El Nino will get worse with global warming.

* How will global warming, as it is accepted today, affect the way we live in, say, 50 years?

The world will be warmer, and some coastal areas will be flooded. There would likely be more hot days and heat waves each year, and fewer cold days.

There should be more heavy rainfall events. Changes in rainfall will cause changes in farming practices.

The competitiveness of our farming may change as the cold areas of Russia and Canada warm up and become more productive.

* Isn't warming due to cities getting bigger and measurements being made in urban areas?

We also have temperature measurements from rural sites well away from cities, from small islands in the middle of oceans, and sea-surface temperatures.

All of these show warming. As well, sea ice is retreating, glaciers are melting almost everywhere, and the amount of snow is decreasing.

This indicates that the warming is widespread, pervasive, and not just restricted to the cities.

* Could the warming be happening because the sun is getting more intense?

We now have several decades of observations of the energy being received from the sun.

There is no evidence the radiation we receive from the sun has increased, but the world has warmed during this period.

So the warming is not caused by the sun becoming more intense.

* Do volcanoes affect global temperature?

When Mount Pinatubo erupted, the global temperature cooled about half a degree and stayed low for a few years.

So, if we had a series of very severe volcanic eruptions this would offset the warming caused by the greenhouse gases.

Together, volcanoes and solar variations have probably caused cooling during the past 50 years, reducing the warming that has been caused by the increase in greenhouse gases.

* Do other human activities affect the climate?

Changing land use, such as clearing forest for agriculture, does affect local climate, but there is no agreement on whether it affects global climate.

Industrial pollution and aerosol gases cool the Earth, offsetting some of the warming caused by the increases in greenhouse gases. They probably caused the cooling seen between 1950 and the 1970s.

8.5

GLOBAL WARMING DOUBTERS MULTIPLY IN THE US

from *The Australian*

> The following selection reveals the disturbing trend that more Americans believe that global warming is not as serious as experts claim. This trend flies in the face of growing evidence that not only is global warming increasing but it is the consequence of human actions and may be becoming irreversible.

Source: "Global Warming Doubters Multiply in the US," *The Australian,* March 14, 2009.

WASHINGTON: More Americans than at any time in the past decade believe that the seriousness of global warming is being exaggerated, a new Gallup poll shows.

Forty-one per cent of Americans told Gallup pollsters they were doubtful global warming was as serious as the mainstream media were reporting—the highest result in more than a decade.

In 2004, 38 per cent of Americans thought news reports exaggerated the seriousness of global warming.

Gallup's 2009 environment poll, which surveyed 1012 adults by fixed and mobile phone, also showed that Americans ranked global warming last out of eight environmental issues they might be concerned about.

The pollution of drinking water was deemed the greatest source of concern, with 84 per cent of respondents saying it worried them.

Other issues that were ranked—and beat global warming by at least five percentage points—were water pollution in general, toxic contamination of soil and water, fresh water supply, air pollution, loss of rainforests, and the extinction of plants and animals.

The number of Americans who thought global warming was already affecting the planet fell from 61 per cent in March last year to 53 per cent this year.

A record high 16 per cent of Americans told Gallup pollsters that they believed the effects of global warming "will never occur."

The poll results suggested "that the global warming message may have lost some footing with Americans," Gallup analyst Lydia Saad said.

"Americans generally believe global warming is real (but) most Americans do not view the issue in the same dire terms as the many prominent leaders advancing global warming as an issue."

8.6

WHO WILL PAY FOR THE ENVIRONMENTAL MESS WE'RE IN?

Shawn McCarthy

As the preceding selections reveal, the issue of global warming has produced passionate debate. The issue divides wealthy states, which remain major sources of carbon emissions but are taking steps to limit them, and less developed countries like China and India, in which carbon emissions are growing rapidly as they use ever more energy to develop economically. The latter fear that their efforts to develop economically would be thwarted if they

Source: Shawn McCarthy, "Who Will Pay for the Environmental Mess We're In?" *The Globe and Mail,* December 4, 2010.

are made to curb such emissions in a significant way. This selection describes how some leaders in the developing world are demanding major infusions of funding from wealthy states if the latter wish them to curb carbon emissions and how these demands are perceived by politicians in the West who are climate-change skeptics as evidence that environmental advocates are merely using unscientific claims of global warming to demand economic assistance for developing countries from wealthier states.

Cancun's white beaches and resort hotels provide a fitting setting for a global argument over the rich world's responsibility for damaging the Earth's environment and the extent of its "climate debt" to poorer nations.

Divisions between the rich and poor—so apparent in such sunny vacation spots - have fuelled bitter debates that threaten to block progress at the United Nations climate summit under way on the Mayan Riviera.

Many leaders from the developing world and Western activists are demanding trillion-dollar reparations for the developed world's damage to the Earth's atmosphere at the expense of the poor. Their argument is an extension of the anti-globalization, anti-corporate credo that assigns moral blame for the vast gap in global living standards.

Representatives from developing countries arrived at Cancun determined to hold rich nations to account for their role in causing what scientists say is a growing climate crisis, one that will hit poor nations the hardest.

However, the United States and the European Union are mired in the worst economic slump since the Great Depression. The heightened level of economic insecurity—and the perception that China is overtaking Western economies—will make it increasingly difficult for those governments to win public support for massive climate-related transfers to developing countries that would have been politically problematic even before the global slump.

At Cancun, negotiators hope to conclude some "building block" agreements on issues of financing and technology transfer that will pave the way for an overarching, binding climate treaty down the road.

Below, a guide to issues, and conflicts that stand in the way.

Carbon Debt

The recognition of differing levels of responsibility between developed and developing countries has been embedded for decades in international agreements that deal with the growing climate crisis.

Based on 160 years of fossil-fuelled economic growth, the industrialized world has emitted an estimated 75 per cent of the man-made greenhouse gases that remain trapped in the atmosphere.

Globally, energy-related emissions have climbed to 29 billion tonnes a year from 200 million tonnes in 1850 as the developed world relied on coal-fired electricity and oil-fuelled transportation to deliver unprecedented prosperity to its citizens.

Governments in the U.S., Europe and Canada have long acknowledged the imbalance and have agreed that the rich world needs to make deep cuts to emissions by 2050 in order to allow for an overall reduction in global levels even as developing countries increase their consumption of fossil fuels such as coal and oil.

The historical argument is being overshadowed by the realization that China has become the world's largest emitter this year and will continue to outpace the United States as it industrializes its economy. However, China's income per person and its emissions per capita remain far below the levels of the United States or Canada.

The Accusers

Bolivian President Evo Morales has been leading the case for the prosecution, calling not only for reparations but also a "people's tribunal" to impose monetary and criminal sanctions on offending rich-world governments and corporations.

Last April, Mr. Morales played host to the People's Conference on Climate Change and the Rights of Mother Earth, which issued a manifesto calling on rich countries to finance the "decolonization of the atmosphere." The Cochabamba Accord was endorsed by activist groups throughout the developed world.

"There is both a legal and a moral obligation to deal with climate debt," says Janet Redman, a co-director of the Institute for Policy Studies in Washington, who helped to draft the document. Among the speakers at Cochabamba was Canadian activist Naomi Klein, a vocal advocate of the need for reparations.

While most developing world leaders steer clear of Mr. Morales's broad denunciation of capitalism, they share his view that the climate debt of the developed world is a fundamental issue at the Cancun talks and cannot be addressed by shuffling aid budgets and offering loans.

The Group of 77, which represents an alliance of poorer countries, has called for annual financial transfers of up to 1.5 per cent of rich countries' gross domestic product by 2020. Applying that figure to Canada in 2010 would require new aid spending of $18 billion, while the American government would have to come up with $210 billion (U.S.).

The Hawks

For many climate change skeptics, demands from the Group of 77 for massive transfers amount to clear evidence of a United Nations-perpetrated hoax that used dubious science to justify a socialist reordering of the global economy.

U.S. Congressman Joe Barton, a leading proponent of the do-nothing approach who is running to become chair of the powerful House energy and commerce committee, rejects the view that carbon dioxide is a pollutant that should be regulated, as the Environmental Protection Agency intends to do.

As a committee member, Mr. Barton has supported British conservative Christopher Monckton, a former political adviser to Margaret Thatcher who has attacked the science of climate change as "flawed" and has accused President Barack Obama of planning to sell out U.S. sovereignty to usher in world government.

Other conservative critics—while not denying the climate-change science—argue that any global agreement that includes large financial transfers would simply be unacceptable.

"Essentially, the right is exploiting the issue of distribution as a way to underscore their belief that any kind of international, UN-based program is going to be inefficient and unworkable," said Jon Entine, a fellow at the conservative, Washington-based American Enterprise Institute. "But a lot of that opposition is from climate deniers who are looking for anything to hang their hats on."

The Canadians

Canadian conservatives have also been suspicious of international demands for major financial transfers. When he was opposition leader, Prime Minister Stephen Harper roundly condemned the Kyoto Protocol, particularly its mechanism for having rich countries purchase emission credits from poorer ones. Instead, he promised a "made-in-Canada" solution.

As Prime Minister, Mr. Harper has agreed to provide "Canada's fair share" of financing for mitigation and adaptation efforts in the Third World, but critics complain that the $400-million allocated so far is largely redirected from other aid programs and comes in the form of loans rather than grants.

In international negotiations, Mr. Harper's government also has been adamant that Canada expects major emerging countries such as China and India to accept binding commitments to rein in emissions, something they were exempted from under the Kyoto deal.

In a speech before last year's Copenhagen summit, Bruce Carson, a former senior adviser in Mr. Harper's office, argued that the Kyoto treaty was fatally flawed because it had set unrealistic targets and that "there were legitimate issues as to whether it was simply a wealth transfer scheme—with nothing to do with climate change."

In Cancun, the Canadian government is looking to scrap the Kyoto deal, rather than extend it past 2012, as the Group of 77 is demanding. Such a move would erase the decades-old distinctions between developing and developed countries.

Cancun and Beyond

An agreement on financing is absolutely critical if the Cancun summit is to be declared a success, and to set the stage for further co-operation.

Negotiators are working on a proposal that would raise $100-billion a year by 2020 through a variety of taxes—on financial transactions, on air travel and shipping—and funnel it through the World Bank and other development agencies. However, leaders from the developing world want the money to be managed by the United Nations itself and are insisting that most of the financing should come from Western treasuries.

U.S. negotiator Todd Stern has insisted that any financial package must be accompanied by an agreement that countries would allow their efforts to be monitored and verified by the UN, a demand that has been rejected by China and India.

Without compromise, the future of the UN process itself is in jeopardy. There are already calls for negotiations to move to the Group of 20, which includes all major emitters but excludes many of the states that are most vulnerable to climate change. But most of the same cleavages that threaten the Cancun talks would exist at the G20.

The more likely outcome is that countries will move in fits and starts to implement their own climate strategies. That approach is bound to fall short of the deep emission reductions that scientists say are necessary to avoid climate catastrophe.

8.7

THE LAST FOREST: THE AMAZON IN THE AGE OF GLOBALIZATION

Joseph A. Page

The next article is a review of a book whose authors argue that concerns about deforestation in Brazil are highly exaggerated. They suggest that the Amazon region was never as important to global climate as many had thought and that if Brazil's government encourages peaceful land reform so that landless peasants can prosper, it will make possible *both* economic growth and environmental protection.

In 1983 Brian Kelly and Mark London published *Amazon*, a comprehensive report on the plight of the largest jungle left on Planet Earth. In it they described efforts by the Brazilian government, big companies and dogged freelancers to extract as much as possible of the abundant natural resources in the region, with scant regard for ecological or human consequences.

The generals then ruling the country feared that if the 2.5 million-square-mile Amazon basin remained underpopulated, Brazil might lose control of it. So the military regime lured settlers with promises of land and technical assistance. The newcomers received neither and faced an uphill struggle to survive. The deforestation to which they contributed raised worldwide alarm about potentially adverse effect on global weather patterns.

Now the authors have taken a fresh look at the dilemma in *The Last Forest* and discover a complex world that has rendered irrelevant once-chic, well-meaning, simplistic pleas from abroad that Brazilians keep their rain forest intact in order to preserve its precious resources and protect the world's climate.

Twenty million people now inhabit the vast Amazon basin, and they are not going anywhere. With the benefits of modern technology, cattle-raising and soybean cultivation in the region make vital contributions to the economy, as Brazil has become the world's leading beef exporter and trails only the United States in soybean shipments. In addition, the discovery of extensive oil and natural-gas reserves threatens to open parts of the

Source: Joseph A. Page, "The Last Forest: The Amazon in the Age of Globalization," *The Miami Herald,* February 18, 2007.

jungle once thought to be impenetrable. Deforestation continues, some of it planned, some of it illegal, much of it senseless. The government has adopted measures to protect the environment but lacks the resources to enforce them.

Kelly and London begin with an account of recent discoveries indicating that the Amazon region was home to permanent settlements more than 10,000 years ago, and that a relatively advanced society of perhaps 100,000 people developed a system of sustainable agriculture that served them for a millennium. For the authors this proves that large numbers of humans are capable of living in the rain forest without destroying it, an assertion undercut by the huge discrepancy between the size of the prehistoric community and the current over-population.

Moreover, some 70 percent of the people in the region now live in cities, many of which replicate the grinding poverty to be found elsewhere in urban Brazil. Manaus, a thriving city of 2 million on the Amazon river in the heart of the jungle, owes its good fortune to the heavy government subsidization of industry in the area. Without this massive public support, the jungle metropolis would return to being a jungle outpost. In the countryside the lack of a working system of land title registration and the absence of law enforcement have stymied would-be settlers, who remain at the mercy of land speculators and large corporations seeking to expand their agricultural and livestock enterprises.

The authors describe efforts by the Movement for Landless Workers to organize the rural poor and invade unproductive land, in order to force the government to expropriate properties and distribute them to the occupiers. This has provoked armed resistance by owners, and a number of Movement leaders and rank-and-file have lost their lives.

The authors see the peaceful achievement of this type of land reform as a way for man and nature to coexist in Amazonia. They argue persuasively that much deforestation involves slash-and-burn efforts by individual settlers desperate to feed their families, without any permanent stake in the land and with little grasp of how to make productive use of the rain forest. But it remains to be seen whether time has bypassed Brazil's chance to create a stable, thriving class of independent farmers, and whether the avowedly collectivist goals of the Movement, which the book ignores, will frustrate this vision.

On the ecological front the authors stress the recent finding that the Amazon basin has always absorbed as much oxygen as it produces. Therefore, the region is not, as some have claimed, the "lungs of the earth." Indeed, instead of contributing to global warming by cutting trees, the people of Amazonia may be victims, as demonstrated by a devastating drought in 2005. Curiously, the authors make only a passing reference to the calamity, which seems to have resulted from the same warming process that caused the flooding of New Orleans.

The Last Forest makes an important contribution to the literature on the Amazon basin. The authors take pains to present the Brazilian side of the international controversy over the destruction of the rain forest and find positive signs in the ways Brazilians have been laboring to reconcile economic growth and environmental protection. The critical question, to be answered over the next 25 years, is whether this response can overcome past mistakes.

Joseph A. Page, a professor at the Georgetown University Law Center, is the author of *The Brazilians*.

Biodiversity

8.8

WERE BISON ONE OF GLOBALIZATION'S FIRST VICTIMS?

Dawn Walton

The following selection describes the claim by a Canadian economist that the virtual extinction of American bison in the 19th century was a consequence of early globalization. Although other factors may have contributed to the reduction in their numbers, the most important was the international demand for bison hides.

The near-extinction of the plains bison in the United States has long been blamed on the advent of the railways, native overhunting and a government policy of slaughter designed to address the "Indian problem."

But a Canadian researcher has discovered that globalization was the real culprit for the decimation of the U.S. bison herd in the 19th century.

M. Scott Taylor, an economist at the University of Calgary who used international trade records and first-person accounts of the hunt, has found that European development of a cheap and easy tanning method after 1870 fuelled that continent's insatiable appetite for bison hides, which could be turned into shoe soles and machinery belts.

"The paper is really about solving a murder mystery and showing that the usual suspects are in fact innocent and that this other suspect—international trade—is the guilty party," Prof. Taylor said.

His 57-page study, which presents an unconventional theory about what happened to the species, was recently published by the National Bureau of Economic Research, a prestigious non-profit think tank based in Cambridge, Mass.

The report deflects some blame from the Americans, but it is also instructive for many developing countries that currently rely on resource exports yet are struggling through civil wars. Few have guidelines governing resource use.

"It is somewhat ironic, that what must be the saddest chapter in U.S. environmental history was not written by Americans; it was instead, the work of Europeans," Prof. Taylor wrote.

An estimated 30 to 75 million plains bison, the lifeblood of indigenous peoples for thousands of years, once filled the continent extending from the northern Canadian prairies to Mexico.

Source: Dawn Walton, "Were Bison One of Globalization's First Victims?" *The Globe and Mail,* July 31, 2007.

Some argue that 75 million figure is too high, and Prof. Taylor puts the number at perhaps 30 million at its peak in the United States. European explorers to the fledging country described it colourfully as "one black robe" of buffalo. (Buffalo is the commonly used, but incorrect name for bison.) By the 1880s, only a few hundred wild plains bison remained on the continent. Estimates vary, but the number was pegged as low as 100 in the U.S. and eight in Canada.

Prof. Taylor, who is also Canada Research Chair in International, Energy and Environmental Economics, recalled that his interest was first piqued while watching a movie that depicted the bison slaughter for robes. He compared the number of dead bison to the number of Americans who could possibly need coats. The figures, he said, didn't make sense.

He started to look through export figures, something other historians and researchers struggled to interpret or dismissed in favour of other attractive explanations.

The U.S. Army and government attempts to eliminate the bison in order to control the natives are well documented, and have been likened to a genocide.

"It would be a great step forward in the civilization of the Indians and the preservation of peace on the [frontier] if there was not a buffalo in existence," Texas Senator James Throckmorton once said.

The market for robes, blankets and meat, as well as the ease of picking off animals from trains for sport, did contribute to the steady demise. So did drought, environmental change and new native hunting methods.

But the bulk of the species was wiped out in the U.S. in just one decade—between the 1870s and 1880s—immediately after the foreign tanning innovation, according to Prof. Taylor.

Hides sold for between 75 cents and $3.50 (U.S.) during that period, and about six million were exported (millions more bison were killed) as European armies were being refitted with bison leather, which was found to be tougher than cattle hides.

The U.S. government, fresh from its bloody civil war, did little to protect its natural resources and fell to the whims of market demand.

The Canadian experience was different than that of the United States, according to historians. There was no hide market in Canada, Prof. Taylor points out. But researchers have fingered the fur trade, indiscriminant hunting by both natives and others, as well as habitat destruction for the loss.

Thanks to a concerted conservation effort, there are now more than 500,000 plains bison in North America, according to the Swiss-based World Conservation Union. Ottawa has pegged the number as high as 720,000, with perhaps 235,000 in Canada.

Despite the comeback, the vast majority of the plains bison are privately owned, many are managed for commercial production like beef, and pure bloodlines have been lost through breeding with cattle.

History could have evolved differently, Prof. Taylor says, but only in regulating the dramatic demise of the bison.

"The buffalo were doomed," he said. "Eventually they would have been gone. They weren't going to be walking down the streets of Seattle and Denver."

Chapter 9

THE FUTURE OF THE NATION-STATE

This chapter begins by examining the various definitions of the state and its evolution from its emergence in Europe to the present. It then discusses different claims concerning how globalization has affected state autonomy and capability and national identity. It concludes by suggesting how states might adapt to globalization in the future—including the return of the classical interstate system, the transformation of the state from providing citizens' welfare to enhancing competitiveness by reducing welfare, the embedding of globalization practices within the state itself, and the adoption of authoritarian measures to strengthen the state.

9.1

STATE AUTONOMY AND CAPACITY IN A GLOBALIZING WORLD[1]

Richard W. Mansbach

The "state" has been the bedrock of "international" relations, but it is a concept about which few agree. As a field of study, international relations evolved as the analysis of the interstate system that emerged after Europe's religious wars and the Peace of Westphalia of 1648, and it sought to analyze the relations among states whose sovereignty was inextricably connected to exclusive control of a defined territory and the borders that enclosed them. Along with hierarchy, in which government acts as an authoritative surrogate for subjects or citizens, exclusive control of territory is the defining attribute of the sovereign state. The state began to emerge following Europe's Middle Ages and only became the world's most prominent political community after 1648. It has continually evolved since. However, we must take care how we use the Westphalian conception lest it "oversimplify and obscure phenomena related to globalization" because "its use as a starting point for investigations of change may lead scholars to exaggerate the magnitude of recent developments in international politics."[2] The central question that this essay confronts is whether or not the authority and capacity of the sovereign state is eroding in the course of globalization.

In what follows, we examine some of the meanings of "state" and briefly trace its evolution. The elements of the ideal state as defined in international relations are well-known—a polity with fixed boundaries and exclusive sovereign authority over a defined territory, the juridical equal of other states, and enjoying a monopoly of the means of coercion within its boundaries. Sovereignty, the result of mutual recognition, has two faces—internal and external—and implies legal independence, political and economic autonomy, and freedom from foreign interference. In fact, as noted earlier in this book, the ideal-type state was never more than an aspiration. Great powers routinely interfered in the internal life of weaker states, boundaries have always been more or less porous, and governments have frequently not enjoyed a monopoly of the means of coercion or exerted control over all their citizens. Indeed, the state is neither a universal feature of political life nor a "given" in global politics. Rather, it is a territorially based community that gradually emerged out of Europe's feudal epoch, and it has varied through time and space. Europe's states triumphed over competing political communities because their centralized organization enabled them to mobilize human and material resources more efficiently than other polities.

We saw earlier how globalization has transcended states' territorial space and how this has profoundly affected the way states function. Some tasks, like waging war, seem less central for many states than they once did. In trying to make sense of such changes, scholars have sought new ways to characterize the state. Thus, the "welfare state" is giving way to a "competition state," a "market state," a "virtual state," a "residual state," and—now perhaps with the recent worldwide financial collapse—perhaps something like a "pump-priming re-regulatory state."

Far from being a universal feature, the territorial state is a relatively recent European invention. Until its emergence, most people were governed by empires, extended families and clans, and nomadic tribes.

From ancient Sumer to the Soviet Union, multiethnic empires have been central features of the global landscape. Most empires lacked *fixed* political frontiers, were expansive, and in some cases put forward claims to universal rule. Some, like Genghis Khan's Mongols, were nomadic, with little concern for exclusive territorial control. Centralization and localization of authority existed side by side, and governance was shared by imperial and local authorities.

The State as an Incoherent Concept

"State" is an ill-defined concept. Classical political philosophers such as Aristotle, Machiavelli, Bodin, Hobbes, Marx, and Hegel had their own definition. Some scholars view the state as an *ethno-cultural* polity, a definition that conflates the usual idea of "state" with "nation." In this case, the state includes a society and its "people" and their unique characteristics. This view, however, is hardly viable for defining failing states in the developing world, like Somalia, or multinational states, like the former USSR or the former Yugoslavia. Institutionalizing a territorial state is elusive where there are violent ethnic conflicts. Additionally, legal and illegal migration of peoples so mixes populations that it is hard to determine who is inside and who is outside the boundaries of their respective nations.

The state is also conceived as a *functional unit*, its emergence reflecting a division of labor and social specialization. In this definition, state building entails political and economic modernization. Another definition, associated with the sociologist Max Weber, defines the state as a *monopoly of legitimate violence within society*. Those holding this view link the emergence of states with warfare and the growth of specialized bureaucracies to wage war. Weber's definition, with roots back to the 16th-century English political philosopher Thomas Hobbes, is an ideal type because most states did not enjoy a monopoly of coercion inside *or* outside their borders until relatively recently and rarely do so any longer. As the historian James Sheehan observes, "The continued presence of groups like the Mafia underscores the state's inability to maintain a monopoly of legitimate violence."[3] Even now, the process of centralizing coercion in many states is incomplete, and drug lords, ethnic separatists, and pirates make a mockery of state control of violence. Weber's concept of the state is more complex than its being no more than a concentration of raw power, as he insists that state coercion be viewed as "legitimate" by society.

Others view the state as a *set of autonomous bureaucracies* apart from the society that it governs. The sociologist Theda Skocpol advocates this view, arguing that the state and its institutions are autonomous and distinct from its society and that the state is a "set of administrative, policing, and military organizations headed, and more or less well coordinated by, an executive authority."[4] The political scientist Stephen Krasner shares this perspective, affirming that "the dominant conceptualization" of the state is as "a bureaucratic apparatus and institutionalized legal order in its totality" and as "an actor in its own right."[5] Krasner's unitary-state perspective comports well with the ideal sovereign state, but for both Skocpol and Krasner, "society" is largely invisible.

In contrast, Marxists view the state as an instrument of a *ruling class* that in time will "wither away," and this definition, unlike the previous one, firmly embeds the state in society. Unlike those who emphasize the central role of war in the emergence of states, Marxists believe that modern states emerged along with the spread of capitalism and the conquest of precapitalist stateless societies. Critical theories that define the *state as a source of harm* evolved from Marxist analysis but abandon historical materialism and focus on the negative consequences of state action. The opposite of the Marxist definition, but one that also retains the role of society, is that the state is a *pluralist community*, that is, an arena of interest-group competition. Somewhere between Marxist and pluralist views are *neo-pluralist* and *corporatist* models that recognize that some interests are underrepresented while others enjoy disproportionate influence in the political process. In some versions of this, such as that of the American sociologist C. Wright Mills, the state is seen to be composed of *ruling elites*.

An extension of pluralism is equating the state with *bureaucratic/governmental* and *organizational politics*. This definition emphasizes that the state is *not* a unitary entity. The bureaucratic model instead stresses how governments are subject to bureaucratic and interest-group infighting and bargaining in which bureaucratic agencies like the U.S.

Departments of State and Defense compete to promote their own interests and policies. They seek larger budgets and support policies to justify those requests. In consequence, there is no place in this model for an objective "national interest," and by the time policies are adopted, they reflect bureaucratic compromises. A variant, the organizational process model, describes policy as a product of the standard operating procedures of large bureaucracies. Each bureaucracy, with its own procedures for managing and responding to routine problems quickly and for defining problems, is responsible for some part of policy.[6]

In the course of globalization, government bureaucracies in different countries may form transnational alliances in opposition to other bureaucracies, including those in their own government. Among such contemporary networks are security officials seeking to prevent acts of terrorism or financial officials trying to stabilize the global financial system. Such networks illustrate how globalized issues may encourage global governance.

The Changing State

International relations scholars have tended to treat states as unchanging territorial communities characterized by the legal privileges associated with sovereignty. In fact, this state, enshrined by international relations theorists, is increasingly recognized today as a mistaken reflection of reality. Early European states did not have separate "domestic" and "international" or "public" (government) and "private" (societal) arenas. The historian Joseph Strayer argues that

> sovereignty requires independence from any outside power and final authority over men who live within certain boundaries. But in 1300 it was not clear who was independent and who was not, and it was difficult to draw definite boundaries in a Europe which had known only overlapping spheres of influence and fluctuating frontier zones.[7]

Medieval Europe was united by Western Christendom but was *not* divided into separate states with exclusive territorial domains. Instead, it was organized into classes: nobility, peasants, clergy, and townsmen.

Philip Bobbitt provides a coherent yet concise account of how states changed over time. According to Bobbitt, the earliest of Europe's states—"princely states"—emerged from medieval Europe in the form of city-states in Italy at the end of the 15th century.[8] Immortalized in Niccolò Machiavelli's *The Prince*, Italy's city-states, unlike the dynastic territories of medieval kings, were urban and geographically compact and had a monetized economy that permitted the employment of mercenaries and the construction of walled fortresses. Their rulers practiced Machiavelli's idea that a prince does not serve his personal interests but rather serves the interests of his state.

Bobbitt argues that the features of the personalized princely states, when exported north of the Alps to the larger states of Spain, England, and France, added dynastic legitimacy, and the states took the form of "kingly states." Kingly states were military machines, reflecting the extension of the king's authority. This logic is visible in the efforts of France's Bourbon kings Louis XIII and XIV to end religious strife within their country, overthrow Habsburg hegemony in Europe, place other members of their dynasty on the thrones of France's neighbors, and achieve French hegemony in Europe. France emerged from the Thirty Years' War (1648) as an archetypal kingly state, legitimated by divine right and dynastic continuity and featuring the centralization of state authority under absolutist sovereigns.

Kingly states were transformed into "territorial" states between the early 16th and late 17th centuries, a period of continent-wide religious wars involving Habsburg Spain's effort to establish imperial dominion over Europe. Unlike the kingly states, "the territorial state was identified by its contiguity." "For the territorial state, its borders were everything—its legitimacy, its defense perimeter, its tax base," and it "was characterized by a shift from the monarch-as-embodiment of sovereignty to the monarch as minister of sovereignty."[9] According to Bobbitt, the territorial state was guided by the principle of *Staatsraison*, defined as "an imperative that compels [the state's] strategic designs" and "identifies the state with the country, the land."[10] Europe's kingly states enshrined the balance-of-power system in the Treaty of Utrecht (1713), thereby recognizing the existence of rules within an interstate society, and the system of territorial states promoted limited warfare to achieve territorial advantages, while avoiding unrestrained warfare.

This situation changed dramatically with the intensification and spread of nationalism during the French Revolution and Napoleonic eras (1789–1815), during which the territorial state evolved into the "state-nation," "a state that mobilizes a nation—a national ethnocultural group—to act on behalf of the State" and "can thus call on the revenues of all society and on the human talent of all persons"[11] The state-nation was energized by mass conscription and transformed its "subjects" into "citizens," who equated their destiny with that of their "nation." The 19th-century British, Russian, and French empires were, in Bobbitt's view, state-nations.

The transition from state-nations to "nation-states" accelerated during the mid-19th century and featured the 1848 revolutions, the Crimean War (1853–1856), broader suffrage in much of Europe, and the unification of Italy (1866) and Germany (1870). Nation-states were perceived as the repository of sovereignty, and citizens assumed primary allegiance to "their" states, regarding other nations as "inferior." The link between citizen and state became still more intimate with the emergence of the modern welfare state in the 19th and 20th centuries.

The Contemporary State in a Globalizing World

The evolution of the state has not ceased, and globalization has been accompanied by continued changes in states' authority and functions. Such changes feature deepening interdependence and growing demands by national and ethnic groups for national self-determination. The world is driven by dynamic and interdependent processes of centralization, which produce "intermestic" politics and decentralization of political authority.

Centralization of authority in large states produces difficulties in managing disparate peoples with disparate needs and interests, while intensifying their desire for local autonomy and governance and nourishment of local culture, norms, and identity. Decentralization simplifies problems of control but limits functional efficiency and economies of scale, while sustaining intimacy and tradition. As a result, the impact of globalization varies, and in some cases, it actually promotes local differences by appearing to erode cherished local mores and beliefs. In other cases, globalization can reduce localism by spreading global values and new ideas and creating new transnational linkages.

The contradictory dynamics of integration and fragmentation pull states in different directions, eroding state autonomy and forcing states to share functions with local groups like ethnic communities and transnational institutions such as global corporations and international organizations. These processes are altering state sovereignty and the meaning of time and space and are again transforming states. The political economist Philip Cerny describes the profound impact of these processes in the economic realm:

> The shift in decision-making power in a globalizing world is differentiating along several dimensions—not merely downward to domestic firms and markets or into different corners of the splintered state, but also upward to international markets and firms and to a range of more or less functionally specialized international bodies.[12]

Sovereignty was a legitimating principle that constituted states, but owing to change, it is increasingly being contested. The sovereign boundaries of states have become porous, and even the United States is largely helpless in the face of migrants moving northward and guns moving southward, or the flood of drugs coming to American cities and towns from around the world. As we observed earlier in this book, one result is the erosion of the distinction between the "foreign" and "domestic" arenas of political life.

Sovereignty and exclusive control of a territorial space are bound up with each other. With globalization, however, as we have seen, the role of territory has changed. The proliferation of subnational, transnational, international, and supranational groups has moved global politics away from the exclusive territorial polities characteristic of the post-Westphalian interstate system. Modern technologies have overcome geography and produced alternative conceptions of space in which, much as was the case in medieval Europe, authority and identities can overlap or, owing to new technologies, can even exist in cyberspace, as is the case with markets. Indeed, markets have become regional and global and are less congruent with national frontiers than in the past.

The global capital market moves investment funds across, over, and under states' borders. Moreover, though transnational corporations typically have a home base, their strategies, production chains, and networks and many of their customers are dispersed overseas. Currency and stock transactions take place in cyberspace, and trade is increasingly conducted between corporate subsidiaries or between transnational corporations rather than between states. (Although there may be territorial sites like the New York Stock Exchange, in which buying and selling take place, stock markets exist largely in cyberspace and could effectively be destroyed as a result of a cyber attack.)

Some globalization enthusiasts even believe that the demise of the state is at hand. Thus, the management consultant Kenichi Ohmae argues that owing to information and communication technologies,

> the nation-state is irrelevant. One of the outward symbols of its existence is the national border, staffed by uniformed officials checking papers and manning barricades. But what use are such border controls in the world of the Internet, for example? Does a stream of data passing along a fiber-optic cable stop at each national border it crosses so that it can be inspected for contraband?[13]

States and Collective Goods

Since the emergence of the state, the essence of its obligations has been provision of collective goods for subjects/citizens, even if only providing collective military security. Collective goods are benefits from which individuals cannot be excluded—such as national defense or clean water—and for which, in consequence, they have little incentive to pay. Hence, governments impose taxes that citizens must pay and enact laws against tax evasion to provide collective goods for society as a whole. According to some observers, however, global economic competition and technological change are reducing the capacity and/or willingness of many states to provide citizens with these goods.

The provision of military security has traditionally been among the most central of the collective goods provided by sovereign states. "Had it not been for the need to wage war," argues the military historian Martin van Creveld, "then the development of bureaucracy, taxation, even welfare services such as education, health, etc. would probably have been much slower."[14] The role of states in providing military security has, however, changed—in some cases dramatically. Following World War II, the development of nuclear weapons, along with ICBMs (intercontinental ballistic missiles), and the fact that they were targeted at cities, meant that territorial states could no longer protect citizens from a devastating attack. Moreover, the irregular and guerrilla wars waged largely by rebels, militias, or terrorists emphasized the political and ideological aspects of warfare rather than its original purpose of seizing territory. Together, the nuclear standoff between the rival superpowers and the spread of irregular warfare eroded the importance of territory in providing security. And in some cases, states have "outsourced" military tasks to mercenaries and private security firms,[15] as did the United States following its intervention in Iraq in 2003. Growing economic interdependence and the globalized market have also raised the costs of warfare for states, and in the West at least, patriotism has declined even while willingness to die for a religion or ideology has increased.

In the economic realm, since the late 19th century and especially after the Great Depression, states have assumed greater responsibility for ensuring citizens' welfare, creating entitlements, and regulating (sometimes planning) national economic, environmental, legal, and social activities. Creating a "welfare state," in effect, became part of the state's mission, and "embedded liberalism"—the provision of welfare domestically along with prevention of destructive economic policies internationally—became the approach of many developed states. However, some critics argue that globalization is reversing what had been the growth of states' obligations to provide welfare because intense global competition forces states to cut costs, reduce taxes, limit welfare, reduce regulations, and thereby improve the competitive position of domestic economic actors in the global market. As a result, there has emerged what Cerny calls the "competition state." "The key to the new role of the state," he argues,

> lies in the way that economic competition is changing in the world. The main task . . . of the contemporary state is the promotion of economic activities, whether at home or abroad, which make firms or sectors located within the territory of the state competitive in international markets.[16]

The public obligations of governments are, moreover, increasingly fragmented and privatized. Indeed, privatization has spread to areas such as education, retirement pensions, and, as we saw, even military security.

In a globalized world, the very meaning of competition itself has changed owing to corporate innovations. No longer does competition take place within defined economic sectors and among similar competitors. Today, competition "is between various economic areas that utilize new technologies in ways that cut across traditional economic sectors, producing new 'value domains' and new customers."[17] Such competition is evident, for example, in Apple's "tablet computer," which combines the elements of a laptop and a smart phone. Such changes create incentives "for companies to move from geographically concentrated production networks to geographically dispersed networks."[18]

If Cerny is right, we would expect a convergence in states' economic and welfare policies because competition would make *all* of them reduce the costs of providing for citizens' welfare. In fact, this has not always been the case. Scandinavian industries, for instance, remain competitive even though their governments continue to provide considerable welfare benefits to citizens. Domestic structures vary in capacity and can modify the impact of globalization. Despite some convergence, there remain differences in areas such as government spending, taxation, and public employment. The capacity of states continues to vary. Some (e.g., Greece, Spain, Italy, Ireland, and Portugal) are finding it necessary to reduce public expenditures dramatically to remain competitive, whereas others (e.g., Germany) have less need to do so. Indeed, less competitive states may even use their lack of competitiveness as an excuse to reduce welfare commitments and service to citizens.

In fact, in the era of globalization, growing numbers of states, especially in the developing world, have fragile institutions and are rent by civil strife. Many are unable to protect themselves or provide citizens with even minimal services. At the extreme are "failed" and "failing" states," for example, Somalia or Afghanistan, which can neither protect citizens from violence nor provide for their most basic needs. In such states, military and security forces have become fractured "states within the state" on behalf of particular leaders or factions. Governments of failed states are controlled by subgroups and are unable to exercise authority over the state's territory. Rather than affording citizens with security, the military security institutions constitute a threat to citizens' security. A deadly combination of predatory leaders, rampant corruption, widespread poverty, income inequality, demographic pressures, fractured elites, refugee flows, vengeance-seeking groups, emigration of educated citizens, and environmental stress have caused state institutions to collapse. Where Europeans imposed borders that inhabitants never accepted and that separated ethnic polities in different states or caged conflicting groups within a single state, postcolonial governments unsuccessfully sought to foster national loyalties and build cohesive nations on the European model. State failure has increased the relative attraction of nonstate identities associated with religion, ethnicity, gender, and clan; and radical groups like Hamas and Hezbolla, and even drug lords and criminal networks, have become popular by assuming the welfare tasks formerly performed by governments.

Conclusion: The Future of the State

It is not surprising that many observers conclude that state autonomy is being eroded by globalization and that competition for foreign investment and market share forces governments to pursue policies desired by transnational corporations and financial markets. After America's subprime mortgage crisis precipitated the worst financial collapse and slowdown in the world economy since the 1930s, neoliberal "casino capitalism" became the target of growing criticism. The economic and financial crises spread by the forces of globalization further reduced the confidence of citizens in their governments and exacerbated what had already become a crisis of authority in many states.

Critics of globalization, citing the Great Recession, have become more vociferous, and political discourse in the United States and other Western countries has revealed rising anger about perceived losses of jobs to emerging-market economies.

Paradoxically, however, in these circumstances, citizens had little choice but to look to the traditional protector and provider of welfare, their respective states. The result was a scramble by governments and central banks to intervene in markets to halt the Great Recession. They quickly produced a barrage of measures designed to prevent additional bank failures, reassure depositors and shareholders, restore consumer confidence, and stimulate national economies as well as the proliferation of new regulations for financial institutions. Moreover, it became clear that countries like China, in which the state remained deeply involved in formulating economic policy, fared better than countries in which neoliberal capitalism remained dominant. China, India, and Russia, as well as other emerging economies, are increasingly attracted to state capitalism, in which governments play a central role in allocating resources, and their relative success has dimmed the attraction of neoliberal market capitalism, with its emphasis on a minimalist state. We seem to be on the cusp of a revival of state capacity.

Globally, the response to these crises has been massive state intervention to aid banks, corporations, and even heavily indebted countries like Greece. States have instituted policies involving greater regulation of capital flows and financial enterprises and deficit spending. "The ideology of the dictatorship of the market," declared French president Nicholas Sarkozy in 2008, "is dead." "Historians will one day see that this crisis marks the real start of the 21st century," a century that will see the "return of politics" in managing national economies, which will prove to be "an intellectual and moral revolution."[19] Whether President Sarkozy's prediction will come true remains to be seen.

The crisis did point up vividly how interconnected the world had become and how important states remain. States, in turn, are adapting, in a continued effort to exercise their traditional tasks, and such adaptation is visible in their responses to the rapid globalization of financial instability. Developing states have formed sovereign wealth funds that allow them a greater voice in the global economy and have forced a shift in global governance from the Group of 7 (G-7) rich states to a larger Group of 20 (G-20), which includes the emerging BRIC economies (Brazil, Russia, India, and China). Opposition to immigration and the belief that the costs of free trade may outweigh its benefits have also intensified and have forced governments to adopt protectionist policies in order to try and shore up porous boundaries.

In fact, although globalization *does* constrain state autonomy in some respects, the globalizing process itself has actually been assisted by the policies of states, and one reason why globalization processes wax and wane is that states—especially the great powers—enjoy some control over them. Some observers go further, arguing that globalization, instead of reducing state autonomy, serves to enhance the power and autonomy of political leaders, who use it as an excuse to weaken domestic actors like labor unions and reduce the state's obligations to citizens.[20] Political leaders use the alleged "constraints" imposed by the need to be competitive in a globalized world as an excuse to reverse the unwilling provision of entitlements such as health care and social security made in earlier decades to groups of citizens, which had imposed fiscal burdens on states. By this logic, globalization actually *increases* the autonomy of states by allying them with the interests of their nation's capitalists and removing the impediments posed by other domestic interests.

All in all, it is difficult to generalize about the impact of globalization on states. Sovereignty is changing, and both international and nongovernmental organizations are increasingly compromising the ability of states to dominate their populations and territory. However, this does not mean that the sovereign state will disappear. Indeed, no other political community has emerged to challenge the state directly, though nonstate institutions, communities, and identities have emerged that share with states their authority over individuals. The state persists but has evolved. It privatizes many formerly public tasks, it is not as anchored in territory as in the past, and sovereignty—though it remains the idea on which states are constructed—provides ever fewer privileges to states, both large and small. In sum, states remain a diverse lot, dissimilar in their nature and practices. How successful they will be in adapting to meet future challenges, of course, remains to be seen.

Notes

1 For an extended analysis of the typology of state definitions presented in this essay, see Yale H. Ferguson and Richard W. Mansbach, *The State, Conceptual Chaos, and the Future of International Relations Theory* (Boulder, CO: Lynne Rienner, 1989), 41–80.

2 Sebastian Schmidt, "To Order the Minds of Scholars: The Discourse of the Peace of Westphalia in International Relations Literature," *International Studies Quarterly* 55:3 (September 2011), 617.

3 James J. Sheehan, *Where Have All the Soldiers Gone? The Transformation of Modern Europe* (Boston, MA: Houghton Mifflin, 2008), 52.

4 Theda Skocpol, *States and Revolutions* (Cambridge, UK: Cambridge University Press, 1979), 29.

5 Stephen D. Krasner, "Approaches to the State: Alternative Conceptions and Historical Dynamics," *Comparative Politics* 16:2 (January 1984), 224–25.

6 See Graham Allison and Philip Zelikow, *Essence of Decision: Explaining the Cuban Missile Crisis*, 2nd ed. (New York: Longman, 1999).

7 Joseph R. Strayer, *On the Medieval Origins of the Modern State* (Princeton, NJ: Princeton University Press, 1970), 58–59.

8 Philip Bobbitt, *The Shield of Achilles: War, Peace, and the Course of History* (New York: Random House, 2002), 81.

9 Ibid., 120, 139, 143.

10 Ibid., 135–36.

11 Ibid., 146.

12 Philip G. Cerny, "What Next for the State?" in Eleonore Kofman and Gillian Youngs, eds., *Globalization: Theory and Practice* (London: Pinter, 1996), 134–35.

13 Kenichi Ohmae, *The Next Global Stage* (Upper Saddle River, NJ: Pearson Education, 2005), 91.

14 Martin van Creveld, *The Rise and Decline of the State* (Cambridge, UK: Cambridge University Press, 1999), 336.

15 See David Shearer, "Outsourcing War," *Foreign Policy* 112 (Autumn 1998), 68–81.

16 Cerny, "What Next for the State?" 124. See also Bobbitt's description of what he calls the "market-state" (*The Shield of Achilles*, 211).

17 David S. Hamilton and Joseph P. Quinlan, *Globalization and Europe* (Washington, DC: Center for Transatlantic Relations, 2008), 22.

18 Ibid.

19 Cited in "France Sets Up Sovereign Wealth Fund," *BusinessDay,* October 24, 2008, http://www.smh.com.au/business/france-sets-up-sovereign-wealth-fund-200810 24-57m1.html.

20 Maria Gritsch, "The Nation-State and Economic Globalization: Soft Geo-Politics and Increased State Autonomy?" *Review of International Political Economy* 12:1 (February 2005), 3.

9.2

ABIDING SOVEREIGNTY

Stephen D. Krasner

In the following selection, the political scientist Stephen Krasner argues that globalization is not historically novel and that states and state sovereignty remain much as they have been for centuries. He suggests that sovereignty

Source: Excerpted from Stephen D. Krasner, "Abiding Sovereignty," *International Political Science Review*, 22:3 (July 2001), 229–51. Notes appearing in the original have been deleted.

has been repeatedly violated and always has been less absolute than it appeared in theory. He terms this "organized hypocrisy." Krasner also argues that sovereignty has four dimensions, which are not necessarily linked, and that one or more of these may be weakened while others may be strengthened. He reviews a variety of phenomena, such as international organizations and nongovernmental groups, that some observers believe reflect eroding sovereignty and concludes that they coexist comfortably alongside sovereign states.

Introduction

The defining characteristic of any international system is anarchy, the absence of any legitimate hierarchical source of authority. Anarchical systems can, however, vary with regard to the specific substance of rules and institutions and the extent to which these rules are recognized and consequential. Writers in the English School tradition have made a distinction between an international system, one lacking a hierarchical structure of authority, and an international society, an international system in which there are shared rules.

The contemporary international system has its own rules and actors. Sovereign states are the building blocks, the basic actors, for the modem state system. Sovereign states are territorial units with juridical independence; they are not formally subject to some external authority. Sovereign states also have de facto autonomy. Although the power and preferences of foreign actors will limit the feasible options for any state, sovereign states are not constrained because external actors have penetrated or controlled their domestic authority structures. . . . An implication of de facto autonomy is the admonition that states should not intervene in each other's internal affairs. Sovereign states are also generally assumed to have some reasonable degree of control over both their borders and their territory

A number of observers have suggested that in the contemporary period the sovereign state is being subjected to unprecedented pressures, especially from globalization and human rights norms which bring the viability of the system itself into question. . . . The analysis presented here concludes that it is too early to schedule a wake for the sovereign-state system. Breathless assertions about globalization and human rights leading to the dissipation of sovereignty have ignored the fact that contemporary challenges are not unique; the control and authority of states has persistently been contested. If the rules of sovereignty are supplanted this could only take place through an evolutionary process in which key actors found that it was in their interest to choose new and incompatible rules and institutions. It is unlikely that key actors will make such choices, given the inherent advantages of the status quo, the ability of states to simply abandon authority claims over issue areas that they cannot effectively regulate, and the fact that sovereignty can coexist with, but not be displaced by, alternative institutional arrangements. Sovereignty is a weak evolutionary stable strategy, one that will be selected by many actors, but that can also persist along with neutral mutants, alternative strategies that are more appealing to specific actors at particular moments.

Defining Sovereignty

In practice the term sovereignty has been used in many different ways. In contemporary usage four different meanings of sovereignty can be distinguished: interdependence sovereignty, domestic sovereignty, Westphalian or Vattelian sovereignty, and international legal sovereignty.

Interdependence sovereignty refers to the ability of states to control movement across their borders. Many observers have argued that sovereignty is being eroded by globalization resulting from technological changes that have dramatically reduced the costs of communication and transportation. States cannot regulate transborder movements of goods, capital, people, ideas, or disease vectors. Governments can no longer engage in activities that have traditionally been understood to be part of their regulatory portfolio: they cannot conduct effective monetary policy because of international capital flows; they cannot control knowledge because of the Internet; they cannot guarantee public health because individuals can move so quickly across the globe. The issue here is not one of authority but rather of control. The right of states to manage their borders is not challenged, but globalization, it is asserted, has eroded their ability to actually do so.

Domestic sovereignty refers to authority structures within states and the ability of these structures to effectively regulate behavior. . . . Authority structures have taken many different forms including monarchies, republics, democracies, unified systems, and federal systems. The acceptance or recognition of a given authority structure is one aspect of domestic sovereignty; the other is the level of control that officials can actually exercise. This has varied dramatically. Well ordered domestic polities have both legitimate and effective authority structures. Failed states have neither. The loss of interdependence sovereignty, which is purely a matter of control, would also imply some loss of domestic sovereignty, at least domestic sovereignty understood as control, since if a state cannot regulate movements across its borders, such as the flow of illegal drugs, it is not likely to be able to control activities within its borders, such as the use of these drugs.

Westphalian or Vattelian sovereignty refers to the exclusion of external sources of authority both de jure and de facto. Within its own boundaries the state has a monopoly over authoritative decision-making. At the international level this implies that states follow the rule of non-intervention in the internal affairs of others. . . .

International legal sovereignty refers to mutual recognition. The basic rule of international legal sovereignty is that recognition is accorded to juridically independent territorial entities which are capable of entering into voluntary contractual agreements. . . . States in the international system, like individuals in domestic polities, are free and equal. International legal sovereignty is consistent with any agreement provided that the state is not coerced. Recognition is associated with a number of other rules including diplomatic immunity, and the act of state doctrine which protects state actions from being challenged in the courts of other countries.

The rules, institutions, and practices that are associated with these four meanings of sovereignty are neither logically nor empirically linked in some organic whole. Sovereignty refers to both practices, such as the ability to control transborder movements or activities within a state's boundaries, and to rules or principles, such as the recognition of juridically independent territorial entities and non-intervention in the internal affairs of other states. A state might have little interdependence sovereignty, be unable to regulate its own borders, but its Westphalian/Vattelian sovereignty could remain intact so long as no external actor attempted to influence its domestic authority structures. A failed state like Somalia in the late 1990s offers one example. States can enjoy international legal sovereignty, mutual recognition, without having Westphalian/Vattelian sovereignty; the eastern European states during the cold war whose domestic structures were deeply penetrated by the Soviet Union offer one example. States can voluntarily compromise their Westphalian/Vattelian sovereignty through the exercise of their international legal sovereignty: the member states of the European Union have entered into a set of voluntary agreements, treaties, that have created supranational authority structures. . . . States can lack effective domestic sovereignty understood either as control or authority and still have international legal sovereignty—Zaire/Congo during the 1990s is an example. . . .

Sovereignty Contested

The basic rules associated with Westphalian/Vattelian and international legal sovereignty have been recognized at least since the end of the eighteenth century, and in some cases even earlier. These rules have been in place during a period of unprecedented material and ideational change in human society.

During the last two centuries, when the rules of the sovereign state system have been widely understood, the world has changed a lot, arguably more than at any other time in human history. Many recent observers have argued that the sovereign-state system is now under unprecedented stress because of two developments: globalization and changing international norms with respect to human rights. Globalization poses challenges to interdependence and domestic sovereignty because it threatens state control. Human rights norms challenge Westphalian/Vattelian sovereignty because they imply that domestic authorities are not free to set their own rules about the treatment of individuals within their borders.

Many observers have suggested that the increase in globalization is a threat to sovereignty. What they usually mean is that the state is losing control over certain activities, but some observers have hinted that this could lead to changes in authority structures as well. . . .

States, however, have always operated in an interdependent international environment. They have never been able to perfectly regulate transborder flows. International capital flows were important in the Middle Ages; the Fuggers, one of the most important German banking families in the early modern period, controlled mines in central Europe and the Alps, had correspondents in Venice, were the dominant firm in Antwerp, the most important financial center of the time, and had branches in Portugal, Spain, Chile, Fiume, and Dubrovnik. . . . European states were more dependent on international borrowing to finance public activities, the most important of which was war, before the nineteenth century, when they lacked the administrative capacity to extract resources from their own economies, than they have been since. It was only in the nineteenth century that the major European states developed sophisticated national systems of finance including revenue collection.

During the nineteenth century the Latin American states were beset by boom and bust cycles linked to international capital flows on which they were heavily dependent. The Asian flu of the late 1990s was hardly the first international financial crisis. Baring Brothers, the British financial institution that suffered a spectacular collapse in 1995 as a result of speculative dealings by a broker in Singapore, would have ceased to exist in 1890 as a result of questionable loans that had been made to Argentina had it not been for the intervention of the Bank of England, the Bank of France, the British Treasury, and J.P. Morgan. The period before the First World War saw net capital flows on a larger scale than ever before or since. For the years 1910 to 1913 foreign investment was equal to 53 percent of British domestic savings, 7 percent of German, and 13 percent of French. Net international capital flows were higher in the nineteenth century. . . .

Capital market integration in the last part of the nineteenth century was so high because of three factors. Technological change dramatically increased the speed of communication, as the telegraph reduced the time it took for information to move between New York and London from ten days to a few minutes; the gold standard encouraged long-term flows by reducing exchange-rate risks; finally, it was easier for governments in the late nineteenth century to make exchange rate stability a more salient policy goal than employment because pressure from labor was weak. While technological change has made communication even easier, exchange rate risks and domestic political pressures weigh against a return to the levels of capital market integration of the late nineteenth century. High capital flows and the rules of sovereignty have coexisted for at least two centuries, even if such flows have made elements of interdependence and domestic sovereignty problematic.

International migration rates reached their highest levels in history during the long nineteenth century stretching from the end of the Napoleonic Wars to 1914. In the century following 1820, 60 million Europeans moved to the labor-scarce New World. . . . Migration resulted in substantial wage convergence between Europe and North America and at least in the United States prompted a political backlash which contributed to more restrictive immigration policies. International trade also increased rapidly during the nineteenth century. Technological changes such as the railroad and the steamship reduced transportation costs, and commodities with high weight-to-value ratios, such as grain, became internationally and intercontinentally competitive. This burst of international commerce was brought to an abrupt halt by the First World War and the ratio of trade to aggregate economic activity remained low during both the interwar period and the Second World War. Trade increased again after 1950, equaling nineteenth-century peaks for many countries in the 1980s and then surpassing them.

In arenas other than economic, the claim that the contemporary era represents a qualitative break with the past should also be met with some skepticism. AIDS, which probably originated in a remote part of Africa, has spread around the world, but in terms of the number of deaths it hardly compares with earlier pandemics, from the bubonic plague in Europe during the Middle Ages, to smallpox which the Europeans brought to the New World, to influenza during the first part of the twentieth century.

The late twentieth century has also witnessed the spread of ideas, including norms such as the rights of indigenous peoples, and popular culture such as MTV. But, here again, the degree of change can be exaggerated. The Reformation transformed the political map of Europe within a decade after Luther had posted his 95 Theses on the door of the Schlosskirche in Wittenberg. . . . The Internet has provided not only very rapid but also widely available and inexpensive forms of communication, but the most dramatic increase in the speed of communication took place not in the 1980s but in the 1860s with the laying of the first transatlantic telegraph cables.

It is not that globalization has had no impact on state control, but rather that controlling transborder movements, not to speak of developments within a state's boundaries, has always been a challenge. The problems for states have become more acute in some areas, but less so in others. There is no evidence that globalization has systematically undermined state control; indeed, the clearest relationship between globalization and state activity is that they have increased hand-in-hand, and in some arenas states are more capable than they have been in the past. Modern medicine has made it easier for public authorities to suppress or cope with epidemics. The level of government spending for the major countries has, on average, increased substantially since 1950 along with increases in trade and capital flows. This ought to be no surprise: governments have intervened to provide social safety nets that make more open economic policies politically acceptable.

In sum, global flows are not new. In some issue areas, such as migration, flows were higher in the nineteenth century than they are now. Government initiatives have not been crippled by globalization. Indeed, the provision of collective goods and social stability have created the conditions that have made higher levels of trade and capital flows politically viable in the postwar period.

While globalization and associated questions of control have raised one set of issues about the viability of the sovereign-state system, especially with regard to interdependence and the control aspects of domestic sovereignty, the spread of international norms regarding human rights presents a second set of challenges. Here the issues are related to Westphalian/Vattelian sovereignty rather than domestic or interdependence sovereignty. Global human rights norms are a direct challenge to one aspect of the authority of the state: its right to regulate relations between its subjects and their rulers free of external interference. Conventional notions of Westphalian/Vattelian sovereignty place authority over relations between rulers and ruled entirely within the hands of national governments; the policies emanating from domestic political structures are not subject to challenge by external actors, especially external actors claiming authority in their own right. Universal human rights norms, in contrast, prescribe standards that all regimes must honor. The state might be the only actor that can establish authoritative rules within its own borders, but universal human rights norms imply that it cannot set any rule that it pleases.

Westphalian/Vattelian sovereignty can be violated in a number of different ways. In some instances external actors such as NGOs, international organizations, or other more powerful states have encouraged regimes to accept standards that they would have preferred to ignore. Human rights NGOs, such as Amnesty International for instance, have publicized what they have regarded as the illicit practices of some regimes, and this in turn has increased pressure from other governments. There have also been more direct cases of state-to-state interventions regarding human rights issues of which military interventions . . . have been the most dramatic.

Westphalian/Vattelian sovereignty can also be compromised through the voluntary actions of political leaders. The European human rights regime, which includes supranational institutions like the European Human Rights Commission and the European Human Rights Court, is one example. . . . This regime was not the result of external coercion or pressure from either public or private actors, but rather of a voluntary agreement, a treaty. By exercising their international legal sovereignty, their right to make contracts, European decision makers violated the Westphalian/Vattelian sovereignty of their own polities.

Among some observers there has been unqualified enthusiasm for contemporary human rights activities, which are seen as changing the basic nature of the sovereign-state system. As in the case of discussions of globalization, such dispositions reflect an element of historical myopia. . . .

Transnational non-governmental organizations (TNGOs) were active in the nineteenth as well as the twentieth century. In their study of what they term transnational advocacy networks Margaret Keck and Kathryn Sikkink point out that such groups were occupied with efforts to abolish slavery, promote the rights of women, improve conditions for workers, and end foot binding in China. . . .

Westphalian/Vattelian sovereignty has been contested among states themselves for an even longer period, at least since the seventeenth century. The right to intervene in relations between rulers and ruled has been justified not only in terms of human rights, but also minority rights, and the need to ensure international security and stability. . . .

As a condition of recognition by the major European powers, the would-be leaders of every state that emerged from the Ottoman Empire during the long nineteenth century—beginning with Greece in 1832, through Romania, Serbia, Montenegro, and Bulgaria as a tributary state of the Empire in 1878, to Albania in 1913—had to recognize the civil and political rights of their religious minorities. . . .

Concern with human as opposed to minority rights, whether religious or ethnic, became more manifest during and after the Second World War. . . . The nineteenth century had witnessed some successes in establishing the rights of broader classes of individuals, especially the abolition of the slave trade and slavery and the movement to secure women's suffrage. The leaders of the United States and some of the other major powers were, in fact, quite anxious about the explicit inclusion of human rights provisions in the founding documents of the United Nations, fearing that this could lead to constraints on their Westphalian/Vatellian and domestic sovereignty, but at the San Francisco meeting a number of smaller countries . . . pressed for explicit human rights provisions. . . . In the end the United States and the other major powers supported the explicit and formal endorsement of human rights. Subsequently there have been many international agreements regarding human rights, including more than twenty United Nations conventions, and the Helsinki and Dayton accords.

In sum, contemporary challenges to Westphalian/Vattelian sovereignty and interdependence sovereignty have many historical precedents. The ability of states to effectively regulate their borders and to exclude external sources of authority could never be taken for granted. Historically some large and powerful states, most obviously the United States, have been very successful at maintaining all elements of sovereignty. Smaller and weaker states have had a harder time.

Sovereignty's Resilience

So here is the puzzle: globalization and alternative normative structures such as minority and human rights have persistently challenged Westphalian/Vattelian and interdependence sovereignty. Economic, demographic, military, and ideational change has been exceptionally dynamic over the last two centuries. Yet no alternative set of institutional arrangements has supplanted the rules associated with sovereign statehood, although new arrangements such as protectorates, dominions, and regional entities have been established and coexisted with the norms of sovereignty. Sovereignty's resilience is striking. . . .

If the rules associated with the sovereign-state system are changing, this could only occur as a result of more incremental developments resulting from the choices of public and private decision makers pursuing their own self-interest in an environment so complicated that they cannot foresee all of the consequences of their decisions. The emergence of the modern state system itself, which occurred over several centuries, offers an historical analogy. States that were juridically independent territorial entities which mutually recognized each other did not suddenly emerge full-blown from the Peace of Westphalia or any other specific historical event. The rules of sovereignty were not explicitly formulated in one organic package by any political leader or theorist. Rather they emerged over time and have been adhered to with varying degrees of fidelity.

The modern European state system evolved from medieval arrangements characterized by formally overlapping structures of authority. The most compelling explanations for the triumph of the national state over other institutional forms point to the ability of states to take advantage of the wealth and military power generated by technological and commercial changes that took place during the late Middle Ages. States, as opposed to empires, or city states, or trading confederations (such as the Hanseatic League) were better able to promote economic development, fight wars, and extract resources. States could more effectively establish uniform weights and measures which encouraged trade and commerce than could city states or city leagues. States were better able to control local political and military actors than could empires. They were more adept at creating the bureaucratic organizations that were necessary to fight effectively with metal, siege guns, and large naval fleets. They were able to extract resources from their own populations, to secure wealth through conquest, to borrow from international financiers, and ultimately beginning in the seventeenth century to establish domestic organizations that could systematically and efficiently tax. Historically, changing material circumstances have led to changes in institutional structures at the international level, most notably redefinitions of the key actors: states as sovereign equals, for instance, versus an imperial center and various lesser entities.

The end of the medieval world, and of city states, empires, and city leagues, precipi-tated by technological change, was supported by new ideas, especially those associated with the Protestant Reformation. Luther's doctrines provided an ideational rationale and legitimation for the position of secular rulers. Will recent changes in technology associ-ated with globalization, and the embrace of human rights norms, lead to new political structures and new rules that will supplant those associated with the sovereign state? Are we in the midst of an evolutionary transformation whose initial steps but not final denouement are becoming more visible?. . .

There are several reasons to suspect that no such transformation is in the offing. First, there are the usual advantages of the status quo. The development of new arrangements requires new investments, while the maintenance of old ones simply involves ongoing expenditures. Once an institution is in place, regardless of how it got there to begin with, it generates shared expectations which become a force for stability. Policy positions are formulated on the assumption that existing practices will persist. Individuals invest in training because they believe that employment opportunities—in the diplomatic corps, civil service, the military—will continue. Complementary cultural practices develop; sovereign states, for instance, may appeal to national loyalties, create flags and anthems, promote the national language, privilege citizens, and establish national holidays. New arrangements might require individuals to invest in new skills, learn new languages, and make different choices for the education of their children, something that they might do but only at some cost.

Second, as suggested by the long-standing challenges posed by globalization and by external efforts to influence relations between rulers and ruled (religious toleration, minority rights, human rights) the actual practice of sovereignty has been characterized by organized hypocrisy. Well-understood rules such as non-intervention in the internal affairs of other states have been violated and these violations have been legitimated by other norms such as minority rights, human rights, and the need to preserve international stability. The reasons given by the major NATO countries for intervention in Kosovo were not much different from the reasons that some of these same states had given for intervening in the Greek war of independence in the 1820s or for brokering a peace settlement that included minority rights at the Congress of Berlin after the first Balkan wars of the 1870s. In all three cases major states legitimated their intervention in the internal affairs of another political entity by appealing to the need to protect minorities and preserve international stability. The existence of multiple norms, rather than being a threat to the rules of sovereignty, may in fact help to preserve them by making it easier for the rulers of powerful states to pursue material and ideational goals in some situa-tions while adhering to conventional sovereignty norms in others. . . .

Third, political actors committed to the sovereign-state system have the option of shedding functions which they cannot manage. Some observers who see globalization undermining sovereignty have correctly pointed out that some states can no longer regu-late international capital flows and as a result their ability to conduct macro-economic policy is constrained. This situation is not, however, a new development. Some smaller states that cannot pursue autonomous monetary policies may simply give up control over this arena. The most extreme examples of this phenomenon are dollarization, with countries adopting a foreign currency, the dollar, and giving up any effort to maintain a national money supply. . . .

Do such moves spell the doom of the sovereign state and the emergence of some alternative institutional structure? This could only be the case if shedding authority in some area—a reformulation of domestic sovereignty—led to conditions that were so problematic that significant political and economic actors would begin to search for new structures that might be inconsistent with the rules of sovereignty. This could, of course, happen. But it is more likely that the economic performance of smaller, weaker states with shaky political regimes will be better if they relinquish control of their own monetary policy, because this will reduce the chances of inflation. Such an outright surrender of macro-economic authority would be more problematic for larger, more powerful states with effective domestic authority structures, because they would find it more difficult to provide social and economic stability for their own populations. . . .

One historical example of the benefits of constraining and relinquishing rather than expanding state authority is the development of religious toleration in Europe. In the medieval period the Catholic Church and secular authority were intertwined. The Protestant Reformation provided an alternative, religiously-grounded rationale for secular authority. Luther argued that the king is ordained by God and God is all-knowing. For European rulers giving up control over religion was not easy: it not only meant abandoning concern for the souls of one's subjects but also weakening one of the foundations for the legitimacy of their own regimes. European rulers did not embrace religious toleration, but confronted with the religious wars of the sixteenth and seventeenth centuries they reluctantly adopted it, and ultimately many adhered to religious freedom which rejected state involvement in spiritual matters. Giving up authority over the way in which subjects interact with the sacred is no small thing. . . . Yet religious toleration and freedom were a consequence of the recognition by political authorities that there were elements of human life that they could not regulate. By redefining the scope of domestic sovereignty they enhanced political stability. Transnational and international ideational and material pressures, globalization, can threaten interdependence sovereignty, but rather than leading players to explore institutional alternatives to domestic sovereignty these threats might simply encourage them to limit the scope of state authority; to alter the nature of domestic sovereignty rather than trying to find alternatives to it.

A fourth reason to expect sovereignty to persist is that claims about domestic authority, the exclusion of external authority, and international recognition and state equality have been compatible with other structures that have existed in the international system. Individual actors have had incentives to develop alternative rules and institutions, indeed, they have done this in the most imaginative ways. But these other arrangements have been neutral mutants that have coexisted with rather than supplanted sovereignty. . . .

The most interesting contemporary example of a neutral mutant is the European Union. After the Second World War, American and European leaders searched for new institutional arrangements. American policy makers were motivated by geopolitical concerns; they wanted a powerful alliance that could balance against the Soviet Union. Rather than following a divide-and-conquer strategy in Western Europe, they supported European unification. European leaders had their own reasons for pursuing such a policy. . . . For Germany's postwar leaders greater European cooperation offered not only economic integration and the strategic advantages of making Germany more secure by making it less of a threat, but also the long-term possibility of establishing a German national identity within a broader European frame of reference. Consistent with the expectations of an evolutionary approach, the current status of the European Union has emerged over a period of time out of complex negotiations designed to deal with specific issues, rather than from some effort to conform with a well understood set of rules and norms. . . . The European Union has territory, recognition, control, national authority, extranational authority, and supranational authority. . . .

The structure of the European Union is hardly settled. It might simply evolve into a conventional federal state. It might become embedded as a distinctly new institutional form, one whose bundle of attributes includes supranational and extranational authority. At the present moment the EU is already a structure that has displaced conventional sovereignty within Europe itself. The member states all enjoy international recognition, but so does the European Union itself. The basic rule of international legal sovereignty, recognizing juridically independent territorial entities, no longer applies in Europe. The EU has no territory separate from that of its members, and its members are not juridically independent. The Union has been a signatory to international accords that fall within its purview including the UN Law of the Seas Convention, various international commodity agreements, the Helsinki Final Act, and several environmental conventions; its member states have also been signatories. It maintains diplomatic representation in a number of countries, as do its member states. . . . The European Union has curtailed the Westphalian/Vatellian sovereignty of its members and altered the structure of their domestic political institutions.

Within Europe the EU has displaced institutional arrangements associated with international legal, Westphalian, and domestic sovereignty. In most issue areas its members have relinquished claims to regulate movements across their borders. Within Europe the Union has displaced conventional sovereignty. In the wider international environment, however, it is a neutral mutant coexisting with political entities that still embrace conventional sovereignty rules.

Institutions change because circumstances, usually material circumstances, change. Historically, some international rules have been annihilated when political entities with asymmetrical power that were previously remote from each other suddenly engaged in direct military confrontations. Absent an invasion from outer space no such dramatic coercive change is in the offing. If the contemporary rules change it will be as a result of incremental choices made by leaders motivated by short-term calculations of interest rather than some comprehensive plan. In the contemporary environment it is difficult to identify why or how such a process might be initiated. Sovereignty rules enjoy the usual advantages of the status quo. When confronted with new material or ideational challenges political leaders have either devised alternative institutional arrangements that have coexisted with but not displaced sovereignty, neutral mutants, or they have simply limited their claims to authority.

New Challenges

There are new challenges to conventional rules but, like past challenges, they will not displace sovereignty. As suggested above, the European Union, while comfortably coexisting with established institutions in the broader international environment, has displaced Westphalian/Vatellian and international legal sovereignty within Europe as well as altering the domestic authority structures of its members including their abandoning claims to regulate transborder flows among member states in most areas. Furthermore, there are at least two actors that are more salient in the contemporary international environment than has been the case in the past—international organizations (IOs) and transnational non-governmental organizations (TNGOs). In addition technology has introduced a new and potentially disruptive form of activity, cyber crime.

International organizations, such as the United Nations, the International Monetary Fund, the World Bank, the World Trade Organization, and many, many others, are more consequential than they have been in the past. These organizations are ultimately beholden to their member states, especially those member states with substantial resources, but officials within IOs can, nevertheless, act on their own within sometimes broad mandates. IOs can be the transmitters of international norms, many but not necessarily all of which have been generated initially within the largest and most powerful polities. These organizations can be instruments for compromising the Westphalian/Vattelian sovereignty of their members. . . . Older institutions such as the IMF and the World Bank became more intimately involved with political questions despite formal prescriptions against such behavior. . . . Adherence to the conditionality terms of international financial institutions is a voluntary act, but such acts can compromise the domestic autonomy of states; better to get the money and acknowledge external involvement in domestic authority structures than to reject such involvement and be impoverished.

The spread of democracy and technological change has made the activities of non-governmental organizations which operate both within and across countries more salient. The Internet has made it easier for poorer, smaller groups, as opposed to wealthier, larger ones like multinational corporations, to organize. The number of NGOs has increased dramatically during the twentieth century from perhaps 200 in 1900 to 4000 in 1980. Keck and Sikkink have argued that NGOs along with foundations, some government bureaucracies, parts of international organizations, the media, and local groups can form transnational advocacy networks that facilitate the exchange of information and alter public policy. There would have been, for instance, no international convention against land mines without the efforts of the International Campaign to Ban Land Mines. . . . Telecommunications technology—telephone, fax, the Internet—has reduced organizational costs for NGOs, making them more potent lobbying organizations than they would otherwise have been, especially in democratic polities. Advocacy networks can organize to pressure international organizations; the Seattle demonstrations against the World Trade Organization offer an example. TNGOs can challenge not only specific policies but also the authority of the state by demanding accountability or shaming political leaders. . . .

Cyberspace will open opportunities for new kinds of criminal or simply malicious activities. Viruses generated in one country can freeze e-mail and destroy files all over the world; individuals in one country can penetrate computer systems in others. Such problematic activities could be dealt with through national legal systems, provided that they have the appropriate laws and enforcement mechanisms, something that cannot be taken for granted. The most troublesome crimes could be those that originate in places that are not effectively controlled by any state. In some places it is easier to have a good Internet connection than to have effective domestic sovereignty.

TNGOs, international organizations, and cyber crime all pose new challenges to state control and in some cases to state authority as well. With regard to the rules of sovereignty, however, the question is this: Will these challenges generate new rules and norms that could undermine or supplant those associated with sovereignty? For TNGOs the answer is no. TNGOs are not alternative governance structures; they are designed to change state policy. For democratic states TNGOs are perfectly consistent with domestic sovereignty; they are just another kind of pressure group, albeit one that might be able to enhance its influence by operating across boundaries. They might, however, puncture Westphalian/Vattelian sovereignty by challenging the legitimacy of existing state practices. Whether or not this happens remains to be seen. Many human rights NGOs, such as Amnesty International, regard the death penalty as barbaric, but this is not likely to change public policy in the United States although other states might be more susceptible to such pressure. For autocratic states TNGOs can contest both domestic and Westphalian/Vattelian sovereignty by arguing, for instance, that governance structures ought to be more democratic, but TNGOs do not claim to offer an alternative to state authority.

International organizations (IOs) are a manifestation of international legal sovereignty. They reflect efforts by political leaders to secure policy outcomes that would elude them if they acted unilaterally. . . . Multilateral organizations may legitimate norms that would be suspect if they emanated from a single state. States, especially individual states, might not be able to fully control IOs, but IOs are a product of international legal sovereignty even if they sometimes undermine Westphalian/Vattelian and domestic sovereignty. . . .

Cyber crime poses a more interesting problem. At modest levels such activities may simply be a cost of doing business in the cyber age but transgressions could become so extensive that they would threaten commerce. In a polity with effective domestic sovereignty cyber crime, like any other crime, could be more or less controlled. In areas without effective political control illicit activities could be much more extensive. This is a problem that calls for the invention of some new institutional arrangements, neutral mutants, that would coexist with sovereign states. . . . Extraterritorial assertions can be a mechanism for compensating for an absence of domestic sovereignty. Cyber crime may generate neutral mutants, . . . but it is more likely to generate additional more extensive extraterritorial assertions by powerful states. Again, this will not displace the conventional rules of sovereignty, but organized hypocrisy, saying one thing and doing another, or endorsing mutually contradictory principles, may become more extensive in the area of criminal activity.

Conclusion

Sovereignty has not been an organically related, inseparable set of rules. Different elements of sovereignty are not logically related, nor have they empirically always occurred together. Political leaders have, for instance, used the international legal sovereignty of their states to compromise their Westphalian/Vattelian sovereignty. Issues of globalization and human rights, which have recently received so much attention, are old, not new, problems. States have always struggled to control the cross-border flow of ideas, goods, and people. The right of rulers to unilaterally and autonomously establish laws for their own polities has been challenged by external actors concerned about international security, minority rights, and fiscal responsibility. Power holders in the present system do not have an incentive to devise a new set of rules that would displace those associated with sovereignty because existing arrangements can coexist with alternatives that can be constructed either voluntarily or through coercion when conventional norms provide less attractive outcomes.

Over the several hundred years during which the rules of sovereignty have been widely understood, state control could never be taken for granted. States could never isolate themselves from the external environment. Globalization and intrusive international norms are not new phenomena. Some aspects of the contemporary environment are unique—the number of transnational non-governmental organizations has grown dramatically, international organizations are more prominent, cyber crime could not exist without cyber space. These developments do challenge state control. A loss of control can precipitate a crisis of authority, but even a crisis of authority is only a necessary but not a sufficient condition for developing new authority structures. New rules could emerge in an evolutionary way as a result of trial and error by rational but myopic actors. But these arrangements, for instance, international policing, are likely to coexist with rather than supplant conventional sovereign structures. Sovereignty's resilience is, if nothing else, a reflection of its tolerance for alternatives.

9.3

FIVE NATIONS BOOSTING THEIR CULTURE OF INNOVATION

Mark Trumbull

In the next selection, the author argues that in today's highly integrated global economic system innovation is the key to competing successfully. Innovation, he points out, is becoming increasingly prevalent in other countries, and the

Source: Mark Trumbull, "Five Nations Boosting Their Culture of Innovation," *The Christian Science Monitor,* February 22, 2010.

United States is no longer unchallenged in this respect. To emphasize his claim, the author describes the different approaches to innovation adopted by Brazil, Singapore, India, Israel, and China.

From Europe to Asia and beyond, the hunger to innovate has created lots of entrepreneurial competition for America. Start-up firms are helping to manage traffic in the teeming cities of Brazil and have allowed less-populous nations such as Israel to become fertile soil for new business ideas. These nations view innovation as a vital source of economic competitiveness. Not that long ago, the United States was the clear world leader in most industries and technology.

Now, while it's hard to put any other nation as "No. 1," America no longer enjoys such a privileged position. The global spread of inventiveness is a disruptive force but also a beneficial one, economists say. If more of the world's people are innovators, more will be creating new industries or solving problems like how to control carbon emissions. "Innovation is growth, and growth creates jobs," says Vijay Govindarajan, who heads the Tuck Business School's Center for Global Leadership at Dartmouth College in Hanover, N.H. And increasingly, he says, innovation is occurring in a global matrix with ideas flowing among developed and developing nations. "The United States can be competitive in the next 25 years only if we embrace globalization 150 percent," he says. "Globalization is like gravity. You can deny it only at your peril." Here's a look at five nations that are using varied strategies to ride the elevator of innovation-led growth.

Brazil

The competition isn't just between East and West. Brazil symbolizes the way continents of the South are ramping up efforts to nurture new businesses. A major government-backed effort to support start-ups includes a growing array of university-based incubator programs. The effort is giving wings to people like Andre Averbug, a business school graduate whose start-up provides software for mass-transit services. "A few years ago, Brazil was seen as a commodity country," he says. "I think Brazil now is being looked at as a good country to do business."

Singapore

This island nation has prospered not just because of investments in education and port infrastructure, but also because of its promotion of start-ups. Its experiments have run the gamut from subsidies for ventures involving targeted technologies to putting up public money alongside venture investors who come to the city-state, Harvard University business expert Josh Lerner writes in a recent report for the American Enterprise Institute. The result: Even though its economy looked similar to that of Jamaica in 1965, per capita gross domestic product has reached $31,400 in Singapore, whereas Jamaica's had edged up to just $4,800.

India

Yes, India is known as a hub of outsourced customer service. But if anyone doubts India's ability to innovate, consider the build-it-yourself automobile. At a price below $3,000, the Tata Nano is providing affordable wheels and generating lots of jobs for people who specialize in assembling the boxed parts into vehicles. "It's as close a thing as we've seen in a long time in the automobile industry to a fresh start," says Eamonn Kelly, a California-based strategic thinker at the consulting firm Monitor Group. He says firms like Tata in cars and Infosys in software have been "quietly reinventing the nature of work," breaking down complex processes into new formulas. India is still in the early stages of discovering its potential. If it can succeed in raising education levels for the vast majority who lack a high-school degree, the flow of ideas from India will expand even more.

Israel

In Israel, a rich crop of enterprises draws strength partly from what may seem like a surprising source: the military. It's not that the start-ups are all defense-related. But the Israeli military is a lean, adaptive organization—and one where citizens serve during early, formative years, says Saul Singer, coauthor of "Start-up Nation," a new book on Israel's entrepreneurial prowess. "The Israeli military is smaller at the top than most, and it forces more authority down," he says. "The sense of improvisation comes from being stressed and short on resources." Another factor: The government of this once-socialist economy has learned to promote free enterprise by getting out of the way.

China

Even as China has leveraged its huge market potential to lure technology partners from overseas, it has also been expanding its ability to generate ideas from the ground up using a self-created array of research universities. China's blend of sheer demographic scale, bottom-up commercial drive, and top-down planning may be rewriting the development rule book. As China plays the traditional game of catch-up, it's also trying to push ahead into leadership positions in key areas such as nanotechnology. The advances come with risks and caveats. Critics see major violations of trade rules. And forecasters have a lively debate going about whether this race-ahead economy is poised for a bust. Alongside these five nations, Europe and Japan remain innovative powerhouses. And Mr. Govindarajan cites other up-and-comers to watch, including Mexico, Vietnam, Turkey, and South Africa. The upshot may be an increasingly two-track process for innovation. He says the new climbers will create more products that filter upward to high-income nations, even as the developed nations still pioneer products that filter downward in a traditional way.

9.4

PAY INCREASES: WAGES ROSE NOMINALLY OVER THE PAST DECADE BUT IF YOU'RE NOT FEELING FLUSHER, YOU MAY BLAME GLOBALIZATION

Heather Scoffield

In the next selection, from Canada, the author contends that wage increases have slowed significantly in recent years owing to the competitive pressures of globalization. In some cases, notably in manufacturing, wages have actually fallen after accounting for inflation.

Have you ever wondered why you haven't felt much richer over the past 10 years?

The answer, according to research by Toronto-Dominion Bank, might be free trade and globalization. TD looked at Statistics Canada figures on pay increases over the past decade, and found that wages for all employees in Canada rose a total of 24 per cent between January 1997, and March 2006, at nominal rates.

But nominal rates include inflation. And while inflation is not very high these days, it does add up over a decade.

So, once inflation is factored out, wages rose a total of only 2 per cent in total over the decade, TD chief economist Don Drummond calculates.

In other words, if you were making $50,000 a year a decade ago, on average you're making $62,000 now in nominal terms.

But once the general rise in prices has been taken into account, in real terms you're only making $51,000—not much of a leap for 10 years' worth of work.

The story gets worse for employees who work in parts of the economy exposed to international competition, TD suggests.

"There is some casual evidence that this competition is influencing Canadian wages as we witnessed a substantial widening of pay in Canada along skill and trade lines in the past decade," Mr. Drummond writes in a recent report.

People who work in manufacturing, for example, saw their wages rise a nominal 16 per cent over the decade, but once inflation is taken into account, they actually had to

Source: Heather Scoffield, "Pay Increases: Wages Rose Nominally Over the Past Decade but If You're Not Feeling Flusher You May Blame Globalization," *The Globe and Mail,* June 28, 2006.

A "Race to the Bottom"?
Competition and Wages

swallow a pay cut of 4 per cent. Those in retail—a sector that has faced big pressure from global giants, such as Wal-Mart Stores Inc.—also saw their wages fall back over the decade.

The largest wage gains were in services, which are insulated from the competition that comes from international trade, Mr. Drummond points out. Childcare workers saw real wage increases of 23 per cent over the decade, although from a very low base.

Managers, business and finance professionals, secretaries and administrators, scientists, civil servants and cooks also pocketed higher wages over the decade.

However, construction workers, who are much in demand these days, have not seen any real wage gains in a decade, the study shows.

Other studies have shown that the United States is experiencing a similar phenomenon. The income gap between skilled and unskilled workers is directly associated with global competition, the studies say.

But it's not as if workers from China are showing up in force at bargaining sessions in North America every time a union tries to negotiate higher wages.

Rather, the trade effect is more indirect. Companies in trouble because of global competition will lay off people, who then often spend long periods of time unemployed and frequently have to settle for a job with lower wages, Mr. Drummond's report says, citing research by the Organization for Economic Co-operation and Development.

9.5

ARMS DEALER'S SAFE HAVEN

from *Canberra Times*

> The following brief selection describes Russia's abortive effort to assist the arms dealer Victor Bout, who was captured in an American "sting" operation in Bangkok and then extradited to the United States to stand trial in New York City, where he was convicted of conspiring to provide weapons to a terrorist organization and conspiring to kill Americans. Bout served as a model for the character of an arms smuggler played by Nicholas Cage in the 2005 film *Lord of War*. Bout and others like him illustrate the growing role of private dealers in arming mercenaries, militias, and other violent groups involved in civil wars and terrorism.

Last week, Moscow stepped in to protect the rights of an upstanding Russian businessman who was arrested overseas. Victor Bout is being held in Thailand on suspicion of plotting to sell Russian-made Igla shoulder-fired missiles to Columbian drug cartels. He was

Source: "Arms Dealer's Safe Haven," *Canberra Times,* April 21, 2008.

poised to sell a mere 100 of these missiles to drug barons, who had been planning to use them to shoot down US helicopters foolish enough to fly over their plantations.

Bout has been accused of selling weapons to the Hutu militants who carried out a monstrous genocide campaign, killing more than 1 million people in Rwanda in 1994. He has allegedly sold arms to other bloodthirsty dictators in Sierra Leone and Liberia and equipped the Taliban. After the United Nations listed Bout as one of the world's most dangerous criminals, he decided to settle in Russia. The government is engaged in a heroic crusade against all those bad businessmen who break the law. But it is not opposed to a Russian businessman offering surface-to-air missiles to Columbian drug lords.

9.6

CONGO-KINSHASA: HUMAN RIGHTS WATCH EXPLAINS CONFLICT

from *Africa News*

Even as globalization has been accompanied by fewer interstate wars, domestic violence of the kind assisted by Victor Bout and similar arms dealers flourishes, especially in parts of the developing world. The globalized world is divided into wealthy countries, which are integrated into the global economic system and have benefited from the mobility of things, persons, and ideas, and impoverished countries, which are the scene of endemic violence. Some of the latter are failed states, in which public institutions have collapsed under the weight of poverty, violence, environmental degradation, and overpopulation. One of these, the Democratic Republic of Congo, is described in the following selection.

Who Is Fighting Whom?

In 2006, Congo held historic elections expected to bring stability to this war-torn country following two consecutive wars between 1996 and 2003, but instead the bloodshed in eastern Congo continued. In January 2008, a peace agreement between the government and a host of Congolese rebel groups brought hope that the violence might end. It did not, and combat resumed a few months later.

In December 2008, the Congolese government struck secret deals with its neighbors, Rwanda and Uganda, both former enemies who had twice invaded Congo, permitting

Source: "Congo-Kinshasa: Human Rights Watch Explains Conflict," *Africa News,* August 10, 2009. Originally published as "Q & A: DR Congo—Dossier for Hillary Clinton's Visit" by Human Rights Watch.

limited joint military operations against foreign rebel groups based in Congo. In exchange, in the case of Rwanda, the Congolese government demanded the Rwandan government cease support for a Congolese rebel group, the National Congress for the Defense of the People, or CNDP, who had received substantial support from Rwanda and had repeatedly routed the Congolese army.

Today, the Congolese national army, known as the FARDC, is currently fighting on two fronts:

Since late January 2009, in the North and South Kivu provinces in eastern Congo, the army has been fighting a Rwandan Hutu militia, the Democratic Forces for the Liberation of Rwanda, or FDLR, first in coalition with the Rwandan army, who carried out operations for 35 days before retreating, and later with the support of the UN peacekeeping mission in Congo, MONUC. Some FDLR leaders participated in the Rwandan genocide in 1994 and then fled across the border to Congo, where they have been ever since. The group is estimated to have about 6,000 combatants. The Congolese government had previously supported the FDLR.

Since December 2008, in Oriental province in Northern Congo, the Congolese army has been fighting a Ugandan rebel group, the Lord's Resistance Army, or LRA. The LRA arrived in Congo in late 2005 and established a base in the remote Garamba National Park, on the border with Sudan. It is estimated to have fewer than 600 combatants. Ugandan forces led the joint operations against the LRA until March, when they withdrew and the Congolese army took over the role. An important number of Ugandan intelligence units based in Congo still continue to assist the Congolese army in the north.

Another 22 Congolese groups have taken up arms, some against the government, others supporting the government, whose authority is weak in eastern Congo. The most important of these groups is the CNDP, backed by Rwanda and formerly led by a Congolese Tutsi warlord, Laurent Nkunda. In January, after a dramatic policy change, Rwanda arrested Nkunda and replaced him with his deputy, Bosco Ntaganda, who was already being sought on an arrest warrant for war crimes from the International Criminal Court.

In March, the government signed a peace deal with the CNDP and other armed groups who agreed to join the Congolese army in its military operation against the FDLR, but the deal is fragile and some groups have already reneged on their commitments. As a result of the deal, 12,000 more combatants have joined the army. Ntaganda, instead of being arrested and sent to The Hague to stand trial, was made a general in the army. See "DR Congo: Arrest Bosco Ntaganda" (February 2009 news release).

The Congolese army has an estimated 120,000 soldiers, about half of them in eastern Congo. The army is ill-disciplined and corrupt. A corporal earns $45US per month, and a general $95US. Troops in the field are not provided adequate food and other supplies, which encourages looting and other criminal behavior.

Humanitarian Situation

Since the start of the military operations against the FDLR, more than 800,000 people have been forced to flee their homes in North and South Kivu, according to the

United Nations. Another 250,000 have fled their homes in northern Congo. The UN estimates that the total number of internally displaced people throughout the DRC is over 2 million.

At least 70 percent of those forced to flee their homes live with "host families" in other communities, and have little or no access to humanitarian assistance.

More than 5,000 homes, and sometimes entire villages, have been burned to the ground in eastern Congo since the military campaign began there in January by both the FDLR and Congolese army soldiers. The LRA has burned hundreds of homes in northern Congo since December 2008.

The UN's Humanitarian Action Plan requested $831US million for 2009, to provide urgently needed humanitarian assistance, but only half of the funds had arrived by June.

There have been 84 attacks on humanitarian agencies aiding people in North Kivu so far in 2009, up from 36 during the same period last year.

Killings and Other Human Rights Abuses

Violence against civilians has increased massively since military operations began. Human Rights Watch researchers documented killings of 1,864 civilians—1,200 in the north by the LRA and 664 in the east, the majority by the FDLR. Both groups are deliberately targeting civilians. See "DR Congo: Massive Increase in Attacks on Civilians" (July 2009 news release).

Nearly half of those killed in eastern Congo were women and children, and 12 percent were elderly. The dead included nine local chiefs and other government officials. In some cases, their heads were chopped off.

The LRA has abducted more than 1,625 Congolese civilians since December 2007, of whom 645 are children, according to the UN. In June alone, 138 adults were abducted. The LRA has a track record of abducting children whom they force to become combatants. In its 23-year conflict with the government of Uganda, the LRA has abducted more than 20,000 children in both Uganda and Sudan.

The Congolese army has been forcing hundreds of civilians to work as porters to carry ammunition or other supplies to and from front-line locations, putting them at serious risk.

According to a mortality survey conducted by the International Rescue Committee, 5.4 million people have died in Congo since 1998, the vast majority from starvation or lack of medical assistance. The death toll in Congo is the largest for civilians in any war since World War II.

Sexual Violence

The United Nations Population Fund (UNFPA), the agency coordinating work on sexual violence in Congo, estimates that 200,000 women and girls have been the victims of sexual violence since 1998. In 2008, it recorded nearly 16,000 cases; 65 percent of the victims were children, mostly adolescent girls.

Rape is increasing. In nine conflict zones visited by Human Rights Watch since January 2009, rape cases had doubled or tripled compared with last year. In over half of the cases, the victims were gang-raped by at least two or more assailants. The youngest victim was 2 years old. The cases of men being raped also appear to be increasing.

According to figures collected by Human Rights Watch, 65 percent of the new rape cases in North Kivu were perpetrated by Congolese army soldiers.

Only 11 percent of donor funds allocated for assistance to victims of sexual violence go to efforts to protect women and girls from rape.

Despite the massive number of rape cases, military courts in eastern Congo convicted only 27 soldiers of crimes of sexual violence during 2008. This year, 17 soldiers have been convicted in North Kivu. In July, a military court found a lieutenant colonel, Ndayambaje Kipanga, guilty of rape. He is the highest-ranking officer convicted to date, but he remains at large. No general has yet been convicted either for his own actions or for failing to control his troops. See "DR Congo: Hold Army Commanders Responsible for Rapes" (July 2009 news release).

UN Peacekeeping

The UN mission in Congo, the world's largest peacekeeping mission, has a budget of $1.3US billion for financial year 2009–10. It will have been in Congo for 10 years as of November 30. MONUC has a Chapter VII mandate under the UN Charter, which means it can use force to protect civilians.

MONUC has 17,000 troops in Congo, of which the majority are in North and South Kivu. It also has 692 military observers, 1,078 police, 973 international civilian personnel, 2,483 local civilian staff, and 619 UN Volunteers. The largest numbers of UN troops in Congo are from India, Pakistan, and Bangladesh. MONUC has no US military personnel. EU countries have contributed 63 military personnel, most of them military observers.

In November 2008, the UN Security Council authorized 3,000 more troops for MONUC, but they have still not arrived. See "UN: Send More Troops to DR Congo" (February 2009 news release).

Financial Assistance

In financial year 2008, the US provided $205US million in aid to Congo. In the same year, the US granted $2.1 billion to Afghanistan.

In December 2008, the US government provided logistical, financial and intelligence support to the Ugandan military for its attack on the LRA leadership in Garamba National Park. The operation failed to apprehend the LRA leader, Joseph Kony.

Congo has 34 percent of the world's reserves of cobalt and 10 percent of global copper reserves. It also has important reserves of gold, cassiterite (tin), coltan, diamonds, uranium and numerous other minerals. According to the UN and international organizations such as Human Rights Watch, the desire to control Congo's mineral wealth by foreign armies and rebel groups has played an important role in the conflict. See "DR Congo: Gold Fuels Massive Human Rights Atrocities" (June 2005 news release).

In 2008, China struck a deal with Congo, offering a $9US billion loan in exchange for copper and cobalt mineral concessions. It is China's largest deal with Africa to date.

Congo has $12US billion in external debt, much of it accumulated during the dictatorship of Mobutu Sese Seko, who ruled Congo for 32 years, till 1997. The US was one of Mobutu's main supporters. To date, Congo has not been granted any debt relief.

Other

Congo is one of the poorest countries in the world. In 2008, it ranked near the bottom of the UN's Human Development Index—177 out of 179.

Congo ranks near the bottom of Transparency International's Corruption Perceptions Index. In 2008 it was 171 out of 180 countries surveyed.

Congo is a member of the International Criminal Court (ICC) and requested the court's prosecutor to investigate crimes in violation of international law committed in the country. Three indictees sought on arrest warrants have been transferred from Congo to the ICC since 2006, but Congo has refused to arrest Ntaganda, now a general in its army. Another Congolese suspect was arrested in Belgium. There are also ICC arrest warrants for three LRA leaders for war crimes and crimes against humanity committed in Uganda. The three leaders are at large and presumed to be in Congo.

Chapter 10

THE CHALLENGE OF NATIONALISM

Nationalism, as the most prominent manifestation of "localization," remains the most obvious way of resisting globalization and reinforcing state frontiers, and it can assume various forms, ranging from imposing and reinforcing traditional norms, values, and practices to resisting free trade and the free movement of people and ideas, and the values associated with these, to aggressive expansion of national boundaries, the effort to achieve economic and political leverage, and the spread of exclusivist and parochial religions or political ideologies. Our first selection deals with the meaning, sources, and consequences of nationalism.

10.1

NATIONALISM AND GLOBALIZATION

Richard W. Mansbach[1]

Global politics, as we have seen, features both globalizing and localizing dynamics. Nationalism remains the most prominent manifestation of localization. It provides people with a comforting territorial home and a community of which they are a part, but it has also promoted xenophobia and war.

Nationalism frequently intensifies as a backlash against globalization based on fear of remote economic forces or of cultural invasion that undermines traditional values and resentment against the limitations on a government's ability to control a nation's economic, political, cultural, or even security destiny, or to halt floods of illegal migrants. Such a backlash is reflected in religious fundamentalism, economic protectionism, anti-migrant politics, and cultural exclusion. In no sphere is the nationalist backlash against globalization more strongly apparent than in a culture that is diluted by urbanization, economic development, global media, and the influx of globalized values. Especially in traditional societies, cultural globalization excites fears of cultural homogenization; the spread of pornography, drugs, sexual promiscuity, and secularism; and of "American" or "Western" hegemony.

Cultural defensiveness is apparent in the political scientist Samuel Huntington's argument that global politics has evolved from an era of clashing states to one of clashing civilizations.[2] Huntington viewed globalization as undermining local cultures anchored in territory. He was a nationalist who feared that relentless globalization would undermine national cultures and perhaps even national independence. He seemed to believe that cultures reflect unbridgeable differences, and he did not account for how cultures have historically evolved owing to the interaction of local and global forces. To critics, he was a xenophobe whose fears were exaggerated. To supporters, he summarized the resentment against a global tidal wave that threatens national identities, boundaries, and traditional values. Whatever one's view, globalization complicates the organizing of different peoples with disparate outlooks and interests while intensifying their desire for national autonomy and local culture, norms, and identity.

The Origins and Meaning of Nationalism

Nationalism constitutes an impediment to globalization. Globalization, as we have seen, may denationalize national practices. Nevertheless, a basic characteristic of global politics is that the world remains divided into groups that mistrust one another. Among the most significant local communities are nations, and nationalism is an ideology that raises these to the acme of human loyalties. Globalization enthusiasts believe that nationalism is waning, but, as we shall see, it remains a powerful though changing force and an appealing ideology. Its persistence reveals an intensification of identity politics in which groups assess goals and policies on the basis of "who they are."

In reacting to the perceived homogenizing impact of globalization, national movements reflect the unleashing and manipulation of old (or forged) identities and memories. In recent years, for instance, Vladimir Putin has revived Russian nationalism by manipulating symbols such as the canonization and reburial of the murdered Tsar Nicholas II and his family, appearing with clergy from the Russian Orthodox Church and alleging threats posed by "enemies" such as Chechen rebels. Resurgent Russian power has in turn aided the leaders of some of that country's neighbors, like Ukraine, to mobilize nationalist sentiment in their countries. For their part, China's communist leaders are asserting Han nationalism in relation to minority issues involving Tibetans and Muslim Uighurs.

"Nation" is a complex idea that denotes a self-conscious group of people who differentiate themselves from others on the basis of characteristics such as language, history, culture, religion, race, or ancestry. Definitions also frequently feature historical events and myths that imply a common origin. In fact, the only consensual attribute of a nation is that its members share a proprietary interest in the community as a whole, sharing a bond that unites them and differentiates them from outsiders.

The question of how nations arise is equally complex. Some argue that nations have their roots in a shared history, often including a common ancestry. Those who hold this interpretation regard nations as objective entities. An alternative to this version of national origin is the view that nations are invented or "imagined" by those who see themselves as sharing a common fate. In this sense, nations are subjective rather than objective phenomena. Individuals "are of the same nation if and only if they *recognize* each other as belonging to the same nation."[3] Notwithstanding their differences, both schools agree that collective memory and identity are crucial to constructing and sustaining a sense of nationality.

Which common features will animate individuals to imagine themselves as part of a nation is by no means predetermined, since identities are a state of mind. In a quest for greater political legitimacy, national leaders may point to new categories of "others" to provide mirror images for their followers. To reinforce national unity, they may emphasize the dissimilarity between their followers' ways of looking at, assigning meaning to, and coping with the world and outsiders. Rituals and symbols are important in this effort, because they reawaken memories of collective myths and important historical events. National feelings can be roused by museums, literature, the history that is taught in schools, national anthems and pledges, national holidays, and even patriotic parades. All of these nourish national identities in generation after generation.

"Nations" should not be confused with "states." Unlike nations, states are territorial entities that enjoy the legal privileges associated with sovereignty and have internationally recognized boundaries. Such recognition affirms that a state enjoys legal control over its territory and is the legal equal of other recognized states, implying that no state has a right to intervene in the domestic affairs of another. Some nations are stateless, for example, the Kurds, who live in several states, including Iraq, Iran, Syria, and Turkey, whereas some states are multinational, as was the Soviet Union.

The Evolution of Nationalism

In the 18th and 19th centuries, the belief spread that nations *should* have their own state homelands. The French Revolution played a major role in linking the nation and the state by shifting the basis for rulers' legitimacy from dynastic inheritance to popular sovereignty. Revolutionary France and then other nation-states were energized by national passions, mass conscription, citizen soldiers, and standing armies.

One result was the emergence of enormous armies driven by aggressive expansionism in the name of the nation, or what the French called *la patrie*. French armies sought to export their national ideals—liberty, equality, and fraternity—on the bayonets of their soldiers. Nation-states were legitimized by the principle of national self-determination, by which the "nation" was deemed the repository of state sovereignty.

The doctrine of national self-determination was very much in the air in the second half of the 19th century, especially as it applied to multinational empires such as Austria-Hungary. The American president Woodrow Wilson made national self-determination one of the core reasons for America's entry into World War I and included it in his Fourteen Points. Wilson's secretary of state, Robert Lansing, was aghast at the implications of the doctrine. "Will it not breed discontent, disorder and rebellion?" he asked.

The phrase is simply loaded with dynamite. It will raise hopes which can never be realized. It will, I fear, cost thousands of lives. . . . What a calamity that the phrase was ever uttered! What misery it will cause![4]

Until the second half of the 19th century, nationalism was fostered as a liberal principle, and national self-determination was seen as a prerequisite for human freedom and political democracy. Liberals like Italy's Giuseppe Mazzini and Hungary's Lajos Kossuth believed that national identities would bring about a republican order in Europe based on popular sovereignty. This view flourished until the failure of Europe's 1848 revolutions.

In the ensuing decades, European nationalism was infected by racial myths and worship of violence, and nationalism became synonymous with exclusion and otherness. During the second half of the 19th century, nationalism fostered three wars that climaxed in Germany's unification in 1870. Germany's Chancellor Otto von Bismarck had never viewed nationalism as a liberal principle, though he rarely hesitated to use national rhetoric to foster German unity. Indeed, in a speech in 1862 he had declared that

the position of Prussia in Germany will not be determined by its liberalism but by its power. . . . Not through speeches and majority decisions will the great questions of the day be decided—that was the great mistake of 1848 and 1849—but by iron and blood.

In Bismarck's Prussia, the nationalist historian Heinrich von Treitschke perceived the nation (*Volk*) as a unique living and evolving community and declared that nations were competitors in a world in which only the strong could survive. This racist version of nationalism would continue to influence global politics until the defeat of the Nazis in World War II.

In the cases of both liberal and malignant nationalism, elites manipulated national identities for different ends. Those like Bismarck manipulated nationalism to reinforce state power and weaken democratic aspirations and institutions. Their example was later emulated by modern demagogues from Italy's fascist leader Benito Mussolini to Serbia's Slobodan Milosevic.

During and after the two world wars, the ideology of self-determination was spread globally by Europe's colonizers and would later become the slogan of those over whom Europe ruled and who sought to bring an end to Europe's overseas empires. Europe's colonial wars were brutal affairs, and European nationalism, abetted by industrialization, made World Wars I and II total, identity-based conflicts. In the 1950s and 1960s, nationalism and national self-determination—enshrined in the UN Charter—were the bases of decolonization.

Unlike the 19th and early 20th centuries, when statesmen invoked nationalism to unify citizens against foreign foes or turn public attention from domestic problems, contemporary nationalism has become a threat to the unity of many states and may escape leaders' control. There is a growing queue of nationalities that want their own state, even if this means the division of existing states, as in the case of Yugoslavia and Sudan, or state failure. In areas of the developing world, especially where national and state boundaries are *not* congruent, ethno-national loyalties threaten the integrity of existing states.

The end of the Cold War witnessed an upsurge in nationalist conflicts. From the bloody breakup of Yugoslavia, with its murderous wars that pitted Serbs, Croatians, and Muslims against one another, and the Rwanda genocide of Tutsi inhabitants to the bloody conflicts that set Sinhalese against Tamils in Sri Lanka, and Kurds, Shia Muslims, and Sunni Muslims against one another in Iraq, ambitious politicians have sought to manipulate national or ethnic divisions. National animosities rent the Soviet Union, and the Soviet nationalities that achieved self-determination continue to quarrel—Armenians versus Azeris, Georgians versus Russians, Estonians versus Russians, and so on. In both developed and developing societies, national groups seek to secede from the states they now share and acquire states for themselves—Spanish Basques, French Corsicans, Belgian Flemish and Walloons, Canadians Inuits, Celtic Scots, and so on.

Since almost any group can claim to be a distinctive "people," there is a risk of fragmentation of political authority into ever smaller and less viable polities. If dwarf polities like Transnistria, Abkhazia, and South Ossetia can achieve independence, is there any limit to the number of potential nation-states?

Contemporary Nationalism and Globalization

In recent decades, nationalism and national self-determination have become significant barriers to globalization. Contemporary nationalism, as the political scientist James Rosenau argues, is "a form of exclusionary localism" because

> it emphasizes boundaries and the distinction between us and them, with the result that even in the United States the idea of a melting pot has tended to give way to what some regard as a multicultural regime in which different minorities stress their ethnic and racial ties even as they downplay the relevance of an inclusive identity that links them to the varied groups that reside in their country.[5]

As an identity, nationalism is associated with closure and with raising barriers to the movement of persons, things, and ideas.

The negative localism associated with nationalism afflicts both the developing and the developed worlds and may assume several forms. One of these is state failure. As we noted in the previous chapter of this book, the failure to build viable nation-states after the decline of colonialism and the post–Cold War upsurge in violence within and across states in parts of Africa and Asia are associated with national, tribal, and ethnic rivalries and grievances, revived and manipulated by ambitious politicians seeking power and loot. In Africa, Europeans imposed states with boundaries that the inhabitants never fully accepted and that divided ethnic groups or enclosed ethnic rivals within the same states.

Negative localism is also visible in the national xenophobia of resident groups opposing the influx of migrants seeking to escape poverty and violence at home, especially since the onset of global economic and financial distress. Among Europeans, migration has fueled nationalism that has increased support for right-wing, anti-immigrant politicians. Residents argue that migrants cannot or will not assimilate into the dominant culture and that they create economic and social problems for their adopted homelands, including lower wages, human trafficking, street crime, and higher welfare costs.

Resentment among Europeans is particularly high in the case of Muslim immigrants, many of whom migrated from their adopted country's former colonial territories. In recent years, the threat of terrorism by Islamic militants and the growing visibility of Muslim symbols ranging from minarets to head scarves have intensified the antipathy of Europeans toward Muslim residents. France, proud of its distinctive secular culture, has witnessed riots by Muslim residents concentrated in the impoverished outskirts of French cities and has banned the wearing of headscarves in French schools and full-face veils in public. Among Europeans, fear of Muslim extremism is highest in Russia, Spain, and Germany,[6] and many Muslim residents in Europe perceive that Europeans are hostile toward them, and they continue to identify themselves as Muslims first and only secondarily as citizens of their adopted countries.[7]

Unlike France, America's multicultural tradition allows immigrants greater latitude to express their identities, but in the United States, too, there is nationalist concern about the assimilation of the country's immigrant community. This sentiment is controversially represented by Samuel Huntington, who argues that Hispanic immigrants are not assimilating into American society. Hispanic migrants, he argues, do not speak English or subscribe to American values.[8] In his view, Hispanics, many of whom are illegal residents, are establishing insulated cultural islands, and their sheer numbers in the United States threaten to overwhelm American culture.

An additional manifestation of nationalism is visible in the spread of protectionist sentiment since the onset of the Great Recession. Globalization is generally seen to have gone farthest and been the least subject to reversal in the economic realm, yet even in this realm nationalist sentiments are strong. Like nationalists of other stripes, economic nationalists evaluate policy in terms of the *relative* rather than *absolute* benefit it affords their nation in comparison with other nations. Indeed, especially since the onset of the Great Recession, trading states have developed a variety of nontariff barriers to free trade—for example, America's antidumping policies, which punish foreign firms that sell their products at "unfair" prices in the American market.

By encouraging economic independence, protecting home industries from foreign competition, and subsidizing "national champions," economic nationalists undermine the essential premise of those who support globalization—that the free movement of goods and services globally benefits everyone. Not surprisingly, economic nationalism has merged with antiglobalization sentiments.

Conclusion: The Revival of Nationalism

Previous eras of interdependence have ended when states confronted political and economic turmoil. As in the 1930s in Germany, Italy, and Japan, the future is likely to see efforts to limit popular discontent by manipulating nationalist symbols and threatening political and economic adventurism overseas. In the face of unemployment, domestic resentment against immigrants who are believed to be competing with citizens for jobs may help strengthen nationalist political parties that seek to "regain control" of national borders already seen to be threatened by transnational terrorism and crime.

Nationalism, however, need not always compete with globalization. People have multiple identities and are simultaneously members of many polities that may overlap. There is no reason, for example, why one cannot simultaneously identify oneself as a Scot, a citizen of Great Britain, and a European.

Nonetheless, the revival of nationalism following the Cold War and its intensification during the global recession pose a threat to globalization. National myths, languages, and memorials have been dusted off, reinforced, or (re)constructed in reaction to globalization. National movements in both developed and developing countries are enjoying a surge in popularity, and nations that had once assimilated and become dormant have reemerged.

Notes

1 For a lengthy and in-depth analysis of some of the issues dealt with in this brief essay, see Richard W. Mansbach, "Nationalism and Ethnicity in World Politics," in Mark Beeson and Nick Bisley, eds., *Issues in 21st Century World Politics* (New York: Palgrave MacMillan, 2010), 108–22.

2 Samuel P. Huntington, *The Clash of Civilizations* (New York: Simon & Schuster, 1996).

3 Ernest Gellner, *Nations and Nationalism* (Ithaca, NY: Cornell University Press, 1983), 7.

4 Robert Lansing, *The Peace Negotiations* (Middlesex, UK: Echo Library, 2007), 57.

5 James N. Rosenau, *Distant Proximities* (Princeton, NJ: Princeton University Press, 2003), 107.

6 Pew Global Attitudes Project, "Islamic Extremism: Common Concern for Muslim and Western Publics," July 14, 2005, http://pewglobal.org/2005/07/14/islamic-extremism-common-concern-for-muslim-and-western-publics/.

7 Pew Global Attitudes Project, "Muslims in Europe: Economic Worries Top Concerns About Religious and Cultural Identity," June 6, 2006, http://pewglobal.org/2006/07/06/muslims-in-europe-economic-worries-top-concerns-about-religious-and-cultural-identity/.

8 Samuel P. Huntington, *Who Are We? The Challenges to America's National Identity* (New York: Simon & Schuster, 2005).

10.2

REALPOLITIK NATIONALISM: INTERNATIONAL SOURCES OF CHINESE NATIONALISM

Lei Guang

Our next selection focuses on the sources of contemporary Chinese nationalism. The upsurge in Chinese nationalism, the author argues, is less an anti-Western phenomenon, a cultural revival, or an effort to achieve greater power than a preoccupation with the country's sovereignty, legitimacy, and territorial integrity.

Source: Excerpted from Lei Guang, "Realpolitik Nationalism: International Sources of Chinese Nationalism," *Modern China* 31:4 (October 2005), 487–514. Notes appearing in the original have been deleted.

Nationalism and China

In recent years, Western interest in Chinese nationalism has increased markedly. Western scholars have used nationalism to frame their study of a diverse set of events in China-from anti-American demonstrations in Beijing after the U.S. bombing of the Chinese embassy in Belgrade, to cultural trends and the publication of best-sellers in China, to China's territorial disputes with its neighbors and the Chinese government's assertive diplomacy in the post-reform period. Seasoned American journalists have also weighed in on the topic, writing popular books about the rise of China and its implications for world peace. Their accounts, along with increasingly assertive defenses of China's national interests mounted by their Chinese counterparts, have helped the discussion spread to the general public in China and in many Western countries.

This growing interest in Chinese nationalism did not develop in a vacuum. It accompanied several changes in global geopolitics and the global economy toward the end of the twentieth century. The most important of these is the demise in the early 1990s of the Soviet Union, and with it the collapse of a relatively stable bipolar world order divided along clear-cut ideological lines. Astute observers of international affairs began to turn their attention to potent subterranean forces of change that had long been suppressed by cold war politics. In this context, nationalism—and increasingly now, transnational terrorism—has emerged as a favorite analytical angle on new, hot global issues. A second major change is simply the emergence of China as a world economic, and potentially military, power. . . .

China's greater power is accompanied by a third change that tends to cloud Western observers' judgment of Chinese worldviews and strategic intentions: China's own down-playing of its communist ideology and its embrace of pragmatism in pursuing its foreign policy. What is filling the vacuum of communism—and what passes as pragmatism, many analysts plausibly conjecture—may simply be old-fashioned nationalism. . . .

In a rudderless world and faced with a new rising power that is very much an unknown quantity lacking a clear ideological track in its strategic vision, scholars and policy analysts alike have unsurprisingly returned to nationalism as the favorite *explanans* of China's foreign policy behavior. And obviously the claim that communism has been replaced by nationalism in recent decades has some validity. Yet the dominant understandings of Chinese nationalism suffer from one major shortcoming: they rely too heavily on our observations about China's antagonistic relations with the West or with Japan, the West's close ally. The strong Western-centric quality of conceptualizations of nationalism in China may be one reason why adding the prefixes "anti-Japanese," "anti-American," or "anti-imperialist" has little serious affect on the meaning of "Chinese nationalism."

It may well be that for the most part, China's main obsession has been with the West. . . . But this emphasis on the Western-directedness of Chinese nationalism, if pushed too far, is problematic in at least two ways. First, it suggests that nationalism does not come into play in China's relations with non-Western states. Yet we know that historically, the PRC's territorial disputes with its neighbors have provided powerful occasions for the expression of nationalism. Second, by delving deeply inside Chinese history to uncover the historical, political, and cultural roots of nationalism, we risk a fundamental conceptual error: neglecting the international sources of ideas and ideals animating contemporary Chinese nationalism.

It has long been controversial to apply the concept of nationalism to the study of Chinese politics. This article contributes to the discussion by highlighting the *international* dimension of Chinese nationalism. Specifically, I consider how some of the prevailing norms of the Westphalian international system have been integrated into and thus made part of the Chinese nationalist discourse. . . .

I begin by briefly surveying the debate on Chinese nationalism in Western scholarship from the 1950s to the 1990s. I then examine several major assumptions underlying these existing understandings. In the third section, I articulate a different conception of Chinese nationalism, which I argue embodies three important norms of the international system. Finally, I illustrate the usefulness of this new conception by analyzing two instances of China's conflicts with neighboring countries.

A Brief Overview of the Debate on Chinese Nationalism

The subject of Chinese nationalism has long been much debated. In the 1950s and 1960s, the debate was largely focused on the nature of Chinese revolution: was the revolution truly inspired by Marxism and Leninism or was it simply a nationalistic movement disguised as communism? . . .

From the late 1960s to the 1970s, nationalism receded from public attention as China was convulsed in ideologically motivated factional struggles over its internal politics. Chinese foreign policy underwent what some have called a process of "ideologization," whereby the guiding principle of "national" interest was displaced by class-based communist ideology. . . . But such ideological interpretations gave way to a realist paradigm in the late 1970s and 1980s, the era of China's skillful triangular diplomacy vis-a-vis the two superpowers. Their study of Chinese foreign policy behavior during this period led some scholars to believe that China had ceased to base its foreign policy on questions of "social systems and ideologies." Instead, Chinese leaders began to adopt "a balance-of-power" approach to protect Chinese interests.

National interests . . . became a concern of those analyzing the PRC's foreign policy behavior in the 1980s and 1990s. Chinese analysts themselves began to explore the notion of national interest systematically. . . . Because of the close affinity between national interest and nationalism, in the 1990s the latter rode on the back of realism to once again become a focal concept for analyzing Chinese politics.

Around the same time, international relations scholars working on China began to emphasize the cultural dimension of its foreign policy. . . . But the cultural realists view China's hard-edged realism as now derived from a historically based *national* strategic culture rather than from the structural dynamics of relations between modern states. The turn to a historically informed and culturally sensitive analysis has given us a more nuanced understanding of the Chinese foreign policy process. But in less deft hands, a cultural approach may lend itself to an essentialist interpretation of the Chinese national culture and its proclivity for certain strategic behaviors.

Against this historical background, scholarly debate on Chinese nationalism in the West reached a fever pitch in the 1990s. A flood of publications on the phenomenon appeared, as scholars from various disciplines addressed a multiplicity of themes and concerns. Some focused on the uniqueness of Chinese nationalism, especially on the blatant statism that set it apart from ethnically based nationalist aspirations. Others tried to discern important historical changes in Chinese nationalism first from the Maoist era to the reform period and then, during the latter period, from state-guided nationalism to popular nationalism and from an affirmative, we-oriented form of nationalism to an assertive nationalism negatively directed against outsiders. Still others analyzed the implications of nationalism for China's relations with the outside world. In this burgeoning literature, Chinese nationalism acquired a long list of qualifying adjectives: confident, muscular, affirmative, assertive or aggressive, incoherent, nativistic and antitraditional, pragmatic, cultural, state-led, popular, "face," and so on. . . .

Key Assumptions Underlying the Debate on Chinese Nationalism

Underlying the contemporary debate on Chinese nationalism are three widely shared assumptions about the phenomenon: its anti-Western orientation, its statist character, and its cultural-historical ambitions. The first assumption is that nationalism in China is characterized by a form of "anti-ism" targeting the West (including Japan). . . . According to this thesis, Western domination was both the catalyst for the culturalism-to-nationalism transition and the object that fervent Chinese nationalists were resisting. Thus, from its beginnings, modern Chinese nationalism took on a basic anti-Western orientation, which was reinforced by subsequent conflicts between China and the West.

Virtually all commentators on Chinese nationalism touch on this anti-Western feature, implicitly or explicitly. . . . As abundant reports on the recent controversies over the embassy bombing in Yugoslavia and the disabled U.S. spy plane make clear, anti-Americanism has not been far below the surface of nationalistic uproars in China. In short, Chinese nationalism is constructed by many authors as a set of ideas, sentiments, and practices directed against the West.

A second assumption behind the debate on Chinese nationalism is its statist character—what some would simply call "state nationalism."

The idea is that China is not, and has never been, a typical nation-state: that is, a nation made up of one ethnic group, which is governed politically by one state. . . . Professing to be a multinational state, the PRC engaged in myriad practices aimed at creating "a new Chinese nation that incorporates all of its nationalities" while at the same time focusing "political loyalty on the state." The outcome might be called the Chinese "state-nation."

Given that the Chinese nation is derived from the state, nationalism in the Chinese context has logically been equated with the quest for state power. . . . The problem with this view is not that it intertwines the Chinese state and nationalism but that it assumes the former to be on a self-aggrandizing course for historical reasons. If the Chinese state seeks to restore its former empire, and if it then creates and manipulates nationalism to serve that goal, we of course should find the rise of Chinese nationalism alarming; it is easy to see why some authors would link Chinese nationalism to possible international aggression. But as I will suggest later, the first order of business for a non-Western state like China is usually less to amass power than to secure and affirm an identity as a nation-state within the framework of the Westphalian state system. Before the international community, such a nascent state must defend and legitimate its sovereign claim over a fixed territory.

Finally, a third assumption is that Chinese nationalism is built on powerful sentiments generated by the "century of shame and humiliation" *(bainian chiru)*. . . . Another eminent scholar of China has asserted that the Chinese are unique among the former colonial or semicolonial peoples in that they "continue to dwell on the idea that they were years ago grossly and cruelly mistreated by others, and consequently they have a huge burden of humiliation that they feel they can live down by being aggressively self-righteous."

From these undoubtedly valid insights, some analysts extrapolate China's ambition to restore its historical greatness. . . . Here Chinese nationalism is taken to represent a backward-looking ideology or strategy, keeping an eye on the past and obsessed with China's historical empire and cultural superiority.

A standard Western narrative on Chinese nationalism today can therefore be summarized as follows: China prides itself as a historically powerful country with a distinguished civilization. Its decline in the nineteenth and twentieth centuries in the face of Western and Japanese incursions indelibly etched shame in the Chinese people and triggered their widespread attempts to reform their political system. Key to this endeavor is the quest for a strong state. Over the past century and a half, various reform and revolutionary movements sought to build up the power of the state with the objective of retrieving China's past glory. Chinese nationalism is thus state-led, anti-Western, and steeped in an acute sense of national humiliation; in a quest for world eminence, it seeks to restore China's historical grandeur.

This narrative does indeed capture many aspects of Chinese nationalism, especially in the context of China's troubled relationship with the West. But its focus on that context is also its main weakness. The problem is essentially twofold. First, an explication of Chinese nationalism based solely on China's encounter with the West makes the concept less useful when China's relationship with the non-Western countries is being considered. And second, looking inward for Chinese nationalism's origins or motivations neglects important external sources of claims around which the state is able to mobilize nationalistic sentiments. . . .

Realpolitik Nationalism?
A Reinterpretation of Chinese Nationalism

To be sure, China's adherence to such international principles as sovereignty may simply be instrumental and self-serving. Rhetoric is cheap. And it is really all that China *can* do in a world dominated by much stronger states. Besides, publicly espousing sovereignty makes China look good in the eyes of the numerous small countries whose legitimate and autonomous self-rule over a fixed national space remains precarious. But astute observers of Chinese politics have also noticed that this cheap rhetoric—a seemingly facile commitment to the Westphalian norms of the modern state system—may have seeped more deeply into the Chinese worldview than is commonly thought. It is plausible that the Chinese leadership has so internalized these norms that they have become part of the modern state's self-identity, around which nationalist ideas, sentiments, and practices can be mobilized.

Consider several recent episodes when nationalistic passions flared up in China. In 2001, the emergency landing on China's Hainan Island by a damaged American EP-3 reconnaissance plane generated an out-cry among the Chinese because of the perceived violation of China's territorial sovereignty by the intrusive American spy plane. Two years earlier, when the United States bombed the Chinese embassy in Belgrade, the anger felt by the Chinese was heightened because embassies are widely considered to be quintessential symbols of national sovereignty. And the spontaneous demonstrations that took place in the streets of Beijing to celebrate China's successful bid for the Olympics and its accession to the World Trade Organization (WTO) in 2001 attest to an intense nationalistic pride over international recognition and acceptance.

Such events highlight the importance of external sources of Chinese nationalism: the Chinese people have internalized some of the prevailing ideas and norms in international politics, however selectively, which then become possible grounds of nationalistic mobilization by China's political leaders and intellectual elites. These ideas increasingly give content and thus coherence to Chinese nationalism. Take as another example a Chinese best-seller in the mid-1990s, *Zhongguo keyi shuobu,* or *China Can Say No.* It is widely regarded, by both its critics and enthusiasts, as evincing a reactionary and emotive form of nationalism. What is most striking about the book is not so much its emphasis on past Chinese glory or on the historical and present-day injustices perpetrated by the West as its trenchant insistence on China's sovereign right to raise territorial claims with other countries, to take back Taiwan, to resist Western human rights campaigns, and to break out of the containment by the United States. Rather than falling back on some grandiose notions of Chinese cultural superiority, the authors suggest that China pursue a geopolitical alliance with Russia and other Asian countries to counterbalance the Americans and their ally in Asia, the Japanese.

We can detect hard-edged realist ideals and ideas about state power and geopolitics clothed in the garb of nationalism in such writings. I call this fusion of political realism and nationalistic aspirations "realpolitik nationalism." The German term *realpolitik* was first coined by Bismarck in the nineteenth century to refer to the stratagems of practical politics. Over time, it has acquired a number of related yet distinctive meanings—power politics among the nations, expansionist state policies for advancing the national interest, politics based on practical or material rather than on normative or moral considerations, and so on. Here, I define "realpolitik" broadly as a nation-state's engagement in power politics in the international arena; its practices range from defending the national interests . . . against other nation-states to striving for dominance or relative gains over its adversaries.

Realpolitik and nationalism are often taken to represent two distinct kinds of historical forces shaping the destinies of nations: the former is characterized by level-headed and steadfast attention to national *interests;* the latter is evocative of powerful normative, and often irrational, *beliefs.* Conventional understandings of nationalism stress its ties to emotions, messianism, and collective identity-making. By contrast, realpolitik is reputed to exert pressure on the modern nation-states from the outside, compelling national leaders to pursue power and their interests in a rational and thus predictable manner. . . .

Animating China's realpolitik nationalism are three interlinked core ideas that organize the existing system among states: the territorial organization of the state, sovereignty (the exclusion of external authority), and international recognition or legitimacy. States exist in bounded territories; within these territories, they set themselves up as the ultimate legitimate power to the exclusion of other authorities, domestic or international; they recognize each other to help ease international transactions and to further legitimate their domestic authority. These principles form the baseline expectations of national leaders as they organize and manage a modern state. In turn, these leaders also inculcate in the citizenry a similar set of values about territory, sovereignty, and legitimacy. Violations of one or more of these principles would then become grounds for collective grievances or backlash against the perceived perpetrators. The process of modern state-building guarantees that Chinese nationalism is infused with the ideas and ideals embedded in the modern state system. . . . In an important way, Chinese nationalism is structured by ideas emanating from the international system.

First, China's national identity is rooted in a strong territorial imagination of the state. Chiang Kai-Shek, arguably China's most ardent nationalist, once declared: "With regard to her geographical configuration, China's mountain ranges and river basins form a self-contained unit. . . . The Chinese nation has lived and developed within these river basins, and there is no area that can be split up or separated from the rest, and therefore, no areas that can become an independent unit." Chiang, like the Communists after him, could not conceive of China independent of these territorial features. A spatial construction has several advantages for a multiethnic and internally differentiated state: It avoids an obviously ethnocultural reference (which was at one time the basis for China's anti-Manchu nationalist revolution). It constructs a we-ness that transcends regional and class differences. Best of all, it accords with the prevailing norm of territoriality (e.g., territorial integrity) at the heart of the modern state system. It is thus not surprising that territorial disputes become potent occasions for the outpourings of nationalistic rhetoric and emotions even when Western countries are not the main adversaries.

Second, sovereign control is an important leitmotif of Chinese nationalism. . . . Over the years, the Chinese leaders have come to embrace an absolutist notion of sovereignty, with watertight boundaries and internal control far more complete than what had ever existed before or appear likely to be present anytime soon. Viewed in this light, China's sovereignty-conscious nationalism seems to be inspired more by a futuristic vision of what a fully sovereign Chinese state *ought* to be like than by a nostalgia for the country's grandiose past. In other words, Chinese nationalism is driven as much if not more by the desire to conform to highly idealized global norms as by feelings of national humiliation and pride issuing from over a century ago.

Finally, modern Chinese nationalists desire international legitimacy. They clamor to increase China's power in the United Nations. They undertake costly foreign aid programs to other countries to improve China's image and strengthen its international position. They take pride in Chinese sports teams winning international honors, and they cheer for China's successful bid to host the Olympics. They question why China has not produced a novelist or scientist worthy of the Nobel Prize, which many see as the pinnacle of global legitimation. Although divided among themselves on the implications of WTO membership, they press for more concessions from the West rather than advocating a complete withdrawal from the international trade system. They feel slighted when China is not treated as an equal in important international matters. They take offense when they perceive external pressure to control China's domestic policies. They yearn for "getting on track with the world". . . , albeit often more on China's terms than on others'.

In short, their quest is for a China that can "stand up as an independent power in the forest of nations.". . .

Chinese Nationalism in the Absence of the West: Territory, Sovereignty, and the Quest for Legitimacy

To illustrate the usefulness of this notion of Chinese nationalism guided by realpolitik ideas and ideals, I turn now to two conflicts that did not involve a direct confrontation between China and a Western power or Japan, but nevertheless sparked an upsurge of Chinese nationalism. As I mentioned at the beginning of this essay, the notion of realpolitik nationalism has the advantage of weaning us from a Western-centric approach that emphasizes the impact of China's historical experience, and thus makes it possible for us to consider Chinese nationalism in non-Western contexts. Realpolitik nationalism also enables us to explore the international sources of ideas and ideals that are then pressed into the service of nationalistic causes. Since my main interest in this essay is conceptual, my empirical discussion here will necessarily be brief and illustrative.

My two test cases are China's confrontation with India in the 1962 border war and its territorial dispute with Southeast Asian countries over the Spratly Islands. Both touch on all issues mentioned above that anchor Chinese nationalism, but I will use the former to examine the role of sovereignty and legitimacy in China's reaction, and the latter to discuss the Chinese territorial imagination of the nation.

First, the Sino-Indian border conflict. In 1962, the PRC fought a brief but bitter war with India in what was the first violent border clash in its history. The war ended in a lopsided victory for China, but it did great damage to the country's international standing and sent bilateral relations into a deep freeze for the next few decades. . . . It is questionable whether China accomplished that goal, given that skirmishes on the border continued in the 1960s and 1970s, and a major confrontation between the two sides was averted only at the last minute in the mid-1980s. However, the Chinese government did achieve two other purposes by the war: consolidating China's sovereign control over Tibet and de-legitimizing India's claim of the McMahon Line as the borderline.

. . . As the dispute with India over the border unfolded in the late 1950s and early 1960s, two factors besides its growing sensitivity to territorial loss appear to have led to a hardening of China's position. One was the Tibet question, and the other was India's refusal to negotiate on the McMahon Line.

As many analysts have pointed out, the Tibetan rebellion in 1959 and its subsequent suppression by China was a turning point in Sino-Indian relations The PRC government staked out its sovereignty claims on Tibet early in the 1950s: From the beginning, it was wary of Jawaharlal Nehru's proposal for a "special" relationship between India and Tibet, because no such relationship was permissible under the modern nation-state system. It was greatly disturbed by Nehru's occasional assertion that China had *suzerainty* rather than sovereignty over the territory. Toward the end of the 1950s, the Chinese came to interpret Nehru's intentions increasingly through the lens of imperialism. . . .

From the viewpoint of Zhou and his fellow leaders, India's challenge to China's sovereignty over Tibet had backed them into a corner; to escape it, they felt they had to exact a strike commensurate with the gravity of the situation.

Another Indian stance that drew a nationalistic response from China was its hard-line attitude toward the McMahon Line. Drawn by the British in a tripartite conference involving British India, China, and Tibet in 1914, the line was intended to mark the eastern border between China and India, but its international legal status was somewhat ambiguous, to say the least. In the years leading up to 1962, India insisted that the McMahon Line was the valid boundary between the two countries, while China disputed its legitimacy on the grounds that no Chinese central government had ever acceded to it. . . . The irony of the whole matter was that China's categorical rejection of the McMahon Line may have been motivated less by a desire to revise the physical boundary it represented than by a determination to alter its symbolic status. The Chinese rhetoric at the time strongly suggested that the legitimacy of the treaty that produced the McMahon Line was the main point of contention. Under such circumstances, a process of renegotiation might well have satisfied China by conferring legitimacy to a new border, even if that border was not in fact significantly altered from the existing line. . . .

The scholarly literature on the Sino-Indian conflict in 1962 has paid ample attention to the role of Indian nationalism but has made little mention of Chinese nationalism. This omission is somewhat understandable, given that the dominant notions of Chinese nationalism were developed to explain China's reaction against the West. As the episodes of EP-3 spy plane and embassy bombing decades later demonstrate, China's protest against the United States was readily cast as a nationalistic backlash, whereas its action against India was not interpreted through the same lens. Yet in the negotiations and events leading up to the war in 1962, Chinese leaders made repeated use of such terms as "national pride" . . . , "national dignity" . . . , and "national feelings." . . .

At the time, there was also limited but targeted mobilization of the Chinese domestic public opinion in support of the government's position. The Nationalist government in Taiwan even set aside its anti-Communist ideology to support mainland China on the border question. . . . Here, realpolitik nationalism transcended the Cold War division.

My second example showcasing a territorial dispute is the ongoing disagreement over the Spratly Islands. . . . The archipelago consists of hundreds of small islands and coral reefs in the South China Sea, claimed or occupied in varying degrees by China (and Taiwan), Malaysia, the Philippines, Vietnam, and Brunei. Covering a vast area, it controls important shipping routes and contains rich oil and gas reserves. In the 1970s and 1980s, China's main quarrel was with Vietnam, and it escalated to an open military clash in March 1988. Since then, China has taken two new tacks: on the one hand, it has directly engaged the sovereignty claims of other disputants besides Vietnam (mainly the Philippines); on the other, it has emphasized joint development opportunities with other littoral countries. But it continues to affirm its public position that the Spratly Islands have always been, and are still, China's rightful territory. . . .

China's dispute with Vietnam and the Philippines over the Spratly Islands has yet to produce a widespread popular backlash on the streets, in part because little has been reported on these conflicts. Instead, much of the action has occurred on the diplomatic front, with occasional armed skirmishes punctuating the diplomatic process. Scholarly books have also been produced to validate China's nationalistic claims. In the 1990s, the nationalist dynamic inside China manifested itself mainly in legislative activities such as its 1996 declaration establishing baselines for measuring the width of the territorial sea and the 1998 adoption of a legal framework to claim rights over a 200-mile-wide exclusive economic zone and the continental shelf. In pressing its sovereignty claims, China used arguments relying both on history (e.g., the Nansha Islands historically have belonged to China) and on international law (e.g., the Chinese claim is widely accepted by other nations and is in accordance with the UN Convention on the Law of the Sea). Throughout this process of claim and counterclaim, territorial integrity was held to be of paramount importance.

Taiwan has largely supported the PRC's claims regarding the Spratly Islands. We saw much the same behavior during the Sino-Indian conflict in 1962. Such a united front presented by the adversaries again suggests that territory . . . transcends political differences once it is linked to perceived national interests. . . .

These examples suggest that Chinese nationalism is a potent force even in the absence of any collision with the West. They also illustrate the argument that nationalism in China emanates from many different sources, including the realpolitik ideas of territory, sovereignty, and legitimacy acquired and internalized in the process of building a modern nation-state. This is not to say that realpolitik nationalism is unrelated to China's experience with the West. Modern Chinese nationalism originated in an age when Western powers repeatedly seized China's territory and compromised its sovereignty. . . . But the concept of realpolitik nationalism enables us to look beyond the historically formed cultural and political attitudes inside China for plausible explanations of behavior that we call nationalistic.

Chinese Nationalism, Realpolitik-Style

Conventional understandings of Chinese nationalism often portray it as anti-Western. They focus on Chinese nationalists' obsession with a powerful state and on their ambition to recover the past glory of China's historical empire. Such understandings clearly underlie the antipathy and fear in the West toward the rise of nationalism in China in recent years. As China's economic power grows, Chinese nationalism is believed to have acquired a material base from which it could wreak havoc on the existing international order. At its most benign, the conventional wisdom goes, the rise of nationalism could mean an unruly China unwilling to subject itself to prevailing international norms; at its worst, it could turn China into an expansionist power fixated on restoring its historical empire.

Analysts of Chinese nationalism often derive their observations about the phenomenon from studying China's interaction with the West. In this sense, their account tends to be overly Western-centric. Intensely interested in nationalism's historical origin, they also tend to look only inside China for ideas, practices, and motivations structuring Chinese nationalism, be these the experience of "the century of humiliation," China's glorious cultural reign in the past, or the pursuit of wealth and power at home. I have focused instead on the international or external sources of ideas and ideals that have informed the Chinese nationalist thinking, emphasizing three sets of ideas emanating from the modem interstate system: territorial integrity, state sovereignty, and international legitimacy. . . .

Realpolitik nationalism is not necessarily directed against the West, although it certainly may be mobilized by the state elites to counter Western pressures. Its power derives not from citizens' depth of feelings about their nation's history or their ethnic identity, but from the key ideas in the international society. It focuses on preserving the nation-state and the nation-state system, rather than on engaging in aggrandizement aimed at recapturing past glories. Contrary to the view that they are a menace to the existing international order, the Chinese nationalists espouse an ideology that may well be in sync with the prevailing norms of international politics. This may be why many international relations scholars increasingly recognize China as among the most orthodox defenders of the Westphalian system. . . . On this account, the challenge that Chinese nationalism presents to the world is not its historical or cultural orientation but its relentless pursuit of power politics according to an idealized construction of the very organizing principles of the modern interstate system.

10.3

CHINESE NATIONALISM: PRIDE AND PITFALLS

Wang Gungwu

> Although the previous article concludes that Chinese nationalism does not pose a serious threat to China's neighbors and in fact reflects the country's

Source: Wang Gungwu, "Chinese Nationalism: Pride and Pitfalls," *The Straits Times,* August 6, 2008.

dedication to interstate practices, those neighbors have become seriously concerned about Beijing's saber rattling and territorial claims. The next selection, written during the 2008 Beijing Olympics, from Singapore's leading newspaper, sees China's nationalism as a relatively recent phenomenon and reflects the nervousness of the country's neighbors.

When Beijing bid for the 2008 Summer Olympics, it wanted to highlight China's successes over the past 30 years. Did it expect that others would do their utmost to highlight China's failures? It probably expected something from the usual suspects and made its preparations for that eventuality.

Nevertheless, it clearly did not expect riots in Tibet, which resulted in burnings and deaths. Once that happened, the chorus of voices already critical of Beijing rose to a crescendo. But what really surprised most people were the reactions of young Chinese to these foreign critics. They protested in the media and on the streets both inside and outside China. The explanations for this phenomenon have ranged from hurt national pride to dangerous, even rampant, nationalism.

The young voices came mostly from the *fenqing* or angry youth. It is hard to determine whether they were angrier inside or outside China. What astonished the international media was the fact that some of the protesters were students studying abroad, among the best-educated and most privileged in China. Certainly, whatever they may think of the Chinese Communist Party (CCP), these young people saw the attacks on China as attacks on the Chinese people.

Is this new? How did this form of nationalism come about?

The record shows that nationalism in China is truly modern. It began to grow only during the 20th century. There is no evidence that it arose from the Opium Wars of the mid-19th century, as some have suggested. Anger at foreign forces at the gate did lead to displays of xenophobia, but there was nothing new in that. That was the norm throughout Chinese history. For centuries, Chinese armies have fought ferociously against anyone who invaded their lands.

Others would date Chinese nationalism to the urgings of Sun Yat-sen, who lived long years abroad and was primarily educated in foreign schools. Yet others would link it to the Chinese students who went to Japan to learn the secrets of Japan's success, and to the *huaqiao* (Overseas Chinese) who had suffered discrimination at the hands of Europeans and Americans.

Certainly, all these contributed to the Chinese wanting a strong China that could restore its greatness. But the anger till the 1920s was never broad-based, nor was it ever directed against China's critics. Among educated leaders, it was often directed against abstractions like racism, imperialism and colonialism—and official historians then traced everything back to the Opium Wars.

What shaped the passionate nationalism that led the Chinese to identify a national enemy came from the conjunction of three events. The first was the rise of the Nationalist Party, the Kuomintang (KMT). By 1927, China was so divided and feeble that Japan intensified its efforts to take control of more Chinese territory. With Japanese advances into Manchuria and contiguous parts of North China, China's survival as a country was at stake.

The second followed from the succession of defeats the KMT inflicted on the CCP, which led the CCP to turn to nationalism to save itself and win support among peasants who never understood the tenets of Marxism-Leninism. That also attracted educated urban youth who doubted the KMT's willingness to fight the Japanese invaders, and they brought along with them their nationalism.

The final catalyst was the Sino-Japanese War of 1937–1945. In contrast to the first war of 1894–1895, which occurred before the rise of nationalism, the second was a life-and-death struggle to save China. Both the KMT and the CCP drew strength from the emotions that sprang partly from anger at China's weakness but most of all from hatred of Japan's ambition to dominate the country. Both the KMT and the CCP became more nationalistic and devoted much energy to shaping nationalism to ensure their legitimacy.

Indeed, that competition continued even after the CCP established the People's Republic of China in 1949. It competed with the KMT in Taiwan for the hearts and minds of the huaqiao while at the same time highlighting its internationalist ideals. When internationalism failed, there remained only nationalism to bolster its right to lead the country.

What became of that nationalism after 1949? At one level, it manifested itself in China playing off the United States against the CCP's former comrades in the Soviet Union. At another level, it was evoked through memories of the patriotic war against Japan. No one could forget that it was the CCP's performance in that war that helped seal its success.

China's remarkable achievements since the reforms of 1978 and after have restored the pride of the Chinese people. As a result, now, when the government tries to please its foreign critics and adjust to their universal standards of correct behaviour, it could be perceived by the Chinese people to be unnecessarily weak. Furthermore, people who have benefited from the reforms feel that the continuing, sometimes carping and contemptuous, attacks on the regime are in fact aimed at China and the Chinese people. Hence their readiness to vent their anger towards the foreign critics.

But their passions should not obscure one undeniable fact: The source of their pride is now China's unity and potential power. There was sympathy for China when it was divided and weak. That was lost when China became stronger. The government is aware of that change as it tries hard to assure neighbouring countries of its peaceful intentions.

It realises that the nationalism of small and weak states could be described as heroic. But the nationalism of a large, populous and technologically superior country, even if justified, would only generate fear and alarm.

Let us hope that the Games will end as Beijing hopes and millions around the world would cheer its success. That will be the time to ask if the Chinese people's pride in China's modernity cannot be celebrated without the need to resort to nationalism again.

10.4

NO REFUGE FOR PATRIOTS IN A GLOBAL SOCIETY

Daniel Flitton

> In the next selection, an Australian author discusses the role of patriotism in a globalized world. He concludes that patriotism, albeit seductive, is out of place, an appeal to emotion rather than to reason, and its results can only harm Australia and the world more generally.

Contrast two events from the week and it is easy to spot a common theme—yet draw entirely different conclusions.

In one example, the Socceroos take to the field in a World Cup qualifier, and people are told to show their national spirit and get behind the Australian team. It's our patriotic duty, after all.

But when the NSW [New South Wales] Government brings down a budget with a plan to put "Local Jobs First"—requiring state agencies to back Australian suppliers ahead of foreign competitors—the measure is decried as rank and silly, jingoism of the worst type.

"I can understand the rhetoric," Trade Minister Simon Crean conceded, "but this is a misguided view in the name of protecting jobs. . . . If we get into a tit-for-tat downward spiral war of protectionism, Australia will be the loser."

All politicians know an appeal to national sentiment makes for powerful rhetoric. Think of all the flag-waving, anthem-singing rituals that are observed to foster a sense of community. Tapping into that popular passion is a means for political success.

Nationalism often guides our everyday choices too. Take, for instance, how the "Made in Australia" on a clothes tag cheers people with the belief that buying local supports jobs down the street. This is despite Australia's steady drift away from manufacturing. Neighbourhood factories are now more likely to be converted into swish inner-city townhouses.

But nationalism is an appeal to emotion, not logic. Advertisers understand this very well. We're told that eating Australian lamb is akin to a form of national service while, at the same time, led to believe that shifting the manufacture of Bonds undies off-shore is an act of high treason.

Source: Daniel Flitton, "No Refuge for Patriots in a Global Society," *The Age,* June 20, 2009.

A campaign to "Buy Australian" is not protectionism; this is simply companies exploiting a market advantage. But when it shifts to formal government policy, this exposes one of the great contractions of modern society—the ongoing appeal of a national economic identity versus the reality of an interdependent global economy. Or put another way, a world at once divided and united.

Before you dismiss this debate as a mere abstract concern, consider the ramifications. One in five jobs in Australia depends on trade. Should other countries look at the NSW Government's actions and retaliate, in effect raising barriers to Australian goods, we lose jobs.

Or think of the sorry recent experience of Indian students in Melbourne, subject to racial abuse that is in part fuelled by misbegotten fear their very presence threatens the chances for locals to gain employment.

But there is an even greater risk. As Prime Minister Kevin Rudd recently warned, the 20th century saw the tragic consequences of rampant nationalism. The bookends for the Great Depression took shape in two devastating world wars. "In seeking to protect itself, each country harmed itself," Rudd said.

The late, great British historian Edward Hallett Carr well understood the intrinsic pull of nationalism over people's identity. In one of his most powerful, yet under-rated essays, "Nationalism and After," he explained how this feeling could be exploited. "Surely the most explicit exaltation of the nation over the individual as an end in itself (is) the mass sacrifice of human beings to the idol of nationalism," he wrote in 1945. This tool generated fatal rivalries.

Modern "globalization" is often said to be the antidote to such bitter competition. Internet phone calls on Skype, for example, make for cheap and instant communication— a way of linking countries and people to help overcome suspicions and deliver lasting peace. Carr was never convinced. "To reduce the time of transit between two capitals from weeks to days or from days to hours," he wrote, "provides no assurance . . . of a growth of mutual understanding and united action."

Nor did he believe the ties of global commerce would remove the threat of war. Modern nations had evolved to protect the individual from the winner-takes-all ravages of an unfettered economy. This trend could not be reversed—nor its demands abated. Protecting one national group would always come at the expense of another.

So now, in the midst of a global economic downturn, Australian society again finds itself grappling with same tensions of national identity. The NSW Government's budget measures are a beginning. Labor is soon to hold its national conference, and already the union movement is squaring off with the Rudd Government over the free trade agreements under negotiation.

Carr saw hope in the prospects of internationalism—not in the sense of a formal authority over national governments, but in recognising equality of human beings. Local loyalties must find a place in a healthy society, he wrote, yet internationalism, like nationalism, must become the social norm. But in practical terms, the world is still a long way from recognising a garment worker in Vietnam has the same rights as one from Geelong.

10.5

PROTECTIONISM WILL ONLY WORSEN THINGS

from *The Business Times Singapore*

> The next selection, from Singapore, warns that protectionist policies by individual countries in times of economic distress will only exacerbate economic conditions. This is an issue to which we shall return in the final chapter of the book.

As the global economic crisis continues to unfold, there are ominous signs of a rise in economic nationalism and even overt protectionism. In the United States, the economic stimulus package is studded with 'buy American' provisions, for products ranging from steel to worker uniforms to computers. In the European Union, authorities are directing banks to lend to domestic entities and are drawing up plans to protect their own 'national champions.' Amid a rising wave of labour unrest, there are calls to protect jobs for domestic workers as against foreigners—and this is evident in Asia too.

During his confirmation hearings, US Treasury Secretary Timothy Geithner referred to China as a 'currency manipulator'—which many observers saw as a thinly veiled protectionist threat. As Harvard Professor Jeffrey Frieden has pointed out, such developments more likely arise from domestic desperation rather than arrogant nationalism. Even so, they do have negative effects on other countries and can provoke hostile reactions. For instance, the 'buy American' provisions being championed by US Congressmen are almost certain to ignite similar demands in the EU. Moves to subsidise only national champions in one country will provoke similar steps in others. The process can snowball from there, with developing countries, too, moving to increase trade barriers and discriminate against foreign companies.

This is a dangerous road for the global economy to take. As it is, with a global recession taking hold, world trade is threatened: the International Monetary Fund (IMF) predicts that the total volume of trade will contract 2.8 per cent this year, after expanding 4.1 per cent in 2008. Tit-for-tat protectionism would make these numbers far worse, and would also aggravate the global recession. The lessons of history are clear on this point. The infamous Smoot-Hawley tariff in the United States during the 1930s was a disaster for the world—and for the US itself. In today's more globalised context, the effects could be even more devastating.

It is not that politicians and policymakers don't know this. But given the current mood, they find it expedient to overlook the external implications of their actions. Such

---

Source: "Protectionism Will Only Worsen Things," *The Business Times Singapore,* February 4, 2009.

implications should be made clear to them, explicitly and publicly. There is a strong case here for heightened surveillance of the actions countries are taking and their effects on other countries. International institutions such as the IMF, the World Bank and especially the World Trade Organization (WTO), need to increase their vigilance in this area.

More policy coordination and collective commitment is also essential. A good start was made at the Group of 20 (G-20) meeting in Brazil last November, when governments pledged not to raise trade barriers. Such commitments need to be reinforced at every opportunity. As WTO director-general Pascal Lamy said in Davos last month: 'The only way to make sure that this crisis doesn't get worse, and longer, is to act together . . . and keep trade open.'

Chapter 11

HUMAN RIGHTS AND DEMOCRACY IN A GLOBALIZING WORLD

Historically, states have limited or violated individual rights for many reasons—for example, to promote their ideology and induce fear. Dictators often force citizens to accept the official ideological, religious, or political view and persecute those who do not do so. Many rulers jail and torture opponents arbitrarily, deny justice and equality to racial and ethnic groups, treat women as chattel, and murder political foes to stifle dissent.

After World War II and the Nazis' murder of millions of Jews and others, individual human rights assumed a greater role in global politics, and observers began to question whether sovereignty should permit governments to treat citizens as they wished. The most important human rights document is the 1948 UN Universal Declaration of Human Rights, a comprehensive listing of civil, political, social, and economic rights. The declaration asserts "the inherent dignity and . . . the equal and inalienable rights of all members of the human family" as "the foundation of freedom, justice and peace in the world." In 1966, the Universal Declaration of Human Rights was reinforced by two multilateral treaties: the international covenants on civil and political rights and on economic, social, and cultural rights. Collectively, the three documents are known as the International Bill of Human Rights. They outline two basic types of human rights—"negative" and "positive" rights. *Negative rights* are those that *prevent* governments from interfering with individual liberty, frequently involving political and civil rights and liberties.

Negative rights include freedom from regulation of speech, the press, or religion as well as others that are listed in the U.S. Bill of Rights. In the West, negative rights are part of the tradition that dates back to the Magna Carta. Many observers believe that democracy is a basic negative right.

Positive rights, which are found in the International Covenant on Economic, Social and Cultural Rights, refer to the obligation of governments, and indeed the international community, to provide for individuals' economic and social welfare—for example, education, employment, and health care. Those who emphasize positive rights see them as prerequisites for negative rights and claim that individual liberty is meaningless without economic and social equality and security. They contend that the absence of such equality and security in the developing world constitutes structural violence.

Positive rights are a more recent development than negative rights, dating back to the expansion of the states' welfare policies in the late 19th and early 20th centuries and to President Franklin Roosevelt's New Deal of the 1930s. Thus, negative and positive rights are often referred to as first- and second-generation rights, respectively. American society still gives relatively less weight to positive than to negative rights, but global norms, as reflected in the UN's Millennium Goals, are evolving toward giving both equal weight.

11.1

NEW RIGHTS ADVOCACY IN A GLOBAL PUBLIC DOMAIN

Paul Nelson and Ellen Dorsey

> Human rights advocacy has changed in recent decades. As the opening selection in this chapter suggests, a "new rights advocacy" goes beyond promoting traditional civil and political rights by advancing economic and social rights as well. Such advocacy, led by transnational nongovernmental organizations, increasingly involves working against neoliberal economic principles, as well as opposing the policies of key international organizations like the World Trade Organization and wealthy countries like the United States while assisting the citizens of poor countries in the developing world.

Introduction

The ascendancy of market-based, liberal approaches to trade, finance and development policy, and the diminishing roles of national government ownership and regulation of enterprises, are among the defining characteristics of world politics since 1980. The accompanying growth of influence by corporations has been well chronicled, as has the less powerful but significant rise of NGOs and popular movements in national and international politics.

. . . This is a political domain in which some—though by no means most—authoritative decisions are made in settings that cross national boundaries. This domain is 'public' in a sense broader than 'governmental': corporations, states, international governmental organizations and civil society organizations participate in authoritative decision-making processes. Moreover, domestic and transnational policy 'spheres' blur and intermingle in trade disputes, environmental policy, and intrastate conflicts, all of which also involve states, international corporations and NGOs and citizens' movements. . . . One of the key characteristics of contemporary civil society activism is a dramatic increase in the application of human rights standards and strategies to economic, social, and development policy issues. Despite some successes elsewhere, NGOs have been largely unable to alter the neo-liberal orientation of development finance, trade, and the regulation of

Source: Excerpted from Paul Nelson and Ellen Dorsey, "New Rights Advocacy in a Global Public Domain," *European Journal of International Relations* 13:2 (June 2007), 187–216. Notes appearing in the original have been deleted.

monetary policy and investment. This article examines the emergence of new strategies grounded in international human rights standards, strategies which represent a new approach by NGOs and which challenge widely held views of the relationship between NGOs and states.

Economic and social rights (ESC) such as the right to food, to health or the broader 'right to development' have long been debated by governments, scholars and NGOs. But recently these human rights have become more prominent in the agendas and strategies of some bilateral development aid donors. . . . and of some NGOs and social movements, which have applied them to more specific policy debates, such as agrarian reform, access to essential medicines, women's reproductive health, and privatization of water supply systems. New and distinct patterns of NGO political action are emerging in advocacy on economic and social rights, as well as in other activism on economic and social policy, which we call the New Rights Advocacy.

We use 'new rights advocacy' (NRA) to refer to advocacy on social, economic or development policy, at local, national, or international levels, which makes explicit reference to internationally recognized human rights standards. . . . [T]wo comments on the definition are needed. First, we do not specify at what levels (national or international) NRA takes place. The advocacy explicitly draws on international standards, but it may draw on international influence to shape domestic policy choices, or on domestic initiatives to influence an international process. Second, we adopt the term *'new* rights advocacy' advisedly. The standards themselves are far from new. Most of the specific standards discussed here (health and food, for example) are mentioned in the Universal Declaration of Human Rights, and given legal standing in the International Covenant on Economic, Social and Cultural Rights. . . . The recent development of the 'right to water' is taken up below.

What is both substantially new and significant is the nature of the advocacy that is outlined here. First, it is characterized by its explicit appeals to human rights standards, by its promotion of both civil and political human rights *and* economic and social human rights, and by the scope of activity and the broad range of actors whose behavior it targets. Second, it assigns accountability for the effects of economic policy in a distinctive way, attempting to develop an important if vague principle in human rights law, that responsibility for fulfilling ESC rights in some circumstances is shared by international actors and wealthy governments. Third, the NRA involves a decisive shift, compared to the established practice of civil and political human rights advocacy, in how appeals are made to international authorities to uphold those rights and in relation to governments whose duty it is to protect those rights. These features lead us to advance two broad arguments: a theoretical argument regarding the models by which we understand NGO involvement in international politics and, by implication, the responsibilities of states and international authorities; and a substantive argument about the significance of human rights in shaping social and economic policy, and the importance of NGOs in promoting economic and social human rights norms.

Theoretically, the rise of New Rights Advocacy challenges existing models for the relations between states, NGOs, and international authority, and clarifies the basis for rule-making in economic and social policy. Prevailing models for understanding NGOs as political actors are inspired largely by civil and political human rights and environmental advocacy, and characterize NGO advocacy as a process of building international support in order to force changes in individual states' behavior. But in a growing number of movements, especially involving economic and social rights, international actors play fundamentally different roles. Here, NGOs often work to weaken the roles of some international organizations, notably the International Monetary Fund (IMF) and the World Trade Organization (WTO), to alter the foreign and economic policies of powerful states, and to protect and broaden the options of national governments. . . .

This shift is momentous for human rights practice, and has important implications for how we think about the state. Many governments and human rights practitioners have historically resisted ESC rights because they are characterized as 'aspirational,' more subjective than civil and political human rights, and because of the difficulty of assigning accountability for ESC rights when most governments have limited control over economic conditions, and limited capacity to provide services. The ascendancy and widespread application of neo-liberal economic policies intensifies this problem for ESC rights by further limiting many governments' control over economic and social conditions.

But this difficulty of assigning responsibility to a single state as sole duty bearer, usually considered a weakness of ESC rights, is being addressed by strategies that seek to transform it in practice into strength, by targeting economic actors—including rich country governments—that create barriers to the realization of specific economic and social rights in national settings. The traditional tension between international NGOs and poor country governments is altered and *sometimes* reversed, as NGOs support and cooperate with governments and work against the constraining effects of trade rules, economic policy conditionality, and corporate leverage.

New rights advocacy is growing in breadth and scope, and has potentially far-reaching significance. First, it calls more serious attention to ESC rights in national and international policy-making. These rights, which are legally and theoretically co-equal with civil and political guarantees such as freedom of speech, and protections against arbitrary detention and torture, have not developed the same support among powerful industrial countries, nor among NGO advocates, that civil and political human rights now enjoy. The Cold War and ideologically driven debates bifurcated the human rights system and relegated ESC rights to a secondary and 'aspirational' status. The new rights advocacy challenges this relative obscurity and calls for reintegration with civil and political rights.

Second, the NRA is the first fundamental challenge to a market-dominated development framework that reshaped national economies and international trade and finance during the 1980s and 1990s. New movements are drawing on human rights standards to challenge the application of market logic to the delivery of water and basic services, to argue for the right to agrarian reform and education, and to assert the primacy of human health considerations in setting national and international policy regarding HIV/AIDS. Resistance to privatization and liberalization plans has been a feature of national politics in developing countries at least since the 1970s. New rights advocacy movements are challenging market-driven orthodoxy at the international institutions with greater political force and legitimacy than critics of structural adjustment policies have previously mustered.

Third, the new rights advocacy entails a fundamentally new understanding of accountability for the failure to meet human rights standards. In traditional civil and political rights advocacy, governments are accused of practising arbitrary detention, torture, or discriminatory access to legal remedies, and international actors are persuaded to exert leverage, pressing the offending governments to amend policies and practices. New Rights Advocacy is not constrained by the sole focus on the state as duty bearer and violator of human rights, targeting many institutions, including international financial institutions (IFI), transnational corporations, trade regimes, rich country governments and poor country governments themselves, whose policies and behavior have an impact on economic and social rights and/or civil and political rights in poor countries. Advocates question the authority of international agencies and rules that weaken states' capacity to meet social and economic rights obligations. They also call upon rich countries to provide more generous and effective development assistance. . . .

This article places this broadening of NGO strategies in the context of the global public domain, and demonstrates the central role of a new politics of human rights advocacy in promoting the relevance and authority of human rights—including ESC human rights—to complex rule-making and policy-making processes. This advocacy involves organizations from human rights, development and environment sectors in establishing new, more complex relationships among NGOs, international organizations and poor country governments. It involves a growing commitment to the entire range of international human rights standards in shaping transnational governance processes, national constitutions and laws, economic and social policies, and the conduct of a range of state, interstate and corporate actors.

The New Rights Advocacy

Development, environmental and human rights advocates are engaged in an important strain of international activity that is not sufficiently explained by contemporary International Relations, social movement or human rights literature. The new political activity draws on human rights norms to shape economic and social policy, entails a wide range of diverse organizations and issue areas, and has sparked regional and international campaigns involving grassroots social movements and NGOs. The number and intensity of these campaigns increased rapidly in the 1990s and the first years of the new century, and focused on specifically defined issues, such as the rights to drinking water and essential medicines, rather than the broader right to food or right to development. This section first outlines the range and breadth of the initiatives; their political implications will then be analyzed through case studies on water and HIV/AIDS.

The expanding interest in economic and social rights encompasses three trends: The first is the move by traditional civil and political rights NGOs to cover ESC rights, exemplified by Amnesty International's adoption in 2001 of a new mission expanding beyond its historic civil and political mandate to include work on ESC rights, or Human Rights Watch's work on HIV/AIDS or property rights for women. The second is the growth of new movements and organizations that explicitly link human needs issues to ESC rights standards, as in campaigns for essential medicines, the right to water, and women's reproductive health rights. Among the leading international NGOs making ESC rights central to their missions are the Center for Economic and Social Rights (CESR), the Center on Housing Rights and Evictions (COHRE), the FoodFirst Information and Action Network (FIAN), and the International Women's Health Coalition. These international initiatives have often been led and even challenged by national NGOs in the countries of the global South, with agendas dedicated to ESC rights.

The third trend making up the new rights advocacy is a rights-based approach (RBA) to development being adopted by existing development, environment and labor groups. International development NGOs such as CARE-USA, Oxfam, ActionAid International, and *Riidda Barnen* (Save the Children-Sweden) are implementing 'rights-based' approaches that parallel similar moves by official development agencies including UNDP, the UN Food and Agriculture Organization (FAO) and the Swedish and British bilateral aid agencies. These official development agencies' interest in rights rarely intersects with the human rights-driven advocacy campaigns. DFI and Sida are both concerned primarily with the benefit that human rights analysis of poverty and social exclusion can have for development program and project design.

NGOs have used a diverse, varied and not always consistent set of strategies as they seek out means of gaining leverage from human rights standards for economic and social policy issues. These methods include the rhetorical referencing of human rights standards to shape and frame policy debates, the application of specific standards to measure and evaluate the performance of government services or development aid projects, litigation of human rights claims before judicial and quasi-judicial bodies, and human rights education to help communities and social movements make the link between social and economic needs and human rights guaranteed by international norms and standards. These methods are often combined in issue-specific advocacy campaigns.

Education advocates, for example, have sometimes made reference to human rights guarantees in a campaign at the international level to encourage investment in guaranteeing access to universal primary education, primarily as a legitimating norm. National campaigns, on the other hand, have made the human rights guarantees more central, as in India, where advocates successfully argued for a national education policy that guarantees universal access to primary education. Advocates for African women's property rights base much of their attack on legal and cultural impediments to ownership and inheritance in the principles of non-discrimination that are enshrined in human rights agreements.

In other settings, education about human rights itself is a central strategy to realize economic and social rights. Human rights education encourages citizen groups to be aware of and to assert their rights in addressing governments and corporations. The Peoples Movement for Human Rights Education is a leading NGO in the field, and the International Women's Health Coalition supports human rights education as a means of strengthening local women's networks' ability to make the case for health services.

Human rights analysis may also be part of an effort to frame—or reframe—an issue, to win international legitimacy for popular socioeconomic struggles. Local and national advocacy for agrarian reform, for example, has broadened its support as peasant movements such as Brazil's *Movimento dos Trabalhadores Rurais Sem Terra* (MST) are linked to human rights-based organizations such as the FoodFirst Information and Action Network (FIAN), which uses urgent action alerts modeled on Amnesty International's prisoner of conscience advocacy. FIAN argues that agrarian reform, which is essential to addressing rural poverty in countries with significant agricultural employment, has been betrayed by official development institutions, and makes the human right to food its basis for making the case for agrarian reform as a human rights issue.

What Is 'New' About the New Rights Advocacy?

What is important about these efforts, and others like them, is the distinctly different pattern of political action involved. While the New Rights Advocacy borrows methods drawn from civil and political rights advocacy of the past, three major distinctions set these movements apart from the patterns outlined in existing models of NGO political action.

First, new rights advocacy addresses policy issues that are already dominated by another strong set of norms, which hold that goods and services are best delivered by markets, and that state guarantees are often inefficient, or worse. NGO campaigning against neoliberal policies is not new, to be sure. . . . But the mobilization of human rights principles and standards against this dominant and controversial set of norms is new. Early efforts to promote civil and political rights confronted the competing norm of sovereignty, and advances in civil and political rights have often involved establishing the principle that human rights agreements give states the authority to investigate, comment on and intervene in the relations of sovereign governments and their citizens.

Human rights advocates devoted considerable political energy to winning powerful governments' cooperation in promoting civil and political rights through their foreign policies. But the core values behind civil and political rights were attractive to powerful—particularly Western—states that were being urged to constrain the sovereignty of other nations by pressuring for political reform. Economic and social rights, on the other hand, are likely to be seen as conflicting with the widely held norms of neo-liberal policy and limited government, held dear by the United States and influential international organizations.

Second, new rights advocacy establishes a different standard of accountability for failures to meet international economic and social rights. Advocates often seek to restrict, not draw on, the influence of international organizations and powerful governments, and NRA tends to involve NGOs in more complex relationships with poor country governments, relations that are sometimes adversarial, sometimes supportive.

Third, new rights advocacy involves a broad range of issues and diverse political arenas (national and international), 'targets' (inter-governmental, governmental, and corporate), and partnerships (among environmental, development, human rights, women, indigenous and children's advocacy organizations). These place NGOs and social movements in a new posture as they attempt to establish the authority of human rights standards, including ESC rights, over social and economic policy-making. . . .

This new dynamic in the emerging global public domain is illustrated by reference to two of the principal social policy debates in contemporary international affairs: the privatization of water systems and the global response to the global AIDS pandemic. The two campaigns illustrate characteristics of other issue campaigns, such as the campaign for access to essential medicines, for the right to agrarian reform, for women's property rights, and for the right to education. They also exemplify the central characteristics of the new rights advocacy: the increasing specificity of campaigns related to ESC rights, their complex relations with governments and international agencies, their appeal to human rights standards as a source of leverage against norms of liberalization and privatization; and the wide range of issues, strategies, and political arenas that they address. Both cases originate with initiatives by local social movements determined to change, or prevent changes, in state policy. Local activists use the language of rights, and international campaigns emerge, also directed at preventing international institutions or rules from blocking human rights-friendly policies.

Conflicting Norms: Markets, Human Rights, and the Case of Water

Human rights standards are being invoked and strategically deployed by advocates for guarantees of universal access to adequate supplies of safe drinking water. The human right to water is recognized in the Convention on the Elimination of All Forms of Discrimination Against Women (CEDAW, Article14(2)(h)) and in the Convention on the Rights of the Child (Article 24), and was reinforced and given a higher profile in November 2002 when the UN Committee on Economic, Social and Cultural Rights issued an explanatory General Comment . . . making explicit the ICESCR's guarantee of a right to water.

Advocates of water rights, however, confront a powerful set of norms in international development and finance emphasizing market mechanisms and the benefits of economic openness and reduced government roles in the economy, norms which have been promoted influentially for more than two decades by the US government and the World Bank and International Monetary Fund. . . . But market-led development, even with the now conventional modifiers that recognize the need for 'broad-based' growth, investment in human capital, good governance, and social safety nets, does not coexist comfortably with a framework for development built on guarantees of universal rights. Asserting universal rights to health, water, or education is in part a means of gaining leverage against market-based development policy.

Consider the use of human rights standards, rhetoric and strategies by advocates opposing the privatization of national and municipal water systems. At least 14 countries in sub-Saharan Africa, and numerous countries and municipalities elsewhere, are implementing or considering dramatic changes to water supply systems. Encouraged by the World Bank and/or IMF, and promoted by several large corporations specializing in water systems management, the new policies involve a shift from state-managed water provision to provision by the private sector, usually international contractors, with fees paid by end users.

There is often a good case for re-working these water systems. Many state-managed systems, while providing drinking water at little or no cost to some citizen-clients, are plagued by high administrative costs, financial losses, leakage, and inadequate coverage, especially of poor 'customers.'

But in virtually every municipality and country where privatization has been proposed or begun, local and national resistance has been vigorous. In Ghana and Bolivia, national governments agreed in 1999 to new water delivery systems, municipal or national, managed by private contractors and financed in part by user fees. Local consumer movements, national NGOs and international NGOs have all been involved in resisting privatization and/or advancing proposals to modify fees and administration. In Ghana, the Coalition against Privatization of Water in Ghana ('the National Coalition') objected to the government's 'fast track' implementation of privatization, the lack of transparency in preparing contracts and transactions, and the perceived favoring of multinational corporations in the sale of public water utilities.

The Ghanaian campaign has succeeded in sparking international support through two mechanisms. First, the World Bank's prominent involvement in the national privatization scheme means that a set of international NGOs that focus on World Bank policy are receptive to the Ghanaian NGOs' case. Washington-based NGOs such as the Services for All and the International Water Working Group were among the earliest international critics of the Ghanaian privatization Second, Ghanaian advocates took steps to link to international opponents of privatization, through speaking tours and by sponsoring an international fact-finding tour to Ghana. The dispute over water privatization in Cochabamba, Bolivia has become a *cause celebre* of the global debates. Citizen organizations resisted a planned contract with a consortium controlled by Bechtel, Inc., which doubled water tariffs for many consumers. Extensive public protests ended with the consortium abandoning its contract to privatize Cochabamba's system, and a lawsuit by Bechtel to recover costs was dropped in January 2006. . . . In Ghana, Bolivia and in similar debates in South Africa, India, and elsewhere, local and national coalitions of poor people's and consumers' organizations press for free access to water and against privatization, making reference to international human rights, or to national constitutional or statutory guarantees.

The rights-based cases against privatization advanced by NGOs and human rights advocates in India and South Africa are among the most potent. In India, human rights arguments are prominent in legal and political challenges to the National Water Policy of 2002, which provided for private ownership and management of water systems. Human rights are similarly invoked in opposition to corporate use of water resources, especially by soft-drink bottlers.

In South Africa, the movement for the human right to water was galvanized by private water providers' use of pre-paid water meters on village and neighborhood pumps. These meters, which allow water to flow only to those who have paid in advance, are manufactured in South Africa and exported, and their use has sharpened the perception that privatized water systems will involve systematic violations of poor citizens' rights. In both cases, local advocates' references to human rights have been picked up, amplified and made more systematic by NGOs working at the global level.

Through the 1990s, international support for local water movements took three primary forms: small solidarity networks with links to a country or city; anti-privatization advocates already working on privatization issues at the World Bank and IMF; and anti-corporate globalization activists led by the Canadian Blue Planet Network, concerned with global water issues. All used the language of rights, but generally without any specific reference to international agreements. For example, international coalitions mobilized individuals and organizations from five continents in support of the claim that 'water is a fundamental, inalienable individual and collective right,' and that 'it is up to society as a whole to guarantee the right of access . . . without discrimination . . .' and call on governments to pledge 'not to privatize, trade, export water, and to exempt water from trade and investment agreements.' International human rights NGOs were not involved.

But the pace and intensity of human rights-related water advocacy has grown rapidly in the 2000s, stimulated both by the pace of privatization efforts and the publication of General Comment 15 on the Right to Water in 2002. Three international NGOs that have begun work on the human right to water since 2003 exemplify the dominant role of the human rights frame in the water debates. The New York-based Committee on Economic and Social Rights (CESR) advocates a human rights-based approach as the best guide to the challenges of water provision. CESR references human rights agreements and affirmations of the right to water in national constitutions, and proposes a standard for policy and litigation by tying the human right to water to the World Health Organization's standards of access to 20 to 40 liters of water daily, 'within a reasonable distance from the household.'

The International Water Working Group (IWWG), a coalition headquartered at Washington, DC-based Public Citizen, focuses its advocacy work on the IMF, World Bank, and the WTO's General Agreement on Trade in Services (GATS). Only in 2003 did IWWG begin making specific reference to water as a human right, and it has now assembled a thorough analysis of the use of prepayment water meters. Other South African and international advocacy organizations take similar positions.

The UK-based NGO WaterAid adopted a 'human rights approach' to its work in 2003. The organization's new framework has implications for its water related project assistance, and has expanded its advocacy work by initiating a critique of 'private sector participation' in water system reforms. . . .

Water advocates are not alone in employing human rights-based advocacy to counter the power of market norms. HIV/AIDS advocacy, discussed below, and some housing, education and welfare rights advocates are making similar strategic use of human rights standards and methods. Often they do so while cooperating with poor country governments against the authority of international institutions and rules, and we now turn to this second distinctive feature of the new rights advocacy.

Beyond the Violating State: The Complex Politics of New Rights Advocacy

The New Rights Advocacy features a new approach to assigning accountability for many failures to meet ESC rights standards. While advocates rely on international human rights norms, they are not likely to call on international agencies or powerful governments to influence a target government's behavior. Rather they enter into more complex and sometimes cooperative relationships with poor country governments, and assign responsibility for the failure to fulfill rights to multiple actors, often including powerful governments or international agencies. Appeals to states' sovereignty, far from being used to resist or obstruct human rights claims, here are aligned with economic and social rights advocacy.

International norms are essential to most human rights and environmental advocacy, including advocacy of ESC rights. International agreements on economic and social rights began with the 1948 Universal Declaration of Human Rights, but were not further specified until the conclusion of the International Covenant on Economic, Social and Cultural Rights (ICESCR). The ICESCR's 30 articles articulate rights to a range of economic and social goods, many of which are further explained by General Comments on Implementation, appended to the Covenant by the Committee on ESC Rights of the United Nations Economic and Social Council.

The international politics of ESC rights, norms and advocacy are different from those of civil and political rights. Civil and political rights strategies tend to rely on the regulatory or diplomatic powers of G-8 governments or international agencies, and advocates devote a great deal of political effort to winning and maintaining the support of such states. Advocacy on economic and social rights often aims to weaken, not reinforce, the leverage of international organizations or G-8 governments. In some cases, new rights advocacy demands an accounting of the finance, trade and development assistance policies of G-8 countries, and their impact on economic and social rights. Frequently, the human rights advocates' support for poor country government initiatives means that *sovereignty and human rights arguments are aligned,* rather than opposed, as is often the case in civil and political human rights.

Some international agencies . . . and powerful governments (particularly the United States) are less friendly to ESC rights than are many poor country governments, and NGO advocates often adopt a broad, two-pronged position: that governments should retain more discretion in making choices regarding their trade and social policies; and OECD governments and international institutions should uphold their obligations for international cooperation and assistance to advance ESC rights in poor countries. This agenda implicitly broadens accountability, shifting from a sole focus on the 'violating state' and assigning co-responsibility to the actors that may create obstacles for those states to the realisation of human rights in a global economy. The precedent has been set by sustained calls for rich governments to increase their support for the UN Fund to Fight Tuberculosis, Malaria and AIDS on the basis of Article 2 of the ICESCR, which sets out the international obligation for assistance.

We are not arguing that poor country governments are freed from responsibility to respect, protect and fulfill economic and social rights: international standards focus on states' duties progressively to realize those rights and to ensure that they are delivered without discrimination. The politics of human rights is now 'beyond the violating state' not because states are no longer accountable for fulfilling ESC rights, but because in a global economy accountability is increasingly shared by corporations, international economic actors and—in some cases—rich donor governments.

HIV/AIDS: New NGO-Government Relationships

Much international HIV/AIDS advocacy has been explicitly linked to international human rights standards, and grounded in and supportive of initiatives by national governments. Advocacy on HIV/AIDS has often been grounded in the assertion that access to care for HIV-infected patients is an essential component of the internationally recognized human right to the 'highest attainable standard' of health. . . . The AIDS advocacy movement is vast and diverse, and our interest is limited to demonstrating the role of human rights principles and methods, and the impact that these methods have had on the pattern of government-NGO contestation and cooperation.

Advocates for a strong, human rights-based response have emphasized four themes since the mid-1990s: the demand for access to medicines, including the effort to overcome WTO trade rules and patent restrictions on their generic manufacture; the protection of people with HIV/AIDS from discriminatory treatment; the call for funding for the United Nations' Global Fund for HIV/AIDS, Malaria and Tuberculosis; and the campaign to influence the behavior of pharmaceutical companies. Médecins Sans Frontières (MSF) and the South African Treatment Action Campaign; traditional human rights organizations such as Physicians for Human Rights, Global Treatment Access Network and the Health Global Access Project (GAP); and AIDS activist organizations in the US and Europe have all provided leadership in the international human rights-based movement on HIV/AIDS.

Advocating for a more adequate financial commitment by wealthy country governments is not a new theme for development NGOs, which have called for more generous official aid allocations for decades. Human rights NGOs joined in the effort to encourage full funding of the UN's Global Fund invoking the human rights obligation of wealthy country governments to contribute and seeking to shift the framing of the development assistance issue, from aid as charity to aid as fulfillment of a fundamental right.

Human Rights Watch's program on HIV/AIDS focuses largely on civil and political rights of HIV/AIDS patients. Applying its established research and documentation strategies, HRW demonstrates that discrimination and stigmatization, and sometimes active and systematic violations of the civil and political rights of people living with HIV/AIDS, contribute to their reluctance to seek testing and treatment. Improved protection of rights against discrimination, under these circumstances, is a step to improve testing and treatment.

But arguably the most dramatic and significant implications of human rights for AIDS advocacy has been manifested in the work on two related issues: governments' policies for the provision of treatment to HIV patients; and the international collision of property rights and human rights in debates over trade rules related to intellectual property rights (TRIPS). In promoting access to treatment, for example, NGO advocates often ally themselves with poor country governments in an effort to limit, change or circumvent the rules or authority of international organizations. Initiatives by national governments have often driven important debates on access to HIV/AIDS medicines, and they have been supported by international advocates and by social movement organizations working on HIV/AIDS issues in the industrial countries.

The interaction among domestic AIDS activists in South Africa, their government and international health and human rights NGOs illustrates the complexity of this new relationship. The South African government was hardly a likely candidate for international NGO support: President Mbeke's administration had placed itself at odds with the international AIDS and medical community through its heterodox positions on the nature of the pandemic. But despite their criticism of the government, domestic and international advocates maintained a strong cooperative element in their relationship with the government throughout the 1990s. Initiatives by the governments of South Africa and Brazil to produce generic versions of patented anti-retroviral drugs led to threats of formal action against them—a suit by the US government against South Africa, and action under WTO rules against Brazil. NGO activists have given unusually strong and direct support to government initiatives, as the following profile of the work of MSF with the governments of South Africa and Brazil demonstrates.

MSF's goals include 'to support health ministries that are fighting to increase access to essential drugs,' and to 'support the implementation of existing trade rules . . . designed to protect' access to these medicines, by informing and advising governments on their options. Facing very high costs for anti-retroviral drugs in its clinical trials in South Africa in 2002, MSF negotiated with the South African and Brazilian governments to purchase and export to South Africa generic versions of the drugs in question, at roughly half the cost of those available from multinational pharmaceutical companies.

South African activists from the Treatment Action Campaign (TAC) participated in the importation of drugs from Brazil, in MSF's clinical trials, and sided with the South African government in the lawsuit against it by the Pharmaceutical Manufacturers Association (PMA). This cooperative strategy was pursued even as TAC continued the advocacy that eventually led to the South African cabinet's November 2003 commitment to making anti-retroviral treatment available in every government health facility to people with HIV. PMA abandoned the legal action soon after TAC entered the case.

This high-profile episode of national policy-setting was intertwined with the debate, at the global level, over the relationship between patent and property rights as outlined in the WTO's TRIPS standards, and the human right to treatment for HIV. The apparent partial victory that AIDS activists won in 2001, when the Ministerial Meeting at Doha reaffirmed that governments' right to act in a public health emergency superseded intellectual property rights rules. Without changing any TRIPS rules, the Ministerial Meeting added a Declaration on TRIPS and Public Health that makes a temporary exception of 15 years, to assure that TRIPS does not prevent countries from taking steps to promote public health.

This ruling opened a further debate over the mechanisms by which poor country governments can act. For governments whose countries lack the capacity to produce their own generic ARVs, a low-cost and efficient mechanism for trade in these generic drugs is essential, and over a temporary mechanism created in August 2003 and adopted in December 2005 by the Ministerial Meeting in Hong Kong. Critics argue that the case-by-case approval approach is a cumbersome mechanism that violates the spirit of the 2001 agreement giving priority to health rights over property rights.

Once again, international NGOs, AIDS activist movements in rich and poor countries and a handful of development NGOs argue for broadening poor country governments' policy choices. The US- and EU-supported solution, one letter argues, locks in a 'burdensome and unworkable' solution, in the interests of ensuring that no generic drugs find their way into industrial country markets. This episode in the debate presents a clear example of how human rights campaigning on economic and social policy put NGOs and social movements in partnership with poor country governments whose policy options are limited by external debt and international financing policies.

HIV/AIDS advocates have also directly engaged the pharmaceutical companies that hold patents on the handful of relatively expensive drugs used to treat HIV infection. Oxfam, for example, mounted sustained advocacy focused on the pharmaceutical giants Pfizer and GlaxoSmithKline, producing two extensive reports and pursuing both public and private efforts to persuade the companies to adjust the prices of medicines to treat HIV/AIDS patients in poor countries. Oxfam's reports on the pharmaceutical industry are directed to the firms themselves and, significantly, to key government bodies such as the UK Parliament, in an effort to shape public and governmental perceptions of the industry and to soften the industry's position in international trade and patent rules.

Learning From Water and HIV/AIDS: Discussion

New rights advocacy, we have argued, is leading to a larger, more influential NGO political presence, elevating the status of ESC rights in economic and social policy debates, and offering an authoritative set of principles for the governance and regulation of corporate and state actors. The water and HIV cases demonstrate the new and varied roles of NGO political action, united by the application of human rights standards to social policy. They display the variety of actors being targeted, the diversity of the institutions initiating human rights-based strategies, and the beginning of impact on policy outcomes, as well as some of the limitations of human rights-based strategies. Finally, NRA is altering popular and scholarly understanding of the contemporary human rights movement. A brief discussion of these factors follows.

The broad range of targets and political arenas targeted by the NRA—including corporations, states and international organizations—is a function both of strategic considerations and of the nature of ESC rights. Recognizing the complexity and costs of fulfilling such rights for very poor countries, the human rights covenants define governments' duty to respect, protect, and fulfill these rights in a much more qualified way than for civil and political rights, obliging governments to 'take steps' to secure the rights 'to the maximum of its available resources,' a process known as progressive realization.

In addition to allowing for progressive realization, the ICESCR also acknowledges that the duty to fulfill ESC rights may fall on the 'international community' as a whole, through the duty to provide assistance (Article 2). For the UNDP, this diffuse duty is an important link in the argument for greater international commitment to a human rights-based development assistance regime.

But for advocates seeking to promote compliance with ESC human rights, the ambiguity poses a challenge, and requires an approach distinct from the appeal to international authority that often provides leverage for civil and political human rights. As Human Rights Watch director Kenneth Roth argues with respect to HIV/AIDS, 'gradualism and shared responsibility make it much more difficult to shame a particular national government for its poor state of health care. . . . Governments can deflect criticism by blaming others. There is no easy way to move beyond this finger-pointing.'

Campaigns on water privatization and HIV/AIDS are both highly critical of the key multinational corporations involved, but the two campaigns differ in the nature and extent of efforts to target the corporations' behavior directly. Water rights advocates excoriate the large multinationals that have made water systems their business, but international NGOs have done relatively little to engage the companies directly, focusing instead largely on the World Bank and IMF. By contrast, the AIDS campaign has engaged pharmaceutical companies directly and extensively. The difference in strategy may flow from the ease with which AIDS advocates assume the moral high ground, with respect to government as well as to the pharmaceutical companies. . . .

These initiatives to assert the authority of ESC rights in social and economic policy are being taken by diverse actors in the global public domain. ESC human rights norms are often being applied and clarified in situations that place them directly in conflict with intellectual property rights or other property rights. In the case of HIV/AIDS, the critical initiatives asserting the right to treatment for HIV/AIDS have been taken by a handful of governments—Brazil, India and South Africa—with powerful encouragement from social movements within their borders, and support from international NGOs and movements.

No governments have taken such clear leadership on the water privatization issue. Local and national consumer organizations and other social movements, with international NGO support, have led the outcry against privatization, and the critique of the World Bank's role. The appeal to human rights to buttress this case began with the largely rhetorical assertion that water is a public good and a right, not a commodity, and has now been refined and strengthened by advocacy organizations in India and South Africa, by international NGOs, and by the UN's Committee on ESC Rights' General Comment 15.

What contributions have human rights standards, strategies, methods and analysis made to policy outcomes? Many of the most important impacts are broad and in process: human rights advocacy, for example, has provided protection to development, labor and environmental activists through programs designed specifically to support and 'defend the defenders.' In other cases, the human rights principle of non-discrimination has been invoked in campaigns to end administrative, legal and police practices that stigmatize or otherwise discriminate against HIV/AIDS patients. Advocacy campaigns are in the early stages of what may, in the end, be a successful reframing of water privatization, where the human rights analysis of water policy has successfully entered the mainstream of debate in international organizations.

Demonstrated impacts on policy outcomes to date have been of three kinds: blocking policy changes at the national level, modifying international rules, and constraining the exercise of international power. Rights-based advocates have succeeded in *blocking policy changes,* in effect upholding the state's obligation to *respect* ESC human rights, by campaigning against certain water privatization schemes. With respect to *international rules,* the clearest but still partial success has come in the deliberations over TRIPS rules in the WTO. Finally, human rights-based campaigns have become an important source of moral suasion in the advocates' efforts to soften the positions of pharmaceutical companies on patent issues, and of the World Bank on water privatization in Ghana and elsewhere.

Whereas HIV/AIDS advocates have had some success intervening in international rule-making to allow domestic production of generic versions of patented HIV medications, water advocates have largely focused on blocking new contracts for private provision of water. To date, advocates have been more successful in mobilizing political support by invoking ESC rights than in using the ESC standards analytically to define the details of policy solutions, although there is evidence of efforts in this area by development practitioners.

Conclusions and Implications for Theory and Practice

The New Rights Advocacy—the expansion of traditional human rights groups' agendas to incorporate economic and social rights, the appearance of new economic and social rights issues campaign and organizations, and the adoption by development organizations of rights-based approaches—is a relatively new phenomenon. But the cases observed here . . . provide enough evidence to reach three early conclusions.

First, the use of human rights standards to influence social and economic policy is growing rapidly. Its *practice* is varied, and advocates rely heavily on the rhetoric of human rights in international circles, even as they experiment with other human rights methods—litigation, investigation and documentation, for example—and occasionally on formal regional and international human rights bodies. . . . Detailed policy proposals explicitly grounded in human rights remain largely the domain of scholars and UN agency functionaries.

ESC rights are attracting broader attention, support, and more careful definition and operationalization, just as civil and political rights did in the 1960s, but their institutionalization is still in an early stage. . . . As ESC rights advocates test the possibilities and the present limitations of their influence, there is evidence of a trend toward broader NGO use of the political, mobilizing, and motivational power of economic and social human rights.

Second, the principal International Relations accounts of NGO participation in international politics—in which NGOs help to bring recalcitrant states under the scrutiny of international agencies and industrial country governments—is in need of revision or supplementation. The political environment in which ESC rights advocacy takes place puts advocates in a different relation to poor country governments, and to sources of political leverage in the international political arena. At times they oppose and condemn the violating state, at others they attempt to shift responsibility for violations to the international level and onto economic actors.

ESC rights advocates do sometimes 'target' governments with external pressure, as in their appeals to reverse water privatization contracts, but the international pressure has come almost entirely from NGOs, social movements and the media, not from international organizations and G-8 governments. This is a new and distinct pattern of political action; rather than an appeal to norms whose resonance is stronger in international arenas than in the target government, much ESC rights advocacy appeals to human rights standards that have stronger support in the countries of the global South than among industrial country governments. It reinforces domestic sovereignty, rather than challenging it, and applies the leverage derived from international human rights to limiting or reforming the influence of international actors. . . .

[F]ulfilling economic and social rights may involve reinforcing international norms, while also calling for greater freedom for national governments and societies to set policy without reference to conditions set by international agencies. The effort to expand access to HIV/AIDS medicines in poor countries, for example, has successfully created temporary exceptions to WTO rules on intellectual property and patents, supporting the initiatives of governments such as India, South Africa and Brazil to produce cheaper generic medicines. . . .

These advocacy strategies do not signal a wholesale reversal by NGOs, which still call for stronger international regulation of child labor, natural resource management, and labor rights. Domestic and international AIDS activists put a great deal of pressure on the South African government of Thabo Mbeki to accept and respond to the epidemiology of HIV, a pattern that conforms to the 'boomerang' model. But the new rights advocacy does represent a significant shift toward a more complex and varied relationship with poor country governments, often strategically supporting and cooperating with national authorities. One effect of this changing pattern is that NGO advocates are likely to have to learn to work without US government cooperation. The United States' aggressive, if inconsistent, support of some environmental and civil and political human rights reforms is unlikely to extend to rights-based claims to social services, or access to land or water, where the Scandinavian and British governments' development agencies have been more sympathetic.

The third theme—the one on which conclusions are most difficult—is the assessment of the New Rights Advocacy's impact. Has the NRA decisively affected policy outcomes, and what role have human rights-based strategies played in those outcomes? Advocacy on economic and social policy to date has not gathered the record of successes that is often attributed to advocates of civil and political rights. . . .

ESC advocates' greatest challenge may be that the rights they advocate confront well-established norms of a market-oriented development paradigm, against which NGO advocates had little success in the 1980s and 1990s. Research is needed to test the impact of ESC rights over the coming decade by monitoring the strategies and impact of advocacy, especially on issues that directly confront norms of liberalization, privatization, and free trade.

Whether such advocacy strategies can succeed, and to what extent, without significant support from the US government or the most influential international organizations, remains to be seen. The answer is, perhaps, even more strongly dependent on whether significant constituencies can be built globally, than in the case of civil and political rights four decades ago. The record of human rights-based advocacy on social and economic policy suggests that broad and diverse configurations of participants can be expected. . . .

11.2

GETTING DOWN TO BUSINESS ON HUMAN RIGHTS

from *The Age*

The next selection describes how the spread of human rights norms has altered the environment in which business operates. It describes the special constraints imposed by such norms on the conduct of extractive industries like mining as human rights norms are globalized.

"The business of business is business," wrote US economist Milton Friedman, but human rights advocates are making it their business to change that. The notion of human rights as solely a government responsibility—or regulation within borders—has shifted, say Castan centre academics Adam McBeth and Joanna Kyriakakis.

The conduct of big business is coming under increasing scrutiny, they say, especially in developing nations and war zones. This gives hope greater protection will be possible in a globalised world. The mining sector is a particular focus. Miners operate in countries where the most egregious human rights abuses—genocide, war crimes and crimes against humanity—can occur. Dr McBeth offers a hypothetical: "If you were to say, 'We're not going to accept what Shell is doing in Nigeria, government needs to hold Shell responsible for that.' Whose laws do you use? Nigeria's? UK's? Netherlands'? The countries of all the shareholders . . ."? This is the new legal frontier: to develop ways of holding multinational corporations—some of them richer than the economies of some states—to account for breaches of human rights standards. "There's been the appointment of the Special Representative of the UN [on business and human rights, in 2005], and there's now a growing recognition that human rights are relevant to the companies and certainly to the World Bank and the various regional development banks," he says.

Source: "Getting Down to Business on Human Rights," *The Age,* October 26, 2010.

11.3

GROUP CRITICISES NARROW
VIEW OF ISLAMIC LAW

from *The New Zealand Herald*

> The following selection describes a meeting in New Zealand at which a
> Muslim group explains that Islamic women are protected by the same human
> rights as other women. When they are deprived of those rights, it is a
> consequence of an unnecessarily rigid interpretation of Islamic law.

The "conservative, literal and narrow interpretation" of Sharia law by Muslim leaders is
the real problem facing Muslims, an Auckland public forum on human rights was told
last night.

Ratna Osman, acting executive director of the Malaysian-based group Sisters of Islam,
said debate was needed for Islam to be better understood.

"But fear has been instilled . . . and we don't talk about things that Muslims are sensitive about," she said.

About 40 people, mainly non-Muslims, attended the "Muslim Women Rights is Human
Rights" forum at the Auckland University of Technology.

Ms Osman's group is opposed to the traditional Muslim teaching that men are superior to women, and criticises Sharia (Islamic) law as being "human constructed" and
"not divine."

Group founder Zainah Anwar said the law was therefore "fallible, changeable, given
a different time and context."

The group also says Islam has no laws making burqa-wearing compulsory.

Race Relations Commissioner Joris de Bres, who has previously said laws banning
Muslims from wearing veils amount to discrimination on grounds of religious belief,
would not comment on whether those forcing women to wear burqas were in breach of
NZ's human rights laws.

Javed Khan, vice-president of the Federation of Islamic Associations of New Zealand,
said he did not share many of the views of Sisters of Islam, which he described as a
"splinter group."

He said a public debate on matters such as the burqa would just raise further confusion about Islam and further isolate Muslim women who wore the garment.

Mr Khan reckoned only about 100 women, from a Muslim population in New
Zealand estimated at between 45,000 and 55,000, wore a niqab or a burqa.

Source: "Group Criticises Narrow View of Islamic Law," *The New Zealand Herald,* July 22, 2011.

11.4

UNITED NATIONS CHIEF CALLS ON US TO HAND OVER INFORMATION

from *The Herald* (Glasgow)

On May 2, 2011, Osama bin Laden, the charismatic leader of al Qaeda and for years a target of America's "War on Terror" owing to his leading role in planning the 9/11 attacks on New York City and Washington, D.C., was killed in a gunfight with U.S. Navy SEALs in his compound in the Pakistani city of Abbottabad. Thereafter, he was buried at sea, and his death was widely applauded, especially in the United States. Could bin Laden have been arrested and tried for the crimes committed at his behest, and was his death a violation of his rights under international law? The following selection describes the controversy that surrounded these questions raised in the international community.

The United Nations top human rights official has called on America to give the UN details about Osama bin Laden's killing and said that all counter-terrorism operations must respect international law.

Navi Pillay, UN High Commissioner for Human Rights, said that the al Qaeda leader, had committed crimes against humanity as self-confessed mastermind of the most appalling acts of terrorism, including the September 11 attacks in New York.

It was always clear that taking bin Laden alive was likely to be difficult, she said, noting US authorities had stated that they intended to arrest him.

This was a complex operation and it would be helpful if we knew the precise facts surrounding his killing.

The United Nations has consistently emphasised that all counter-terrorism acts must respect international law, Ms Pillay said.

While many world leaders applauded the US operation that killed the al Qaeda leader, there were concerns in parts of Europe that the United States was wrong to act as judge, jury and executioner.

US Attorney General Eric Holder defended the action as lawful yesterday, but some in Europe said bin Laden should have been put on trial.

It was quite clearly a violation of international law, said former West German Chancellor Helmut Schmidt, adding: The operation could also have incalculable consequences in the Arab world in light of all the unrest.

Source: "United Nations Chief Calls on US to Hand Over Information," *The Herald* (Glasgow), May 4, 2011.

Ehrhart Koerting, interior minister in the city state of Berlin, said: As a lawyer, I would have preferred to have seen him put on trial at the International Criminal Court.

Gert-Jan Knoops, a Dutch-based international law specialist, said bin Laden should have been arrested and extradited to the US.

He drew parallels with the arrest of former Yugoslav president Slobodan Milosevic, who was put on trial at the war crimes tribunal in The Hague after his arrest in 2001.

The Americans say they are at war with terrorism and can take out their opponents on the battlefield, Mr Knoops said. But in a strictly formal sense, this argument does not stand up.

Reed Brody, counsel at New York-based Human Rights Watch, said it was too early to say whether the US operation was legal because too few details were known.

We would want to know what the orders were, what the rules of engagement were. We want to know exactly what happened . . . and what the US alleges that bin Laden was actually engaged in, he said.

Is the world a better place because bin Laden is not here? People can obviously answer that question. But does that mean you have the right to violate protocols of human rights or international law to do that? Then no.

It may be that we may never know enough.

In Brussels, EU Home Affairs Commissioner Cecilia Malmstrom wrote in a blog: It would have been preferred to see bin Laden before a court.

In Italy, former prime minister Massimo D Alema, from the centre-left opposition, said: You don't rejoice at the death of a man.

Maybe if bin Laden had been captured and put on trial it would have been an even more significant victory.

Meanwhile, Mr Holder said: If he was captured and brought before a court, I have no doubt he would have been charged with the most serious crimes, including the mass murder of civilians that took place on 9/11, which were planned and systematic and in my view amounted to a crime against humanity.

11.5

AS MUSLIM WOMEN SUFFER, FEMINISTS AVERT THEIR GAZE

Robert Fulford

The final selection describes how a female journalist in Sudan invited fellow journalists to witness her being flogged for the "crime" of wearing trousers! The author of the article goes on to argue that Western feminists have not been sufficiently concerned with the ways in which Muslim women may be oppressed when governed by Islamic law.

Source: Robert Fulford, "As Muslim Women Suffer, Feminists Avert Their Gaze," *National Post,* July 25, 2009.

Lubna Ahmed al-Hussein, an angry Khartoum journalist who works for the UN in Sudan, has started a campaign against shariah law by elevating a local police matter into an international embarrassment: She's invited the world to witness her judicial flogging, thus making her case part of the struggle between religious traditionalists and independent women—a struggle that now may encompass the quadruple murder that was revealed a world away, in Kingston, Ont., on Thursday.

In Khartoum, the General Discipline Police Authority patrols the streets, charged with maintaining shariah standards of public decency. Recently it raided a restaurant and arrested 13 women, including al-Hussein, for the crime of . . . wearing trousers.

Since 1991, that's been a violation of the Sudanese criminal code. More precisely, it is classified as a violation of public morality. While erratically enforced, the rule is serious enough to carry a penalty of 40 lashes. Ten of the women arrested with al-Hussein pleaded guilty and received a reduced sentence of 10 lashes. But al-Hussein and two others demanded their day in court and al-Hussein decided to provoke a scandal by distributing 500 personal invitations to her trial. She expects to be found guilty (she won't be allowed a lawyer or a chance to speak), so she informed her guests that they'll also be expected at her flogging.

The French government has condemned the law, and in Cairo the Arabic Network for Human Rights Information (ANHRI) has launched a campaign to defend al-Hussein and the others. ANHRI also protested a suit brought by the police against another journalist, Amal Habbani, for an article praising al-Hussein ("A Case of Subduing a Woman's Body"). The police claim that the mere act of defending female pants-wearing also violates General Discipline.

When stories such as al-Hussein's flash around the world, there's usually a missing element: The feminist movement rarely becomes part of the narrative. The rise of shariah law constitutes the major global change in women's status during this era, yet Western feminists remain pathetically silent.

Feminist journalists like to speculate about the future of activism among women today, but you can leaf through a fat sheaf of their articles without encountering a mention of Muslim women. Feminist professors, for their part, show even less interest. Trolling through the 40-page program of the European Conference on Politics and Gender, held in Belfast last winter, I found feminist scholars (from Europe, the United States and Canada) dealing with women's political opportunities, the implications for women of new medical technology, the politics of fashion and even women's response to climate change. What I couldn't find was even one lecture or discussion devoted to so-called "honour killing." Nor was there any mention of the thousands upon thousands of women routinely flogged, raped, imprisoned or stoned to death, often with the tacit or explicit agreement of Islamic governments.

The recent Kingston murders—in which a Quebec couple stand accused of killing their three daughters (and the man's first wife) because, according to one relative, the daughters had adopted disgracefully Western habits—apparently demonstrate that the oppression of women can be imported into countries where it has no support in law. Honour killing, far from being an isolated remnant of a primitive past, seems to be increasingly widespread.

Ayse Onal, a leading Turkish journalist, says in her book, *Honour Killing: Stories of Men Who Killed*, that in Turkey alone honour killings average about one a day—1,806 were reported in the period between 2000 and 2005, a number I found astonishing. The justifications for this crime, passed by word of mouth, apparently encourage young men and boys to consider it appropriate punishment for even trivial offences of females. Onal quotes a 14-year-old boy who slit his 16-year-old sister's throat in the public market of the town of Urfa. Asked if he was remorseful, he explained that she had been "going about in cafes" and he had cleansed his dignity by killing her. Sentenced to 10 years, he served 34 months. (The use of brothers to commit the vile deed is a particularly horrible aspect of honour killings. In the Kingston murders, it is worth noting, one of those arrested was the alleged killer's 18-year-old son.)

Once in a while, a few women in the West notice. On Monday, Pamela Geller, a conservative blogger in the United States, suggested that women everywhere should stand up for al-Hussein. She called the silence of women's movements "scandalous, shameful, complicit in the horrible suppression of women in Islam." But more typical is the feminist blog of Deborah Kate, who acknowledges that feminists have been accused of ignoring Muslim women. Kate comes out against stoning, enforced marriage, female circumcision, etc., and wonders idly whether countries guilty of crimes against women deserve sanctions like those levelled at South Africa in its apartheid days. No, she decides, exhibiting the fondness for fashionable moral relativism that is now epidemic in feminist circles, "I realize I cannot force my version of feminism upon non-Western women."

Chapter 12

IS GLOBALIZATION A GOOD THING?

Globalization poses significant normative questions, the central topic of this chapter. The materials that follow encourage you to think through the variety of arguments urging or opposing greater globalization. Those critical of globalization—ranging from Marxists and anarchists to nationalists, environmentalists, and labor unions—make a variety of claims. Among other things, they argue that globalization is antidemocratic, reduces wages, lowers environmental and safety standards, increases inequality within and between states, reduces welfare, undermines unique traditions and cultures, and encourages irresponsible, risk-taking economic behavior. In contrast, globalization enthusiasts argue that it increases overall wealth and efficiency, provides an unprecedented range of consumer goods at affordable cost, spreads democracy and human rights, reduces the probability of war, and eradicates reprehensible local practices and customs.

12.1

GLOBALIZATION: LOVE IT OR LOATHE IT?[1]

Richard W. Mansbach

Globalization has passionate supporters and critics, a fact that owes much to the contradictions apparent in globalizing trends. On the one hand, Joseph Stiglitz, a Nobel Prize winner in economics, argues that globalization has favored special interests in the West at the expense of the developing world. "But even when not guilty of hypocrisy," he concludes, "the West has driven the globalization agenda, ensuring that it garners a disproportionate share of the benefits, at the expense of the developing world."[2] On the other, globalization enthusiast Jagdish Bhagwati cites declining poverty, especially in India and China, and concludes,

> So when we have moved away from the anti-globalization rhetoric and looked at the fears, even convictions, dispassionately with the available empirical evidence, we can conclude . . . that globalization helps, not harms, the cause of poverty reduction in the poor countries.[3]

Laissez-faire capitalism, based on free trade, free movement of investment, deregulation, and market competition, seems to be responsible for *both* the rising standards of living and the spread of financial crises and panics. Globalization connects people more closely, exposes them to new ideas, and gives them access to unprecedented amounts of information, while simultaneously producing a sense of vulnerability to remote forces that threaten people's livelihood, welfare, and cultural uniqueness. To some, globalization is the face of modernity that promises the demise of war-making states and the eradication of harmful social mores. Globalization spreads wealth and innovation while also spreading disease and crime. Globalization popularizes democracy while, in some respects, making the world less democratic.

Criticisms of Globalization

The "Democratic Deficit"

Critics of globalization claim that the institutions that are the pillars of globalization—corporations, international institutions like the World Trade Organization (WTO), and regional groups like the European Union—arc not accountable to voters and rob citizens of a democratic voice in determining their future. They decry the erosion of state capacity as detrimental to citizens, arguing that states exist to protect citizens' welfare. Democracy, in their view, was created by nation-states and affords citizen participation in decision making and a national identity.

Sovereignty, which should ensure a state's freedom from foreign intervention, frequently fails to do so and does not protect states from pressures from international organizations and corporations that compete with one another. As a result, states are surrendering responsibility for citizens' welfare. According to critics, even during the global financial crisis that began in 2007, the behavior of banks and corporations showed scant regard for public welfare and, despite high unemployment, corporate and bank executives received enormous financial bonuses.

Citizens have little voice in the boardrooms of corporations, in remote international bureaucracies like the WTO, in economic markets, or in unelected nongovernmental organizations (NGOs). Instead, corporations are accountable to managers and stockholders. Corporate policies may be good or bad, but what matters is that neither governments nor citizens have a voice in determining those policies. International institutions like the International Monetary Fund (IMF) impose conditions on states that borrow from them, which governments have little choice but to accept. Thus, in 2010 Greece was forced to impose painful austerity policies on its citizens in return for loan guarantees from the European Union and the IMF. In sum, globalization, critics argue, has created a "democratic deficit" by empowering institutions that are not accountable to citizens and forcing governments to pursue economic, political, and social policies that their publics have not approved and sometimes vigorously oppose.

"Casino Capitalism"

"Casino capitalism"[4] and market competition are viewed by globalization critics as limiting states' capacity to determine their economic destinies. As the collapse of

America's subprime mortgage market and the subsequent global financial crisis reveal, rapid movements of capital can trigger financial volatility and even financial collapse. Global competition among states to increase exports and attract investment, argue critics, is responsible for reducing the ability of governments to provide citizens with welfare and social security. Unregulated market competition forces countries to shed jobs, reduce taxes, end welfare policies, and reduce wages in order to become more efficient in a competitive capitalist world. Thus, globalization produces a change in states' priorities as the imperative of global competition reduces the provision of welfare for citizens and concentrates wealth in ever fewer hands.

Growing Economic Inequality: Distributive Injustice?

The result of changes in government policies, according to critics, has been an increase in economic inequality between and within countries. The claim that economic inequality accompanies globalization is hotly debated. Indeed, the answer is colored by different definitions of "inequality" and "poverty" and by disagreement about how to measure them. Does inequality mean income differences, unequal opportunity, or what? Does it refer to inequality between countries, genders, ethnic groups, or individuals? Such differences in definition lead to different answers about whether global inequality is growing.

Conclusions about inequality also depend on how inequality is measured. If we are comparing individuals, then inequality may appear high owing to debt burdens that are the result of neoliberal economics. Inequality appears to be growing *within* states, especially between rural and urban regions, threatening social stability. Urban–rural inequality also results from the policy of developed countries to limit agricultural imports from poor countries. Household incomes are also becoming more unequal, largely as a result of differential access to technology.

Market capitalism has enriched some countries more than others. For example, free trade has benefited exporters of labor-intensive goods like China and India more than it has low-income, commodity-dependent countries like the Ivory Coast. Central Europe and Latin America have grown less than East and Southeast Asia. Indeed, measuring inequality is muddied by the impact of two countries, China and India. Conclusions about inequality depend heavily on whether or not these two countries, which account for most of the reduction in world poverty, are included in the analysis. If the calculations account for these countries' huge populations, it appears that global inequality is less than if we count all countries equally regardless of population.

A "Race to the Bottom"

Critics believe that global competition, the absence of democracy, and inequality produce "a race to the bottom." Owing to globalization, corporations move to countries with low wages and poor environmental and labor standards to remain competitive. Globalization opponents claim that huge movements of capital have produced a global labor market in which workers compete with one another. Although capital is mobile, workers are less so, placing them at a disadvantage. If workers seek higher wages, corporations leave and move elsewhere. According to critics, such "outsourcing" first led to an outflow of jobs from rich countries like the United States to poor countries in Latin

America and Southeast Asia, which, in turn, are losing jobs to China and India. Marxist critics go further, arguing that globalization is a form of "imperialism." Nevertheless, all of globalization's critics agree that there is a need for enforceable global safety, environmental, and labor standards.

Cultural Erosion

Some critics also claim that the information and communication technologies of globalization are spreading a global culture, originally American, based on individualism, secularism, consumerism, neoliberal capitalism, and liberal democracy that undermines traditional cultures and the authority of traditional elites. Globalization, they suggest, is producing a superficial consumerist culture that promotes individualism and greed, spreads pornography, and erodes moral standards. Mass media controlled by the West, along with migration and tourism, result in what critics view as cultural uniformity that is evident in dress, diet, advertising, and political views. Some critics contend that cultural uniformity constitutes a form of Western neocolonialism that leaves no role for non-Western values. To buttress this claim, they point to the dominance of English as the single language of economics and technology.

National and religious groups bridle at the threat they perceive to their uniqueness, dignity, and values. The resulting erosion of local mores and traditional values produces resentment, which results in a backlash by those seeking to protect their cultural uniqueness. The spread of Islamic fundamentalism is partly a reaction to the secularism of globalization.

Migration, Crime, Terrorism, and Disease

In enabling migration as part of an effort by poor people seeking jobs in wealthy countries, globalization, argue its critics, also promotes transnational criminal networks, the spread of disease, and transnational terrorism. Illegal migrants enjoy fewer rights than citizens and are thereby denied human rights. Migration also disrupts local communities and encourages transnational criminal industries in drug smuggling and human trafficking. Migration frequently involves trafficking in women and children as part of the global sex trade and demand for domestic servants. As a result, women are particularly vulnerable to human rights abuses associated with globalization.

Transnational criminal networks have made use of globalization much as have other business enterprises, utilizing partnerships, diversification, and financial expertise. Guns, for instance, flow southward from the United States to Mexico, arming the Mexican drug cartels, while drugs flow northward. Moreover, cooperation between terrorists and drug cartels is widespread, with drug profits providing terrorists with hard currency to buy weapons and corrupting government officials, thereby undermining state institutions in countries like Mexico and Jamaica. Terrorists and rebels, as well as criminals, use new technologies to coordinate in cyberspace, launder funds, and create a demand for the illegal transnational trade in arms. The UN estimates that there are about 500 million small arms circulating in the world. A single Russian arms dealer, Viktor Bout, is said to have evaded UN arms embargoes and provided weapons to the Taliban in Afghanistan, the Hizbullah in Lebanon, and Islamic militants in Somalia.

Disease is also globalized as migrants and tourists travel around the world. In recent decades, SARS, H1N1 influenza, and HIV/AIDS have spread along with globalization.

The Antiglobalization Movement

The critics of globalization have mobilized to reform and even reverse globalization. It is widely believed that the antiglobalization movement began to coalesce into the 1999 protests against the WTO in Seattle. Additional protests, some violent, have taken place in Washington, D.C., Genoa, Prague, Québec City, Seoul, and Pittsburgh. Hundreds of groups with different objectives were involved in these protests.

The diverse movement that appeared in Seattle coalesced into the World Social Forum (WSF), which initially gathered in Brazil, in 2001. The WSF was intended to be the antithesis of the proglobalization World Economic Forum of public and private economic leaders, which gathers every year in Davos, Switzerland. According to its Charter of Principles, the WSF opposes globalization, as well as the transnational corporations, the governments of wealthy states, and the international institutions that foster globalization. The Final Declaration of the 2009 WSF meeting, which took place during the global financial crisis, took a radically anticapitalist position, declaring, "We won't pay for the crisis. The rich have to pay for it! Anti-imperialist, anticapitalist, feminist, environmentalist and socialist alternatives are necessary."[5]

In Praise of Globalization

Advocates of globalization seem to be looking at an entirely different world than globalization's critics. They interpret differently the same issues discussed by critics and reach opposite conclusions. Many look forward to a world without independent states and foresee transnational corporations, international economic institutions, and global civil society as the means to efficiency, prosperity, peace, and cosmopolitanism. Expanding global governance, they believe, spreads progressive norms that improve women's status, enhance human rights, and encourage cooperation in curbing environmental deterioration. The result is growing recognition of collective problems through the formation of new international rules and mechanisms.

States and Democracy

Globalization's advocates view sovereign states as war-making machines. Despite popular sovereignty, decisions about war and peace and the distribution of wealth, they argue, remain in the hands of small elites that encourage nationalism to produce unity. Its supporters argue that globalization has reduced the likelihood of war by increasing interdependence among peoples, spreading democratic values, and reducing nationalism. Globalization is replacing ideologies that divided the world in the 20th century with a single ideology based on liberal democracy that will ensure a "democratic peace."

In response to critics who cite a "democratic deficit," proglobalizers contend that technologies such as the Internet and cell phones provide new opportunities for democracy and the exchange of views, along with unprecedented access to information. Such technologies make possible "electronic democracy." Advocates praise globalization processes that deepen interdependence, spread human rights norms, increase humanitarian relief, promote NGOs and governance, erode state exclusivity, encourage migration, and mix cultures. For such reasons, supporters of globalization see the erosion of state autonomy as a great accomplishment.

Greater Wealth

Independent states, contend globalization enthusiasts, are economically inefficient. In contrast, globalization has alleviated poverty and has reduced inequality, reversing a long-term trend. Growth rates in poor countries have accelerated, becoming even faster than in rich countries, and the number of those living in poverty has declined precipitously. Where income inequality is growing, it is because wage increases in highly globalized countries have risen more quickly than they have in less globalized countries. In any event, efficiency, advocates believe, is more important than inequality because it means that overall wealth is growing and poverty is declining. Thus, in recent decades the poverty rate in East Asia declined from 80% to less than 20%.

Why has wealth increased? Proglobalizers contend that prosperity is a result of the free movement of capital and labor, and competition among states and corporations. The free market gives consumers a greater choice of inexpensive goods and reduces inflation. Although obsolete industries decline and workers lose jobs, innovative industries thrive and increase employment, leading to growth and higher living standards.

Global Culture

Globalization advocates deny that a global culture is overwhelming local cultures or that new technologies are not beneficial. Critics, globalization advocates claim, underestimate the resilience of local cultures and their tendency to assimilate global values. Globalization encourages a healthy mixing of cultures that involves the exchange of ideas and styles in cyberspace and in the course of travel and migration. Globalization is also bringing an end to reprehensible cultural anachronisms such as female genital mutilation in Africa and "honor killings" in the Islamic and Hindu worlds. Migration may have negative aspects, but labor mobility is imperative to achieve economic efficiency. The alternative to moving surplus labor from poor countries to rich countries is exporting jobs from rich countries to poor ones, where less expensive labor and less state regulation reduce production costs. Moreover, aging populations in rich countries means growing welfare costs to support the elderly and fewer young workers to pay the taxes needed to pay for the rising health and retirement entitlements of the elderly.

Globalization advocates conclude that new technologies are spreading progressive ideas that make it harder for authoritarian regimes to act abusively toward their citizens. Access to information creates an informed citizenry and fosters individuals' ability to mobilize in cyberspace, thereby contributing to a diversity of views and the networking of NGOs for civil society.

Conclusion

Notwithstanding the arguments of globalization's advocates and foes, any final judgment of such a complex process must be mixed. Globalization increases interdependence but does not eliminate interstate rivalries. Wars among states have become rarer, but civil strife has spread. Globalization limits state capacity, triggering public pressure on governments for protection from external forces, while enhancing opportunities for global trade. Globalization enriches many but spreads economic crises swiftly. Cultural globalization pits the virtues of tradition against the virtues of change and diversity. Political globalization is accompanied by a proliferation of international organizations and NGOs while reducing state autonomy. Civil society and governance spread but do so only slowly. At the end of the day, globalization seems a modernizing force to many, yet for many others it is perceived as threatening, something to be feared and resented.

Notes

1 For a lengthy and in-depth analysis of some of the issues dealt with in this brief essay, see Yale H. Ferguson and Richard W. Mansbach, *Globalization: The Return of Borders to a Borderless World?* (Abingdon, UK: Routledge, 2012), chapter 6.
2 Joseph E. Stiglitz, *Globalization and Its Discontents* (New York: W. W. Norton, 2002), 7.
3 Jagdish Bhagwati, *In Defense of Globalization* (Oxford, UK: Oxford University Press, 2004), 66.
4 See Susan Strange, *Casino Capitalism* (Manchester, UK: Manchester University Press, 1997).
5 "Final Declaration of 2009 World Social Forum Meeting in Brazil," http://www.haitianalysis .com/international-relations/final-declaration-of-2009-world-social-forum-meeting-in-brazil.

12.2

WHO SAYS GLOBALIZATION IS BAD?

from *The Nikkei Weekly*

As part of modernization and the spread of ideas, globalization is enabling workers to move from poor countries to seek a better life and is putting an end to reprehensible cultural traditions, such as India's caste system. The next selection, from a Japanese newspaper, describes how economic reforms in India allowed a lower-caste Indian to move with his firm to Japan and thereafter to prosper. It argues that globalization is reducing wealth disparities and global poverty. Nevertheless, in addition to making "winners," globalization also results in "losers," who resent and are hostile to globalization. Governments, the author concludes, have an obligation to assist the latter.

Who says globalization is bad?

Some blame trend for spreading disparity, yet poverty has declined; better to glean positives, cushion negatives than jump ship, turn inward. There was a time when

Source: "Who Says Globalization Is Bad?" *The Nikkei Weekly,* March 30, 2009.

Hunachgiry, 34, could not have even imagined working in Japan. Today, however, he works for the Japanese subsidiary of a leading Indian information-technology firm. He is the first from his small village in southern India to go abroad.

India's over 3,000-year-old caste system is a symbol of class-based disparity. Low-caste children are left uneducated, and adults have limited job options. Hunachgiry is of a lower caste, but his life began to change in 1991, when India, in response to the currency crisis, implemented policies to liberalize its economy.

These included deregulation, opening to foreign capital, and job training. Credited with the invention of zero, India has long been known for high mathematical aptitude among its people. And the new government policy was immediately effective, allowing more people to reach their potential.

On His Feet

Now a college graduate with computer programming skills, Hunachgiry earns 7 million yen ($71,000) annually—far beyond the dreams of his fellow villagers, who generally live on only about 200,000 yen a year. He feels India has become nearly caste-free in the last 20 years. The new wealth of emerging economies like India, China, Brazil, Indonesia and Mexico has resulted in a rapidly growing middle class.

And as globalization has fused regional economies together, the old structure that concentrated wealth in developed countries has begun to change.

The Gini coefficient, which indexes overall income disparity on a scale of 0-1 (small to large), fell from 0.67 in 1970 to 0.61 in 2006 on a global basis, according to U.S. Columbia University Prof. Xavier Sala-i-Martin. World Bank statistics show that the population of the poor—defined as those who live on $1.25 or less a day—has decreased by 500 million people over 25 years. These are indicators of the spreading benefits of economic growth. And so, speaking macroeconomically, there is insufficient evidence to suggest globalization has made things worse, as some contend.

Sala-i-Martin notes that since the beginning of the new century, even Africa has begun to shake off poverty. It would be egotistical for developed nations, now in recession, to advocate moves against globalization after having benefited so much from it. Doing so would deprive people in the developing world of their right to a richer life.

On the other hand, globalization does force many people to face a harsh reality. One 44-year-old man, laid off in November by an appliance maker in Morioka, Iwate Prefecture, sent out 30 copies of his resume in hopes of getting another manu-facturing job. He came up empty, and in late January, he settled into Tsukui Corp., which provides care-giving services. The kind of job he wanted had simply "evaporated," as the global recession coincided with a corporate shift to optimum global labor procurement.

This reality nurtures hostility against globalization. Case in point: The Pew Research Center of the U.S. asked people in various countries whether they believe that world trade is beneficial to their countries. Comparing results from 2002 and 2007, the per-centage of positive responses dropped most in the U.S., often considered the biggest believer in free markets.

Go It Alone?

Globalization brings both darkness and light, but if we choose isolation as a result, the world will be pushed into a balanced contraction. What is needed now is the wisdom to draw the positives from globalization while cushioning the negatives.

Many countries pursuing social democratic ideas and those valuing market economies have fundamentally similar policy priorities, such as guaranteeing basic living for the poor and unemployed, assisting part-time workers toward self-sustainment, and balancing labor-market needs.

The weak should not just be rescued, but rather helped back into the labor market. Collectively, these are sometimes known as "trampoline policies." As Prof. Kenzo Kashino at Tezukayama University put it, "Safety nets represent the cost of protecting the free market."

While social democracy values redistribution of income by greater taxation on higher-income earners, market economies tend to support corporate tax cuts and similar measures to promote growth and attract investment. Opinions are also divided over labor regulations, but such hurdles are not impossible to clear.

There are signs that the world is becoming more inward-looking, with moves to pull back from globalization in favor of easy dependence on government and opposition to market mechanisms. Such reflex actions, however, will not improve the current situation. It is important to prevent a U-turn against globalization out of desperation.

12.3

"THE GLORY OF GLOBALIZATION"

Samuel J. Palmisano

> The following selection contains the remarks of Samuel J. Palmisano, chairman, president and chief executive of IBM in which he praises the results of globalization in general and for Canada in particular. Palmisano equates globalization with innovation, arguing that claims that it produces "a race to the bottom" or cultural erosion are baseless and that globalization should not be feared. Instead, there are steps countries can take such as improving education that will stimulate innovation.

No matter where we look today, it seems we find ourselves looking at planet Earth. Whether we are talking about the environment, or economics, or geopolitics, or communications and technology, the discussion inevitably evolves to a global perspective.

Source: Samuel J. Palmisano, "The Glory of Globalization," *National Post,* July 21, 2007.

But when we consider this global picture, is the smart response for Canada hope or fear?

Recently, IBM hosted a forum in St. Petersburg, Russia, to discuss the issues surrounding business and technology innovation. We conduct gatherings like this regularly around the world, bringing in government, business and academic leaders. This session was our most heavily booked ever—with a waiting list of CEOs and 430 high-level attendees from 55 countries, including Canada.

These leaders don't come to hear IBM sales pitches for our products and services—and those are never mentioned. In fact, these forums aren't even like most innovation-themed conferences. We don't focus on products, services and technologies at all. Rather, we consider the more complex and important forms of innovation—business processes, management systems, policies, culture and basic business models. And as probably won't surprise you, this topic is top of mind for CEOs and other leaders today.

However, something different happened this year in St. Petersburg. As each discussion proceeded, the CEOs and government officials couldn't stop debating and discussing something else: the issue of globalization. Is it good or bad? Deflationary? Culture-erasing? A challenge to how we run our organizations? The way out of poverty and obscurity for billions? Something that exacerbates the gap between haves and have-nots? All of the above?

These exchanges only strengthened my belief that globalization and innovation are not, in fact, separate phenomena. They are two sides of the same coin.

Globalization is the new playing field, the arena in which the competitive game from now on will be played—whether that game is economics, technology, politics or culture. And innovation is the only way you are going to win in that arena.

Pretty straightforward. But by missing this key interconnection between innovation and globalization, critics in Canada and around the world misunderstand what globalization is all about.

In the countries of the developed world, some people worry about globalization's economic impact. They see it as a "race to the bottom" and fear its effect on their own job security, wages and standard of living. A recent survey IBM conducted along with The Economist Intelligence Unit ranks Canada fifth in a worldwide "financial sophistication index" used to trace the impact of globalization across 35 of the world's most critical national economies. Obviously, there is worry over whether Canada will continue in that position or sink in the rankings as such countries as India (ranked 28th) and China (ranked 32nd) continue to modernize.

But there also are critics in the developing world, who fear globalization for other reasons. They are concerned about its supposedly "homogenizing" effect as a threat to their culture and traditions. They believe globalization is simply another word for colonization.

While these fears are understandable, I think they are largely unfounded—and that came through loud and clear in St. Petersburg. First, global integration is about much more than lower costs. If it were only cost, why would Canada rank sixth in the world in another IBM study that collated public-domain statistics concerning inward investment projects established by multinational companies involved in manufacturing, services and R&D in 2005?

The forces driving global integration are deeper and subtler, and they offer opportunities to everyone, not just low-cost providers, who sooner or later find their competitive advantage has vanished.

Second, far from moving us toward a common global culture, I am convinced that global integration is driving greater differentiation. Increased economic value is flowing to countries and companies who figure out their strengths and what makes them special. For sure, the countries and companies represented at our forum are focused with laser-like attention on what their unique strengths are, and on how each of them should adapt to the challenging and ultimately promising reality of global integration.

What these leaders were concerned with, above all, was the question of what needs to be done. The serious response is not to deny what is happening, nor to point the finger at others. The serious response is to take meaningful and responsible action now.

That encompasses the need to tackle declining education systems, short-termism in our thinking, inadequate investments in infrastructure, under-utilization of ageing populations in many countries, smart economic incentives and so forth. But in the end it always comes back to innovation. This is the case no matter which aspect of globalization we consider today. The innovation of Canada and its 33.3 million people is the country's key to competing and winning in the globally integrating world.

The good news is that there has never been a better time to be an innovator. Exceptional talent and technical capabilities are everywhere. And any country, company or institution—or individual—can tap into them whenever it wants. Canada, where more than two-thirds of the adult population uses the Internet, already is well-linked to the world. By combining technology and expertise, invention and insight, small companies can be global, and established corporations can be more agile. Developed nations can market their unique skills, and developing regions can compete and dramatically improve their people's standard of living.

Globalization has arrived—in all its controversial, disruptive and historic glory. The challenge before us is to address the serious issues it raises—not just for established institutions, but for the billions of people, both in the developed and developing worlds, who do not yet see themselves as its beneficiaries. If we believe that the opportunities we face are greater than the dangers, then we had better demonstrate the enormously liberating and innovative potential of global integration—not just in words, but in deeds.

12.4

ROLE OF GLOBALIZATION AFTER THE CRISIS

from *Chinadaily.com.cn*

The next article, by a World Bank chief economist and senior vice president for development economics, describes how the global recession triggered criticism of globalization. The author warns, however, that countries will lose

Source: "Role of Globalization After the Crisis," *Chinadaily.com.cn,* January 6, 2010.

more by isolating themselves from globalization than by adapting themselves to it and points out that countries like India and China have continued to do well owing to their reliance on producing what they can produce most efficiently ("comparative advantage"). The author warns that alternative policies would be self-defeating and describes what countries should do to profit from their comparative economic advantage.

The world economy has just been through a severe recession marked by financial turmoil, large-scale destruction of wealth, and declines in industrial production and global trade. According to the International Labor Organization, continued labor-market deterioration in 2009 may lead to an estimated increase in global unemployment of 39–61 million workers relative to 2007. By the end of this year, the worldwide ranks of the unemployed may range from 219–241 million—the highest number on record.

Global growth in real wages, which slowed dramatically in 2008, is expected to have dropped even further in 2009, despite signs of a possible economic recovery. In a sample of 53 countries for which data are available, median growth in real average wages had declined from 4.3 percent in 2007 to 1.4 percent in 2008. The World Bank warns that 89 million more people may be trapped in poverty in the wake of the crisis, adding to the 1.4 billion people estimated in 2005 to be living below the international poverty line of $1.25 a day.

In this climate, globalization has come under heavy criticism, including from leaders of developing countries that could strongly benefit from it. President Yoweri Museveni, who is widely credited for integrating Uganda into world markets, has said that globalization is "the same old order with new means of control, new means of oppression, new means of marginalization" by rich countries seeking to secure access to developing country markets.

Yet the alternative to global integration holds little attraction. Indeed, while closing an economy may insulate it from shocks, it can also result in stagnation and even severe homegrown crises. To ensure a durable exit from the crisis, and to build foundations for sustained and broad-based growth in a globalized world, developing countries in 2010 and beyond must draw the right lessons from history.

In the current crisis, China, India, and certain other emerging-market countries are coping fairly well. These countries all had strong external balance sheets and ample room for fiscal maneuver before the crisis, which allowed them to apply countercyclical policies to combat external shocks.

They have also nurtured industries in line with their comparative advantage, which has helped them weather through the storm. Indeed, comparative advantage—determined by the relative abundance of labor, natural resources, and capital endowments—is the foundation for competitiveness, which in turn underpins dynamic growth and strong fiscal and external positions.

By contrast, if a country attempts to defy its comparative advantage, such as by adopting an import-substitution strategy to pursue the development of capital-intensive or high-tech industries in a capital-scarce economy, the government may resort to distortional subsidies and protections that dampen economic performance. In turn, this risks weakening both the government's fiscal position and the economy's external account. Without the ability to take timely countercyclical measures, such countries fare poorly when hit by crises.

To pursue its comparative advantage and prosper in a globalized world, a country needs a price system that reflects the relative abundance of its factor endowments. Firms in such a context will have incentives to enter industries that can use their relatively abundant labor to replace relatively scarce capital, or vice versa, thereby reducing costs and enhancing competitiveness. Examples include the development of garments in Bangladesh, software outsourcing in India, and light manufacturing in China. But such a relative price system is feasible only in a market economy. This is why China—which appears to be faring well in the crisis, meeting its 8 percent growth target in 2009— became an economic powerhouse only after instituting market-oriented reforms in the 1980s. Indeed, all 13 economies with an average annual growth rate of 7 percent or more for 25 years or longer, identified in the Growth Commission Report led by Nobel laureate Michael Spence, are market economies.

Pursuing its comparative advantage strengthens a country's resilience to crisis and allows for the rapid accumulation of human and physical capital. Developing countries with such characteristics are able to turn factor endowments from relatively labor- or resource-abundant to relatively capital-abundant in the span of a generation.

In today's competitive global marketplace, countries need to upgrade and diversify their industries continuously according to their changing endowments. A pioneering firm's success or failure in upgrading and/or diversifying will influence whether other firms follow or not. Government compensation for such pioneering firms can speed the process.

Industrial progress also requires coordination of related investments among firms. In Ecuador, a country that is now a successful exporter of cut flowers, farmers would not grow flowers decades ago because there was no modern cooling facility near the airport, and private firms would not invest in such facilities without a supply of flowers for export.

In such chicken-and-egg situations, in which the market alone fails to overcome externalities and essential investments go lacking, the government can play a vital facilitating role. This may be one of the reasons why the Growth Commission Report also found that all successful economies have committed, credible, and capable governments. The world is now so far down the path of integration that turning back is no longer a viable option. We must internalize lessons from the past and focus on establishing well-functioning markets that enable developing countries fully to tap their economies' comparative advantages. As part of this process, a facilitating role for the state is desirable in developing and developed economies alike, although the appropriate role may be different depending on a country's stage of development. Ultimately, in today's complex and interlinked world, even the most competitive economies need a helping hand as they climb the global ladder.

12.5

CASINO BANKING DOES
MORE DAMAGE THAN RIOTS

Joan Smith

> The following selection attacks the irresponsible behavior of bankers whose unsupervised activities in buying and selling assets ("casino capitalism")— some legal and some illegal—played a major role in the global financial crisis that began in 2008 and still remains a threat. The author argues that the damage done by these bankers is significantly greater than that of the riots that swept London and then other British cities between August 6 and 10, 2011, and that shocked the British public. She concludes that Great Britain's Prime Minister David Cameron, who denounced the rioters for "criminality, pure and simple," would do well to pay attention to the moral implications of the activities of bankers involved in "casino capitalism."

Another week, another banking scandal: on Friday, a day after the Swiss bank UBS announced it had lost the staggering sum of £1.3bn, one of its star traders appeared in court charged with fraud and false accounting. The hugely embarrassing announcement from UBS came three years to the day since the collapse of Lehman Brothers, suggesting not much has changed in the high-risk world of casino capitalism.

Initial reports concentrated on Kweku Adoboli's lifestyle, which sounded par for the course for a young man with a well-paid City job—long hours, flat in fashionable Stepney, parties. For once, though, the narrative of an abrupt fall from grace rang hollow. It isn't as though the big banks disapprove of the kind of casino capitalism its traders get involved in; on the contrary, they seek out and encourage risk-takers, rewarding them handsomely as long as they make huge profits.

The people who work on "delta one" desks at big banks bet on the direction of share prices and other assets. It's what Jerome Kerviel did at Société Générale in Paris in 2008, eventually losing the bank an eye-watering £4bn. But if he'd made that amount no one would have batted an eyelid. These young men (they mostly are men) don't make anything useful and they don't improve the lot of humanity one jot; they're gamblers, pure and simple.

Three years into the world banking crisis, there's still a tendency to hate "bankers" in general while having a fascination for the high-octane lifestyle of City traders. That's why people buy books like *The Wolf of Wall Street* by Jordan Belfort, a broker who ended up

Source: Joan Smith, "Casino Banking Does More Damage Than Riots," *Independent.co.uk,* September 18, 2011.

in prison, with its front-cover boast that "I partied like a rock star and lived like a king." Labour's former City minister Lord Myners had a different author in mind when he made a speech in the House of Lords about banking last week, quoting Hunter S. Thompson's assessment of the music business as a "shallow money trench . . . where thieves and pimps run free and good men die like dogs." Myners added drily: "As he is claimed to have said, it also has a negative side."

That negative side includes destroying jobs among people employed in the banking sector and beyond, and reducing the value of pension funds. UBS had to be bailed out by the Swiss government in 2008, and only last month it announced 3,500 job cuts. Last week's loss is expected to lead to more job cuts, while a drop in the value of UBS shares is likely to affect pensioners whose funds are invested in the company.

It's shocking to most people that the decisions of a handful of traders can have massive effects on their lives yet the Government endlessly delays regulation; only last week, following publication of the Vickers report, the banks were given an astonishing eight years to ring-fence their high street functions from their riskier investment operations.

The language of morality comes easily to David Cameron when he's talking about young people breaking into Comet, but it's different when financial institutions encourage reckless behaviour. How many reminders does the PM need that the culture of risk among City traders is one of our most urgent moral problems? Riots destroy property and lives in a limited area, but this white-collar vandalism threatens entire financial systems.

12.6

COALITION FIGHTS GLOBALIZATION: EMPLOYEES TRAIN FOREIGN WORKERS, THEN LOSE THEIR JOBS

Jane M. Von Bergen

> The next selection describes how one American saw his job at J. P. Morgan Chase & Co. outsourced and how, as a result, he decided to use the Internet to mobilize others in the same situation and lobby to prevent additional outsourcing of U.S. jobs.

J. Scott Kirwin's Web site sells a T-shirt that says "My job went to India and all I got was a stupid pink slip."

Source: Jane M. Von Bergen, "Coalition Fights Globalization: Employees Train Foreign Workers, Then Lose Their Jobs," *The Philadelphia Inquirer,* March 2, 2004.

Kirwin's not sure if his specific job went to India, but he knows about the pink-slip part. After training employees of an Indian company to handle J.P. Morgan Chase & Co.'s software, he was out of work. Since then, Kirwin, 37, of Wilmington, has found a mission—and so have hundreds of displaced information-technology workers.

They are part of a national grassroots movement that is making alliances with manufacturing groups and organized labor to fight globalization and the loss of jobs to overseas companies and foreign guest workers.

"I just think what is happening is wrong," said Kirwin, who started the Information Technology Professionals Association of America last year. "I'm like a little poodle nipping at their legs, but if I save jobs, it will be worth it."

Driven by anger and a sense of betrayal, Kirwin and other displaced programmers, analysts and Webmasters have the technical savvy to blast their message via the Internet.

On Kirwin's Web site are more than 100 links to grassroots and labor groups: the Texas Labor Champions, the Oregon Association of Tech Professionals, even one called Outsource Congress.

One link leads to an unemployed Connecticut programmer, John Bauman, and six longtime friends, who started The Organization for the Rights of American Workers in 2002 after realizing that only two of a dozen friends still had their jobs.

About half had trained their replacements—foreigners on temporary worker visas, who, they suspected, would eventually move the work abroad.

Last Tuesday, Bauman went to a news conference in Washington of the Jobs and Trade Network, an alliance of manufacturing groups, trade unionists, and displaced information-technology workers. They came to support a bill by Connecticut Sen. Chris Dodd to bar federal tax dollars from being used to take government work offshore.

Next month, Bauman's group and others will protest at an International Business Machines Corp. shareholders meeting. IBM's outsourcing has made it a lightning rod on the issue.

"We're doing it for our kids," said Bauman, who has been unemployed for 16 months and whose grown children have been unable to use their own software training. "Their jobs are going down the tubes."

Another link from Kirwin's Web site leads to Mike Emmons, 41, a Florida programmer, who, in 2002, after working with Siemens AG for five years, faced the choice of immediate termination or training his replacements, workers on foreign visas.

Emmons found Siemen's plan to move jobs abroad and shared it with politicians, including his congressman. But after learning that John Mica, a Republican, had accepted contributions from Siemens in 2002, he decided to run against Mica this fall.

To Emmons, the use of foreign guest workers and the offshoring of jobs are linked. "It's the golden egg that Congress has given the companies to take the jobs offshore," he said.

In Wilmington, Kirwin said he hoped to "create a sense of consciousness among IT workers." He said he feared that the coming generation of potential technology workers would have no place to learn and advance—to the detriment of America's future.

Advocacy, though, has not helped him support his wife and child. He is on his third job since losing his J.P. Morgan work last year.

"Here I am, at the most experienced in my life, and I'm making less than I did in 1999," he said.

12.7

DEMOCRACY OR ANARCHY?

Peter McKenna

The next article is a review in a Montreal newspaper of a book that describes how opponents of globalization have organized to gain democratic control over globalization and wrest power from undemocratic institutions such as corporations and international organizations like the International Monetary Fund and World Bank. Such organization involves extending global civil society, or what is called the "new democracy movement." The book also describes the tactics of the democratization movement and why, in the authors' view, that movement is critical to the world's future. The reviewer, however, has certain doubts about the argument, especially its theme that one should trust the antiglobalization movement more than one's own government.

GLOBAL SHOWDOWN: HOW THE NEW ACTIVISTS ARE FIGHTING GLOBAL CORPORATE RULE, By Maude Barlow and Tony Clarke, Stoddart, 228 pp., $29.95

How many of us would know whether Reclaim the Streets, the Direct Action Network or SalAMI are part of an emerging, youth-backed, global civil-society movement? Very few, one would hazard to guess. But as the April 20 opening ceremony for the Summit of the Americas in Quebec City rapidly approaches, the numbers are likely to improve substantially.

In their book *Global Showdown*, lefties Maude Barlow of the Council of Canadians and Tony Clarke of the Polaris Institute of Canada shed some much-needed light on this popular movement.

Both the authors and the protest groups are in agreement on what is driving economic globalization, singling out for particular scorn companies like ExxonMobil, Pharmacia Corporation and McDonald's. Like a good part of the movement itself, it's fair to say that neither have seemingly met a transnational corporation that they didn't dislike or distrust. To reverse global corporate rule, they call upon governments and political leaders not only to sever their incestuous relationship with a bevy of corporate greed-mongers, but also to re-energize the regulatory-minded state to strengthen democratic processes and to ensure sustainable communities.

Source: Peter McKenna, "Democracy or Anarchy? Authors Provide Insiders' Look at Anti-Globalization Protest Movement," *Montreal Gazette,* April 14, 2001.

Additionally, they admonish the United Nations to dust off its original mandate, taking ownership of global economic governance away from out-of-touch international financial institutions like the World Bank and the International Monetary Fund.

With this set of objectives in mind, *Global Showdown* chronicles the emergence of a sophisticated global civil society or "new democracy movement"—flexing its growing collective muscle against the Multilateral Agreement on Investment in 1998, the December 1999 Millennium Round of World Trade Organization-sanctioned talks in Seattle and the April 2000 WB-IMF meetings in Washington.

These dastardly villains are joined by compliant and puppet-like governments, sovereignty-infringing international trade compacts like the 1994 North American Free Trade Agreement and the proposed Free Trade Area of the Americas and, most important, socially irresponsible transnational corporations.

Repeatedly, the book rails against the reckless manner in which this illegitimate junta embraces unfettered capitalism, globalized markets and shrinking governmental control and regulation, thereby creating the conditions for an unjust and unequal global dispensation.

According to Barlow and Clarke, the stakes are incredibly high: the very ecological survival of the planet, cherished democratic principles and human-rights protection are at risk, as are public services like education and health care.

After examining the above-mentioned "what" and "why," the authors turn their undivided attention to detailing the "how" of this so-called "vigilante citizen movement." United in defying "global corporate governance," yet benefiting organizationally and tactically from the "Fast World" of globalization itself, the movement advocates "culture jamming," "direct action" and "civil disobedience." And in a highly synchronized fashion, in some cases solely designed to shut down high-level international gatherings like the Summit of the Americas, demonstrators avail themselves of what's known within the protesting ranks as "affinity groups" (groups operating under shared decisions), "convergence centres" (where protesters regroup for food, medical assistance and support) and "flying groups" (free to roam wherever they are needed).

Barlow and Clarke argue that the protests are mostly peaceful in nature (and should remain so), notwithstanding Seattle's epic running street battles involving scads of riot police brandishing truncheons and sundry tools of the "security" trade.

"Most protesters were armed with nothing but a bandanna soaked in vinegar, to protect their eyes and noses from pepper-spray and tear gas, and jackets with hoods to fend off the elements," they write. Indeed, unlike past social movements, this one has a decidedly youth-infused underpinning; or as some critics refer to them pejoratively: the purple-haired, body-tattooed, nose-pierced and multiracial hordes of anarchists. This youth component, however, may prove to be its life-line to longevity.

While *Global Showdown* is thought-provoking, highly readable and a useful primer for anyone interested in learning more about this global civil-society movement, it does tend to suffer from its own ideologically blinkered mindset.

This led me to several nagging questions: for instance, how is it possible to square Barlow and Clarke's notion that the Canadian government (and its many departmental entities) is in open collusion with big business, given the recent bureaucratic bungling over allegations of mad-cow disease in imported Brazilian beef? In addition, how do the authors reconcile their strident opposition to free-trade arrangements and global markets with the fact that a large majority of Canadians appear to welcome them? Moreover, what happens to individual interests and issues of accountability—clearly sacrosanct principles of democratic pluralism—when the demands of groups (like the Council of Canadians) take precedence in our political system?

In the final analysis, Barlow and Clarke are asking us to put our trust in a civil-society movement rather than governments and a profit-driven business community. But how can we be sure that by doing so we are not simply replacing one group of elites (and their policy prescriptions) with another? As one organizer at January's World Social Forum in Brazil remarked: "What civil society movements need is our own international forum, where we can develop and promote our own agenda and strategies for transforming the global economy."

After reading *Global Showdown*, all of us will have to weigh carefully what amalgam of the government-corporate-civil society triangle best creates a more just, environmentally friendly and equitable planet for the world's inhabitants.

12.8

BLACK BLOC & BLUE: {A LOOK AT THE ANARCHISTS WHO MAY POSE THE BIGGEST SECURITY THREAT}

Kathryn Blaze Carlson

> Although the antiglobalization movement as a whole tends to demonstrate peacefully, there is a violent minority. This minority of violent demonstrators frequently includes members of the Black Bloc, anarchists who oppose all authority. As a result, there is a need for security preparations, such as those taken by Canada for a 2010 meeting of the Group of Twenty (G-20) in Toronto.

When security experts talk about the problems posed by protesters at this month's G20 summit—the activists who present the "chief threat" to the city and its guests—they are largely talking about a collective of elusive protesters hooded and clad in head-to-toe black.

Source: Kathryn Blaze Carlson, "Black Bloc & Blue: {A Look at the Anarchists Who May Pose the Biggest Security Threat}," *National Post,* June 15, 2010.

Antiglobalization Demonstrators

The Black Bloc, which grabbed international attention for its raucous appearance at the 1999 World Trade Organization protests in Seattle, is not a group, but rather a tactic used by self-described anarchists who promote violence in the form of property damage and direct confrontation with police.

"They are the chief threat—they are the people we know are going to turn up and cause problems," said John Thompson, a security expert and president of the Toronto-based Mackenzie Institute, an organization that focuses on political instability and organized violence. "They are adrenaline junkies who are there to elicit confrontation."

The loosely connected activists sport hoods or balaclavas to conceal their identity and, while protesters do not often organize prior to an event, their all-black uniform gives them an air of solidarity.

Peter St. John, a University of Manitoba professor who specializes in security issues, said the Black Bloc is a "sophisticated" and "radical" movement with a history of violence and a penchant for "shop-smashing."

"These people are doing more than protesting—they are using violence to advance their agenda," said Mr. St. John, citing Black Bloc-led vandalism at the Vancouver Olympics as an example. "And when you start using violence, you're really coming under the rubric of a terrorist organization."

He said recent revelations of government spending on items like the notorious $57,000 "fake lake" will only serve to strengthen the international movement of mostly young men and women—a movement that despises all things corporate and Western.

Ironically, however, protesters engaged in the Black Bloc movement are partly to blame for the whopping $1 billion G8/G20 security tab, according to Mr. Thompson.

"These guys are the ones who have driven the costs up—you know they're going to turn up and you know they're going to break windows, trash cars and get into confrontations with police," he said. "What the Black Bloc protesters do is basically an extreme sport at public expense."

Although Constable Wendy Drummond, a spokeswoman for the G20 Integrated Security Unit, would not address the Black Bloc movement specifically, she said the unit is "prepared for any eventuality."

Ben Schumin, a self-described anarchist who has participated in upward of a dozen Black Bloc protests, including the 2008 G20 Summit in Washington, D.C., said the security unit is right to prepare for a violent Black Bloc appearance at the June 26 and 27 gathering of international leaders.

"There are some people who wear the all-black simply to send a radical message, but there are also those who will be willing to get violent," he said, adding that he does not support radical tactics, and will not be at this year's summit. "A lot of the people who cause the biggest problems are the ones who come in from out of town—the locals don't want to mess up their own bed."

A cursory glance at anti-G20 websites proves that out-of-province protesters will, indeed, make their way to Toronto, with one Montreal-based group calling for protesters to "attack the G20." Meantime, a music video entitled "Crash the Meeting," which was posted by a self-described anarchist to a blog called the Guerilla Underground Network, calls on anti-capitalists to "leave Bay Street blazing" and features historic footage of black-clad protesters.

Mr. Schumin, who offered a rare glimpse into the inner workings of the movement, said that while the Black Bloc is not a group, per se—even the capitalization of the movement is debatable—there are those who make regular appearances at events and who co-ordinate via email.

"Oftentimes there's no plan at the outset, but usually you have a couple people who will take charge a bit," he said, adding that Black Bloc participants will often "de-bloc" at the end of a protest, shedding their black attire in order to mesh with the general public.

Mr. Thompson said any violence perpetrated by Black Bloc participants will be the exception rather than the norm, but warned that a radical minority can still leave a mark.

"About 90% of the people who find themselves in a riot are just watching, and about 8% to 9% will follow the example of the 1% to 2% who are instigators," he said. "The Black Bloc is a gathering of that 1% to 2% types—they will always start something."

The Black Bloc

– Clad in head-to-toe black

– Hooded or sporting a bandana in order to conceal identity

– Male or female, likely young

– Supports property damage and/or violent police confrontation as a means to convey an anti-capitalist message

– May correspond with fellow Black Bloc protesters via email, but could simply show up solo at an event wearing black

– May be equipped with protective gear, such as knee pads and bicycle helmets

– Likely living in the Western world

12.9

FAIR PRICE FOR COCOA BEANS

Humphrey Hawksley

> The reliance of many poor countries, especially in Africa, on selling commodities overseas is one major reason why poverty is perpetuated. Wealthy countries tend to raise barriers to imports of commodities and subsidize their own agricultural products, thereby making it impossible for

Poverty and Protectionism

Source: Humphrey Hawksley, "Fair Price for Cocoa Beans," *The Korea Herald,* August 24, 2007. Originally published as "Like Wages for Chocolate" in *YaleGlobal Online,* August 21, 2007.

Note: Humphrey Hawksley is the author of "The History Book," a novel about corporate social responsibility.

farmers in the developing world to compete. Such issues, as we saw earlier, were largely responsible for the failure in 2006 of the Doha Round of trade talks. In addition, commodity prices frequently do not keep pace with the costs of finished goods that poor countries need to import. The Ivory Coast in West Africa, which depends heavily on the export of cocoa beans, illustrates the problem.

Soufre, Ivory Coast—In recent years the question of Africa has shifted from a moral and humanitarian challenge to a strategic one. Since the end of the Cold War in the early 1990s Africa has relied mostly on the free market system for its economic development. But the continent has slipped backwards, and the UN estimates that between now and 2015 the number of those workers living with their families on less than $1 a day will actually increase by 20 percent.

While the causes are multiple, alternatives to the Western democratic model are beginning to push their way through. Economically powerful, yet authoritarian China offers its own definition of human dignity which, it maintains, should be measured not by holding elections but by dragging people out of poverty. And extreme Islam spreads an inspirational anti-Western doctrine designed specifically to draw in the poor.

Almost half a century ago, Africa found itself similarly courted as newly independent nations chose between the ideology of the West and that of the Soviet Union. In 1960, Harold Macmillan, then British prime minister, declared that "winds of change were sweeping through Africa." He argued that one of the great issues of the 20th century was whether the "uncommitted peoples" of Africa would swing away from the Western powers.

Now, his latest successor, Gordon Brown, has taken up the baton. Addressing the United Nations July 31, Brown spoke of "the dignity of individuals empowered to trade and be economically self sufficient."

A key difference between 1960 and now is that half a century ago the commodities such as cotton, cocoa and coffee were largely seen as a source of wealth for Africa. Now because of globalization of media and the rise of non-governmental organizations, they have come to be seen as a symbol of exploitation.

Many multinational corporations stand accused of taking huge profits while those who farm their raw products become poorer.

African poverty, therefore, has become a test for economic globalization. One of its pivotal concepts is that whether you work in Shenzhen, China, sewing jackets, or in Soufre, the Ivory Coast, farming cocoa, you can improve your standard of living by hooking up to the international supply chain.

Globalization based on supply chain is an outgrowth of the economic systems of Western democracies. Therefore, its failure to deliver becomes the West's failure, too. A reversal requires a sea change of thinking from big business.

One example of the link between globalization and African poverty is the chocolate industry that accepts the use of child labor to farm cocoa, chocolate's raw product. Children are kept out of school and forced to work on farms to meet the world's craving for chocolate and profit drive by the multinationals. Some are sold as child slaves, but most are put to work because cocoa farmers are too poor to hire adult labor.

Down a barely passable road, about two hours drive from the town of Soufre, Sanogo Lamine, 70, said he had been growing cocoa for more than 30 years. In his first harvest, in 1974, he was paid 300 West African francs, about 60 cents, a kilo. This year, his cocoa beans sold for exactly the same 60 cents a kilo.

When he began farming, Lamine saw a bright future. Now, his extended family barely makes a subsistence living. Of his seven children, three have gone to the cities to try to earn enough for the family to survive. Had the cocoa price kept pace with inflation, members of his family could have earned enough to build proper houses, go to college and progress from generation to generation.

Instead, they live in mud huts and remain illiterate.

When asked how much he needed to live on, Lamine totted up the present-day costs of farming equipment and fertilizers. "About three times what we are paid now," he replied.

That figure roughly matches the 325 percent increase of U.S. inflation between 1974 and 2007, a rise that would be reflected in the wages, marketing costs and product price in selling a bar of chocolate. The benefits, therefore, reach almost every stage of the supply chain stage except the farmer himself.

The industry does not reveal its total annual revenue, but it's thought to be between $50 and $70 billion. According to some independent estimates, an allocation of between 0.5 and 1 percent of revenue would be enough to ensure community development such as the building of roads, schools and clinics.

It should be delivered not as aid, but in the price actually paid for the cocoa, which would, as Brown put it, speak toward the "dignity of individuals empowered to trade."

Yet this is precisely what the chocolate industry refuses to do.

When challenged about cocoa prices, the industry claims helplessness because prices are dictated by unpredictable international commodity markets. It cites free market doctrine with an ideological fervor comparable to that of Red Guards waving Mao Zedong's Little Red Book as if minor reform to the commodity markets would ruin Western life as we know it.

The Ivory Coast produces almost 50 percent of the world's cocoa and derives 90 percent of its foreign earnings from the trade. From independence in 1960, under the pro-Western authoritarian regime of President Felix Houphouet-Boigny, it became a jewel of Africa. The president ensured cocoa prices did not drop below a minimum level and many Ivorians felt secure and prosperous.

Houphouet-Boigny's death in 1993 coincided with the post Cold War call for free market democracy and with the removal of cocoa price guarantees. This led to increased poverty and ethnic tension exploited by new and weaker leaders. By 2000, the Ivory Coast was heading for civil war.

Having put their trust in Western trade, millions from the Ivorian cocoa belt and tens of millions elsewhere in Africa feel let down. They see themselves at the bottom of an international supply chain that refuses to spread wealth to the poorest and weakest. It is only natural that they seek alternatives.

Similar feelings were prevalent in 1940s China, 1930s Germany and turn-of-the-20th-century Russia. The alternative systems that took control then shook the world.

Today, a confident China bankrolls bad government in the Sudan and Zimbabwe and in the scramble for natural resources, has aspirations to control politically uncommitted swathes of the African continent. Extreme Islam has taken grip in Somalia, Nigeria and beyond and creeps toward cocoa farms of the Ivory Coast.

While inflexible thinking about state control over the economy by the hard left contributed to the collapse of communism, it may be the inflexibility of the free market right that threatens the future of Western liberal democracy.

The chocolate industry could set an example by taking steps to move away from this fraught course. They could at least ensure that the income of those farming cocoa is enough for a family to live on.

Chapter 13

ALTERNATIVE GLOBALIZATIONS

The divisions between advocates and opponents of globalization are at the heart of Manfred Steger's distinction between *"globalization"*—"a set of social processes of increasing interdependence"—and *"globalisms"*—"political ideologies . . . that endow globalization with their preferred norms, values, and meanings."[1] Steger identifies three conflicting ideologies or "globalisms" that contest the meaning of globalization and the ability of agents to shape its social processes. These are *market globalism, justice globalism,* and *jihadist globalism.* "By the end of the 1990s," he writes, "market globalism had managed to spread to all parts of the world by employing its dominant codes and hegemonic meanings through its powerful arsenal of ideological representation, co-optation of loyal elites, and economic power."

Despite their formidable efforts, however, the dominant vision of neoliberal globalization became increasingly tarred by the reality of growing social inequalities and rising cultural tensions. "Global justice" networks sprang up, and justice-globalist demonstrations erupted.[2]

Influenced by "Green Politics"[3] and socialist principles, globalization critics advocate a reformed alternative globalization that would promote social and economic justice and move beyond the dog-eat-dog competitiveness of neoliberal capitalism. Instead of being imposed from above by international institutions, wealthy states, and transnational corporations, economic and social institutions would be shaped from below and would reflect the needs and aspirations of local groups.

Then came the terrorist attacks of September 11, 2001, carried out by al Qaeda, led by Osama bin Laden and Ayman al-Zawahiri, whose followers declare their objectives to be the end of the interstate system, capitalism, and globalization and the worldwide unification of the nonterritorial and nonstate Muslim community of believers. The 9/11 attacks popularized a romanticized, historically based Islamic version of globalization. For the sociologist Manuel Castells,

> the explosion of Islamic movements seems to be related to both the disruption of traditional societies (including the undermining of the power of traditional clergy), and to the failure of the nation-state, created by nationalist movements, to accomplish modernization, develop the economy, and/or distribute the benefits of economic growth among the population at large.

Islamic globalism thus opposes capitalism, socialism, and nationalism, all perceived as "failing ideologies of the post-colonial order."[4] However, Islamic globalism is not only a reaction to Western colonialism. It is also an effort to return to a glorious past as an alternative to secular modernity. As such, it appeals strongly to Muslims who are minorities in non-Muslim societies, in which they find themselves isolated from the indigenous culture of the majority as well as from their own national and cultural roots.

Notes

1 Manfred B. Steger and B. Manfred, *Globalisms: The Great Ideological Struggle of the Twenty-First Century*, 3rd ed. (Lanham, MD: Rowman & Littlefield, 2009), 17.
2 Ibid., 15, 16.
3 Matthew Paterson, "Green Politics," in Scott Burchill, Richard Devetak, Jack Donnelly, eds., *Theories of International Relations*, 4th ed. (New York: Palgrave Macmillan, 2009), 260–83.
4 Manuel Castells, *The Power of Identity*, vol. II, 2nd ed. (Oxford, UK: Blackwell Publishing, 2004), 17.

13.1

BEYOND NEOLIBERAL GLOBALIZATION: ANOTHER WORLD

Donald W. Bray and Marjorie Woodford Bray

The first selection in this chapter denounces the dominant role of neoliberal economic principles, giant transnational corporations, and the United States in contemporary globalization. Instead, it embraces changes in many practices ranging from what is taught in academic subjects and the global structure to economic planning, improving the quality of life, especially in the developing world, and reemphasizing international law. The authors also seek to enhance global democracy and the direction of globalization from bottom-up rather than top-down, a shift in which labor unions and local community groups would play a key role. The article concludes by describing a new world of "humanistic globalization" to replace "neoliberal globalization."

Globalization has become the predominant framework for the analysis of the world political economy. The literature is replete with telling criticism of the consequences of globalization controlled by neoliberal ideology, namely, social and economic injustice and despoliation of the environment. What needs to be done is to construct an alternative

Source: Donald W. Bray and Marjorie Woodford Bray, (November, 2002), "Beyond Neoliberal Globalization: Another World," *Latin American Perspectives* 29:6, 117–26.

model of global change and to elaborate a political agenda for its implementation. Establishment theorists, stung by widespread antineoliberalism mobilizations including ones in Seattle and Washington, DC (right in the neoliberal heartland), have rallied to resist the challenge to their model of a corporation-dominated world. They have responded with "phase 2 reform" as damage control for the current world system (transperialism) through trickle-down economics. This is avoidance of what really is demanded by our time: transcending neoliberalism to achieve *another* world.

The essential elements of another world are personal well-being, environment enhancement, social justice, human rights, space for personal creativity and technical innovation, enlightened international law and regulation, the end of the war system, the politics of individual and group fulfillment, the promotion of cultural expression and preservation, and citizen control. The literature explains why the present world system is generally detrimental to the attainment of *any* of these goals.

Making Another World

The Seattle and Washington protesters' slogan "Nix It or Fix It" suggests that the present neoliberal world system is fixable. Reformist formulations are variously called *"alternativa,"* "the third wave," "inter-American dialogue," "the new architecture," "tinkering," "phase 2 reform," and so forth. All of these prescriptions leave large, mainly transnational corporations in command, subject only to limited public supervision. These power relationships cannot be fixed by tepid reform; they have to be superseded.

Corporations have the legal status of individuals, and this leaves their leaders mostly free from responsibility for their actions. They constitute the new ruling class and have little or no commitment to the well-being of anyone or any place. The market has been reified as the actor responsible for all economic transactions. Under current law the basic duty of corporate management is to seek profits. If corporations are to continue to exist, requirements to protect the environment and community well-being and to enforce core labor standards should be written into the laws of incorporation. They should have privileges, not rights. Restructuring must place the world under the control of its citizens and remove the "citizenship" of corporations.

The present degree of interdependence of world technology and production precludes deglobalization or complete local self-sufficiency. The system is fragile and could collapse at any time. A collapse would bring misery even deeper and more widespread than is now experienced by the most poverty-stricken. Reglobalization not deglobalization is required, and it can be accomplished in a way that will provide for considerable local control, including autonomy for indigenous peoples.

Desirable reglobalization will require a rethinking of many values and practices. In the universities, all academic fields are due for revamping. Accounting, for example, should validate positive social outcomes in a "new-world" accounting system. Social efficiency should be entwined with production efficiency. Science should be weaned from its dependence on warfare research. A larger segment of the social sciences should be directed toward policy questions. Alongside market-based economics, a field of instrumental economics should go beyond the critical perspectives afforded by the study of political economy to propose socioeconomic *objectives* and the politics of their attainment. Companion fields to instrumental economics could be developed in public administration and political science. Political science has already begun to go beyond the animals-in-a-cage "rational choice" approaches to address useful political outcomes. International law and organization should become a premier field of study. Humanitarian law is already a percolating subject. The principal argument made on behalf of neoliberal globalization is that the present exploitation of labor in poor countries will ultimately lead to sufficient technology transfer and local capital accumulation to generate general economic uplift. The four tigers, Taiwan, South Korea, Singapore, and Hong Kong, are cited as precedents. Hong Kong and Singapore are small entrepots where capital has accumulated for many decades. Special circumstances also render Taiwan and Korea unsuitable as models of capitalist development through foreign investment. In these cases the United States government provided billions of dollars of cold-war-inspired capital during a critical stage of growth. What would have happened if India or North Korea had received commensurate amounts? In any case, the time when the export-led/foreign-investment model might work has passed, as Sri Lanka, Tunisia, Honduras, and many other countries have learned. The collapse of the Argentine economy in December 2001 has been a devastating blow to the neoliberal model. But even if the model could ultimately be successful, it is becoming politically impossible to sacrifice present generations for the promise of satisfactory conditions of life at some future time. Globalized information has intensified political restlessness and response. In Venezuela a seemingly stabilized political party system imploded overnight when the populist leader Hugo Chavez ran for president under the banner of opposition to neoliberalism. Another startling development is the national plebiscite organized by the Brazilian Catholic Church to question payment of the foreign debt and an International Monetary Fund (IMF)-imposed austerity program.

Given the present state of technology, there is no need to sacrifice present generations. Development is a problem of political agenda and political power. Success will require change in the power structure. Control of the world will be wrested from the hands of transnational corporations. The resources, experience, and knowledge assembled in these corporations are not the problem; the problem is the unsupervised and uncritically evaluated purposes to which they are put. In this regard, the Enron Corporation scandal is instructive. While Enron management was only fleecing consumers, including state and local governments *as* consumers, the game was tolerable to the establishment. Only when *capital* (investors' holdings) was purloined by management was moral indignation seriously aroused.

A persistent myth is that since planned economies did not work in the Soviet systems, planning does not work. In reality, planning becomes ever more imperative as free-marketeering impels the planet toward ecological and social disaster. "New-world" planning should, indeed, learn from Soviet shortcomings. Individual creativity and expression should not be stifled; entrepreneurship should be prized. Market allocations should be encouraged within planning guidelines. Runaway greed should be muted by reallocation of benefits in accordance with world, national, and local priorities. Under new-world planning, living conditions in the South would be raised to acceptable levels by redirecting existing resources and organizing education and production in terms of locally determined goals and available resources and revenue generators. Present international debt obligations that have already returned huge amounts to lenders would be cancelled. In advanced industrial societies the abolition of avoidable misery should be more important than the excessive production of goods and services. All of this has to be done in the context of devising effective mechanisms for moving capital from areas of surplus to areas of deficit.

The Measurement of Progress

Some cynical manipulators of the postmodern age have abandoned the idea of progress while clinging to the corporate bottom line as reality incarnate. One exemplar of this position, Lawrence Summers, secretary of the treasury in the year 2000, is reported to have written a memo while working for the World Bank suggesting that the underdeveloped world was underpolluted: people living in those regions had such short life expectancies that they would die before contamination of their environment would affect them. Progress is a relative thing, but assessing it is not beyond the ability of the human mind. Measured by the state of the human condition, current trends are generally retrograde. Under present circumstances the establishment has a vested interest in belittling the idea of progress, except as measured by profit. Thus the establishment favors measuring development as per capita income, concealing distribution. U.S. journalism and scholarship generally accept this evasive measure rather than the physical-quality-of-life index (PQLI) that measures the human condition. Neither progress nor the PQLI is an illusion. The people of the world know better.

Globalization's Unsteady Regional Instruments

Both consensus and rivalry mark the push by corporate captains for the expansion of free-trade areas. There is world capitalist consensus about the desirability of using regional agreements to reduce tariffs and government restrictions on investments and profit remittances. At the same time there is rivalry over the domination of regional markets and which single currency to impose. These contradictions are evident in the tug-of-war between the European Union (EU) and the United States exemplified by the George H. W. Bush-initiated effort to continue U.S. hegemony in Latin America through the proposed Free Trade Agreement of the Americas (FTAA).

The establishment and expansion of trade agreements provide some space for progressive results. The corporate forces won the day with the North American Free Trade Agreement (NAFTA), an agreement that does not now include effective mechanisms for the protection of the environment and the enforcement of core labor standards. The struggle over the enactment of NAFTA, however, forged an alliance among labor and other groups that is a foundation of the world antiglobalization movement. This movement prevented the U.S. Congress from granting President William Clinton fast-track authority to negotiate a hemispherewide agreement. Popular pressure could force future negotiations to include a social charter guaranteeing labor standards, human rights, and preservation of the environment. Negotiations surrounding modification and expansion of trade agreements are a better forum for applying trade-union and social-movement pressure than would be an effort to force the World Trade Organization (WTO) to enforce social charter-rights.

Meanwhile, in August 2000, the heads of 12 South American nations signed a declaration calling for combining MERCOSUR (Brazil, Argentina, Uruguay, with Paraguay) and the Andean free-trade agreement. South American elites are now threatening, in the words of President Ricardo Lagos of Chile, to "speak with one voice," and popular organization could force that "voice" to include demands for a social charter. The same could occur with a revision of NAFTA. A NAFTA that now *degrades* the quality of life for most citizens of participating countries could—under social-charter provisions—uplift standards.

International Law

The twenty-first century may see the subjection of international power to effective legal restraint. The principal impediment to international law and cooperation is the United States, which clings to its economic and military custodianship of the world. In Africa, the United States contracts out some of its intervention activities to U.S.-based private paramilitary organizations. A law-based world is nascent in the UN Charter and numerous other treaties, conventions, and resolutions. The basic problem is that the United States will not sign on to the world consensus favoring the extension of international agreements.

There has been palpable initial progress in the fields of human rights, democracy, and social betterment. Global institutions are emerging to restrain future power wielders who would commit gross violations of citizen rights. Early instances of this trend are the arrest of the former Chilean dictator Augusto Pinochet by the United Kingdom, the citing of international law by a Japanese court to end the exclusion of the foreign-born from stores, the granting of civil rights to foreign workers in South Korea, and the establishment of a world criminal court—to mention only a few. To date, the United States has not joined the world criminal court for fear of punishment of its own international abusers. There was, for example, a case in a Belgian court against Henry Kissinger alleging violations of the genocide convention.

A voluntary code of conduct for transnationals was in the making at the UN Transnational Centre until the Centre was closed down by William Thornburgh, whom President George H. W. Bush insisted on having appointed as an undersecretary general. The trade-off was to be the honoring of the U.S. financial obligation to the organization- a promise that was not kept during his administration. Secretary General Kofi Annan is now promoting a voluntary compact that commits transnational corporations to protect labor standards, the environment, and human rights. This may be a small step in the right direction.

The anti-UN spirit of the assault upon the Transnational Centre by the elder President Bush was matched by his son, who in June 2002 in an address at West Point claimed for the United States the unilateral right of anticipatory military action—the "with us or against us" doctrine. His declaring for the United States the right of preemptive military attack was a historic departure from international law and the UN Charter. What he proposed went well beyond accepted standards of what is the legitimate right of self-defense.

From Nontransparency to Megademocracy

A grand hypocrisy of the day is that the United States and other industrial countries call for "transparency" in South-country business and government while exercising star-chamber control of the world economy behind the closed doors of corporate board-rooms and the WTO. In secret sessions, unaccountable to those impacted, planetary robber barons confect the maximization of corporate profits. Unconsulted are the billions of citizens attempting to survive on less than two dollars a day. This arrangement prevails in what is sometimes referred to as the "free world." Megademocracy, in contrast, would be a global system of and by and for the *people* of the world. (That is definitely *not* what U.S. President George H. W. Bush meant by a "new world order.") Creating megademocracy should be at the top of the twenty-first century agenda. It is a breathtaking challenge for a new generation. It is doable.

Globalism From Below

The achievements of capitalism have, of course, been transformative. Marx himself saw capitalism as creating the necessary basis for the development of socialism by building the infrastructure required for an abundance of production that would be adequate for all. But capitalism is ruthless. It does not revere the best of the past. Capitalist cosmopolitanism destroys group traditions; although it allows some to prosper mightily, it does not value ways of life that contribute to the well-being of the ordinary citizen. Moreover, the development of capitalism has mostly benefited the North. Traditional colonialism depleted its subjects of their natural wealth, leaving few and contradictory improvements in the quality of life. What is more, modern capitalism continues to make its profits by exploiting the cheap labor in the South as part of the modern technological industrial process. This cheapens labor in the North as well, and the income gap between the top and bottom quintiles is increasing. Finally, the dynamics of unfettered capitalism have begun to threaten the survival of an environment in which it is possible for the human and other species to continue to exist.

The common interests of those attuned to these issues—preservation of the past (particularly by indigenous groups), the exploitation of labor and the environment—are bringing people together all over the world. Many of them have formed cross-border alliances. This has been identified as a crucial sector of global civil society, but international civil society is not sufficient. Not unreasonably, these groups have grown to distrust government. Government is essential, however, to control and restructure the institutions of capitalism. World and national government institutions effectively representing the interests of ordinary people will be required to bring economic well-being, education, health, leisure, and pleasure to the lives of all.

The Citizenship Movement

A new movement that declares fundamental human rights as entitlements of citizenship is now confronting neoliberal policy makers at national, regional, and world levels. The right to a livable environment, a decent livelihood, housing, education, recreation, health care, and more is being asserted as the patrimony of citizenship. This appeal has its strongest mobilizational effectiveness in Brazil but is spreading to other countries. The compelling implication of the movement is that there must be a different world system in order for its demands to be met. The UN "Geneva Process," which seeks the elimination of poverty in the world, carries a similar implication.

Within the citizenship thrust is the awareness that the people who cross borders seeking livelihoods in the North or elsewhere also have rights that deserve recognition. If capital and goods can flow freely but labor is frozen in place within country limits, capital will find the cheapest labor and the world wage level will be lowered.

Organized Labor and Organized Communities

Crucial to the achievement of another world is the role of communities based on work, geography, ecology, religion, youth, gender, race, culture, sexual orientation, and shared interests. Among these, labor unions are fundamental. They must be organized more strongly at all levels of confrontation with corporate power, especially in the global theater. Cross-border organizing and network building is imperative if the internationally owned megacompanies are to be brought to heel and citizens are to reclaim the world. Unions should return to their original vision of building a better society and eschew economistic business unionism under corporate domination. They should forge multiple alliances with progressive groups as an expression of "social-movement unionism."

Organization of poor people to demand their rights is burgeoning throughout the world. Many were present in the Seattle and Washington and subsequent gatherings against the WTO, the World Bank, the IMF, and the FTAA. Latin America has been preeminent in community organizing. Conspicuous Brazilian examples are the Landless Movement and the implementation of community-based budgeting in cities governed by the Workers' party. Similar efforts include the mushrooming of spontaneous neighborhood committees and worker-managed factories as a response to the economic and political collapse when neoliberalism crumbled in Argentina. In Havana, Cuba, the institutionalized Popular Power system is also tapping neighborhood energies through locally initiated social development workshops. Neighborhood organizing has changed the political calculus and the nature of popular struggle, becoming a wellspring of future possibilities.

The Activism Imperative

Globalization has placed everyone's life in the world matrix. Not everyone will (as some already do) have cousins on three continents, but increasingly our reference will be globeland as well as homeland. Significant world events will be everyone's events. Many people's working and leisure lives will take them far afield. The world as it is now will not do. Changing it will not be easy. Some people are too preoccupied with survival, and many have become disillusioned over failed efforts. The role of aware educators with teaching grounded in authentic Freireian methods will be vital. Uncooptable leaders are essential. Change will be facilitated by the use of the Internet for information and for organizing. Without national and international activists to prevent them, the transnationals will continue to buy legislatures and courts with abandon and the U.S. hegemon will continue to structure the international system for the benefit of corporate profit. Without activists the promise of the twenty-first century will remain unfulfilled.

Evidence of the response to the need for activism was demonstrated in January 2002, when 16,000 activists gathered in Porto Alegre, Brazil, to exchange ideas and experience in the global quest for another world. The international antineoliberal-globalization movement had become a political force of historic proportions. Yet, a basic arena for struggle remains at the national level. Despite transperialism's semisuccessful efforts to liquidate regulation of their economies by nation-states, the consequences of neoliberal globalization and corporate scandals have activated popular demands to impose national government regulation of economic life.

Another World

The progressive theorists and activists of the past century contributed monumentally to the improvement of social conditions, but the socialist project was sidetracked by faulty analysis and by misunderstanding of people's needs and aspirations. Fun, diversity, social and political openness, stimulation, innovation, face-to-face human interactions, spirituality, and the right to be apolitical are as basic to the human spirit as security and vocational opportunity. The price of social justice should not be drabness and coercion. That the Cuban Revolution appreciates most of these realities helps explain why it has survived while others have failed.

Shared popular culture, particularly music, is a hallmark of globalization. It is a planetary bond, especially for youth. When political messages appear in the music they tend to be supportive of the environment and of international cooperation. Although this music is disseminated by the global media, one does not discern endorsement of neoliberalism. To that extent it is music of another world—of the world to come.

Another world will be grounded in the rights of citizenship—not the limited U.S. concept of civil rights but the full range of economic and social rights. The world will move ever closer to implementation of the Universal Declaration of Human Rights because of the economic abuse inherent in neoliberalism. Not only has neoliberalism not led to democracy, it is *incompatible* with democracy. The mere holding of elections is not democracy. Social democracy has failed to control elite domination. Meaningful citizenship will be exercised at three levels: local, national, and international.

The achievement of citizenship rights has been placed in temporary jeopardy by the U.S.-led War on Terrorism. This "war" is being used as a magician's cloak to suffocate meaningful world discourse and change. This effort is too contrived, however, to stay on the center stage of world attention for long. Overriding imperatives will force a return to more pressing issues.

In another world transperialism will be replaced by a world system under which production and distribution of goods and services are guided by citizen needs. The conditions of life will be a choice, not a market determination. Neoliberal globalization will be overcome by humanistic globalism.

13.2

CHOOSING WEALTH OR WELLBEING

John Langmore

> Our next selection provides an account of why material welfare is not sufficient in the eyes of many Australians who are concerned about their wellbeing, job security, and future quality of life. The article suggests that Australians believe that their "way of life is threatened by commercial pressure, materialism, drugs (legal and illegal) and a steady decline in manners and morals." This perception has undermined Australians' faith in neoliberal capitalism and its emphasis on materialism.

Social surveys show that most Australians are paradoxically both relatively comfortable with the national situation but also unsure about longer-term prospects. There have been 15 years of relatively rapid economic growth, for which there is widespread appreciation.

Though most have a general sense of material wellbeing, at the same time there are widespread insecurities and fears. Many Australians worry about job security.

Opinion polls show that the proportion of those who prefer higher public spending on health and education to lower taxes has risen steadily since 1990 to a substantial majority. Services for which most respondents are willing to pay quite a bit more tax or a little more tax include health and Medicare, primary and secondary education and the environment. It is, therefore, an amateurish electoral misjudgment for some politicians to claim that tax cuts are the highest political priority.

Advocacy of further tax cuts demonstrates ignorance of voters' preferences, or readiness to succumb to the constant clarion call from the rich and privileged.

While most Australians are optimistic about their personal futures, their confidence in the future quality of life is declining.

Social researcher Hugh Mackay identifies an underlying, rather wistful concern that the Australian way of life is threatened by commercial pressure, materialism, drugs (legal and illegal) and a steady decline in manners and morals. Public discourse stirred during

Source: John Langmore, "Choosing Wealth or Wellbeing," *Canberra Times,* October 17, 2007.

2006 and 2007. Complaints about the low level of public debate became increasingly common as the level of debate started to rise. Unease about Australia's values and direction grew. One underlying cause of unease is the current economic ideology, sometimes misnamed economic rationalism and often described internationally as neo-liberalism or the Washington consensus. As this ideology is a direct descendent from 19th century liberalism, it is accurate to use the descriptive term economic liberalism. At the extreme, however, economic liberalism can and does become market fundamentalism. The economic liberal fog has obscured voters' preferences. Liberal economists have been so preoccupied with maximising individual income that other aspects of wellbeing have been excluded.

Their recommendations for achieving individual income growth have been minimising public expenditure and taxation, privatisation of public enterprises, and deregulating the financial and corporate sectors. Many have been so obsessed with efficiency that harmony, social justice and environmental responsibility have been forgotten. Two of the clearest outcomes of the economic liberal ascendancy are a striking dichotomy, for while the strategy has been associated with a long period of economic growth, market fundamentalists have actually made no progress at all towards their principal goal of contracting public expenditure and taxation. Public expenditure and taxation, as proportions of national income, are higher than ever.

Economic growth has been achieved by abandoning the main economic liberal goal, which is in itself a clear reason for moving on.

One feature of economic liberalism is the obsession with individual income maximisation to the exclusion of other dimensions of wellbeing. National public policy still focuses on gross domestic product growth and devalues many policies which would contribute to wellbeing and equality of opportunity. This is not simply an expression of ideology, however, but also reflects the interests of the powerful in preference to those of the whole population. While economic liberalism has been so strongly entrenched, rigorous evaluation of the wider consequences of the policy has been downplayed. The economically successful proclaim the dominant ideology while the sceptics become disillusioned and resigned. Together with the Howard Government's repression of public discourse and dissent, this political atmosphere has generated a widespread sense of powerlessness and political passivity.

The ascendency of liberal economics meant that big political issues such as economic strategy, income distribution, social and environmental policy and provision of public services, appeared to have been settled, leaving only technical and marginal issues for discussion.

The quality of both personal and public life has been undermined by preoccupation with individual income and material accumulation and neglect of broader concerns.

Acquisitiveness has stimulated the growth of individualism and commercialisation in Australia, as in the United States. Constant emphasis on material goals and denigration of generosity and cooperation has damaged the quality of Australian community life.

The successful have a growing, complacent sense of entitlement which undermines mutual responsibility, while lower-income earners have been marginalised.

In the rest of the developed world, people have reacted against the extremes of market fundamentalism.

In the largely social democratic countries of the European Union, the ideology has never been dominant.

Australian public policy has yet to catch up with the defeat of the market fundamentalist advocates in Britain and the US, but criticism of economic liberalism is increasing. Most of us know intuitively there is much more to life than possessions and consumption, and this has caused some reaction against assertive materialism. Allowing the intermediate goal of economic growth to dominate national life has been a misjudgment of this era.

There is widespread and growing recognition that, as well as income, wellbeing also depends on many other factors. Quality of life is more than standard of living. Our happiness depends on such qualities as loving and being loved, security, autonomy, productive work, enjoyable leisure, achievements and harmony. Going for growth at all costs underestimates the social and environmental costs of growth. The goal of economic security has a vital place in any framework for public policy, but so does improving the quality of life and the common good, for they put economic growth in a wider perspective. Many of us sense a lack of balance which we would like to improve by reducing work pressure and building capacity for relationships, cultural and spiritual vitality, sport and other relaxations. Why not recognise that Australians work the longest average hours in any OECD country and gradually reduce standard working hours, rather than increasing pay as the reward for growing productivity?

This would also allow a more equitable sharing of available work by increasing total employment. . . .

13.3

WORLD: WORLD SOCIAL FORUM 2011, SO INTRICATE, YET SO PERFECT: THE REALITY OF AFRICA

Sachin Jain

The World Social Forum (WSF) was established in 2001 as a forum for social movements and nongovernmental organizations (NGOs) to represent the interests of less developed countries. It was intended as an alternative to the World Economic Forum, which meets annually in Davos, Switzerland, and

Source: Sachin Jain, "WORLD: World Social Forum 2011, So Intricate, Yet So Perfect: The Reality of Africa," Asian Human Rights Commission, March 18, 2011.

reflects the interests of the leaders of global capitalism. It is described as "an open meeting place where social movements, networks, NGOs and other civil society organizations opposed to neo-liberalism and a world dominated by capital or by any form of imperialism come together to pursue their thinking, to debate ideas democratically, to formulate proposals, share their experiences freely and network for effective action."[1] The following selection describes the 2011 annual meeting of the WSF in Dakar, Senegal, which focused on the economic and social problems confronting sub-Saharan Africa. The author expresses concern over the growing influence of NGOs from the developed world, compares Senegal with India, describes the legacy of colonialism in both countries, and argues that many of the challenges confronting Africans are the result of European neocolonialism. He then reflects on the history and evolution of the WSF and the problems it seeks to deal with.

This year, the World Social Forum (WSF) raised several new questions but there are many older questions that we still need to find answers to. Since we met in Senegal, it was quite natural that the focus of discussion was the African question, which proved to be a fruitful learning ground for civil society groups. Situated in the eastern part of the continent, Senegal is considered a resource-rich region of Africa, yet its first major highway was constructed just four years ago. It is said the Senegalese president spent the largest chunk of the country's budget on building the road, yet it peters out into a desert.

WSF 2011, organised in the Senegalese capital of Dakar, attracted more than 50,000 people pursuing the vision of creating a better world. But I have been observing a worrisome trend in this forum over the 10 years that I have attended its deliberations—you get a sense of the growing dominance of NGOs over people's movements at every step. Many of these organisations were, in fact, present this year to advertise and publicise themselves. The ruling political party of China put up a stall. Also participating were USAid and a host of other International funding agencies that push a liberal neo-colonial and capitalist approach to development agenda along with the financial resources they disburse. There should be no illusions about the kind of linkages these groups seek to establish with the WSF vision of building a new world order.

My African interlude began with one of those unpleasant encounters that bring to mind my own country—the Dakar ambience is so like India! The moment I alighted from the Iberia Airlines flight I proceeded to the immigration department to complete the formalities for entering the country. After stamping my passport the immigration officer said something to me in French, which I couldn't understand. He then called me aside to the door and, gesturing with his fingers, whispered, "Money, money."

That was my first experience of Senegal. I pretended as if I hadn't understood. But the thought germinating in my mind was that whatever people said about African countries being corrupt was true. I must admit I was a bit scared as well.

I learned later that not just in Senegal but other African countries as well people in government service (teachers, revenue officials, nurses, etc.) often didn't get their salaries for six months at a stretch, while 2–3 months' salary of many petty officials would even 'disappear.' That creates the ideal environment for corruption to flourish. The only visible symbol of governmental administration is the police, clad in military uniform, armed with weapons, menacing. At first I could not tell whether they were guerrilla fighters or city police. That's the look the colonial powers groomed in their police to stamp their power across the globe, especially after the first and second world wars, I thought to myself.

It is, indeed, a matter of regret that African countries, once the victims of Spanish and French colonialism—just like India was subjugated by the British—and now free nations manifest their freedom only superficially while continuing to remain under the control of European powers.

Senegal is a country where the majority is Muslim and the native language is Wolof, yet 80% of the people speak French and it is compulsory for students to learn the language. Even the signboards of shops and commercial establishments are in French. It's like in India where the middle class sacrifices itself on the altar of English, the only difference being that we Indians have ourselves opted for language colonialism whereas the Senegalese had no choice.

Naturally, there are economic and diplomatic dimensions to the subjugation of African nations by European entities. Their natural resources have been systematically looted. Modern Europe, whose beauty is so widely lauded, was built with the resources sent from African countries, from wood and stone to art and cultural materials. Even sand! And the situation today is that Senegal is trapped in a web of poverty where it has little choice but to remain the bonded slave of Europe.

Every third Senegalese is a painter, their paintings beautifully depicting the symbiotic links between nature, resources and the people. They illustrate the relationship between man and woman and the link between gender and social change.

Impressive artistry, but have you ever heard of Senegal being a centre of great art? You probably haven't, because the country's art comes to the world via Europe, where its identity is lost in transit. These priceless works of art, which the Senegalese artist completes in 7–8 days, fetches him a remuneration of just Rs. 1,000–2,000 (15–20 Euros), which is the cost of a frugal meal in Paris.

The Senegalese are also master craftsmen in wood. Only African artistry can achieve such intricate carvings on statues made from the teak, ebony and Sheesham. Yet I found they earned a meagre Rs. 700–800 for 10 days of artistic labour during the days of the WSF when they sold their wares to the congregation of visitors.

I talked a bit to one such individual who told me this was perhaps the first time he had seen so many people from countries other than European. He was keen to sell his wares to Asians even at lower prices. Sitting on the roadside selling his paintings and woodwork he greeted me with a query, "Namaste. India?" As I nodded in assent, he came closer to me and said, "Take something, anything." He could speak just a couple of sentences in English. "You Indian, you are my friend, you are my brother, I give you good price." He then touched a finger to my wrist saying, "Same colour. We are brothers."

An African-Asian bond was established. I could not understand how we had become so far apart in the first place. But I could sense why Mahatma Gandhi chose Africa to launch his journey into public life. It wasn't just a matter of history and politics but of human civilization, of creating and diffusing familial ties.

Around 50% of the participants in the Dakar WSF were European and 45% African. The Europeans, Coca Cola can in one hand, almost always used one word in their conversations—capitalist. At night many of them partied in bars, discussing and analyzing the daily goings on at WSF. But there was not a single session in the entire proceedings where colonialism (history, present and future) figured in the discussions. No one had the courage to open up those pages of history that described how African nations had come to such a pass and who was responsible for their plight.

Some of them did suffer a sense of guilt which they sought to mollify by paying whatever the taxi drivers demanded without bargaining, as if by doing so they were returning something of what their forefathers had taken away from here.

Some days earlier, French president Sarkozy had visited Senegal to discuss possible ways of helping the country free itself from its pitiable plight, even suggesting that there may be some benefit in remaining a colony of France. It is in the context of such ideas and views prevalent among the dominant nations that organising WSF is so important and relevant to those of us with an alternative worldview.

African Society in a Neo-Colonial Framework

Africa is now becoming a colony of newly developed countries like India and China. Walter Fernandes, a well-known social scientist from the continent and an expert on the subject of displacement caused by development, reports that the rich capitalist class and their governments are currently in the process of usurping 40 million hectares from the Saharan nations. Most of these countries are under the control of dictators and lack any vestige of democratic functioning. At the same time, their people are denied even the basic facilities for living.

Representatives from Sudan and Congo who had come to attend the WSF organised in the African nation of Senegal from February 6 to 11, 2011, related how it took people two years to walk across the Sahara, the world's largest desert, when they decided to migrate from their homeland in search of a better life. They had to then sail across the Atlantic Ocean in tiny boats to reach European shores. Many died on the way. Many others were caught while slipping across the borders into European countries. The inhuman face of international diplomacy can be seen in the way they were transported and dumped back into the desert from where they had sought to escape. European countries like France, Italy and Spain are now paying around Rs. 10,000 million every year to African and Middle East countries to ensure that they make the necessary arrangements to prevent people from crossing European borders. The developed countries see the influx of migrants as having a deleterious impact on their resources while damaging their image in the eyes of the world, Over a million people from Kenya, Namibia, Congo, Algeria and other African countries are forced to migrate every year to escape their pitiable living conditions but they are not permitted to enter these European countries.

The face of colonial development and progress stands exposed. The colonizing powers first create scarcity conditions and then enslave the people of the country they target.

They know that it is necessary to control culture, education, resources and language in order to enslave a society or a country. This process is still under way in the African continent today. But the ways in which colonization is taking place are changing.

A country like India, which was once itself enslaved and a victim of servitude, has over the past two decades adopted neoliberal policies for its economic development. It is cutting down on governmental support/subsidies for agriculture and social welfare while at the same time increasing allocations for developing an industrial-capitalist framework. The bottom-line is how to increase the growth rate.

Wealth has, indeed, increased but imbalances in its distribution have increased even more starkly and rapidly. Today in India, a single industrial house, the Ambani family, controls 5% of the country's gross domestic product (GDP). Around 70% of India's resources have been captured by 7% of its people. It is these Indian industrial houses that are now targeting Africa to expand their colonial empires. This class has begun exploiting the industrial expansion policies of African nations to take control of the continent's natural resources.

China is already sending its citizens to cash in on the employment opportunities that are being generated there. In this way, countries that were once categorized as 'developing' are now adopting colonial practices, the greatest irony being that we are now beginning to enslave those societies that have always been closest to us.

There is one other commonality that is clearly evident—African society is also the victim of capitalist policies.

In spite of being rich in resources, you will get a clear idea of the distressing state of the country's economy if you venture into the older quarters of the capital city of Dakar, where you will come across vendors on footpaths and in small shops selling second-hand clothes for children, men and women. The distressing fact is that the second-hand goods are coming into the market from Europe, which means that even the fashion trade is controlled by that continent. When we tried to snap photographs of the vendors they pleaded with us not to do so. They didn't want anyone to see their condition, which is becoming permanent, the norm.

The state of health facilities in the city will bring tears to your eyes. The people have no access or right to government or public health services. The maternal mortality rate is a distressing 1,000 per 100,000 births because there are no health facilities for women. Even private health facilities are skeletal, their reach being limited only to the capital. I'll quote just one example to illustrate the pitiable health situation in the country. Rami, one of our companions from the Palestine, came down with the flu and had a throat infection. It took us two hours to locate a doctor to attend to him and he charged 26,000 CFA Francs (the Senegalese currency) as consultation fees, which equals around Rs. 2,600. The antibiotics and paracetamol we bought for his treatment cost another 49,000 CFA Francs (around Rs. 4,900)! Can anyone really dare to fall sick in a country where the average monthly income is less than Rs. 2,000?

I roamed the city, bargaining like a tourist. But in the nine days I was in the country I did not come across a single individual who raised his/her voice while talking. They always listened respectfully to what I had to say, with no sign of guile or crookedness. I have noticed that even the immigration official lowered his gaze while asking me for a bribe and smiled when he didn't receive one. Can one imagine a more civilized people?

Yet they were subjugated, colonized and enslaved. We found evidence of the violent, inhuman and frightening face of apartheid in a 5 sq km island situated in the Atlantic Ocean some 15 km from Dakar. Known as Slave Island, this is the area closest to the rich, developed nations of the world.

In earlier times Africans were captured from different regions and brought here as slaves. It was from this island that they were dispatched into slavery in groups to different parts of Europe and America. One can still see those 80 to 150 sq ft rooms in which 15 to 30 people were imprisoned. They were allowed out only once in the day to relieve themselves. The insanitary conditions caused epidemics that killed thousands of Africans. Young girls were subjected to virginity tests and virgins were kept in separate rooms to be sent later to different places for sexual exploitation. If they became pregnant they were abandoned in forsaken places. Since this was the sole pathway to freedom, many girls sought to get pregnant as quickly as possible.

Official statistics covering over 300 years around the 14th and 15th centuries reveal that as many as 15 million people lost their lives during this period of the slave trade. Those who attempted to escape either drowned in the ocean or were attacked by sharks. Only the healthy ones weighing over 60 kg were sent across the ocean into slavery. The underweight were fed a special diet to increase their weight to qualify for slavery.

The people living on the island today relate the story of how the pope himself came here once from the Vatican to apologise for the depressing role played by the church in the practice of slavery. They told him yes, they could forgive him for this bitter truth of history but they could never forget it. Indeed, mankind has committed grievous sins in its history that cannot be forgotten.

The question we need to ask ourselves today is why European and American countries are still unwilling to fully reject an ideology steeped in apartheid and colonialism.

WSF 2011: Searching for Direction in People's Movements

The WSF came into being to explore a possibility. We knew that a society built on the superstructure of the current global economy based on capitalist policies could never be free from feudal and colonial exploitation. We needed to dream of building a new world and have faith in our ability to create such a world. But building a new dispensation would require analyzing and reviewing the direction in which the world is proceeding. So we decided to gather together every year in this forum to examine where our world is heading.

This year's WSF organised in Senegal was significant for two reasons. First, it was organised on African soil. Second, the people's movements and activist groups who assembled in Dakar sought to understand how they could strengthen themselves for their struggle to change the political contours of the world. The organisation of the event may have been found wanting in many ways but it nevertheless provided the ideal opportunity to examine the critical Middle East and African question.

It was a time of turmoil in the region. Even as 50,000 people gathered to explore the way to democracy and happiness, in neighbouring Egypt hundreds of thousands of people came out into the streets to free themselves from the clutches of dictatorship and fight for the restoration of democracy in their country. It was an exhilarating experience to watch people at the forum excitedly discussing Egypt and tracking whether Hosni Mubarak had abdicated power or not. A large rally was organised in Dakar in support of the people's movement in Egypt, which ended in a demonstration before the Egyptian embassy.

It was during these days that a similar political environment was building up in many other African and Middle East countries like Tunisia, Algeria, Yemen, Iran and Libya. And groups from around the world were rallying in solidarity with these people's movements. For those 10 days, newspapers across Africa and Europe devoted most of their space to report what was happening in Egypt and these other countries because of its spill-over implications across the region. From this you can get a sense of the political climate across the Middle East and Africa.

Incidentally, around 1,000 delegates were activists from countries like Burma and Congo who had sought political refuge in France, South Africa and other countries after being forced to flee their home countries because of their participation in revolutionary struggles.

This year the focus at the Dakar forum was on international migration, democracy and the political character of different countries, the exploitation of land and natural resources, and other related issues.

Over 50,000 social activists from across the globe gathered in the first week of February in Dakar, the capital of Senegal, a country situated in the western fringe of Africa, to participate in WSF 2011. This series of global meetings has been held regularly every year ever since the first forum was organised in Porto Allegro, Brazil, in 2001. It provides a platform for social activists from across the world to share their ideas, strategies and struggles for creating a new and better world.

The first WSF was a response to the World Economic Forum organised at Davos in Switzerland. It boldly articulated the stand that it is possible to create a world in which basic human needs would gain precedence over ever-growing corporate rapaciousness and exploitation. Ten years have gone by during which WSF has sought to unite social movements across the world struggling against the forces of neoliberal capitalism and militarism, seeking a world order based on social justice and dedicated to humanity.

The chain of global meetings held in Brazil, India, Kenya and now Senegal reveal that the political orientation of not just local, national or regional forums but even the WSF is veering leftwards. In Africa this year, the attempt was once again to link local conditions with the global struggle for justice and equality.

The main agenda of the Dakar forum was the current recession in the global capitalist economy, which is impacting most severely on the poorest countries in the world. Its effects are clearly evident in the turmoil we are witnessing in the financial, energy and food sectors of most countries as well as the climatic changes taking place the world over. Privatisation of public resources under the neoliberal policies supported by global institutions like the World Bank and International Monetary Fund has had its most deleterious effect on countries in the African continent.

Keeping in mind the current global economic conditions, the Dakar forum focused on three main ideological issues: the growing criticism of capitalism, the growing strength of the struggles against capitalism and imperialism, and using democratic and traditional methods as an alternative to repression and exploitation.

The six-day forum began with a huge rally from downtown Dakar to the university, where the programmes were subsequently organised. There was unbounded enthusiasm among the participants, the diversity in the messages sporting the banners they carried and the slogans they shouted pointing to how wide range and depth of the concept of social justice. The rally ended with a speech by Bolivia's leftist president Evo Morales. Denouncing imperialism in no uncertain terms, he underlined the importance of WSF, pointing out that it is like a school where activists learn how to develop, consolidate and strengthen their social revolutions to make them more effective.

A host of activities were planned on the forum agenda. The first day was devoted to Africa and emigrants from the continent. The daughters of Franz Fanon and Malcolm X participated in this session, discussing the legacy of their famed fathers. There was also a session chaired by former Brazilian president Luiz Inacio Lula da Silva in which he urged stronger ties between African and South American countries. Brazil is not just home to WSF but to the largest number of African emigrants.

The next two days of introspection brought out the wide range of concerns and rights issues that had brought participants together from across the globe. The evenings were devoted to music and cultural programmes as well as informal meetings. The last two days were devoted to the coordinators of various organisations, networks and revolutionary groups who expounded their plans of action for a better world based on the collective thinking of the forum. The closing ceremony had organisations making their announcements and reiterating their responsibilities.

In the initial years the WSF concept was of a platform where civil society groups could sit together and reflect on their common concerns. It was conceived to assist and strengthen grass roots organisations so they could grow and develop rather than to create a one-point programme to pursue any special agenda. But the forum became increasingly open to criticism for its inability to articulate a stand on several issues, especially with many organisations coming forward to seek help for furthering their political agendas.

In the first forum in 2001, a consensus was reached on the influential role played by Washington in the privatization of global resources. In subsequent forums one sees a tendency to view governments as part of the problem. This led to the organisers excluding governments, political parties and armed terrorist organisations. However, subsequent global political developments over the past decade point to a polarization of left forces, most clearly seen in South America than elsewhere. As a result of this process most participants today enthusiastically accept the view that political parties and governments can be used as weapons to resolve the problems raised by the crisis of global capitalism.

As in previous years, most of the delegates this year were from the host nation. In addition there were large contingents from neighbouring African countries. There were also a large number of delegates from France, Senegal's earlier colonial master. The preponderance of Francophone countries from Africa meant the language of discourse was mainly French, unlike earlier forums, which were mostly multilingual. This led to many delegates from former British colonies like Nigeria and Kenya feeling a sense of neglect.

Until now, most forums had attracted more than 100,000 delegates, hence the 50,000 who congregated at Dakar made WSF 2011 look comparatively small. The largest forums organised until now were in Brazil and India, which have a population far larger than Senegal's 12 million. But since it is the host nation that usually contributes the most delegates, the Dakar forum should not be seen as being unsuccessful.

Every forum has had its own style and character. Unfortunately, the Dakar forum will be remembered for its limited size. Truly, this is unfortunate since this forum had tremendous potential. Africa is certainly no stranger to the WSF process, having hosted the forum more times than any other continent.

The Dakar forum had to contend with many logistical problems. The local committee given the responsibility of organizing the event was not up to the task. In spite of this it refused any international assistance. It was thus inevitable that the forum suffered from a problem that is the hallmark of all WSF's—chaotic organisation. There was little concept of punctuality. Many delegates found it difficult to locate the venue of their sessions. The extra classes organised by the university to make up for the loss caused by a strike a few days earlier compounded the problem. As a result, in many cases the students shooed the delegates away from their allocated locations. This surprised many delegates, who felt that the organisers should have made some attempt to invite students to participate. Some haphazard attempts were made to put up tents to keep the sessions going but the general confusion prevailing led to many sessions being cancelled or organised with no contrast to the schedule.

The greatest setback was the backlash from the successful rebellions in Tunisia and Egypt to overthrow their dictatorial governments. It generated a fear in Senegal's president Abdoulade Wade that such an organised and disciplined assembly of social activists may somehow catalyse the fall of his own government. The help and permission of the host government is crucial for organizing food, housing and other necessities for such a large assembly. But in Senegal, an unwilling president tried instead to ruin the forum.

One issue of discussion in the forum was whether it is at all necessary to organise such a gathering of social activists from around the world considering the large capital expenditure involved, its organisational shortcomings and the environmental impact. What mostly happens is that NGOs with time, financial resources and visa facilities find it easier to participate in such forums than grass roots organisations, who do not have such facilities or resources.

Participants of WSF 2011 discussed the issues of concerns in detail. The focus was on Migration, Land and other resource grabbing, dying democracy, challenges for people's action, rapid expansion of corporate control over political economy, climate change etc. There were discussions and sessions on the concept of de-growth. We also learned about the agriculture and food crisis from various aspects, like future trading, price volatility, increasing corporate control over agriculture across the world. But at a point of time we, the participants of this grand global event almost failed to discuss the role of justice institutions and seek the possibilities for collective action to activate them. In India we have enormous number of institutions having mandates to protect fundamental rights of the people and simultaneously protect democracy, but we find these institutions like National Human Rights Commission and Right to Information Commissions have started becoming a party in the rights violation. It was not a coincidence that people of Middle-East and Arab countries or even in some of the African countries are now marching towards changing rules of injustice in respective countries, they now feel they are in practice are the colony of their own exploitative rulers. Their rulers don't believe in democracy, transparency and accountability at any level, and if all such things are asked, bullets and guns will facilitate them.

[Grammar and spelling as in the original essay.]. We have seen earlier in Pakistan, where government ruled the Supreme Court and in India recent ex-Chief Justice of Supreme Court is being charged with corruption. This is not a case from a particular country, but in most of the under-developed and developing countries, judiciary has become a patron to the anti-people policies and integral part of the state system rather then providing justice to people and make state systems accountable. We all are concerned about the media freedom but it was a fact that we need to focus our ideological opposition against increasing corporate control over media and state supported violence against journalists, but somehow knowingly-unknowingly debate on organised attacks on free media were not there on the discussion forums. It is a global trend that all the countries now do every thing what they want to do by making laws and policies to justify all sorts of actions. We all found that land grabbing is not a un-organised strategy, State is with the capitalist corporate and in fact resource grabbing exercises are being performed in a legal framework by following a structured plan, but there are no policies to protect tribal from eviction and forced displacement. The state authorities for ensuring smooth displacement can rape tribal women, patriarchal society keep silent on these inhuman actions. Firing is justified, if people ask for democracy and accountability in the governance system, and out judicial system keeps silent on these incidences, because judiciary also want to be under umbrella of larger state machinery sp that its own wasted interest are protected. It is in deed a fact that existing justice institutions are being used purposefully to serve the purpose of the elitist, capitalists and politically powerful.

Various countries are deeply involved in justice reforms but primarily they want to ensure that corporate interests are protected first, so debt and capital rules are being changed, special courts are established, single window system for land control are in place, police services stand with industries, land ceiling acts have been changed and so on; but there are no steps to protect farmers, so that they don't commit suicide, acts are their to protect Women, Children, Dalits, Tribal from exclusion and caste based exclusion and violence, but not practiced because it will be an efforts towards power sharing and changing power relations.

Fundamentally; an integrated stroke oriented approach with focused issues making dent on the structural causes of Exclusion, Exploitation, Violence, Injustice, Hunger & Poverty, Eviction and Displacement needs to be defined and accomplished through forums like WSF.

Several activists suggested that instead of holding such forums it might be a better idea to organise virtual forums. But it should be noted in this context that, even now, face-to-face encounters are seen as better than virtual encounters, with many universities pulling back from virtual classrooms in online education to opt for actual classes instead.

Even after a decade of successful organisation of these forums, the future of the WSF is still in a limbo. The international organizing committee met at the end of the Dakar forum to discuss future strategy. When the first forum was held in Porto Allegro, it was decided to hold these meetings to demand social and economic justice from the perspective of the global south. However, the original enthusiasm has paled in the face of the organisational difficulties. Many delegates would still like to come to such forums once every two years. As long as the WSF is held the fight for social justice will not falter. But there is need for a review.

Note

1 "WSF 2011," http://fsm2011.org/en/wsf-2011.

13.4

WORLD CIVIC FORUM TAKES MIDDLE ROAD

Park Sang-seek

> In the following selection, a South Korean observer describes the first meeting of the World Civic Forum, which took place in Seoul in 2009. The author explains how the World Civic Forum is different from either the World Economic Forum or the World Social Forum. Whereas the World Economic Forum reflects the positive view of contemporary neoliberal globalization in the developed world and the World Social Forum, the negative view of this form of globalization in the developing world, the World Civic Forum, which consists mainly of university academics ("epistemic communities"), seeks to reconcile the contrasting views of the other two and foster a genuine global community to confront the challenges that face both the developed and the developing worlds.

The World Civic Forum had its inaugural meeting in Seoul on May 5–8. The founding of this forum has significant historical implications for the future development of international civil society and a global community.

There are already two similar world forums—the World Economic Forum (based in Davos, Switzerland) and the World Social Forum (based in Porto Alegree, Brazil). Therefore, it is necessary to examine the significance of the third international non-governmental forum in comparison with the existing two.

The main difference between the Cold War and post–Cold War periods is that the former was characterized by the global ideological confrontation between the communist and Western blocs and the global economic division between the developed and developing worlds.

In the post-Cold War era the world still suffers from two pairs of conflicts: intra-state and inter-state political conflicts underpinned by ethno-religious divisions and the aggravating North-South divide.

The bifurcated world in the two eras has a similarity as well as a difference—similar because one pair of conflicts is political and the other pair economic in both eras. They are different because the ideological conflict in the former era has been replaced by the ethno-religious conflict in the new era, which the North-South divide has aggravated.

Source: Park Sang-seek, "World Civic Forum Takes Middle Road," *The Korea Herald,* May 9, 2009.

The main agenda and tasks of the United Nations are how to deal with these new divisions and old confrontations. It mobilizes all kinds of peace keeping and peace-building mechanisms to solve the ethno-religious conflicts, while employing various means to reduce and eradicate the wealth disparity in the world.

The World Economic Forum (commonly called the Davos Forum) was officially launched in 1974 following the collapse of the Bretton Woods fixed exchange rate mechanism.

In contrast, the World Social Forum started in 2001 when globalization began to accelerate. Both were to deal with the problem of the North-South divide.

However, their approaches oppose each other.

The WEF holds that the developed and developing worlds can co-prosper through neo-liberalism, while the WSF rejects this view, arguing that neo-liberalism makes the North-South divide worse, by benefiting only the developed world. Their respective official purposes and agenda reveal that the WEF represents the interests of the developed world and the WSF those of the developing world.

Although both forums' participants encompass a wide range of political, economic, social, intellectual, mass media and civil society leaders, global business leaders dominate the WEF, and neo-Marxist and socialist leaders the WSF. Therefore, it is no surprise that the former wants to preserve the existing international economic order and supports globalization, while the latter wants to create a new world order and opposes globalization. In a sense, the WEF represents the forces of globalization and the WSF the forces of deglobalization.

Their attitudes toward civil society organizations also reveal their ideological differences. Business leaders are the main decision makers in the WEF while NGOs act mostly in an advisory capacity. In contrast, NGOs are the main players in the WSF.

In this connection, it is interesting to note that the UN attends both forums—directly through the Economic and Social Council in the case of the WEF and indirectly through UNESCO in the case of the WSF.

Since the UN is a strong advocate of the growth of global civil society organizations, it is no surprise that it participates in these forums, which may help it achieve its dual goal—peace and development. But the UN needs to carefully watch and guide the operations of these forums so that they do not aggravate the North-South divide and consequently obstruct or retard the creation of a global community.

How the newly-created World Civic Forum can contribute to the goals and objectives of the UN should be evaluated in this context. In terms of participants, the WCF also encompasses a wide range of civil society leaders as the WEF does. The main difference, in this regard, is that the WEF is dominated by global business elites and the WSF by non-partisan NGOs and social movements, whereas the WCF is led by diverse epistemic communities (particularly universities).

Most important, however, is that the goals and objectives of the WCF are to synthesize those of the other two forums. It sides with neither neo-liberal nor neo-Marxist/socialist ideologies. Neither does it support the position of the developed world nor that of the developing world. Its ultimate goal is to build a global community through replacing dehumanized civilization with a new humanitarian civilization.

In other words, it tries to sublimate both approaches and find a synthetic solution. This mean that it puts more emphasis on universal values and the active role of civil society in global governance rather than economic prosperity (as the WEF does) and social justice and equality (as the WSF does).

This difference is well reflected in the WCF 2009 Declaration on Building a Humanitarian Planet. It calls for civic values for social justice, civic engagement in public and global governance, and civic action for the global agenda. This is the reason the UN hosts the WCF jointly with Kyung Hee University.

Globalization increases and expands interactions and interdependence among international actors (such as states, governmental organizations, social movements and multinational companies), erodes state sovereignty, destroys cultural diversity, and creates and expands international networks among different peoples. In the process, global issues (climate change, energy shortage, etc.) occur. To deal with them, universal values (human rights, human security, tolerance, shared responsibility, etc.) will be nurtured and consolidated by all humanity. This trend will ultimately contribute to the emergence of a global community.

The developed world argues that the resolution of political conflicts will lead to economic prosperity, while the developing world asserts that the wealth disparity between the two worlds is the main cause of political conflicts. The WEF supports the first view and the WSF the second view. The WCF believes that both issues are intertwined and international conflicts are caused by many factors.

Now, we have three non-governmental forums of deliberative democracy in three different continents. We should welcome them, because they represent one of the three pillars of the global order—international civil society. (The other two are states, and international governmental organizations.)

13.5

IRAN PAPER SAYS JUDICIAL UNION AMONG ISLAMIC NATIONS IDEAL, POSSIBLE, INNOVATIVE

from *BBC Monitoring Middle East/Hamshahri*

The final selection in this chapter is from an Iranian newspaper that describes the positive reaction of an Iranian official to a proposal for forming an "International Judicial Union" among Islamic states. The author explains the way in which such an institution could unite Islamic societies, codify Islamic law, and facilitate Islamic globalization.

Source: "Iran Paper Says Judicial Union Among Islamic Nations Ideal, Possible, Innovative," *BBC Monitoring Middle East*—Political, December 6, 2007. Text of commentary by Seyyed Ebrahim Ra'isi published as "An Efficient Legal Center in the World of Islam" in the Iranian newspaper *Hamshahri* on December 4, 2007.

Deputy Judiciary Chief Seyyed Ebrahim Ra'isi said: "The proposal for the formation of an International Judicial Union among Islamic countries by the head of the Judiciary comes in a year that has been designated the year of Islamic solidarity by the supreme leader of the Islamic Revolution. The unique characteristics of Islamic countries and the strengths and capabilities they possess make this proposal ideal, possible, one that is rooted in an Islamic identity and is a new and innovative plan."

Through this plan, the Muslims of the world can take control of the legal initiatives of a third of the world. In view of the ever-increasing role of the law in different human societies and bearing in mind various economic, social, political and cultural reasons, they can use the first-class capabilities available to them and, despite the political challenges, they can bring together legal views and stances and prepare the necessary grounds for the unity of the Islamic nations.

A proud past can be re-created through this legal institution in sensitive and critical periods. It can be a powerful Islamic legal center that is influential, alongside the other noteworthy facilities in Islamic countries, in making the decisions of the Islamic world effective in the international arena, which is the main aim of this plan.

Today's Islamic world has the richest natural resources on earth such as oil and gas. It is also home to some of the most important strategic areas in the world such as the Suez Canal, the Strait of Gibraltar, the Dardanelles and the Strait of Hormoz. It makes up a huge proportion of the world's population, and, more important than anything else, it has the Islamic civilization.

Another salient and key point which has prompted this proposal is found in the nature of Islam which seeks to unify the world and not fragment it. More than any other model throughout history, Islam is based on globalization. Indeed, it was Islam that, in only a short span of time, presented globalization founded on a common belief and faith for the first time in history in various legal, economic, social, political, scientific and cultural arenas. It is a religion that gave the world the first global economic and commercial system in history; the Silk Road [Route] from China to the coasts of the Mediterranean being a tangible symbol of this Islamic global economic system. It is a religion which by stating "we did not send you other than as a kindness to the world" stands beyond political, racial, national and tribal borders and with the slogan of an ideological boundary and by placing the Islamic nation at its center, it presented the framework for a single, global government.

The capabilities and latent potentials, which exist in Islamic countries, demonstrate that if they were to come together in legal or non-legal unions as a consolidated collective, then through the ancient culture and civilization they share, supplemented with their [Islamic] values and principles, this union could achieve the necessary dynamism. Subsequently, alongside other symbols such as Hajj [the pilgrimage]—which is symbolic of globalization on a scale that no other political or religious school of thought can boast—and without having to depend on intermediary organizations, the media or mechanisms and technology, every year it could create miracles as the only cultural connection between the Islamic nations. They should use this [union] as a model in their global struggle so that when need be, they can use it to defend their Islamic culture and identity.

Initially, this union can be formed through a favorable response from many of the Islamic countries, then gradually all the countries can join. The success of such a legal union is clear from the beginning. This is because it will share a common basis, such as the Noble Koran and will have a rich foundation of Islamic laws along with the principles of divine government, the interests of the Islamic nation and the protection of mankind. It will be assisted by a shared Islamic culture and the fact that the weltanschauung [the overall perspective from which one sees and interprets the world] of all Islamic countries stems from the religion and arises from a precise, systematic and comprehensive divine worldview.

It is hoped that with the formation of this union, alongside other Islamic unions such as the Inter-Parliamentary Union, and by codifying unchanging regulations and laws in different fields, the Islamic countries can enjoy an integrated legal system. It is clear that with unified views in legal matters new horizons will be opened up for the Islamic countries.

It seems that today, courts in all the Islamic countries apply Islamic laws, at least in personal matters. If this interaction results in the rich and resplendent laws of Islam also being applied to civil, legal and penal matters, and the experiences being used, then an effective step forward will have been taken.

Chapter 14

THE FUTURE OF GLOBALIZATION

Will globalization persist, will it assume another form, or will it be reversed? Large and expansive empires have repeatedly united and governed diverse peoples, only to collapse and divide into small, local polities. Thus, the ancient Mediterranean region at the height of the Roman Empire was highly integrated, but in the end it collapsed under the external pressure of nomadic tribes and dissolved into the highly localized feudal system of medieval Europe. In China, even during the warring states era, a sense of cultural unity produced a common identity among the Han Chinese, notwithstanding localized security and economic arrangements, yet through the centuries Chinese unity has waxed and waned. Out of medieval Europe, with its small, localized polities, there emerged large territorial states. The cultural cohesion afforded Europe by Christianity ended with the Reformation and the religious wars that divided the continent into Catholic and Protestant adversaries.

A form of globalization also characterized the world of Europe's colonial empires from the 17th to the early 20th century. Economic interdependence deepened when mercantilism gave way to economic liberalism and free trade. As the Nobel Prize–winning economist Paul Krugman declares, "Our great-great grandfathers lived, as we do, in a world of large-scale international trade and investment, a world destroyed by nationalism." Krugman quotes John Maynard Keynes's description of prewar Europe:

> The inhabitant of London could order by telephone, sipping his morning tea in bed, the various products of the whole earth . . . he could at the same moment and by the same means adventure his wealth in the natural resources and new enterprises of any quarter of the world.

"But then," continues Krugman,

> came three decades of war, revolution, political instability, depression and more war. By the end of World War II, the world was fragmented economically as well as politically. And it took a couple of generations to put it back together. So, can things fall apart again? Yes, they can.[1]

Note

1 Paul Krugman, "The Great Illusion," *New York Times*, August 15, 2008, http://www.nytimes.com/2008/08/15/opinion/15krugman.html.

14.1

GLOBALIZATION AND THE FUTURE: UNSTOPPABLE OR REVERSIBLE PROCESS?

Richard W. Mansbach

> This essay, which introduces the final chapter of the book, synthesizes much of what has been said in earlier chapters in an effort to peek into the future of globalization.[1]

Globalization has had to confront strong head winds in the years following the global spread of America's subprime mortgage crisis. National boundaries had already thickened after 9/11 and the threat of continued transnational terrorism. The threat of economic protectionism was already visible with the collapse of the Doha Round of global trade talks, and the multilateral virtues of global governance were under strain from America's unilateralist policies—the invasion of Iraq, reluctance to support the International Criminal Court, and refusal to join the Kyoto Protocol to the UN Convention on Climate Change. Other indicators of a slowing of globalization included growing public concern about the outsourcing of jobs from the developed world, resistance in Europe and the United States to the flow of migrants and asylum seekers fleeing poverty or violence, the failure of the 2009 Copenhagen environmental summit, and Europe's difficulties in constructing a unified response to the threat of sovereign default by some of its members.

The global financial crisis revived questions about the dark side of globalization, casting doubts on the wisdom of neoliberal capitalism and its future, and the need to renew state intervention in global economic and financial markets. The crisis also produced a retreat into nationalism and protectionism. Do unregulated markets really benefit the global economy and enrich states, or do the practices of unaccountable banks and corporations entail unjustifiable risks?

No less an advocate of globalization than the journalist Thomas Friedman recognized the potentially damaging impact of "millions of investors moving money around the world with the click of a mouse," which he dubbed "the Electronic Herd."[2] Concentrated in global cities like New York and London, the "Herd," Friedman conceded, could bring down governments and could discipline a national economy "either by the herd avoiding or withdrawing its money from that country."[3] Credit-rating agencies like Moody's, which Friedman labeled "the bloodhounds for the Electronic Herd,"[4] played a major role in the threat of sovereign default by Greece and elsewhere in Europe in 2010–2012 by downgrading the rating of their bonds.

Counterglobalization Currents

The years following the onset of the global recession witnessed an acceleration of negative localism and opposition to cultural, economic, and political globalization, as well as pessimism about globalization's future. The revival of nationalism, as we saw earlier, remains an obstacle to globalization. Although globalization may erode national identities, this very process may trigger efforts to reinvigorate nationalism. Fear that global culture eats away at local values stimulates a backlash, especially in traditional societies, as well as efforts to adapt globalization to local circumstances.

As we noted earlier in this book, recent decades have witnessed secessionist yearnings of national groups such as Bosnian Muslims, Chechens, Albanians, Tibetans, China's Uighurs, and Sri Lanka's Tamils, suggesting that human loyalties are still anchored in nations. Governments, moreover, have manipulated national sensitivities to promote unity and national pride, as did China in hosting the 2008 Beijing Olympics. In sum, nationalism is anchored in territory and erects boundaries—both antithetical to globalization.

Disillusionment with neoliberal economics, heightened by the global economic malaise, has been accompanied by renewed efforts to firm up state borders and reassert state sovereignty. Regulation, especially of financial institutions, is again looked upon favorably, and the neoliberal preference for market-based solutions is no longer automatically assumed to work best. Governments have responded with deficit spending that accounts for larger shares of GDP, which in turn has produced pressure for cutting national budgets and the virtual, if temporary, takeover of key financial institutions. In the United States, President Barack Obama moved toward more activist government, an effort that has met stubborn opposition from the Republicans. State intervention, justified as an effort to ease the effects of recession, reveals a retreat from neoliberal economics. Growing sovereign wealth funds (government investment portfolios) in emerging economies reflect the spread of state capitalism and are favored over private investment.

Elsewhere, state failure is isolating many people from globalization. The absence of state authority in countries like Somalia or the western regions of Pakistan makes them asylums for terrorists, narcotics traffickers, and pirates and threatens to spread disorder across entire regions. Somali pirates prey on shipping in the Arabian Gulf and Indian Ocean. Mexico is at war with drug gangs that purchase arms in the United States. Civil war among national, ethnic, and tribal rivals afflicts large areas of the developing world.

Civil wars and poverty trigger migration, even as immigration controls in the United States, the European Union (EU), and elsewhere are tightened, and in wealthy countries, the issue of economic migration from poor countries is a focus of passionate controversy. In addition to intensifying opposition to migration, the economic recession slowed migration to wealthy societies. By 2009, reverse migration had begun as Mexicans from the United States headed south and the governments of Spain and Japan provided cash incentives for migrants to return home. Antimigrant sentiment in the United States and Europe is partly a result of high unemployment, and one consequence was a significant reduction in the remittances sent home by migrants, which constitute a source of income for developing countries. Migration from poor to rich regions provides young workers and taxpayers to support the growing welfare costs in aging societies but simultaneously poses problems of assimilation. However, the alternative to admitting migrants to rich countries with declining populations may be the outsourcing of industries to developing countries.

Countries also erected new barriers to trade after the onset of the global recession. In addition to higher tariffs and subsidies for "national champions," barriers to the movement of capital proliferated. Protectionism breeds conflict. China's reluctance to allow the value of its currency to rise in relation to the U.S. dollar, its management of capital flows, its passage of an antimonopoly law to prevent foreign takeovers of local companies, its requirement that high-tech products contain "indigenous innovation," and its export controls on raw materials all provoked protests in Europe and the United States, inducing them to file complaints before the World Trade Organization.

The unanswered question is whether economic nationalism is a long-term trend and a source of political divisions or a temporary retreat in the face of economic hard times. Although by 2010 global trade had begun to grow once more, protectionist barriers, once in place, may be difficult to remove.

Opposition to global governance remains strong. This is evident in failed efforts to curb global warming. In 2007, China overtook the United States as the world's leading source of carbon emissions. The transformation of China and India into economic giants has complicated the task of dealing with global environmental challenges. Developing countries like China and India are unwilling to limit carbon emissions because to do so would slow economic development, but they are also likely to be the worst affected by global warming. Unwillingness to sacrifice economic development, intensified by the slowing of economic growth, remains a major obstacle to environmental cooperation, especially between rich and poor countries. In negotiations on limiting carbon emissions in preparation for a meeting in Copenhagen in 2009 to replace the Kyoto Protocol, China and India argued that Americans remain higher per capita sources of carbon emissions than their citizens, while Washington contended that China's and India's rates of increasing carbon emissions are higher. And the Obama administration has been unable and/or unwilling to confront congressional and public opposition to expensive programs to reduce carbon emissions.

What Next?

How does it all add up? The question of whether globalization is reversible is complex. Each trend seems to trigger resistance that makes visible opposing trends. Centralization of authority creates pressures for its decentralization and vice versa. Globalized values produce efforts to defend local cultures, and free trade calls forth demands for protectionism. Cultural globalization has rested on the spread of free market capitalism based on values such as political democracy, individualism, secularism, and consumerism, which are viewed as necessary for economic development but are resented because they undermine traditional cultures and mores that anchor communities psychologically.

Nationalism may imperil globalization, yet global culture may place "nations" in danger of losing what makes them distinctive in terms of religion, history, and language. Demographic trends in the developed and developing worlds produce greater migration, and greater migration triggers nationalist opposition. Unilateral policies produce demands for multilateralism, and multilateralism with the need for compromise will create pressures to act unilaterally.

On the one hand, globalization has been encouraged by states, especially in the developed world, in their own interest, even while in some respects it reduces state autonomy. In other words, states voluntarily limit their autonomy and then complain about its loss. In return, the apparent decline in autonomy provides political leaders with justification for pursuing policies while denying responsibility for them.

Political globalization and steps toward global governance include the establishment of international institutions like the International Monetary Fund, the World Bank, and the World Trade Organization. Other institutions like the UN, the EU, the African Union, and NATO (the North Atlantic Treaty Organization) have helped create global order by undertaking humanitarian intervention and aiding the reconstruction of failed states (plus Russia). Finally, the shift in economic influence from the Group of 8 (G-8) of wealthy states to the Group of 20 (G-20) suggests the flexibility needed to co-opt developing countries like Brazil, China, and India into assuming responsibility for more global governance. Governance has also assumed the form of an incipient global civil society built on a dense network of nongovernmental organizations (NGOs). However, efforts by international institutions, NGOs, or states to foster global governance may produce a backlash.

Even in the absence of the global economic slowdown, there would be resistance to neoliberal globalization. Environmentalists who believe that the outsourcing of industry to developing countries leads to a "race to the bottom" by making it easier for firms to evade environmental regulations, members of labor unions in developed countries who see their jobs disappear and believe that lower labor costs result in the exploitation of local workers and the erosion of welfare and safety rules, and local businessmen who find themselves unable to compete with giant transnational corporations will continue to resist globalization.

In the end, we probably should reject the dichotomy between a globalized world and a world of independent and sovereign states. Like most dichotomies, it forces us to make an "either/or" choice instead of viewing the world as dynamically moving back and forth between extremes. The two worlds—globalized versus interstate—are ideal versions of a messy reality.

Nevertheless, globalization has revolutionized global politics. Interconnectedness, the essence of globalization, exists despite head winds. Spreading information technologies continue to make state frontiers porous and will continue to foster interconnectedness. States remain, but they have been penetrated by global economic, political, and cultural forces over which they exert only limited control. Global markets, along with giant corporations, distribute global resources and alter the well-being of individuals everywhere, sometimes for better and sometimes for worse. Although individual countries like

North Korea and Myanmar may opt out of globalization, they must pay high costs for doing so.

For many people, national and communal identities will compete with other identities. Migration continues despite efforts to slow it. Violence and famine will send people across borders, and prosperity elsewhere will attract them. Notwithstanding setbacks in countries from Venezuela and Russia to Thailand and Zimbabwe, democratic aspirations are spreading to new countries, especially in the Middle East. Nevertheless, perceptions of intrastate and interstate economic inequality (whether correct or not) and a backlash against alleged cultural homogenization and the erosion of traditional values will continue to mobilize opponents of globalization.

The institutions of globalization, from transnational corporations to international organizations, remain in reasonably good health. A variety of NGOs, the elements of global civil society, continue to provide humanitarian relief and protection for civilians despite the opposition of authoritarian regimes like those of China and Russia. International organizations, aided by NGOs and wealthy states, continue to intervene to restore peace or provide for the welfare of citizens living in countries that have failed or are in danger of doing so, and the norms that underpin interstate and transnational collaboration remain intact. Such efforts reflect globalization's importance and involve the recognition that it is impossible for states to isolate themselves from global crises and currents.

In the coming years, globalization will be tested by ethnic and religious sectarianism. We live in a turbulent era. At present, it is not clear whether major states have the political will or vision to oppose oppressive regimes such as those in Zimbabwe and Iran or provide the resources for international institutions to sustain global order. Humanitarian intervention has been haphazard, depending on the attitude of major powers like the United States and China. The record is not encouraging and provides the evidence for Robert Kaplan's apocalyptic vision of a world dominated by "poverty, the collapse of cities, porous borders, cultural and racial strife, growing economic disparities, weakening nation states," a world of "disease pandemics like AIDS, environmental catastrophes, organized crime."[5] The kind of chaos described by Kaplan is likely to afflict areas in the developing world where poverty, population growth, ecological disaster, and corruption promote state failure. Disorder, religious fanaticism, and ethnic secession remain threats to globalization.

Spasms of local or regional violence, as well as terrorism, may lead to authoritarian solutions and renewed efforts to isolate societies. This was the path taken by Chile, Uruguay, and Argentina in the 1970s. Contemporary Russia illustrates how creeping authoritarianism can occur as a way of restoring "order." As long as globalization does not rob states of political independence, governments will view events through the prism of the national interest, especially as long as issues like those dividing Indians and Pakistanis and Israelis and Palestinians persist. Where such conflicts fester, leaders will find it expedient to whip up nationalism against real or imagined foes. Whatever form it assumes, tomorrow's world is likely to be complex and unpredictable.

The rapid spread of financial and economic distress globally that began with America's subprime mortgage crisis reveals that major economic outcomes remain the result of market forces that governments can soften but cannot resist. Asia's 1997–1998 financial contagion was a harbinger of the later global crisis. The institutions of globalization did not serve Asia well at that time, but Asia's economies recovered quickly, and Asians did not turn their backs on globalization. Asia's experience suggests that while the world may seek a different institutional architecture in which more countries have a greater voice, it will not reject globalization in a wholesale way.

The future of globalization is becoming clearer as the global recession wanes. Trade conflicts have remained tolerable. Nationalism remains a threat, even in Europe, where divisions exist over matters such as aid to economic laggards like Greece and Ireland, but it has not undermined the key international and nongovernmental institutions of globalization. Everywhere states responded to the economic crisis by assuming a more significant regulatory role, but this may merely reflect a rebalancing after decades of neoliberal capitalism. Antimigration sentiment remains strong, but demographic and economic realities should limit its worst consequences. Environmental nationalism persisted, in part because of the economic crisis, but may ease in the face of intensified environmental problems, technological improvements, and growing evidence of negative consequences.

Prospects for global governance are modest. International organizations reflect institutional globalization but, for the most part, lack authority beyond that conceded to them by leading member states, whether in matters of nuclear proliferation, environmental standards, or reform of global financial markets. The failure of the United States and China to assume leadership on such issues is a reminder that major states still play a key role in global governance.

None of this means an end to globalization, though it may be slowing. A negative reaction to the excesses of neoliberal economic policies is, as we have seen, already visible. After all, globalization is a highly complex, multidimensional phenomenon that defies simple predictions. Thus, globalized violence—world wars or international terrorism—complicates the transnational movement of people, as tourists, businessmen, or migrants. Global diseases and crime interfere with the movement of persons and things but not the movement of ideas or cultural norms. Global economic crises produce self-interested protectionist policies and nationalist sentiments that can slow additional economic globalization.

In the end, although some observers are convinced that globalization is neither inevitable nor irreversible, some factors make it unlikely that globalization will be reversed. The most important is the spread of technologies that allow instantaneous global communication and the rapid movement of people and things. Although some countries have tried to impose national controls on technologies like the Internet, these efforts have met with mixed success. A second factor is the presence in most countries of wealthy globalized business and knowledge elites that have an interest in fostering globalization. Another is the challenge of issues that individual states cannot effectively manage. There is, of course, no logical necessity for actors to cope with collective dilemmas, but there is considerable incentive for them to do so. A fourth factor is the growing economic and political specialization of countries and the integrated networks of transnational corporations.

Globalization will have its ups and downs in the coming years, but it is unlikely to be reversed barring a major global war or an economic catastrophe such as the collapse of the U.S. dollar.

Since history is not linear, we should not expect globalization to be linear either. Some trends will increase globalization, even as others impede it. Some eras will witness rapid globalization, while others will entail its retreat. There is no teleology to globalization, only contingencies and possibilities. There is no simple strategy to enhance globalization, reverse it, or end it.

Notes

1   For a lengthy and in-depth analysis of some of the issues dealt with in this brief essay, see Yale H. Ferguson and Richard W. Mansbach, *Globalization: The Return of Borders to a Borderless World?* (Abingdon, UK: Routledge, 2012), chapters 9 and 10.
2   Thomas L. Friedman, *The Lexus and the Olive Tree*, rev. ed. (New York: Farrar, Straus and Giroux, 2000), 13.
3   Ibid., 110.
4   Ibid.
5   Robert D. Kaplan, *The Ends of the Earth: From Togo to Turkmenistan, From Iran to Cambodia, a Journey to the Frontiers of Anarchy* (New York: Vintage Books, 1996), 436.

14.2

GLOBAL NEWS STORIES VS. GLOBAL ISSUES

Park Sang-seek

The following selection observes that, with the global financial crisis that originated in the United States, the American model of neoliberal capitalism has been increasingly assailed, especially outside the West. The Korean author lists what he regards as the 10 most challenging items on the global agenda, most of which, from pandemic diseases and identity conflicts to international terrorism and governance crises, are related to globalization. He observes that global challenges have not elicited the global cooperation needed to manage them effectively and that the main obstacle to doing so remains nationalism. His pessimistic conclusion is that the "greatest challenge to humankind now is how to shift the traditional sources of identity to the modern one—the global community."

Source: Park Sang-seek, "Global News Stories vs. Global Issues," *The Korea Herald,* January 6, 2009.

Time magazine and the Associated Press recently selected their top 10 news stories of 2008. Five of them are identical: Obama's win as U.S. president, the global economic crisis, the Russia-Georgia war, the terrorist attacks in Mumbai and the earthquake in China. If they had published their results in the last week of December, they surely would have included the Israeli attacks on Gaza in the list.

News organizations usually select top news items on the basis of "newsworthiness," not implications for or possible impact on the future of humanity as a whole. However, sensational news items often reveal the symptoms of global issues.

For instance, the epicenter of the global economic crisis is the United States, which has been in control of the global financial system. The existing international financial order established at Bretton Woods was almost exclusively designed by the United States to impose the principles and rules of its capitalist economic system.

This system has been challenged and opposed by developing countries ever since, while Western countries have basically supported it. This difference deepened the East-West conflict during the Cold War period because the communist countries formed a united front with the Third World against the capitalist world economic order. Another example is the terrorist attacks in India. The cause of the incident can be found in the essential nature of terrorism.

The world needs to pay more attention to global issues rather than global news stories because if the former are resolved, the latter will no longer become newsworthy.

Here are the 10 most serious global issues that have and will have the most profound impact on the fate of humanity. They are, not in order of importance, political terrorism (domestic and international), proliferation of weapons of mass destruction, the international economic order, environmental degradation (particularly climate change), poverty and wealth disparity (within and between states), identity conflicts (ethnic, regional and religious), pandemic diseases, governance crises (failed state, rogue state, corruption, etc.), resources depletion (energy, water, food, etc.), and the knowledge divide.

Broadly speaking, there are three kinds of terrorist movements in terms of their goals: religious movements, ideological movements and ethnic movements. Geographically, there are local, regional, national and international organizations.

According to the list of terrorist groups made by the U.S. State Department there are 44 terrorist groups. Of them 23 organizations are Muslim movements and 9 Marxist. Out of the 44 organizations only two (al-Qaida and AUM) have a global goal and others seek either the overthrow of the existing regime or the establishment of a separate state.

The problem relating to terrorism is that most nations are only concerned with the organizations threatening their own security. This is why nations rarely take joint action against any terrorist organizations. More importantly, Muslim terrorist organizations are mostly aiming at the overthrow of Israel or the establishment of a Palestinian state in Israel and are openly or silently supported by some Muslims in the world.

Proliferation of WMDs cannot easily be solved, mainly because the Nuclear Non-Proliferation Treaty has two conflicting rules: the classification of states into nuclear and non-nuclear powers and the privilege given to the nuclear powers. The five nuclear states are allowed to have their nuclear weapons, while non-nuclear powers are prohibited to do so. Non-nuclear powers can hardly accept these rules. The NPT also has a provision stipulating that the nuclear states ultimately abandon their nuclear arsenals.

Another serious challenge to the NPT is that some non-nuclear states are informally accepted as de facto nuclear states. North Korea claims that it is one such state.

Unless and until this illogical provision and practice are rectified, there will be more Irans. It is good news that recently prominent American pundits have jointly called for the denuclearization of the world. This is exactly the raison d'etre of the NPT.

The existing international economic order should be urgently revamped. Of course, it will not be replaced by an entirely new order, but is likely to be gradually transformed into a system that is governed by a consortium formed by G20, as a new international financial system will be established through the G20 conference.

Here again is a formidable obstacle. G20 encompasses groups representing different positions, from conservative to radical: the United States, the EU, China and Japan as well as Brazil representing a variety of Third World positions. The key issues are principles of supervision of the international financial institutions and the mechanisms of supervision. The United States desperately tries not to lose its hegemony over the international financial institutions because otherwise, its political and economic hegemony in the world will most likely diminish. Other great powers will use the international financial crisis as an opportunity to establish a multi-polar world order.

The UN Millennium Summit adopted a lofty declaration, and based on the declaration, the Millennium Development Goals were adopted to reduce and ultimately eradicate poverty and wealth disparity in the world.

Developed and developing countries lock horns on this issue. Developing countries demand more aid and preferential treatment of their exports, while developed countries call for good governance and the eradication of corruption as a prerequisite. It is not surprising that this perceptional difference has been the main obstacle to the WTO trade negotiation processes.

The MDGs include eight goals (ending hunger, universal education, gender equality, child health, maternal health, combating HIV/AIDs, environmental sustainability and global partnership). The irony is that without global partnership, the other seven goals cannot be achieved. Despite the pressure of globalization on global partnership, nations are unable to form a common front to overcome poverty and wealth disparity.

Identity conflicts have become a major source of domestic and international conflicts since the end of the cold war. They threaten and undermine not only the peace and stability of nations but also cause international conflicts. Moreover, they become a breeding ground for terrorism. The sources of identity—ethnicity, religion and region—are so deeply embedded in everybody's psyche that it is extremely difficult, if not impossible, for a person to overcome them and shift to another.

Another problem with identity is that one can hardly maintain dual identities. We expect that the rapid process of globalization in every field of life will erode the traditional sources of identity, but the speed of erosion is too slow and geographically uneven. The global epistemic community holds that humanity can shift its identity from the traditional community based on ethnicity, nation or religion to a community of universal values. But the fight between the forces of globalization and those of particularism aggravate identity conflicts.

Concerning the problem of pandemic diseases, there is no doubt that the poorer countries become, the more pandemic diseases they have. We see here a close relationship between the problem of poverty and the problem of pandemic diseases. Under the circumstances, if one problem is solved, a solution for the other will also be found.

Governance crises are closely related to the increasing number of failed states, rogue states, identity crises, power struggles, etc. Good governance is required of all organizations at all levels, private and public. Bad governance is more likely to happen in non-democratic and poor states. It also exists at international organizations. Serious scholarly debates are going on about how good governance can be realized.

Traditional forms of governance may not be suitable for modern organizations. Even representative democracy is viewed as an archaic form of governance. The necessity of UN reform is no longer questioned, but nations are divided on how the UN should be reformed.

Environmental degradation is so widespread and serious that it needs an immediate cure. It encompasses climate change, loss of biological diversity, deforestation, desertification, reduced fresh water and marine pollution. All these problems cause food scarcities.

Here is again the North-South conflict in a different form: resource poor countries blame the industrialized countries for environmental damages and demand compensation in the form of economic and technological aid, while the industrial countries are hesitant to do so because they cannot decelerate industrial development.

All nations agree on the necessity for environmental protection, but are divided on the ways and means and speed for accomplishing the set goals. Consequently, there have emerged six interest groups: the EU, the United States, the non-European developed countries, the newly industrialized nations, island nations and the least developed countries. No matter what kind of programs the UN adopts, they will hardly reach consensus.

The last global issue is knowledge divide. This concept includes digital divide. Even in this area developed and developing countries disagree on how knowledge can be shared by all humanity.

No one questions the close relationship between poverty and knowledge. Developing countries ask for aid for educational development in their countries and the loosening of intellectual property rights. Yet developed countries demand better governance and management, gender equality for educational development, and the reform of educational systems and programs, while insisting on the strict protection of intellectual property rights. In this context, it is a welcome development for all countries that the theory of knowledge as a global common good is promoted by some prominent scholars.

What are the main obstacles to all these global issues? Nationalism based on traditional sources of identity is the ultimate source of conflicts. The greatest challenge to humankind now is how to shift the traditional sources of identity to the modern one—the global community. Nations will not abandon the traditional ones in the foreseeable future, but they will be forced to realize that unless they do something about the existing international order, the international order itself will force them to do so. We should celebrate the New Year with this mission in mind.

14.3

GLOBALIZATION IN RETREAT

Walden Bello

The next article is highly pessimistic about globalization's future. Written by the Filipino academic Walden Bello, it begins by summarizing the views of optimists, who foresaw a "borderless world." Bello argues that, in fact, nation-states have not lost their importance as the optimists had predicted: State capitalism has become popular, international economic institutions have grown weaker, and trade liberalization has stalled. Why was globalization "in retreat"? Bello identifies six reasons for this: (1) globalization itself was "oversold"; (2) major leaders have refused to cooperate in confronting global challenges like global warming; (3) the United States, while preaching free trade, has not practiced it; (4) the spread of poverty and inequality; (5) an obsession with economic growth; and (6) the opposition of the antiglobalization movement. The article concludes that although globalization may be resuscitated if it is reformed, this will not be a simple matter.

When it first became part of the English vocabulary in the early 1990s, globalization was supposed to be the wave of the future. Fifteen years ago, the writings of globalist thinkers such as Kenichi Ohmae and Robert Reich celebrated the advent of the emergence of the so-called borderless world. The process by which relatively autonomous national economies become functionally integrated into one global economy was touted as "irreversible." And the people who opposed globalization were disdainfully dismissed as modern day incarnations of the Luddites that destroyed machines during the Industrial Revolution.

Fifteen years later, despite runaway shops and outsourcing, what passes for an international economy remains a collection of national economies. These economies are interdependent no doubt, but domestic factors still largely determine their dynamics.

Globalization, in fact, has reached its high-water mark and is receding.

Bright Predictions, Dismal Outcomes

During globalization's heyday, we were told that state policies no longer mattered and that corporations would soon dwarf states. In fact, states still do matter. The European Union, the U.S. government, and the Chinese state are stronger economic actors today than they were a decade ago. In China, for instance, transnational corporations (TNCs) march to the tune of the state rather than the other way around.

Source: Walden Bello, "Globalization in Retreat," *Foreign Policy in Focus*, December 27, 2006.

Moreover, state policies that interfere with the market in order to build up industrial structures or protect employment still make a difference. Indeed, over the last ten years, interventionist government policies have spelled the difference between development and underdevelopment, prosperity and poverty. Malaysia's imposition of capital controls during the Asian financial crisis in 1997–98 prevented it from unraveling like Thailand or Indonesia. Strict capital controls also insulated China from the economic collapse engulfing its neighbors.

Fifteen years ago, we were told to expect the emergence of a transnational capitalist elite that would manage the world economy. Indeed, globalization became the "grand strategy" of the Clinton administration, which envisioned the U.S. elite being the primus inter pares—first among equals—of a global coalition leading the way to the new, benign world order. Today, this project lies in shambles. During the reign of George W. Bush, the nationalist faction has overwhelmed the transnational faction of the economic elite. These nationalism-inflected states are now competing sharply with one another, seeking to beggar one another's economies.

A decade ago, the World Trade Organization (WTO) was born, joining the World Bank and the International Monetary Fund (IMF) as the pillars of the system of international economic governance in the era of globalization. With a triumphalist air, officials of the three organizations meeting in Singapore during the first ministerial gathering of the WTO in December 1996 saw the remaining task of "global governance" as the achievement of "coherence," that is, the coordination of the neoliberal policies of the three institutions in order to ensure the smooth, technocratic integration of the global economy.

But now Sebastian Mallaby, the influential pro-globalization commentator of the Washington Post, complains that "trade liberalization has stalled, aid is less coherent than it should be, and the next financial conflagration will be managed by an injured fireman." In fact, the situation is worse than he describes. The IMF is practically defunct. Knowing how the Fund precipitated and worsened the Asian financial crisis, more and more of the advanced developing countries are refusing to borrow from it or are paying ahead of schedule, with some declaring their intention never to borrow again. These include Thailand, Indonesia, Brazil, and Argentina. Since the Fund's budget greatly depends on debt repayments from these big borrowers, this boycott is translating into what one expert describes as "a huge squeeze on the budget of the organization."

The World Bank may seem to be in better health than the Fund. But having been central to the debacle of structural adjustment policies that left most developing and transitional economies that implemented them in greater poverty, with greater inequality, and in a state of stagnation, the Bank is also suffering a crisis of legitimacy.

But the crisis of multilateralism is perhaps most acute at the WTO. Last July, the Doha Round of global negotiations for more trade liberalization unraveled abruptly when talks among the so-called Group of Six broke down in acrimony over the U.S. refusal to budge on its enormous subsidies for agriculture. The pro-free trade American economist Fred Bergsten once compared trade liberalization and the WTO to a bicycle: they collapse when they are not moving forward. The collapse of an organization that one of its director generals once described as the "jewel in the crown of multilateralism" may be nearer than it seems.

Why Globalization Stalled

Why did globalization run aground? First of all, the case for globalization was oversold. The bulk of the production and sales of most TNCs continues to take place within the country or region of origin. There are only a handful of truly global corporations whose production and sales are dispersed relatively equally across regions.

Second, rather than forge a common, cooperative response to the global crises of overproduction, stagnation, and environmental ruin, national capitalist elites have competed with each other to shift the burden of adjustment. The Bush administration, for instance, has pushed a weak-dollar policy to promote U.S. economic recovery and growth at the expense of Europe and Japan. It has also refused to sign the Kyoto Protocol in order to push Europe and Japan to absorb most of the costs of global environmental adjustment and thus make U.S. industry comparatively more competitive. While cooperation may be the rational strategic choice from the point of view of the global capitalist system, national capitalist interests are mainly concerned with not losing out to their rivals in the short term.

A third factor has been the corrosive effect of the double standards brazenly displayed by the hegemonic power, the United States. While the Clinton administration did try to move the United States toward free trade, the Bush administration has hypocritically preached free trade while practicing protectionism. Indeed, the trade policy of the Bush administration seems to be free trade for the rest of the world and protectionism for the United States.

Fourth, there has been too much dissonance between the promise of globalization and free trade and the actual results of neoliberal policies, which have been more poverty, inequality, and stagnation. One of the very few places where poverty diminished over the last 15 years is China. But interventionist state policies that managed market forces, not neoliberal prescriptions, were responsible for lifting 120 million Chinese out of poverty. Moreover, the advocates of eliminating capital controls have had to face the actual collapse of the economies that took this policy to heart. The globalization of finance proceeded much faster than the globalization of production. But it proved to be the cutting edge not of prosperity but of chaos. The Asian financial crisis and the collapse of the economy of Argentina, which had been among the most doctrinaire practitioners of capital account liberalization, were two decisive moments in reality's revolt against theory.

Another factor unraveling the globalist project is its obsession with economic growth. Indeed, unending growth is the centerpiece of globalization, the mainspring of its legitimacy. While a recent World Bank report continues to extol rapid growth as the key to expanding the global middle class, global warming, peak oil, and other environmental events are making it clear to people that the rates and patterns of growth that come with globalization are a surefire prescription for ecological Armageddon.

The final factor, not to be underestimated, has been popular resistance to globalization. The battles of Seattle in 1999, Prague in 2000, and Genoa in 2001; the massive global anti-war march on February 15, 2003, when the anti-globalization movement morphed into the global anti-war movement; the collapse of the WTO ministerial meeting in Cancun in 2003 and its near collapse in Hong Kong in 2005; the French and Dutch peoples' rejection of the neoliberal, pro-globalization European Constitution in 2005—these were all critical junctures in a decade-long global struggle that has rolled back the neoliberal project. But these high-profile events were merely the tip of the iceberg, the summation of thousands of anti-neoliberal, anti-globalization struggles in thousands of communities throughout the world involving millions of peasants, workers, students, indigenous people, and many sectors of the middle class.

Down but Not Out

While corporate-driven globalization may be down, it is not out. Though discredited, many pro-globalization neoliberal policies remain in place in many economies, for lack of credible alternative policies in the eyes of technocrats. With talks dead-ended at the WTO, the big trading powers are emphasizing free trade agreements (FTAs) and economic partnership agreements (EPAs) with developing countries. These agreements are in many ways more dangerous than the multilateral negotiations at the WTO since they often require greater concessions in terms of market access and tighter enforcement of intellectual property rights.

However, things are no longer that easy for the corporations and trading powers. Doctrinaire neoliberals are being eased out of key positions, giving way to pragmatic technocrats who often subvert neoliberal policies in practice owing to popular pressure. When it comes to FTAs, the global south is becoming aware of the dangers and is beginning to resist. Key South American governments under pressure from their citizenries derailed the Free Trade Area of the Americas (FTAA)—the grand plan of George W. Bush for the Western hemisphere—during the Mar del Plata conference in November 2005.

Also, one of the reasons many people resisted Prime Minister Thaksin Shinawatra in the months before the recent coup in Thailand was his rush to conclude a free trade agreement with the United States. Indeed, in January this year, some 10,000 protesters tried to storm the building in Chiang Mai, Thailand, where U.S. and Thai officials were negotiating. The government that succeeded Thaksin's has put the U.S.-Thai FTA on hold, and movements seeking to stop FTAs elsewhere have been inspired by the success of the Thai efforts.

The retreat from neoliberal globalization is most marked in Latin America. Long exploited by foreign energy giants, Bolivia under President Evo Morales has nationalized its energy resources. Nestor Kirchner of Argentina gave an example of how developing country governments can face down finance capital when he forced northern bondholders to accept only 25 cents of every dollar Argentina owed them. Hugo Chavez has launched an ambitious plan for regional integration, the Bolivarian Alternative for the Americas (ALBA), based on genuine economic cooperation instead of free trade, with little or no participation by northern TNCs, and driven by what Chavez himself describes as a "logic beyond capitalism."

Globalization in Perspective

From today's vantage point, globalization appears to have been not a new, higher phase in the development of capitalism but a response to the underlying structural crisis of this system of production. Fifteen years since it was trumpeted as the wave of the future, globalization seems to have been less a "brave new phase" of the capitalist adventure than a desperate effort by global capital to escape the stagnation and disequilibria overtaking the global economy in the 1970s and 1980s. The collapse of the centralized socialist regimes in Central and Eastern Europe deflected people's attention from this reality in the early 1990s.

Many in progressive circles still think that the task at hand is to "humanize" globalization. Globalization, however, is a spent force. Today's multiplying economic and political conflicts resemble, if anything, the period following the end of what historians refer to as the first era of globalization, which extended from 1815 to the eruption of World War I in 1914. The urgent task is not to steer corporate-driven globalization in a "social democratic" direction but to manage its retreat so that it does not bring about the same chaos and runaway conflicts that marked its demise in that earlier era.

14.4

GLOBALIZATION COMES UNDER SIEGE

Thomas J. Duesterberg

> According to the next selection, written shortly before America's 2008 presidential election by Thomas J. Duesterberg, president and CEO of the business research organization Manufacturers Alliance/MAPI, the growing opposition to globalization could prove harmful to major American corporations. Duesterberg begins by citing evidence of growing opposition to globalization. He then argues that both China and Europe are pursuing regional economic arrangements that might leave American firms out in the cold and that a variety of other factors are increasing the attraction of marketing goods locally rather than globally. Finally, American workers and consumers are less convinced than in the past of the virtues of economic globalization.

A few short years ago, Thomas Friedman crystallized both academic studies and leading opinion about the inevitable advance of global integration in his book *The World Is Flat*.

Source: Thomas J. Duesterberg, "Globalization Comes Under Siege," *Industry Week,* July 2008.

More recently, no matter where one turns, there is evidence of reaction against, and resistance to, globalization. Is this just one of the periodic swings in public opinion and political rhetoric (noted academics like Alan Blinder share this view, too), or has the tide turned strongly enough to roll back the changes of the last few decades? Given the current strength in U.S. manufacturing exports and weakness of domestic demand, this is a crucial question for industry leaders.

The signs of anti-globalization sentiment are legion, both here and abroad:

- U.S. presidential candidates are calling for revising NAFTA and halting further trade agreements;
- tainted toys, drugs and food imported from China and elsewhere have revived fears of the safety and quality of imports;
- the accumulation of vast foreign currency holdings by "sovereign wealth funds" is stoking fears of foreign purchases of strategic U.S. firms;
- the rise of new nationalized foreign firms, especially in the natural resources industries, is raising fears of unfair competition, outright economic nationalism and national competition for scarce resources;
- worldwide food shortages have caused many countries to limit exports of food commodities;
- and large-scale movement of workers across borders has provoked a fierce debate over labor competition and fears of disruptive waves of immigration.

The culmination of these disparate anti-globalization elements was the vote in the U.S. House of Representatives to scuttle ... the U.S.-Colombia Free Trade Agreement, [ratified by the U.S. in 2011], and to dismantle the "fast-track" rules which have allowed U.S. trade negotiators to complete trade agreements and ensure an up-or-down vote in Congress since 1974. According to trade expert C. Fred Bergsten of the Peterson Institute for International Economics, the vote to end fast-track "instantaneously destroyed the credibility of the United States as a negotiating partner in the eyes of the world."

Taken together, these forces represent the most serious threat to global integration and free trade since the end of the disastrous protectionist era bookended by the two World Wars. Even though the purely economic case for further trade liberalization has not been repealed, especially for the increasingly trade-dependent U.S. manufacturing sector, even a victory by free trade proponent John McCain in the 2008 presidential election will not be enough to offset a Democratic Congress and emotional anti-global sentiment.

Here are a few tentative observations about the climate for globalization in the years ahead.

First, China and the European Union will not stand still; both are pursuing enhanced regional economic integration. The United States can ill afford to be left out, especially in the vital Asian markets. Additionally, economic nationalism in Russia, China and Latin America will only be further provoked by protectionist sentiments in the United States.

Second, high transport costs, economic nationalism and political instability in the developing world are all likely to persist and strengthen the case for producing locally for foreign markets.

Finally, U.S. proponents of further global economic integration will need to sharpen their arguments and find new ways to soften trade's impact on domestic workers and consumers through enhanced education and training programs and more openness to global safety and quality standards. The upcoming presidential election will be a major test of whether we will move forward or backward.

14.5

NEWS OF GLOBALIZATION'S DEATH VASTLY EXAGGERATED

John Hancock and Robert Greenhill

Not everyone is pessimistic about the future of globalization. According to the next article, coauthored by a counselor at the World Trade Organization and an officer at the Davos World Economic Forum, the global recession is ending, and globalization has not been eroded by it. Efforts to liberalize trade have resumed; protectionism has remained muted; and major emerging economic powers such as China, India, and Brazil have eagerly embraced globalization. The article concludes that the reasons for the staying power of economic globalization are the strength of multilateral economic institutions, the strong support of transnational corporations for globalized markets and global economic strategies, and the simple fact that globalization is better than any alternative.

What happened to the end of globalization? For months we've heard that the economic crisis would lead to a wave of protectionism, trade conflict and "de-globalization." But far from unravelling, the world economy seems likely to emerge from the crisis more, not less, globalized.

The feared protectionist backlash has not materialized. On the contrary, according to a recent WTO report the crisis has actually spurred more efforts to liberalize trade than to restrict it, as a way of cutting import costs, attracting investment and boosting competitiveness. Tariffs remain historically low, anti-dumping actions are down a quarter from 2001, and free-trade agreements, like the one recently concluded between the EU and Korea, are expanding.

Economies are moving even faster to open up to foreign investment. According to the UN, four-fifths of policy changes since 2007 have been in the direction of more

Source: John Hancock and Robert Greenhill, "News of Globalization's Death Vastly Exaggerated," *The Toronto Star,* December 6, 2009.

liberalization—reducing restrictions, cutting red tape, signing investment and double tax treaties—not less. Nowhere is the drive for openness more striking than in the telecoms and IT sectors, key arteries of a globally integrated economy.

For every country like North Korea trying to stay out of globalization, there is a China, India or Brazil moving in. The decision to replace the G8 with the G20 is merely the most visible sign of how much more integrated and multipolar the post-crisis world will be. From coordinating monetary and fiscal stimulus, to cooperating on tax and banking regulations, to passing the EU's Lisbon Treaty and possibly expanding the Eurozone, the unmistakable trend is toward more globalization.

So why didn't globalization implode? One reason is that the international economic system has proven stronger than even its defenders had hoped. Multilateral trade rules have been respected, and any conflicts resolved, not through a replay of the 1930s, but through the WTO's "trade court." The IMF and World Bank have also been surprisingly agile and effective—channelling more funds to crisis-hit countries more quickly and with fewer strings attached.

A bigger reason is the rise of global companies. Corporate interests now transcend borders through a complex web of supply chains, offshore alliances and global market strategies—made possible by new transport and communications networks that increasingly "hard-wire" globalization. When more than half of world trade now takes place within multinationals, "protectionism" starts looking at best passé and at worst self-destructive. Companies, as much as countries, want to keep global markets open.

The biggest reason is that globalization is better than the alternatives. As devastating as the present crisis has been, it comes on the heels of two decades of historically high global growth, the unprecedented rise of millions in the developing world, and a unique period of relative international peace—brought about in part because the great powers are now so economically and institutionally intertwined.

Critics of globalization talk about the need for a "new model," but few alternatives have been forthcoming. And no one seriously proposes a return to the economic nationalism and isolationism of the first half of the last century. There are many challenges today: unemployment, the environment, international disparities and systemic risks in the financial sector. Yet most proposals to address these challenges—restoring economic growth, reducing global warming, improving development assistance or enhancing financial oversight—involve more globalization, not less.

Does this make globalization inevitable? Hardly. One reason for the endless predictions of globalization's demise is our collective memory of how the late 19th century's version came crashing down in the early 20th century amidst war, depression and resurgent nationalism. Globalization is a human creation, the result not of unstoppable technology but of our ideas and choices. Who can guess whether a perceived inability to deal with rising unemployment, wealth disparities or shifts in geoeconomic power could potentially send globalization into reverse?

Nevertheless, what is striking about the modern phase of globalization is its resilience. It survived the Asian financial crisis, the dot-com bubble, the 9/11 attacks—and now it looks likely to survive the "Great Recession" as well. World trade is rebounding. Investment flows are expected to return to pre-crisis levels by 2011. And growth forecasts, especially for Asia, are being repeatedly revised upward. This surprisingly rapid turn-around from crisis to recovery would have been inconceivable without the flexibility and durability of today's open and integrated world economy.

The one unambiguous lesson from the economic crisis is that we have never been more interdependent. We must rethink and redesign our systems of global cooperation to match this inescapable reality. Deeper globalization—not de-globalization—is the future we will need to grapple with. It is arriving sooner than we think.

14.6

THE WORLD MAP 50 YEARS FROM NOW

from *The Christian Science Monitor*

The chapter's final selection, written some years before the global financial crisis, describes the prescient views of four observers of key trends in global affairs. One is the simultaneous fragmentation of states, even as they are integrated, for better or worse, in the course of globalization. The second is the introduction of technologies that overcome national boundaries and link diverse societies. The third is the proliferation of management networks in emerging economies that transcend national frontiers, and the fourth is the emergence of numerous new and smaller states. However, the meaning and role of their boundaries will be different in a variety of ways.

Pull of Unity, Push of Splintering

United Nations Secretary-General Boutros Boutros-Ghali spoke to Monitor contributor Lucia Mouat in New York:

We are confronted by two different things. One is fragmentation. When the UN was created we had 51 member states. Today, 50 years later, we have 185 members. The civil war in Yugoslavia is an example of this fragmentation of the family of nations. The UN has participated in this through its role in decolonization. But at the same time, we are confronted by something new which I call globalization, problems in the field of communication, disease, drugs, environment—Chernobyl is an example—that have no borders.

Over the next 50 years we will be confronted by this dialectic relation where on the one side you will have more globalization, and on the other side we may have more fragmentation.

Source: "The World Map 50 Years From Now," *The Christian Science Monitor,* October 18, 1995.

It is a big challenge, but I believe the UN has the capacity to manage the globalization and contain the fragmentation if it receives the support of member states.

New Borders Belong to the Efficient

Kenichi Ohmae, author of "The Borderless World" (1990), "The End of the Nation-State" (1995), and other books, spoke from Tokyo:

What will happen to the world's nations depends on how well we harness technologies.

The Internet community, for instance, ignores national borders. Companies can use technologies to transfer services across countries. You can have an efficient production plant in South Dakota or in India.

Worldwide autonomous regions of production are being created, from Bangalore to Singapore. More natural units of economy are emerging. The ideal is 3 million to 5 million people, very visible to world investors and consumers, but not so complex to govern.

By 2010, the world will develop into a network of similar production communities, emerging states that don't need military force, large land masses, or natural resources.

New Zealand and Ireland, for instance, are attracting companies because they have enlightened workers who communicate well with the world, a deregulated economy, high educational level, and reasonably high unemployment.

Bangalore uses satellite dishes to connect with the world, avoiding the bad land lines that are common in India. It's wired itself to the world community. It's even building its own small power plants.

In Dalian in northeast China, half of the industrial investment is foreign, and the city is becoming less connected to Beijing.

The emerging states of the world are those with credible management teams.

Over the past 30 to 40 years, national leaders have fought for broader alliances—the EU, NAFTA, ASEAN—to deal with the problems of the traditional nation state. Once you form these alliances, however, the bureaucracy becomes overwhelming to administer the larger unit. This pushes people to find more basic units of commonality with historical, ethnic, linguistic, or technological bonds.

The EU attempt to end nation-state borders has forced its people to establish their identities along ethnic lines. Smaller units will emerge as national borders break down. The identity of Catalonians in Spain is stronger today, and they may form a new state.

As NAFTA grows, what will Nova Scotia have in common with Vancouver? Canada's cities and provinces will look south, not to Ottawa: British Columbia will look to Washington State, Ontario will join the Great Lakes area.

The same is true with Mexico: The northern part can join the US and leave the south isolated from prosperity.

In China, the government cannot control 1.2 billion people under one doctrine, with so many tribes and dialects. The only way is military force to keep unity.

Deng Xiaoping created economic zones with autonomy to deal with foreign investors, but Beijing doesn't get the money. Now it is tightening the controls with national taxes, but to no avail. No one sees the value of central government. The southern provinces have gone too far to be called back by Beijing.

In Russia, that country may not be the optimal economic unit in the 21st century. If Siberia is split into autonomous units, then Russia may prosper. But Moscow will never do it. It'll see a challenge to its authority in Siberia.

Hundreds of New Flags Will Unfurl

Richard C. Carlson is the chairman of Spectrum Economics in Palo Alto, Calif. He is the author of "Twenty Twenty Visions: a Long View of a Changing World" (1991) and, with Bruce Goldman, "Fast Forward: Where Technology, Demographics, and History Will Take America & the World in the Next Thirty Years" (1994).

The concept of national borders has shifted throughout history and will continue to change. The most rigid concept of borders—a physical barrier that severely limits the passage of people, products, and information—reached its peak during the cold war when several Communist nations—e.g., Albania and North Korea—tried to completely cut themselves off from the world.

This attempt at isolation was both doomed to failure and doomed these nations to ultimate economic and political collapse. No period of human history, before or since, will have had such rigid borders.

The questions for 50 years from now are not just where will the borders be, but which borders will be left, if any, and what will these remaining borders mean? Several things are nearly certain:

- Borders will be meaningless for information flows. Any attempt to stop audio, video, and data from moving anywhere at any time will be hopeless.
- Money, which now is little more than bits of data, will move instantly and without restriction around the planet. Money in most of the world will be denominated in one to three world currencies.
- Products will move without restriction among developed and undeveloped nations, but there will still be limited residual restrictions on product movements between developed and undeveloped nations.
- Borders will become meaningless for the movement of people among developed nations, but severe border restrictions will remain between the developed and undeveloped world and among undeveloped (and collapsing) nations. Going from England to the United States will be like traveling from Kansas to Nebraska.
- Borders will lose much of their meaning for language. Translation will be automatic, and everyone of consequence under age 30 will probably speak English.
- National citizenship will have two meanings in the developed world: membership in nation-based social-welfare systems (with most of the younger generation opting out of these collapsed or collapsing systems) and national voting.

There will be only one border that really counts by 2050, the border between the modern, developed world and the world of chaos.

The developed world will include most of the Americas (Brazil being the big question mark), Europe, Japan, and much of Asia. Within this world borders will be largely meaningless.

The world of chaos will include most of Africa, Pakistan, Bangladesh, parts of India, and parts of China, where demographic, economic, and political troubles will have overwhelmed social order and cohesion. Border conflicts will continue in these tragic parts of the world.

In the interim decades, the world has many border conflicts to look forward to. Borders are far from settled in most of Africa, the Middle East, Central Europe, and most of the former Soviet Union.

China may well attempt to maintain its political cohesion by trying to expand its own borders through military force into Russia and Southeast Asia. Russia, Japan, and the US cannot tolerate such behavior. Any such attempt would only hasten the political collapse and division of China.

Strangely, the world will have more borders as well as fewer. Many large nations will break down into smaller more "autonomous" regions where attempts will be made to protect language and cultural cohesion.

These attempts will ultimately fail under the information onslaught of world technology, but meanwhile the world will see dozens if not hundreds of new flags unfurled from Catalonia (Spain) to Quebec.

Mega-Networks Redraw Asia Map

John Naisbitt, author of "Megatrends" and the soon-to-be published "Megatrends Asia," gave this assessment in an interview from Cambridge, Mass.:

The cross-border economic activity of the 57 million Overseas Chinese [outside China] is a country all by itself, outranked only by the US and Japan.

Their family businesses in Southeast Asia are networks of companies. They are not a nation-state, but a network of networks. The world is moving from a collection of nation-states to a collection of networks. And Asia is where the action is going to be.

CREDITS

1.2   Material reprinted with the express permission of: "Montreal Gazette Group Inc.," a Postmedia Network Partnership.

1.3   Used by permission from *China Daily*.

1.4   Reprinted with permission from YaleGlobal Online. Copyright © 2005 Yale Center for the Study of Globalization.

1.5   Used by permission from *China Daily*.

2.2   Used by permission from the American Academy of Political and Social Science.

2.3   Used by permission from *China Daily*.

2.4   Used by permission from Ronal Deibert and Rafal Rohozinski.

2.5   Used by permission from The Philadelphia Inquirer. Copyright © 2012. All rights reserved.

2.6   Material reprinted with the express permission of "National Post Inc."

2.7   © The Globe and Mail Inc. All rights reserved.

2.8   © Sydney Morning Herald, July 31, 2010.

2.9   Used by permission from The Toronto Sun/Sun Media Corporation.

2.10 U.S. State Department (Bureau of International Information Programs).

3.1   Used by permission from American Academy of Political and Social Science

3.2   Reprinted by permission of the WTO (World Trade Organization).

3.3   © The Globe and Mail Inc. All rights reserved.

3.4   By Ron Scherer. Reprinted with permission from the August 16, 2010 issue of *The Christian Science Monitor*. © 2010 The Christian Science Monitor (www.CSMonitor.com).